THE WORLD OF MONEY MANAGEMENT

America's Leading Experts Share Their Views on
Investment Management and the Value of Consulting

Compiled and Edited by
Sydney LeBlanc and Lyn Fisher

©2004, Fisher LeBlanc Group, Logan, UT/San Diego, CA

All Rights Reserved. No part of this publication may be reproduced, stored in a retrieval system, or transmitted by any means (electronic, mechanical, photocopy, recording, stored in a database or otherwise) without the prior written permission of the publisher and the copyright holder. Fisher LeBlanc Group, 90 North 100 East, Ste, 4, Logan, UT 84321

Disclosures/Disclaimers: The material included in *The World of Money Management* is provided for informational and educational purposes only. The opinions and theories expressed throughout the chapters are strictly those of the authors of their respective chapters and not necessarily those of their firms or the editors and publishers, and are subject to change without notice. The authors and/or compliance boards representing their firms have written/and or reviewed and approved the text contained in the book. While the editors and publishers agree with the tenets presented, no endorsement is implied.

Note: *The World of Money Management* is intended for *professional use only*, it is not intended for individual investors. This book contains no investment recommendations and should not be construed as specific tax, legal, financial planning or investment advice. Financial advisors who choose to pass text contained herein to investors should do so with the approval of their firm's management or legal and compliance departments. The text is not NASD-approved for the general public. Information was obtained from third-party sources, which we believe to be reliable, but not guaranteed. Money management firms participating in the creation of this book purchased multiple copies from Financial Forum Publishing for their own distribution.

Copyright of all material submitted and published is held by the publisher, Financial Forum, Inc.

Copies of this book are available for purchase through Fisher LeBlanc Group. Discounts given for volume purchases. For more information, call 435.787.2900.

Publisher:
Financial Forum Publishing
435.750.0062

ISBN# 0-9745175-3-4
Printed by Monroe Litho

DEDICATION

To the professional men and women who demonstrate higher principles and ethics, practice higher standards of care, and devote themselves to providing the highest level of service and advice to their individual and institutional clients.

CONTENTS

Preface viii
Acknowledgements.. x
Forward xi
Introduction xii

PART I: THE MANAGER/CONSULTANT/INVESTOR TRIANGLE

CHAPTER 1
The Value of Professional Money Management 3

CHAPTER 2
The Value of Investment Management Consulting.................... 7

CHAPTER 3
Consultant: Educator and Confidante. 15

CHAPTER 4
What Will It Take to Make It a Profession? 19

CHAPTER 5
Instilling Trust and Eliminating Investor Fear 27

CHAPTER 6
Defining Investor Responsibility 33

PART II: THE COMPLETE CONSULTANT: PROCESS AND VALUE

CHAPTER 7
Data Mining 41
The Client Questionnaire and Beyond

CHAPTER 8
Effective Risk Management.. 47
Increasing the Probability of Investor Success

CHAPTER 9
The Investment Policy Statement 61
A Blueprint for Guiding the Investment Process

CHAPTER 10
The Art and Importance of Asset Allocation 75

CHAPTER 11
Manager Search and Evaluation 85
A Magic Formula?

CHAPTER 12
Evaluating Investment Manager Performance 91

CHAPTER 13
Performance Reporting and Client Meetings 111

CHAPTER 14
Consultants and Managers 119
Maintaining the Symbiotic Relationship

CHAPTER 15
The Value of Advice..125
Is It Worth the Fee?

CONTENTS

PART III: A Discussion of Various Investment Strategies and Disciplines

CHAPTER 16
Balanced Portfolio Management 131

CHAPTER 17
Core Equity Management 135

CHAPTER 18
Bonds For All Seasons 141

CHAPTER 19
Growth Investing 153
The Hunt for Outsized Returns

CHAPTER 20
International Equity 163

CHAPTER 21
The Value of Value Investing 171

CHAPTER 22
Relative Value 179
Everything is Relative

CHAPTER 23
Passive and Active Management 187
A Balanced Perspective Emerges

CHAPTER 24
Behavioral Finance and Value Investing 201

PART IV: Eye On the Investment Portfolio

CHAPTER 25
Identifying Investment Manager Skill 217

CHAPTER 26
The Significance of Style Drift 225

PART V: Wealth Management Solutions

CHAPTER 27
Separately Managed Accounts 237

CHAPTER 28
Client-Focused Investment Solutions 249

CHAPTER 29
Multiple Style Accounts 253

CHAPTER 30
The Mysterious UMA 261

CHAPTER 31
Serving the Ultra High Net Worth Market 269

CONTENTS

CHAPTER 32
Absolute Return Opportunities and 279
Risk Mitigation with Hedge Funds

PART VI: THE FUTURE

CHAPTER 33
Technology Today 290

CHAPTER 34
The Financial Advisor of the Future 299

Associations and Designations 311
Author Biographies 313
Corporate Profiles 329
2004 - Money Manager Chart 355

▻ This symbol appears on client application chapters. See chapter footnotes for additional information.

PREFACE

In the investment industry and financial advisory business knowledge is the key to success. Federal Reserve Chairman Alan Greenspan recently put it: "As market forces continue to expand the range of providers of financial services, consumers will have more choice and flexibility in how they manage their personal finances. They will also need to learn ways to use new technologies and to make wise financial decisions."

Sound, well-informed advice from experienced, professional financial advisors can help investors make correct choices. The disappointments of the past few years have, however, badly eroded investor confidence in the quality and integrity of the sources of that advice. Research scandals, accounting scandals, the rise and fall of the Internet bubble of the late 1990s – all these setbacks have left portfolio managers and financial advisors under a cloud of intense skepticism, if not outright distrust.

This situation is easy to understand, but less easy to correct. When bad news strikes, investors often conclude their financial advisors *must* be at fault – even if their portfolios are actually *outperforming* the market on a relative basis. This is especially true when the newspapers are filled with stories of corporate malfeasance or cozy insider relationships. At such times, it's painfully easy for individual investors to conclude that *their* interests are not being served.

There is no single solution to restore Wall Street's credibility. However, for advisors and money managers who can clearly demonstrate a superior understanding of the investment process, the current climate could be a tremendous opportunity for both personal and professional growth.

This is particularly true for those professionals within the money management industry who have embraced the fee-based advisory model. They bring a special set of skills to the table – detailed knowledge of the capital markets and the elements of portfolio construction, together with a business model that puts their interests on the same side of the table as their clients. It's a combination that most competitors in the financial advice industry cannot even begin to match.

The key is knowledge. In an era of more modest returns – and more realistic future expectations – financial advisors and portfolio managers will have to demonstrate the value they offer. They will need to document the value they create, whether through customized asset allocation planning, tax-efficient portfolio management, investment manager research and selection, estate planning or any of the other services that they provide.

Continuing education – and the credentials that go with it – can play a vital role in making the case for an investment advisory relationship. Organizations such as the Association for Investment Management Research (AIMR), and the Center for Fiduciary Studies are excellent standouts among the many organizations currently providing recognized courses of study and professional designations. AIMR's Certified Financial Analyst (CFA™) credential is a globally recognized standard for measuring the competence and integrity of financial analysts, and one of the most highly regarded designations in our industry.

Also, new to the industry is the Accredited Investment Fiduciary Auditor (AIFA™) designation introduced in 2002 by the Center for Fiduciary Studies. Professionals holding this particular designation must demonstrate that they fully comprehend all pertinent issues

PREFACE

surrounding the fiduciary to adequately evaluate an independent investment process.

In addition to these vital designations, many investment consulting firms have developed their own inhouse training and certification programs.

Developing the tools is one thing, spreading the knowledge is another. As an introduction and a guide to the best practices in our industry, *The World of Money Management* should become a key text, supplementing and enhancing the many training programs now available. I strongly recommend *The World of Money Management* as a valuable work for investment advisors, consultants, and their clients.

Christopher L. Davis
Executive Director
The Money Management Institute
Washington, DC

ACKNOWLEDGEMENTS

Our biggest challenge in producing the *World of Money Management* was the sheer enormity of developing and overseeing the entire project, and then completing it against a completely unrealistic deadline. From beginning to end—obtaining the participation of talented managers and industry specialists for each of the 34 chapters and the eventual publishing—this book was the result of extremely hard work provided by more than 75 dedicated individuals.

First, we want to our express our gratitude to the supportive money managers who joined us in undertaking this immense project. Without their participation, we would not have been able to publish the book as expeditiously as we did. With numerous "moving parts" to the book, i.e. interviews, writing drafts, editing, management and compliance approvals, layout and design, proofing, and printing, it took organization and teamwork to accomplish the many tasks.

A very special thank you goes to sponsors AIM Private Asset Management Inc., BlackRock, Brandes Investment Partners, Eaton Vance Distributors, Inc., ING, Madison Equity Group, Mariner Investment Group, Nuveen Investments, Rorer Asset Management LLC, Roxbury Capital Management, Russell Investment Group, State Street Global Advisors, and Franklin Templeton Private Client Group. Another big thank-you goes to industry contributors Daniel R. Bott, Frank Campanale, Scott MacKillop, Barry Mendelson, Richard Iwanski, Jennifer Arnold, Steven Maslow, Thomas O'Keefe, Leonard Reinhart, James Seuffert, Alan Sislen, Ron Surz, Rich Todd, Donald Trone, Lewis Walker, Drew Washburn, Jack Waymire, and Stephen Winks.

An extra note of appreciation goes to John Nersesian and Alan Williamson at Nuveen Investments; Bob Jamo and Mark Spina at ING; and Ed Blodgett and Barry Gillman at Brandes Investment Partners for believing in our project and joining us in the initial stages; this gave us the momentum we needed to launch the book. And to our friend, MMI executive director Chris Davis, for his encouragement and industry perspective.

We appreciate the extraordinary efforts of the remaining members of all the teams working behind the scenes at the investment management and consulting firms. They number in the dozens. Their quick response and follow-through was instrumental in helping us achieve our goals. Our researchers, editors, and writers deserve a big dose of appreciation, and we thank Jonathan Barnett, Arianne Colton, Steven Drozdeck, Lida Gray, Alison Hobbs, Rebecca Kirby, John Keefe, Gina Lauer, Channary Leng, Montgomery LeBlanc, Cami Miller, Whitney Oswald and Allen Plummer for their valuable contributions to this project.

Special recognition goes to our families, friends, associates, and many kind financial advisors who offered advice and counsel throughout the process. Without the generous help from everyone above, we would still be on page one.

—Lyn Fisher, Sydney LeBlanc

FORWARD

The Prudent Process and the Managing of Assets

According to investment management and fiduciary experts Donald B. Trone, William R. Allbright, and Philip R. Taylor, one of the most important ingredients in the "procedurally prudent process" is *the management of investment decisions*, not the act of *making money*. In their widely acclaimed book, "Procedural Prudence," which was written for fiduciaries of pension plans, trustees, and investment management consultants, the authors maintain that any individual who exercises discretionary authority or control over assets is considered a fiduciary and, therefore, responsible and accountable by law to act in a prudent manner over those assets.

States ERISA Sec 409 (a), *"Any person who is a fiduciary with respect to a plan who breaches any of the responsibilities, obligations, or duties imposed upon by this title shall be personally liable to make good to such plan any profits of such fiduciary which have been made through use of assets of the plan by the fiduciary, and shall be subject to such other equitable or remedial relief as the court may deem appropriate, including the removal of such fiduciary."*

It is vital for any financial advisor, planner, consultant, wealth manager, money manager, trustee, family office specialist, or other financial services professional who oversees and makes decisions regarding the management of assets, **to thoroughly understand the key steps in the investment management process.** Moreover, it is important that the financial professional explain these steps, as well as the responsibilities, to the client.

In addition to the prudence and investment management expertise, the perfect equation for any successful client-consultant-money manager relationship is one of trust/responsibility/accountability. This book attempts to cover the many aspects of this alliance. We hope you enjoy it, and that it offers avenues of education in an entertaining and informative way.

— Editors

INTRODUCTION

In the early 1960s, institutional-caliber money management became the calling card for an elite group of visionary consultants—pioneers who paved the way for future financial advisors and consultants to offer value-based investment management consulting for a fee instead of transacting products for a commission. Today, high net worth individuals, foundations and endowments, family offices, small business owners, and other investors of various shapes and sizes all rely on the skill and experience of managers, consultants and advisors for high-level counsel. Fortunes are made, capital is protected, and lives are enriched through competent investment management and investment consulting, two time-honored professions advanced by talented practitioners.

Most recently, the promulgation of fee-based business, the growth of investment management consulting, and the demand for professional advice by investors have resulted in the increased recognition of these professions. With this growth and popularity comes the need for more education—for the advisor and for the client. Industry organizations offer online studies, university classes, national and regional conferences, workshops, certifications, designations, and more to help fill these needs. Courses that led to such prestigious designations as Chartered Financial Analyst (CFA®), Certified Investment Management Analyst (CIMA), Accredited Investment Fiduciary Associate (AIFA™), and others were created to better serve clients, especially the affluent individual, family, and small- to mid-sized institutions. As a result, higher standards of professional, ethical, and fiduciary conduct are now expected—and delivered. And as more advisors make the transition to the "advice" business, and as the value of this advice becomes the element of differentiation, professional training (coupled with the professional education) will remain at the forefront of our industry. Teaching has become the mantra for a growing number of money managers and industry specialists who are eager to contribute their knowledge of marketing, practice management, and other educational skills to those "in the trenches" who need them most. These managers and specialists—many of whom are contributors to this book—are on the frontline making a significant difference in the lives of advisors and consultants, and those of their clients. They are an endless source of ideas, insight, and support.

Additionally, the current move toward total wealth management, which offers all-inclusive services to high net worth and ultra high net worth individuals and families, is being embraced by a cross-section of advisors, consultants and financial planners. Planning, solutions, and ongoing management in such areas as investing, estate and retirement planning, tax efficiency, business succession, insurance, mortgage advice, legacy planning, and charitable giving is a significant and responsible move on the part of the financial services industry. This move is being accelerated by wise financial professionals who have strategically aligned themselves with experts like CPAs, attorneys, business and insurance consultants and others to form "wealth management teams." Members of such teams also consider continuing education and professional designations an important component of their differentiation and their value to clients.

It is apparent today that individual investors are evolving. Investors are expecting—and are entitled—to see Wall Street adopt a higher standard of care, and industry change-makers like fiduciary expert, Donald R. Trone for example, are single-handedly helping raise those standards of care through his work for the Department of Labor and his organizations, the Center for Fiduciary Studies and Foundation for Fiduciary Studies. Fiduciary standards, ethics, accountability, responsibility, concern and care for the client are what industry pro-

INTRODUCTION

fessionals strive for. For the clients' sake, advisors and consultants understand the need to reinforce their education and to continue reflecting on—and elevating—their own core competencies in order to best serve their audience.

The authors, contributors, editors, and publisher of *The World of Money Management* hope this book will be a helpful resource for you, the 21st century financial advisor and investment management consultant. Some of the industry's best minds have pooled their talent to provide you with an educational guide through which to learn more about—or update you on—the vital components of successful asset management and investment consulting. *The World of Money Management* is a journalistic endeavor undertaken with respected money managers and financial services industry experts. The chapters in the book are the result of a collaboration of ideas and intellectual discussion with 30 strategic partners. Some managers chose to present editorials highlighting their investment style expertise, and others chose such areas as asset allocation, risk management, and active versus passive investing. Supporting this effort were esteemed experts in various specialties as performance attribution, separately managed accounts, style drift, and the consulting process. Throughout the book, you'll read opinions, analyses, scholarly research, and entertaining views from well-known (and a few emerging) industry professionals. Some you will be in agreement with; some not. But all should be thought-provoking and worthy of intelligent dialogue with colleagues.

The book serves as a "big picture" compendium of ideas, information, and knowledge, on other such topics as separately managed accounts, investment disciplines, style drift, performance attribution, behavioral finance, manager search and evaluation, technology, fee justification, and much more. Each chapter is a self-contained topic, categorized into sections of similar interest so you can either read sections at a time, one chapter at a time, or the entire book from front to back. Since the book showcases various authors, the task of keeping a consistent flow of writing style and the consistent use of terminology throughout was difficult, and we attempted to accomplish this as best we could. Text is written primarily in the third person, however, the first person occasionally surfaced. You also will see the terms "financial advisor," "advisor," "wealth manager," "investment management consultant," and "consultant," used throughout all chapters—sometimes interchangeably—as well as "manager," "money manager," and "investment manager," in similar fashion. Our intention is to pay respect to the individual title of choice, while recognizing the various distinctions in each as well.

Enjoy reading *The World of Money Management*. We hope you will keep it close at hand and refer to it as a frequent resource. We welcome all opinions and comments. You may contact authors, editors, and contributors directly for more information on any topic contained in this book.

Sydney LeBlanc
Lyn Fisher
Co-Directors, Fisher LeBlanc Group
info@fisherleblanc.com

PART I

THE
MANAGER · CONSULTANT · INVESTOR
TRIANGLE

1

THE VALUE OF PROFESSIONAL MONEY MANAGEMENT

Sydney LeBlanc with Frank Campanale
Former President and CEO
Smith Barney Consulting Group

"If an advisor doesn't know why he or she should be using professional money managers, they must be hiding under a rock."

— Comment by a well-known manager
overheard at a key industry conference.

Professional money management is most often highlighted in terms of its value to clients, but what sort of value does it hold for advisors and consultants? This question must be asked—and answered—throughout this book to confirm its own value to the reader. Industry firms emphasize professional asset management, especially on a fee-based compensation foundation, but fewer than half of industry advisors have transitioned their businesses.

Why the reluctance?

Has industry leadership failed to adequately communicate the value professional management holds for advisory practices or are advisors simply afraid to change? If the former, what should firms be doing now to make the message more effective; if the latter, how can the importance of changing to accommodate the value being sought by the marketplace be translated?

In reality, the answer lies in all of these questions. Yes, much of firm management has failed to adequately communicate the message, but advisors also have a responsibility to investors to provide the best advice possible at the best price. In other words, the primary responsibility of advisors is to do the right thing for the client. In today's world, this requires a decided shift in focus on the part of firms as well as the advisors who work for them.

The setting for the remaining chapters in this book will be framed by the premises set forth in this chapter. To fully appreciate the methods and expertise available from professional management, one needs to first recognize not only the need for—but the full value of— that management.

The World as We Knew It

Many new advisors emerge from their training with a pretty good idea of how to sell and what types of products are available. Increasingly, firms are changing the focus from "providing a list of products for new advisors to sell" to approving a menu of services provided by professional money managers. The trainees have just enough knowledge to present such a menu of services to clients. But the change in focus is not properly followed through. This problem stems from the fact that firms require these same trainees to revert back to a production-focused mode of operation; they must attain enough critical mass to support themselves within that first year—a very short period of time in which to get a new business up and running from scratch. A trainee at any other company might certainly be allowed two or three years to reach such a point.

Further, these new advisors are measured against production quartiles during that first production year. This means not only do they have to worry about being self-supportive by the end of year one, but during that year they operate with the ever-present reality that they are being measured quarterly against their peers with a *production* benchmark, not a relationship-building measurement. The powers-that-be deliver this edict, so the branch manager is under pressure to ensure the new trainees operate within the first two quartiles which, in turn, keeps the pressure off of the branch managers. This is an unrealistic, pressure-cooker type of environment that sets up new advisors for failure rather than success.

Today's client is demanding that advisors hear a different message from management, one that is followed through and completely supported. Clients demand that advisors become interested in their personal situations in order to make their investments work for them on a multi-level basis. This requires considering a client's liabilities as well as assets and getting to know that client in face-to-face meetings; this translates into allowing clients to be involved in their own futures.

Operating Without Professional Management

There are plenty of old-timers — pure product sellers — still in the business. They grew up in the business by getting on the phone, selling stocks, bonds, mutual funds, or the "product of the day." These brokers have been tremendously successful with that process and many have no interest in becoming a "new" financial advisor or consultant, investing in training programs at Investment Management Consulting Association (IMCA) or achieving the Certified Investment Management Analyst (CIMA) designation. They consider themselves *sales people* and see no need to change.

These professionals have done well conducting business the traditional way and don't want to "fix" something they don't consider broken. But these people are missing some links that hold the process together. And those missing links secure the future of both new and more seasoned advisors.

Advisors who do not use outside management easily can gain a distorted view of their own ability during exceptionally good markets such as those of the late 1990s. Unfortunately, some begin to think they are geniuses. They may have transitioned to the fee-based concept, amassing hundreds of millions of dollars in assets and are trying to manage it all themselves. When these accounts suffered the consequences of the bear market, many of these advisors lost their businesses. They overestimated their ability to manage portfolios, and they neglected to diversify their book of business, which could have ensured that a down cycle in one area would not have put them out of business.

Another internal problem advisors face is competition among firm departments. In the old, product-based mentality of the business, the internal mutual fund division, the annuity department, the fixed income department, unit trusts—all were competing for client dollars from advisors. Focus was on getting those dollars from advisors, not on helping advisors properly serve their clients. Professional portfolio management allows the advisor and the internal departments of the firm to adopt a client-centered perspective with a holistic approach that helps clients solve problems and achieve their goals.

The Advantages of Professional Management

Today, practitioners working for a large firm have access to all the products and investment solutions available to properly serve their clients. They can be confident in the quality of those products, that they have been vetted through a thorough due diligence research process, and can confidently include those products in the toolbox housed within the firm's warehouse of client solutions. This allows the practitioner to assemble a portfolio that will drive the investment strategy toward reaching the goals of a specific client.

Ideally, this advisor would be able to offer all of these different tools—separately managed accounts, mutual funds, tax-advantaged products, and more—in one place, on one platform, under one master account number so that the client could receive a comprehensive, single report that he or she could understand. The Multiple Style Portfolio (MSP) products are one way to accomplish this, but in the long run, the long-term relationship the advisor is trying to build with the client will require more.

The Unified Managed Account (UMA) solution also will give advisors a platform that allows discretionary investment advisory that is product-neutral and completely fee-based. The UMA solution approaches the ideal, but because the concept is beginning to gain recognition through the industry, full realization is still years away.

In Conclusion

In the meantime, professional portfolio management allows advisors to focus on what is going to drive a family's retirement, the college education for the children, or the career change the parent wants to make. It also drives the knowledge, experience, and wisdom of the advisor. This is what clients are mandating.

Adequate and effective training of the advisor to develop a client's investment strategy, the wisdom gained from experience, and an arsenal of such tools as professional portfolio management to implement on the client's behalf are all imperative. The focus of this book is to educate advisors about the money management and consulting processes, and to illustrate how professional portfolio management can open the door to advisors in their quest to develop a profitable business model for themselves and, in the process, to do the right thing for their clients.

❖❖❖

The World of Money Management

2

THE VALUE OF INVESTMENT MANAGEMENT CONSULTING

Sydney LeBlanc with Alan Sislen, President
Managed Account Perspectives, LLC

"The real need in most investment relationships is not for more investment management, but for more management management..."
— Charles D. Ellis, Managing Partner, Greenwich Associates

One of the industry's great thinkers, Charles Ellis, owns the above quote and said it simply and eloquently in his highly acclaimed book, "Winning the Loser's Game." He says the role of the investment management consultant is to *manage*, not to make investment decisions. And, as vital conduits for providing highly skilled investment management expertise to the mass affluent, wealthy families and small to mid-sized institutions, consultants are important components of the investment process.

Echoing this sentiment is respected fiduciary expert and author Donald R. Trone who also believes consultants (as fiduciaries) manage the investment process and without this vital oversight "other components of the investment plan can be neither defined, implemented, nor evaluated."

These and other industry leaders have a keen understanding of the "new" world of investment management, and how *management* is a key to developing a successful consulting practice.

The Need for Consulting

The investment management consulting discipline has its roots in the institutional markets. Historically, investment management consulting was an exclusive and prestigious service offered to wealthy families and individuals, well-known foundations and the largest pension plans of Fortune 500-type companies. Individuals and smaller plans had no cost-effective access to this "institutional-type" of investment management, often provided by bank trust departments or consulting firms that catered to the affluent. The number of investment consultants was limited, and costly fees and account size minimums made it impossible for the retail investor—who could have benefited from these services—to access them.[1]

Today, with increases in fiduciary liability, trusted consultants who provide a high degree of standards and accountability are in high demand. The need for consulting services provided by objective, independent third parties has never been greater. As a result, more advisors are stepping up their education and entering the world of investment management consulting. They are focusing on the emerging affluent, the mass affluent, high net worth, and the ultra high net worth audiences. Improved and accessible technology, industry association training and certification programs all help the advancement of consulting and a creation of a "culture of value" for clients.

According to the Investment Management Consultants Association (IMCA), as of mid-March 2004 there were approximately 3,800 consultants holding the designations of Certified Investment Management Analyst (CIMA) and/or Certified Investment Management Consultant (CIMC). (The designation of CIMC is no longer being offered.) Compared to the mid-80s, when few, if any, advisors held these prestigious designations, this figure represents a growing number of advisors who desire education, training, and professional advancement of standards. Increasingly, advisors are changing their business model from a commission-based practice and transitioning to an advice-based model.

In this role, the investment management consultant—as Charles Ellis stated in his quote at the beginning of this chapter—primarily is responsible for the *management* of investment management, not for the actual *investment* management. Consultants are trained to help the client manage the manager through a disciplined process, and to manage client expectations. The structured process they follow is essential for all assets under management and required for ERISA accounts. This consulting process consists of—but is not limited to—the following six steps:

- Comprehensive client discussions about short- and long-term financial needs and objectives along with risk tolerance, which results in a written investment policy statement
- Development of an asset allocation strategy
- Search and selection of investment managers and/or investment vehicles
- Ongoing monitoring and evaluation of the investment manager, portfolio performance, rebalancing, and other pertinent activities
- Oversight of management and custodial fees and expenses
- Client meetings on a quarterly (or as needed) basis to evaluate progress toward their financial goals and to review manager performance

The consulting process and the advice model provide a high degree of accountability because the consultant is viewed as an objective third-party expert, and minimizes any perceived consultant conflicts of interest.

The Value of Investment Management Consulting

Benefits to the Consultant

An investment management consultant has the opportunity to work with the nation's most talented money managers. High net worth clients, foundations and endowments, and corporate pension plans demand the knowledge and expertise of a consultant's investment process. Following are a few attractive benefits of being part of the consulting community:[2]

Institutional clients use consultants exclusively: Institutions represent the most sophisticated level of clients in the industry. States, counties, municipalities, unions, corporations, charitable organizations and other institutional clients extensively use the consulting process to help reduce risk, improve consistency of performance, and maximize their rate of return.

More time to maintain client relationships: Consultants have fewer, but larger, clients so that time saved can be spent building and servicing clients in a meaningful way.

Eliminate the possibility of conflicts of interest: By charging a fee, rather than collecting transaction-generated commissions, potential consultant conflicts of interest are minimized because the consultant also takes himself or herself out of the investment management equation, and leaves the portfolio buying and selling decisions to the manager.

Institutional caliber talent for the client: Consultants have access to numerous professional managers, gaining the benefit of their talents, experience, and various investment styles.

The client's partner: A consultant is on the same side of the table with the client. No longer on the firing line making individual security recommendations and possibly suffering the consequences, the consultant is in a position to objectively review results and make appropriate recommendations to clients. Due to the fee-based nature of the process, the client has a better understanding of costs, and the consultant has a more predictable revenue stream.

A powerful team for the client: A consultant can suggest a team of professional managers, employing their investment styles to help clients achieve their investment goals. Professional managers can obtain the best possible sources of research and investment information. The consultant now becomes an important client resource, helping to determine investment objectives, proper asset allocations, assisting in manager selection, and reviewing performance.

The consulting process embodies planning: The main reason many individuals never achieve their financial goals is that they never establish them or create and implement a plan to achieve them. The consulting process requires that the consultant and client create a plan to achieve goals, periodically monitor the implementation of the plan, and revise the plan when needed.

Steady growth and less volatility: All consultants are necessarily committed to the asset allocation process as a method of reducing risk and, thereby, increasing the potential for success of the client's overall portfolio. By diversifying a client's portfolio over various asset classes, the client's reliance on results from any one asset category is decreased, and potential for better overall performance is increased. The very nature of the consulting process increases the probability of clients achieving their financial goals at an *acceptable risk level*.

Lower costs for the client: Clients are becoming more and more fee-sensitive, and one of the major reasons that some advisors may lose clients is that clients feel fees are too high. Typically, clients pay lower fees using the consulting process, and they better understand the fees. The consulting process helps retain clients by helping them understand their costs.

Explaining the Value of Consulting to Clients

Today, most financial professionals understand the advantages of consulting—not only to their own practice, but also to their clients' long-range financial goals. However, describing the true value of a finely tuned process that a consultant places over and above the "selling" of an investment product is not always an easy task.

Simply, a newly transitioned advisor can explain that it is the consulting process through which the most value for the client is received. Here are key points for advisors and consultants to examine before discussing the process with clients or prospective clients:

- First, a consultant is not a money manager. Consultants help clients hire portfolio managers. The consultant is, therefore, an intermediary between their clients and the experts who make the day-to-day investment decisions. A consultant's job is to ask vital questions, probe for objectives, and help clarify which strategies can best result in success (or avoid failure). The process assists with the delicate task of finding one or more suitable and appropriate investment managers. This process takes skill, experience and information, all qualities that qualified consultants have in common. One of the benefits of working with a qualified consultant is that they and/or their firms provide value added services such as on-site meetings and due diligence reviews of the investment management firm, keeping a protective eye out for legal, management and performance changes, or anything else that may affect investments.

- Additionally, certain areas of tax-efficient investing can be explored, as well as better and more timely reporting which is made possible through integrated technology currently available to consultants. Most consultants have developed working relationships with CPAs, business and estate planning attorneys, and insurance professionals. These individuals are valuable resources who are rich in expertise and can be available as allies. One key benefit is the security clients feel when they have confidence in their team of investment professionals.

- Finally, why hire a consultant? It is not reasonable to expect even highly experienced investors or trustees to be able to keep up with the overflow of information that affects investments today. For one thing, most do not have access to the technology used to conduct manager searches, monitor performance or assure proper asset allocation. For another, investors do not have the expertise or time to conduct due diligence of money managers or to stay abreast of changes in the management team. This is all part of the consulting process and the value of advice.[3]

Summary

A good consultant should more than earn his or her fee; and a good consulting relationship empowers the client to make more intelligent decisions that are fueled by the wisdom of experts. As more informed investors learn about the consulting process, they will turn to investment management consultants to protect them from unnecessary risk, help them stick to a long-term strategy, and to implement a disciplined process to ensure their goals are achieved.

❖ ❖ ❖

---

1 The Value of Investment Management Consulting, ICIMC, Editor Sydney LeBlanc, 1998
2 Adapted with permission from "Eleven Persuasive Reasons to Become a Consultant," John F. Holman and Robert D. Hogue, www.horsesmouth.com 2000
3 The Value of Investment Management Consulting, ICIMC, Editor Sydney LeBlanc, 1998

Editor's note: Thanks to Don Trone for his permission to reference text from, "The Management of Investment Decisions," by Donald B. Trone, William B. Allbright, and Philip R. Taylor. 1996. All rights reserved.

Commentary and Observations
By Alan Sislen

Challenges for the Consultant

Competition is a major issue. Many advisors are now trying to get a foothold into the ultra high net worth marketplace. Some of the major challenges the consultant faces today is how to be — and remain — an excellent relationship manager, offer superb service and advice, and how to become highly knowledgeable and educated. The consultant also must keep current about the capital markets and the development of new financial instruments, since they are constantly evolving.

Unfortunately, good advisors and consultants who are incredibly knowledgeable from an academic standpoint, at times cannot seem to persuade the client to do what is ultimately in the client's best interest. Consultants who are skilled in the technical areas potentially could increase their business two-or three-fold if they took a more holistic approach with clients, understanding them from the inside out, giving them the benefit of professional advice and then persuading them to take action.

Taking more of a wealth management approach is another challenge as the competition for the affluent individual continues to heat up. Some advisors and consultants feel they cannot be experts in all areas. Obviously, it is easier for the professional who works for the larger firm because of the expert resources that are available. The wealth management approach is more difficult for the independent investment consultant, in terms of capital outlay for technology, staff members or partners in areas of accounting, estate planning, insurance and business consulting. However, those who make the often difficult leap into this lucrative market, seldom have regrets.*

Education and Designations

As more consultants and advisors earn designations, the better it is for the industry. It raises the bar and the standards for everyone. But it's not simply the credentials that are important — it's how the client and the consultant relate to each other, and how comfortable they feel in the relationship. People entrust their money to those they have confidence in, no matter what designations a financial professional holds, no matter what initials are on their business cards.

The certifications and designations serve multiple purposes. First, in addition to the valuable education provided, they clearly demonstrate to clients that the consultant has reached a certain level of expertise. From a competitive standpoint, designations help differentiate a consultant in a crowded marketplace. They also provide the consultant a level of confidence knowing that their knowledge level is a step above much of their competition.

Most investment management consultants attend formal and informal training and educational industry functions. Many consultants are members of professional associations that have standards, codes of ethics, certification programs and advanced training programs. Designations are granted to qualified consultants who complete a detailed course in the process of investment management consulting. Programs typically cover all aspects of investment management consulting including: Investment policy, manager analyses and selection, performance measurement, asset allocation, modern portfolio theory, the tax-exempt market, ERISA-related

Editor's note: for more information on cost and budgeting see Chapter 34

standards, and ethical considerations. Those holding designations must uphold the high code of ethics and standards and meet continuing education requirements established by the association to maintain their designations.

Consultant Accountability

Generally speaking, consultants provide guidance and make recommendations. In most cases, the client is ultimately responsible for deciding what he or she is going to do. The often quoted doctor analogy can apply here: A patient visits the doctor for an ailment. The patient is examined, a diagnosis is given, and advice for treatment is recommended. Ultimately, the patient decides whether he or she wants the particular treatment or not. The Investment Advisers Act of 1940 defines an advisor as an individual or firm that provides guidance and advice for a fee. In most cases, consultants do not make the actual decision for their clients; they are accountable for providing guidance and advice.

On Technology

The use of technology is increasing in the investment management and the consulting business. However, clients are looking for solutions; solutions that will lead them to their destination. How they get there, and with what technology, isn't as critical to them. Technology has a place, but clients only care about seeing the results of the technology. Advisors and consultants can run their practices more efficiently and with greater accuracy with the programs available today. But, it still comes down to the relationship. Clients don't care to know, for example, how all their account information is pulled together and shown on one statement; or, how their portfolio performance was consolidated onto one page. They just want their financial life simplified.

Technology-Enabled Investment Products and Services

Technology has helped create new investment products and services, such as separately managed accounts (SMAs), multiple strategy portfolios (MSPs), and unified managed accounts (UMAs). One question consultants raise about these new products and services is whether their role, as perceived by the client, is enhanced or reduced. Early in the life of SMAs, financial consultants constantly raised the concern that their clients viewed *them* as the portfolio manager. Wouldn't their role be lessened if investment managers were hired? Over the last 15 plus years, that concern has virtually disappeared as the financial consultant assumed a far more valuable role, that of relationship manager to the client. Clients appreciate their consultants being their advocate, and significant value is now placed on this role.

The same issue has frequently been raised about MSPs, because the MSP sponsor, typically, has greater responsibility for determining asset allocations, rebalancing, tax considerations, and management of concentrated sector, issue or industry weightings across multiple investment managers or portfolio "sleeves." Freeing up the consultant's time from these more mundane tasks that technology can facilitate, the consultant can now provide the client with more time to discuss the client's goals, objectives, risk preferences and progress toward financial goals. Like the institutional marketplace of 30 years ago, the consultant has the opportunity to provide the client with more value, not less.

For consultants transitioning to a fee-based business, as well as established financial consultants, SMAs, MSPs and UMAs are a win-win-win. They are good for the client because they provide simplicity and a higher level of advice and guidance; they are good for the consultant because client relationships are solidified and the consultant's perceived value is increased; and they are good for the sponsor firm because more predictable revenue is generated and client satisfaction and retention increase.

In Summary

To truly serve their clients, investment management consultants must be able to react to an ever-changing industry. That job can be rewarding as well as challenging because consultants constantly must educate themselves on new and innovative investment solutions, investment principles, and technological advances.

As any consultant knows, *the management* of investment management is not a job to be taken lightly. It is important to always keep in mind a client's goals and objectives, and work in partnership with that client. Consultants must continually educate clients and they must always be aware of the clients' current financial and personal situation. They must formulate an investment and/or wealth management plan to carry the client through their lifetime, and to safeguard remaining assets for futures generations. Their role is not so much to manage client accounts, but to manage clients' expectations and investment decisions, that is, to help the client manage the critically important investment management process. Thus, the rewards of helping clients is mutually gratifying to the investor as well as to the consultant, who leads the client down the best path toward attaining their personal dreams and financial goals.

❖❖❖

3

CONSULTANT:
EDUCATOR AND CONFIDANTE

Daniel R. Bott Sr., CIMC
Managing Director, Investment Officer
Bott & Associates

The money management process is not all that complicated. Or is it? The methods utilized range from the very basic allocation of mutual funds from a boiler-plate brochure, to a highly sophisticated study program with certification exams that have up to a 50 percent failure rate. A vast array of well-defined information, accompanied by many research resources, is available about the consulting process.

The same thing can be said, however, for becoming a brain or heart surgeon, or even a welder. Still not complicated?

Money management, like any other process or profession, requires knowledge and skill to be successful. Typically, seasoned professionals will attain a high level of wisdom stemming from trial, error, and recovery. Industry experience suggests that a large number of investors (high net worth, small to mid-sized institutional) continue to make the mistake of hiring an investment advisor or portfolio manager without using the services of a consultant. Consequently, these investors later discover that significant capital is lost, or opportunities missed, due to lack of knowledge and experience.

If an investor wants to achieve a fairly high level of success in investing, it requires a disciplined process. Most investors, however, are not interested in becoming professionals in the investment business. This is why they have not learned how to "make money with money."

One would be hard-pressed to find an advisor or consultant with clients who previously were not riders on an emotional roller coaster, making one rash financial decision after another. To end their emotional ride, industry professionals need to educate investors with market history facts. This, of course, takes time. Consultants and advisors should plan on three to five years to turn a client into an excellent investor. In the meantime, to create low client turnover and high client retention, consultants must work to meet client objectives as well as instill a high level of confidence in their professional capabilities.

Absolutely essential is the need to teach clients about the money management process.

They need to understand that bumps in the road are nothing more than rough spots, and to be shown historical perspectives of similar occurrences. The more educated the client, the more comfortable he or she is with a plan of action, and the more patient he or she is about following the advisor's investment recommendations.

Successful Consultants are Educators

The most successful consultants and advisors are those who take the consulting process seriously and also are skilled educators to their clients.

10 prominent traits of the highly successful consultant as educator.[1]

1. Believes that an informed investor is a more successful investor
2. Probes for information and facts about the investor
3. Qualifies as a talented interpreter of information
4. Skilled as a communicator of facts and numbers
5. Diligent implementer of agreed-upon recommendations
6. Makes the process simple and gets to the point quickly
7. Explains and does not leave room to assume
8. Does not confuse simple facts with current trends
9. Has confidence and maintains a long-term perspective
10. Evaluates a plan that currently is not working, and communicates needed changes simply, or redefines the plan with current factual information

Above all, the consultant must continue to do research, maintain a focus on the process, hold to a discipline, and implement the plan by communicating so the investor understands what is happening and why.

In more detail, here are the ways these 10 traits can make a skilled consultant an excellent educator to the investor.

- If the consultant works in abstract terms and doesn't buy into the idea that "a well-informed investor is a better investor," then he or she should forget about the rest of the traits. If the consultant doesn't take the lead as an educator, then sooner or later the investor will lose faith when something doesn't go well. That fear will cause the investor to become defensive, most likely, at the wrong time.

Consultant: Educator and Confidante

- History and factual information on the markets are tools of the trade for the consultant; however, the consultant also needs to have a handle on the investing history of each *client*. This information helps the consultant better understand some of the investor's hang-ups or confusion about certain aspects of the markets or about their risk levels.

- The consultant must act as an interpreter. The consultant already should have an opinion of the market conditions and, based on his or her own research, have evaluated areas to avoid. However, a truly valuable consultant is one who takes great effort to understand the underlying biases of each and every investor.

- Being a good communicator really helps when trying to deliver a concept; however, consultants who don't understand the concept themselves already are behind the eight-ball. A great way to deliver a message is through charts, graphs or a PowerPoint presentation. Keep it simple, and try to get to the point quickly.

- Once the consultant makes a recommendation, it is important to illustrate how that recommendation will appear within the new asset mix, and be ready to implement it. The consultant must be diligent without being pushy. Consultants who have done their homework can show the investor exactly how to move forward.

- Consultants shouldn't assume the investor understands what they are saying. They must explain a concept in multiple ways, making sure not to insult a client's intelligence. First, the consultant must explain to the investor what the recommendation should *not* do, i.e., lose all of their money. The consultant must explain how liquid the investment may or may not be, how the recommendation affects the entire asset mix, and how important it is to follow through with the recommendation. Remember, the investor can't really assess the "greatness" of the consultant's idea. It is up to the consultant to show the benefits of the plan and the negatives for not doing it. The consultant also must explain that he or she has taken all of the risks into consideration and that the rewards of the plan outweigh the risks.

- In today's world of continuous and timely news, investors are bombarded with differing opinions and news. A good consultant must be ready to explain how, and if, current events will affect an investor's investments and whether a well-thought-out investment policy should be modified because of some news event or a new investment fad. The consultant of today must stay abreast of the information that investors hear through the media; otherwise, they may not know what chatter-of-the-day is hitting their clients' ears.

- Successful consultants must exude confidence; if they don't, the investor will not share in that confidence. Investors don't pay consultants for uncertainty; they assume the consultant has the knowledge to make an educated assessment. Most investors know their consultant doesn't have a crystal ball, and they don't expect perfection. They do, however, expect the consultant to be knowledgeable and confident in their recommendations.

- If a recommendation doesn't go as planned, the consultant must come up with a plan to resolve the problem. Often, time does not heal a bad situation. In general, investors decide to exit an investment or move their account simply because their consultant didn't educate them or remedy a bad situation.

- On the other hand, when things go well, the consultant must remember to rebalance the client's portfolio so a great situation doesn't slip away. This is, arguably, one of the most difficult, but most valuable, recommendations that consultants can make to their clients. Investors inherently want to reward good results with more money; however, the consultant must be ready to show clients that above-average returns generally regress to their mean average. Allowing over-allocation in a high-priced segment of the portfolio to go unattended is just as bad as recommending an investor make an investment to an overpriced segment. Consulting is a value-added proposition. Consultants must use all of their skills to protect profits. The best way to do this is to educate the investor on the laws of regression and remind them to trust professional experience.

Education Equals Trust

In summary, a successful investment management consultant and/or highly skilled advisor must be a successful educator. A successful educator must be prepared with information, be able to deliver the information in an understandable way, be confident in his or her recommendations, and be ready to implement them.

Remember, the consultant is the knowledgeable professional in the investor/consultant relationship. That's how trust is developed and maintained in good markets and bad.

❖❖❖

---

[1] These 10 traits were created by, and are the original property of, the author Daniel R. Bott Sr., CIMC

4

WHAT WILL IT TAKE
TO MAKE IT A PROFESSION?

Donald Trone, AIFA™, President and Founder
Foundation for Fiduciary Studies

"Society depends upon professionals to provide reliable fixed standards in situations where the facts are murky or the temptations too strong. Their principal contribution is an ability to bring sound judgment to bear on these situations. They represent the best a particular community is able to muster in response to new challenges."

—— Dr. Robert Kennedy
"Why Military Officers Must Have Training in Ethics"

In a time of crisis and scandal, the need for professionals is the most acute. A profession is characterized as a vocation that has defined practice standards integrated with ethical procedures and is supported by required advanced training and education. There must be a means of measuring both objective and subjective decisions made by the professional. The business of providing investment advice, relative to other professions, is in its infancy, but its importance to the fiscal health of the nation cannot be under-emphasized.

The vast majority of the country's liquid, investable wealth is in the hands of investment fiduciaries – the more than five million people who have the legal responsibility for managing someone else's money and who serve as investment committee members and trustees. These investment fiduciaries rely heavily on investment advisors to assist them in the management of their fiduciary duties and responsibilities. Even retail and high net worth investors (non-fiduciary accounts) often turn to investment advisors for objective advice and guidance.

Despite the critical role investment advisors play in the management of the nation's wealth, we must honestly assess whether the business of investment advice has reached professional status. Does it have defined practice standards? Are the practices integrated with ethical procedures? Are there requirements for advanced training and education? Regrettably, the answer is no— at least, not yet.

Defining the Advisor's Professional Role

To earn professional status, an investment advisor must be willing to accept fiduciary status. In fact, by functional definition, every professional (regardless of the associated business) is held to the fiduciary standard of care associated with that profession. In other words, the professional has the fiduciary responsibility to manage and make decisions consistent with the profession's defined practice standards.

One regulatory body must be responsible for the oversight of the profession. Today, investment advisors can choose between two: the Securities and Exchange Commission (SEC) and the National Association of Securities Dealers (NASD). In some limited cases, investment advisors *could* choose not to come under any regulatory authority at all (by staying below a state's client *de minimus* requirements)!

The SEC is the most logical sole regulatory choice since it already holds the registered investment advisor accountable to a *fiduciary standard of care*. In contrast, the NASD defines for brokers a *suitability standard of care* which is intended to address the execution of transactions and the selling of financial products. The NASD rules are simply not intended to cover situations in which a broker is called upon to provide comprehensive and continuous investment advice. Confusion on the part of investors between the roles of "advisor" and "broker" has been the source of numerous regulatory complaints.

One of the shortcomings of the SEC, however, is that *the regulator* has yet to define the specific practices that detail a *fiduciary standard of care*. We can approximate the scope of the fiduciary standards by examining regulations, regulatory opinion letters, and case law, but specific details are lacking.

Defining the Practices That Detail a Fiduciary Standard of Care

Defined practice standards must be adopted if an *industry* is to mature into a *profession*. Investment advisors lack such defined practices, so where should we turn—to the regulators, or to the industry itself? The Foundation for Fiduciary Studies is a not-for-profit organization launched in the fall of 2000 to bring together industry veterans and fiduciary experts to define the practices that detail a prudent investment process.

The Foundation began its task with several objectives:

1. To define practices that are applicable to both investment advisors and to investment committee members and trustees.
2. To define practices that detail a prudent investment process from beginning to end. The emphasis is on *practices,* which define the breadth of a subject, as opposed to *standards,* which define

the depth. The foundation recognized that the first challenge was to reach an industry consensus on defining the practices before allocating additional time to defining standards.

3. To define practices that are comprehensive, but not cumbersome, and to employ a language the layperson can understand. Every consideration was given to reducing ambiguity and subjectivity so that the practices could be easily communicated to as broad an audience as possible.

4. To define practices that are applicable to any fiduciary engagement. Rather than focusing on the differences between fiduciary accounts, the emphasis was on identifying the practices that are equally applicable to retirement plans, foundations, endowments and private trusts – referred to as the horizontal integration of the fiduciary practices.

The Foundation began by analyzing existing fiduciary legislation: (1) Employee Retirement Income and Retirement Act of 1974 (ERISA); Uniform Prudent Investor Act (UPIA); and Uniform Management of Public Employees Retirement Systems Act (UMPERS). Upon examination, it was determined that seven standards of care are contained in all three acts. The Foundation coined the term, *Uniform Fiduciary Standards of Care*, to denote these seven specific fiduciary standards of care:

Uniform Fiduciary Standards of Care

1. Know standards, laws, and trust provisions
2. Diversify assets to specific risk/return profile of client
3. Prepare investment policy statement (IPS)
4. Use "prudent experts" (money managers) and document due diligence
5. Control and account for investment expenses
6. Monitor the activities of "prudent experts"
7. Avoid conflicts of interest and prohibited transactions

In turn, the simplest investment process that can be constructed from the seven *Uniform Fiduciary Standards of Care* is a *Five-Step Investment Management Process*:

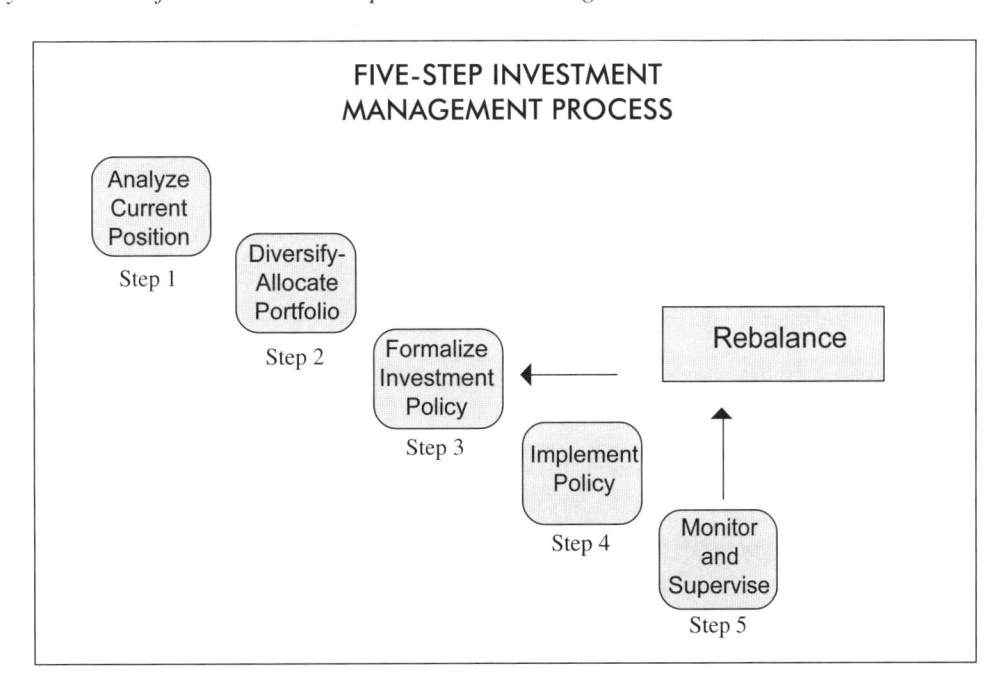

FIVE-STEP INVESTMENT MANAGEMENT PROCESS

- Step 1: Analyze Current Position
- Step 2: Diversify-Allocate Portfolio
- Step 3: Formalize Investment Policy
- Step 4: Implement Policy
- Step 5: Monitor and Supervise
- Rebalance

The seven *Uniform Fiduciary Standards of Care* and the *Five-Step Investment Management Process* framed a prudent investment process; however, certain details were still missing. To complete the picture, and to aid in the visualization of the intersection between the *Uniform Standards* and the *Five-Step Process*, a matrix was constructed:

The vertical axis of the matrix is the seven *Uniform Fiduciary Standards of Care*. The horizontal axis of the matrix is the *Five-Step Investment Management Process*.

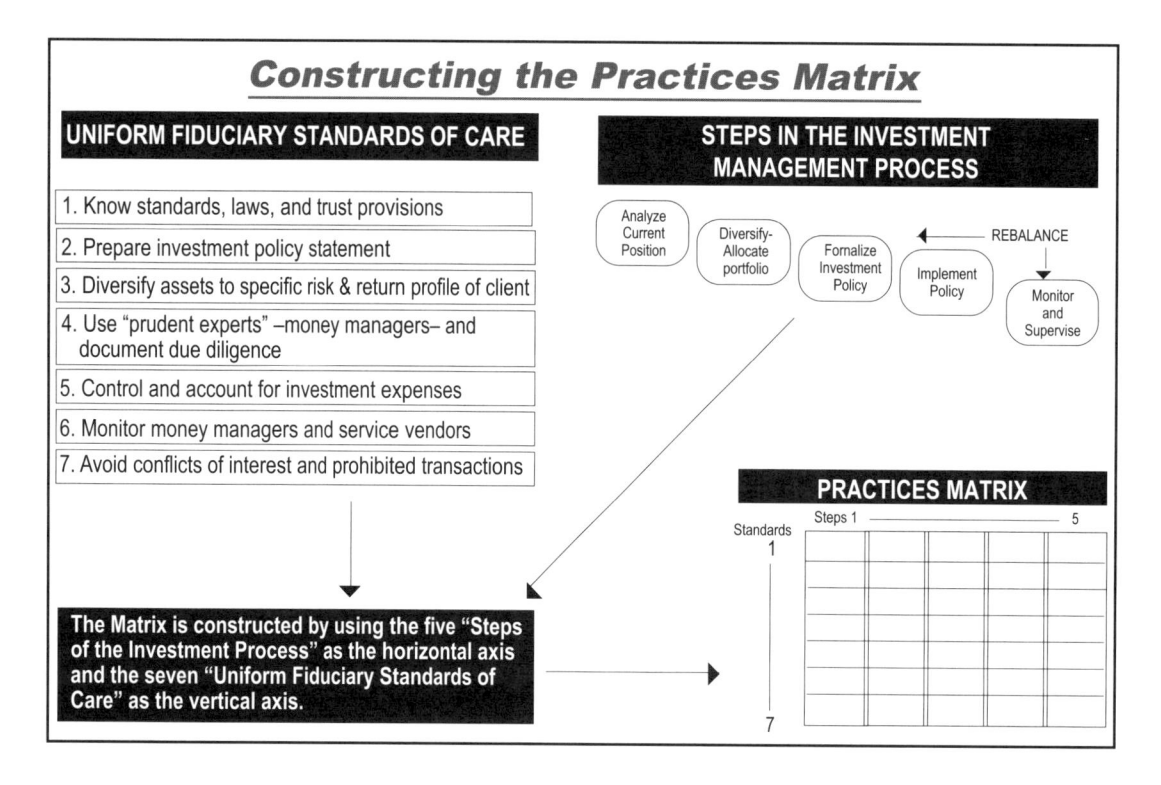

Constructing the Practices Matrix

UNIFORM FIDUCIARY STANDARDS OF CARE

1. Know standards, laws, and trust provisions
2. Prepare investment policy statement
3. Diversify assets to specific risk & return profile of client
4. Use "prudent experts" –money managers– and document due diligence
5. Control and account for investment expenses
6. Monitor money managers and service vendors
7. Avoid conflicts of interest and prohibited transactions

STEPS IN THE INVESTMENT MANAGEMENT PROCESS

Analyze Current Position → Diversify-Allocate portfolio → Formalize Investment Policy → Implement Policy → Monitor and Supervise ← REBALANCE

The Matrix is constructed by using the five "Steps of the Investment Process" as the horizontal axis and the seven "Uniform Fiduciary Standards of Care" as the vertical axis.

PRACTICES MATRIX: Standards 1–7 (vertical) × Steps 1–5 (horizontal)

The logic behind the construction of the matrix is to ensure the identification of all practices needed to define a prudent investment process that meets a fiduciary standard of care.

Each cell of the matrix should have one or more identified *Practice(s)*. When the matrix was completed, 27 discrete *Practices* were identified. To facilitate the ordering of the *Practices*, each one is grouped under the most appropriate *Step of the Investment Management Process*.

    Practice No. 1.1 Investments are managed in accordance with applicable laws, trust documents, and written investment policy statements (IPS).

    Practice No. 1.2 Fiduciaries are aware of their duties and responsibilities.

    Practice No. 1.3 Fiduciaries and parties in interest are not involved in self-dealing.

    Practice No. 1.4 Service agreements and contracts are in writing, and do not contain provisions that conflict with fiduciary standards of care.

    Practice No. 1.5 There is documentation to show timing and distribution of cash flows, and the payment of liabilities.

    Practice No. 1.6 Assets are within the jurisdiction of U.S. courts, and are protected from theft and embezzlement.

What Will It Take?

Practice No. 2.1 A risk level has been identified.

Practice No. 2.2 An expected modeled return to meet investment objectives has been identified.

Practice No. 2.3 An investment time horizon has been identified.

Practice No. 2.4 Selected asset classes are consistent with the identified risk, return, and time horizon.

Practice No. 2.5 The number of asset classes is consistent with portfolio size.

Practice No. 3.1 There is detail to implement a specific investment strategy.

Practice No. 3.2 The investment policy statement defines duties and responsibilities of all parties involved.

Practice No. 3.3 The investment policy statement defines diversification and rebalancing guidelines.

Practice No. 3.4 The investment policy statement defines due diligence criteria for selecting investment options.

Practice No. 3.5 The investment policy statement defines monitoring criteria for investment options and service vendors.

Practice No. 3.6 The investment policy statement defines procedures for controlling and accounting for investment expenses.

Practice No. 3.7 The investment policy statement defines appropriately structured, socially responsible investment strategies (when applicable).

Practice No. 4.1 The investment strategy is implemented in compliance with the required level of prudence.

Practice No. 4.2 The Fiduciary is following applicable "Safe Harbor" provisions (when elected).

Practice No. 4.3 Investment vehicles are appropriate for the portfolio size.

Practice No. 4.4 A due diligence process is followed in selecting the custodian.

Practice No. 5.1 Periodic performance reports compare the performance of money managers against appropriate index, peer group, and IPS objectives.

Practice No. 5.2 Periodic reviews are made of qualitative and/or organizational changes to money managers.

Practice No. 5.3 Control procedures are in place to periodically review money managers' policies for best execution, soft dollars, and proxy voting.

Practice No. 5.4 Fees for investment management are consistent with contracts and service agreements.

Practice No. 5.5 "Finders fees," 12b-1 fees, or other forms of compensation for asset placement are appropriately applied, utilized, and documented.

Integrating Fiduciary Practices with Ethical Procedures

A well-defined code of ethics should be based on fiduciary practices that serve as the working guide for investigating and distinguishing "right" from "wrong." However, ethical behavior cannot be controlled simply with a checklist of rules and regulations—it also must be a state of mind and an attitude. Ethical behavior requires critical intelligence, factual information, and a commitment to doing what's right.

Investment advisors should take a page from religion and medicine and consider the value of Casuistic Decision-Making (CDM)—defined as the application of principles to aid in investigating and judging "right" from "wrong."[1] As it pertains to developing the investment advisory industry as a profession, CDM is the application of the previously defined fiduciary practices to help clarify legal, ethical, and moral decisions made by investment advisors.

The fiduciary P*ractices* are intended to be maxims that serve as illuminators—not as directives. The *Practices* enable the investment advisor to enter into each decision-making situation armed with an intelligible, prudent investment process that brings fiduciary and ethical imperatives into practical application. The focus should be on *prospective* procedural process rather than *retrospective* judgment-passing.

Regulations are widespread in the investment industry, so it would seem that nearly every decision faced by an investment advisor would be controlled by a set of prefabricated rules and regulations. Yet, industry scandals clearly demonstrate that regulations alone will never fully protect the investor.

CDM encourages and inculcates standards of care for investment advisors that are *higher* than the law requires. It bridges the gap between what is required by regulators and what is in the *best interests of the investor*. This trite phrase appears throughout regulations and industry marketing slogans, but the scandals clearly prove that those words have lost their intended meaning. CDM helps to prioritize the natural tension that exists between the four polarities of an advisor's investment decisions: (1) What is in the best interests of the investor; (2) What is required by law; (3) What is in the best interests of the advisor; and, (4) What is in the best interests of the advisor's firm.

Quadrilateral Tension of Investment Advisory Decisions

- What is in the best interests of the client?
- What is in the best interests of the advisor's firm?
- What is in the best interests of the advisor?
- What do regulations require?

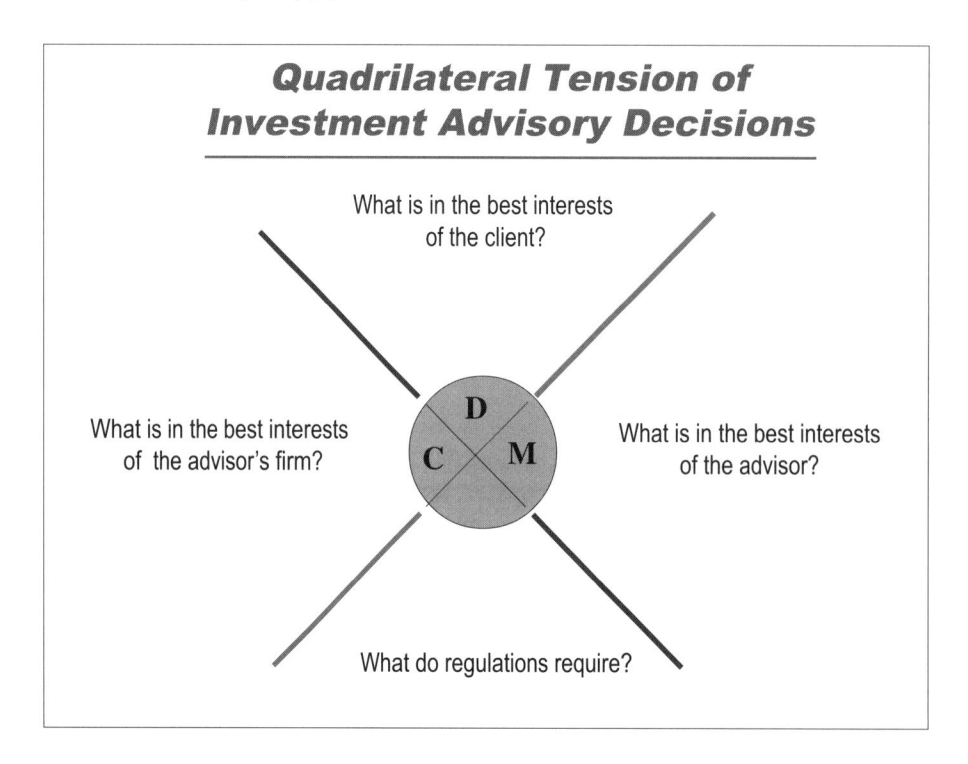

(CDM)

What Will It Take?

Unfortunately, some advisors will hide behind the *letter* of the law to escape the higher demands of the *spirit* behind the regulations. Less ethical advisors and, in some cases, entire investment advisory firms will find ways to camouflage their self-interests behind a systematized scheme of codified conduct.

The Requirement for Advanced Training and Education

Defined practice standards of care integrated with ethical procedures lead to the identification of learning objectives for advanced education and training. The investment industry offers a plethora of outstanding training and professional designation programs, but a defined curriculum for investment advisors has yet to be identified.

We would suggest that upon completion of a training program, the advisor should, at minimum, be able to:

1. Articulate the legal and regulatory environment impacting investment fiduciaries
2. Articulate the steps of a prudent investment process
3. Describe the process for conducting an asset allocation study
4. Prepare an investment policy statement
5. Conduct due diligence on separate account managers and mutual funds
6. Implement an investment strategy with active and/or passive funds
7. Monitor and supervise the activities of an investment program
8. Analyze an investment program's expenses and fees
9. Analyze an investment program for possible prohibited transactions and conflicts of interest
10. Deliver performance measurement reports
11. Customize fiduciary services to different market segments

Furthermore, the key learning components of this chapter still lack traditional academic rigor–no doctorate is offered in investment fiduciary responsibility!

In Summary: Pulling it all Together

What will it take to turn the investment advisory business into a profession? The requirements bear repeating. Investment advisors must:

- Be willing to acknowledge their fiduciary status, and communicate the same to their clients
- Be regulated by one entity – preferably the SEC
- Adhere to defined fiduciary practice standards of care
- Apply an ethical decision-making process in conjunction with the defined fiduciary practices
- Complete advanced education and training on fiduciary responsibility and portfolio management

The investment advisor's most important role is to *manage* the client's overall investment process, otherwise the client's investment strategy cannot be defined, implemented, or evaluated. Defined fiduciary practices can help the advisor to: uncover investment and/or procedural risks not previously identified; assist in prioritizing investment management projects; and establish benchmarks to measure progress. Most importantly, professional fiduciary standards of care coupled with an ethical decision-making process can provide the foundation and framework to keep the advisor from making ad hoc investment decisions.

❖ ❖ ❖

Editor's note: More information on Mr. Trone's work can be found at Fiduciary 360 http://www.fi360.com.

---

1 The author acknowledges the significant influence of the book "Situation Effects" by Joseph Fletcher (1905—1991) [Westminster Press, 1966] for this section of the chapter.

5

INSTILLING TRUST AND ELIMINATING INVESTOR FEAR

Thomas O'Keefe, AAMS, Founder and President
National Association of Investment Professionals

"Our greatest challenge now is to turn around the public environment from one of skepticism and doubt to one of confidence and trust. Unremitting stories of scandals, misdeeds and alleged wrongdoing have shaken the public's trust in us, as well as our confidence in ourselves."

— Marc Lackritz, President of the Securities Industry Association, 2003 annual conference in Boca Raton, Florida.

Trust is of primary importance in a civilized world. From neighborhood stores to major stock exchanges, these various markets operate—and rely—on trust. But when Enron filed for bankruptcy in December of 2001, it soon became clear that investors' trust was taken for granted and abused not only in one company, or sector, but across our total market system. High standards of integrity dipped to their lowest point in recent history.

One need only to review a recent study[1] done by the Securities Industry Association (SIA) on the concerns investors have about investing in the stock market to realize there is a serious problem with trust in our industry. In this study:

- 60 percent expressed high levels of concern about accounting fraud at U.S. corporations

- 57 percent said they were concerned about corporate governance
- 43 percent volunteered dishonesty as the main issue facing the securities industry today, up from 41 percent in 2002
- 66 percent cited the industry's reluctance to punish wrongdoers as a big problem

A December 3, 2003, *Wall Street Journal* article cited a study done by the Spectrem Group of wealthy investors for the period of 2001-2003 that found:

- Mutual fund assets dropped to 6 percent from 11 percent of total assets for this class
- Mutual funds were the second-least popular asset class among high net worth people, beating only stock options and restricted stock as a class
- Managed accounts during the same period grew from 13 percent to 26 percent of total assets
- Interestingly, *individual stocks and bonds* grew as an asset class from 26 percent to 31 percent
- 67 percent said they plan on investing their hordes of cash in individual stocks over the next 12 months

Clearly, there is growing mistrust of the financial services industry among the investing public because the same survey points out that *the advice they sought from advisors and brokers dropped 27 percent*! Yet, the survey also tells us that investors are trusting *someone* to give them advice on which individual stocks and bonds to buy, but whom are they trusting for this advice?

The reasons for the growing mistrust are obvious. After all, many investors lost a great deal of money in the market from March of 2000 to the spring of 2003. We know, to a great degree, these losses were caused by some analysts hyping stocks in the media and on road shows that had nowhere near the value they were purported to have. And, to make things worse, daily revelations were made over the last few years about how Wall Street and big corporate insiders were using tie-ins, excessive commissions, "flipping," "laddering", "spinning", and other questionable activities regarding the creation of worthless special purpose entities by accounting firms.

From the peak of the bull run to late 2002, the market shrank by more than $6 trillion. In fact, by November of 2002, the Bloomberg Internet Index had shed $1.7 trillon in market value alone. Of the 280 stocks in the index, 79 were down 90 percent or more from their 52-week high. Another 72 were down 80 to 89 percent. This wasn't a correction – it was a crash!

Then came the stories of bad governance in the corporate boardrooms as well as at the largest, most prestigious trading exchange in the world—-the New York Stock Exchange. As soon as NYSE president Dick Grasso was shown the door after disclosures of his excessive pay package, the public was hit with yet another barrage of controversy regarding mutual fund late trading and sales practices.

Up to this point, 95 million U.S. investors thought they could at least trust mutual fund companies – even if they believed major Wall Street firms were riddled with corruption. But now, even that belief has been thrown onto the pile of urban legends. In fact, in a survey done by *Sound Money* on National Public Radio, 59 percent of those surveyed thought that the mutual fund industry was rigged against the individual investor. In the same survey, close to 80 percent of those questioned said they would withdraw their money if a mutual fund company was accused of wrongdoing.

A great many brokers and advisors have left the industry. But that's not all bad. The state of flux in our industry is creating a great opportunity for smart advisors to re-establish trust and to capture more assets from the investing public. Financial advisors, consultants, financial planners, wealth managers, and brokers are an integral part of the solution.

The advisors who are providing the solutions are the same people that investors are flocking to for advice. These professionals are managers of the hopes and fears of each and every client and prospective client under their counsel. Since most investors tend to base their investment decisions on emotions rather than intellect, it is vital to teach them how to control emotions like fear, for example, while promoting the emotions of trust and respect.

A Case in Point

The National Association of Investment Professionals (NAIP) is very fortunate to have a large percentage of its members who are very successful advisors. We asked one of these members for advice on how *he* has built trust over a 20-year period with his clients. Don Barry, an advisor who works with a well-respected regional firm in the Midwest, has a far-reaching reputation for being not only a consummate professional, but also an individual of high integrity. The following are Mr. Barry's core beliefs, laced with some humor, concerning investor trust:

- We must be concerned about rebuilding the clients' hope for the future. We are stuck with finding an intellectual solution to an emotional problem, but it can be done. The disappointment investors feel is simply the gap between expectations and reality. For example, after four years of double-digit returns, what do you suppose the average investor expectation was for the fifth year? Keeping your clients' expectations realistic should be a blindingly obvious goal.

- Ask indepth questions, listen carefully, then ask more questions. This is *absolutely* essential for engendering trust, as well as for gathering information.

- The process by which you get to know a new client is a big issue in building trust. Imagine coming in for the investor/advisor interview and the first question from the advisor is, 'how much money do you have to invest today?' The second statement the advisor makes is about a great, new fund the investor needs. Some advisors try too hard to establish a relationship, and think one way is to 'buy it' with expectations that incite greed on the prospect's part with the latest hot-dot. Building trust begins with giving advice, not selling products.

- If you have to use the word "trust" in a conversation about yourself, there is a high likelihood you don't have it and never will. You can use the word trust as it refers to a type of account; after that, don't use it again. Once lost, it is almost never regained, in any circumstance. Think of your own experience— once a person admits a mistake to you, you are willing to forgive and go on. The people who have the biggest problems are the ones who deny the mistake and try to cover it up.

- Disclosure, even at the cost of losing a prospective client, is a necessary part of the investment process, not only because of trust, but also because it is the right thing to do (and, oh, by the way…it's the law).

- The investor also must feel the advisor or broker is technically competent and knows more than the investor about the complicated areas of investing. This is one of the reasons new brokers and advisors have such a hard time obtaining accounts from friends and associates. An advisor will have a higher credibility level with a prospect they don't know, rather than with the guy who used to crush beer cans on his forehead.

- The impression an advisor gives others is also important. What we wear, say, and our environment all play a part in the trust equation. Most people trust doctors in a white lab coat. But what would you do if a physician in a clown suit, big red nose and huge shoes came in and asked you to get undressed, stick out your tongue, and say 'aaahh?' It's no surprise that bankers used to wear three-piece suits in times past, and even more so after many banks went broke in the 1930s."

In Conclusion : Take Time to Reflect

Investors continue to fear fraud and dishonesty in our industry today. To alleviate those fears and to establish trust, advisors should make sure they truly listen to their clients, are empathetic, and treat them as they would want to be treated. Acting ethically in the best interest of the client does not mean one must be an ascetic, on the contrary. Instead, it will create a differentiation in the advisor's practice to which investors will be drawn.

> Now is the time for advisors to be introspective. Ask these few questions, and add to this list .

1. What do investors fear most?
2. How do we eliminate these fears?
3. What are investors now doing to alleviate their fears?
4. How can we be part of the solution?
5. What qualities are the most significant in the trusted advisor?
6. What are the vital steps in re-building investor trust?
7. In re-building this trust can we make it a win-win for both our clients and ourselves?

Discovering the answers to these questions can help advisors better understand their clients – and themselves. And understanding clients goes a long way toward building and maintaining trust over the long term, in good markets and bad.

❖❖❖

---

[1] SIA annual investor survey- Paris Interactive, "Investor's Attitudes Toward the Securities Industry, 2003" November 2003.

Building Trust and Establishing Credibility

An interview with Steven S. Shagrin, CFP and million-dollar advisor at a major wirehouse.

Editor's Note: *The following interview by Tom O'Keefe with Mr. Shagrin is a good example of one high-level advisor's beliefs on the aspect of client trust. Mr. Shagrin also is a retirement counselor, enhanced lifestyle planner and holds a JD degree.*

O'Keefe: Why do many investors feel a sense of betrayal or have skepticism about financial advisors in particular?

Shagrin: Many investors feel that the financial services industry is in business only for WIIFM - that is, "What's in it for me?" and responsibility to investors is last on the list.

O'Keefe: Can trust be regulated?

Shagrin: No, trust is an attitude and a feeling investors have as a result of the exercise of proper responsibility. It cannot be regulated the way measurable and tangible activities can be.

O'Keefe: Are disclosure and accountability vital building blocks to trust?

Shagrin: Yes, but words on paper are only that — words on paper. And the words and paper are only as good as the integrity that backs them up.

O'Keefe: From your experience what do investors fear most? How do you best allay the fears?

Shagrin: Number one, they fear uncertainty. You alleviate this fear in part by positioning the investor's portfolio in a diversified manner which, in correlation with their values and motivations, goals and objectives, most closely matches their comfort level, as well as their need for return and accessibility.

O'Keefe: How difficult is it for a financial advisor to change the perception that they, as a group, are untrustworthy?

Shagrin: It's easily done individually, one-on-one with investors we work with. As a group, it's by not doing things that put us in the news in a negative light.

O'Keefe: Describe what you feel are the vital steps to take to "re-build" or "re-confirm" the investors' trust.

Shagrin: Full and complete disclosure of costs and whose "fingers are in the till."

O'Keefe: What qualities are the most significant in the trusted advisor?

Shagrin: Good listening skills, compassion, and understanding of the client's innermost concerns and needs.

O'Keefe: Use a sample scenario or two in which an advisor may find himself/herself having to defend or discuss the issue of trust

Shagrin: Anyone who was sold a mutual fund may ask the advisor to defend their recommendation, especially for those fund families recently in the news for bad behavior. Also, investors steered into specific companies later found to be defrauding the entire investment community.

O'Keefe: Does an advisor have to earn an investor's trust, or should it be implicit?

Shagrin: It has to be earned, it's no longer implicit. It's not so much a *challenge* for advisors to meet, but more of an ongoing, unwaivering *obligation.*

O'Keefe: Some firms talk a good "put-the-client-first" game, but continue to give lip service. Explain why this is harmful to the advisor as well as the client.

Shagrin: Remember the story of "The Boy Who Cried Wolf?" That's what investors feel like these days — the townsfolk who responded to the cry for help so many times and were fooled. Investors seem to have lost all trust and faith in the financial services industry.

O'Keefe: What would be the perfect environment (if cost, firm politics, personalities, time restraints, talent were no object) in which financial professionals could develop trusting relationships with investors?

Shagrin: If everyone worked on a "fee-only" basis, with investments secured through a central clearinghouse with full disclosure and the same level of transactions costs for all, institutional as well as retail. Advisors would be compensated for advice, not for being hucksters of financial products.

6

DEFINING INVESTOR RESPONSIBILITY

Jack C. Waymire, President
Paladin Investor Resources

Clients and prospective clients are apprehensive about investing these days, and with good reason. Financial headlines are screaming about impropriety in the financial services and mutual fund industries. Investors get jittery when they hear that companies are under scrutiny by the Securities and Exchange Commission (SEC) and other regulatory entities. As much as they want to invest for the future, clients and potential clients want to be reassured that they are doing the right thing, and that their assets are in good hands.

This is where a competent advisor comes in. Advisors need to be ready to educate their clients not only on the basics of money and portfolio management, but also on the workings of the financial services industry. They need to be able to explain how and why unlawful trading practices happen, and, at the same time, explain how regulatory agencies act quickly to make sure other abuses don't occur. That's why it is also important for an advisor to view a client's financial situation from their side of the table.

Investors Need Guidance

The primary goal of most investors is saving for retirement. This means that if something goes awry in an investment plan, the results can be catastrophic – deferred retirements, part-time jobs, reduced standards of living, and financial insecurity late in life when they can least afford it.

Client application

For these reasons alone, it is important to impress upon investors the need to select a qualified advisor, one who can explain to them how their hard-earned retirement funds are being invested. Teaching clients how to invest does not mean they all will want to manage their own assets. An industry research report shows that only 16 percent of investors with more than $75,000 manage their own assets, while 84 percent use the services of a personal financial advisor. Consequently, one of the most important skills an investor must learn is how to identify a highly capable advisor.

Just as people hire CPAs and attorneys, they also should seek the help of advisors and consultants to assist them with their financial goals. But there is a big difference between hiring a CPA to prepare a tax return and selecting an advisor who will map out an individual's financial future. If a CPA makes a mistake on a tax return, the error is often easy to correct. If an advisor makes a serious mistake, however, it can impact the financial well-being of an investor for years. Consequently, an advisor must impress upon prospective clients the importance of selecting a well-qualified professional.

The wise advisor helps guide a client or prospect through the investment or wealth planning process so they feel comfortable with the plan and understand the process. If an investor does not take the time to obtain this minimal amount of knowledge, who can they blame when their financial expectations fall short?

Investor Versus Advisor Responsibility

One of the primary responsibilities of an investor is to provide their advisor with complete financial and personal information.

Investors must communicate:
- Their psychological pre-disposition with regard to investing. Is the client an aggressive investor or does he/she just expect high returns? There is a big difference. Their return objectives must be consistent with their risk tolerance.
- What they expect from the advisor in terms of return on investment.
- The conditions under which the advisor could be terminated.
- A comprehensive profile of their current situation – including all assets and liabilities.

Advisors also have specific responsibilities with regard to their clients. Investor-advisor relationships are not just one-way streets.

Advisors must:
- Obtain comprehensive information so they can formulate appropriate strategies that will match an investor's expectations.
- Provide suitable solutions based on the characteristics of particular investors.
- Provide solutions that are free of any conflicts that may impact the investors' performance, risk, or expense.

Defining Investor Responsibility

Advisors must:
- Keep clients informed about market events that may impact their assets, especially in down markets.
- Provide regular (at least quarterly) performance reports as a primary ongoing service that documents results.

Tutoring the Investor

Investors often use subjective processes for evaluating advisors because they rely on input from friends, family or quick sales presentations. They use gut instincts to make their selection, rather than using an objective process to determine whether a certain advisor has the knowledge to handle their particular financial situation.

Investors who don't know what to look for in a financial advisor set themselves up for disappointment and even disaster. If they don't ask the right questions of an advisor or fail to provide the information an advisor needs to put together a comprehensive financial plan, they probably won't see their assets accumulate in line with their expectations. Even worse, they can fall victim to inexperienced advisors or brokers who may be more interested in making commissions than helping an investor create a wealth management strategy.

It is not an advisor's fault that investors will spend more time planning their next vacation than their financial futures. It is, however, their responsibility to teach investors how to take responsibility for their finances.

The Trusted Advisor

In recent years, financial associations and advisors have been helping investors learn how to select qualified financial advisors. The media and the Internet also offer articles and tips on how to select an advisor. Advisors themselves can help by providing prospects reprints of educational articles or directing them to financial association websites that provide a checklist of what to look for before choosing an advisor.

Part of the selection process is intuitive, but the foundation of a trusting relationship with a quality advisor is based on two vitally important characteristics: competence and integrity. One without the other is not worth much. For example, how valuable is competent advice from a dishonest source or incompetent advice from an honest one? The answer is, not much.

In addition, investors need to understand the importance of credentials or designations earned by an advisor. If an advisor carries a certain designation(s) behind his or her name, such as Certified Financial Planner (CFP), Certified Financial Advisor (CFA), Certified Investment Management Analyst (CIMA), Certified Investment Management Consultant (CIMC), or Chartered Financial Consultant (ChFC), for example, then an advisor must explain what these credentials mean, even if a client doesn't think to ask. These credentials show that an advisor has gone the extra mile to educate himself or herself on important financial matters affecting their profession.

Advisors also should briefly explain to clients the technology they use to develop investment solutions. For example, various software systems help advisors and money managers with asset allocation, optimization, manager search, investment policies, rebalancing, and performance reporting services. Competent, trustworthy advisors use these sophisticated tools to add value to their investment services.

Often a client selects an advisor as a result of a referral from a source the investor trusts: CPA, attorney, friend, family member, or co-worker. While this can be a helpful method of finding an advisor, it is not always the best way. Different investors have different needs, and they need to find an advisor who can best help them map out and implement their investment strategy.

The Advisor Selection Process

Investors need accurate and complete information that will help them determine the quality of the advisors they are evaluating. A detailed data-gathering process can help. An investor can ask for a Request for Information (RFI), which contains questions about education, experience, certifications, services, association memberships, and current client data. This request gives advisors a chance to explain their experience and services and helps an investor to evaluate an advisor based on his or her financial expertise.

After evaluating an advisor's background, the next step is for an advisor to provide a disclosure: sources and amounts of compensation, compliance record, and conflicts of interest are examples. For example, an advisor might disclose that he or she is putting some of the investor's assets into proprietary products.

The last document an investor should require from advisors is a signed statement that describes the treatment the investor can expect from the professional. For example, is the advisor willing to put the investor's financial interests ahead of his or her own? The advisor should disclose all potential conflicts of interest that would impact the investor's performance, risk or expense.

When investors have the RFIs, disclosure documents, and statements of intentions from several advisors, they can compare the responses and select the two or three advisors that most closely match their expectations. These "finalists" are invited to participate in interviews that will determine the eventual "winner."

This process benefits the advisor as well as the investor. The advisor gets a chance to describe his or her strengths and investment philosophy, while the investor gets all the information he or she needs to determine whether the relationship match is a good one.

Measuring Performance

Numerous services measure the performance of money managers; however, there are no technological tools to measure the performance of advisors. Advisors may explain that they provide non-discretionary services and the investors are the actual decision-makers. But in most cases, advisors control or influence the choices that are being made by investors. That includes strategy, asset allocation, manager selection, rebalancing, and retention decisions. As a result, the U.S. courts are increasingly ruling that influence is control, which creates fiduciary status for many advisors. (See chapter 4). Even if it is not a legal requirement, advisors need to provide investors with some measuring tools that they can discuss at periodic financial updates.

Lack of measurement also opens the door for inexperienced advisors to compete with high-quality advisors and consultants. Since there is no way to measure or document results, inexperienced advisors can use hindsight to select hot-performing managers and claim the manager's returns as their own track record. It is our opinion that these advisors are deliberately misleading investors when they use the managers' track records as their own and yet it is a wide-spread practice that is referred to as "selling the hot dot." This misrepresentation is a major disservice to investors and the quality advisors who actually produce competitive returns for their clients.

There should be a way to evaluate the results of advisors based on the return objectives and risk tolerances of investors. It could be as simple as taking the total return the advisor produced for all of the investor's assets, or of a representative account and comparing it to benchmarks or returns produced by other advisors for investors with similar characteristics.

Discretionary Services

Investors are increasingly interested in discretionary services that transfer decision-making authority to financial professionals, where many people believe it belongs. This is a higher level of service that produces several operating efficiencies for the investor. However, it requires an even higher level of trust because of the discretionary nature of the relationship. It's a good idea for advisors to explain to the prospect and client the various discretionary services available.

When firms begin offering discretionary services, a popular strategy is to have third parties exercise the discretion. That explains the popularity of overlay management products that are run by third-party providers. As an alternative, advisory companies also can acquire software that enables a small number of staff to run multiple overlay products.

Another form of discretion is the management of a portfolio of mutual funds by an RIA. This is referred to as a manage-the-manager program and is practiced by advisors who custody assets at third-party custodians.

The industry has resisted providing discretionary services; however, it is the preferred level of service for a high percentage of investors.

Monitoring

All quality advisors provide their clients with quarterly performance reports that describe recent, year-to-date, and since-inception return on their investments. An advisor should always be willing to discuss the status of a client's account at any point in time. Communication with a client should not be limited to pre-set meetings, and an advisor should have an open-door policy.

The information contained in a quarterly report should explain:

- Recent Market Environment
- Cash Flow
- Asset Allocation
- Performance
- Risk Characteristics
- Current Holdings
- Sales of Securities and the Tax Consequences
- Purchases of Securities

Conclusion

Advisors cannot expect investors to be as trusting as they have been in the past because of the market and industry issues that have surfaced since spring of 2000. That means advisors and consultants must be prepared to prove that they are competent and trustworthy.

Since both competency and integrity are difficult for investors to measure, it makes a proof statement problematic: It will not be enough to say "you can trust me with your assets." Advisors must be willing to offer background information and disclosures that will prove they are competent and trustworthy.

❖ ❖ ❖

Editor's note: This article is an extremely valuable pass-along tool for advisors or consultants who need assistance in fully explaining investor responsibility to their clients. For reprints, go to http://www.fisherleblanc.com.
Important: Before distributing to investors, please have materials approved by compliance and/or management.

PART II

The Complete Consultant: Process and Value

7

DATA MINING THE CLIENT QUESTIONNAIRE AND BEYOND

Lewis Walker, CFP®, CIMC, CRC®
President, Walker Capital Management Corporation
President, ICIMC, 1999-2000

Data mining means going beyond gathering data for the basic client questionnaire. An understanding of the client's core values and objectives is vital to the relationship, and is the result of face-to-face conversations over lunch or dinner, in relaxed atmospheres, during unguarded moments. It is an exercise in human communication, verbal and non-verbal, that leads to important discoveries and creative solutions.

The client's investment questionnaire involves the often-daunting task of data gathering. Many times, the client has a difficult time rounding up relevant personal and financial documents in one—or two—fell swoops. Both the advisor and the client need a system to organize the data and have the patience to wade through it.

Money, securities, and other assets may be on deposit at multiple institutions. Important paperwork and files may be held by various advisors and financial firms since, in many cases, no single advisor "owns the client relationship." One of the primary benefits an advisor provides a client is a process to define their goals and objectives so they match that client's particular lifestyle, beliefs and interests.

Often, clients walk into an advisor's office not really knowing what they want to accomplish. Sometimes "save for retirement" is the immediate issue, but there may be other yet-to-be-discovered reasons the client is there, and it is up to the advisor to uncover them. That's why one of the simplest questions to first ask a client is, "What do you expect me/my firm to do for you?" At the same time, advisors need to convey to clients that they have the expertise and experience to draw up a financial or investment plan that will carry that client through life and beyond, in terms of legacy and estate distribution objectives.

The investment questionnaire is a critical document. Locating the client's various assets and sources of income is the basis for formulating an accurate financial plan. Risk tolerance, time horizons and a client's financial situation must all be taken into consideration. From a compliance standpoint, the questionnaire is a necessity. But that does not mean it has to be looked upon with dread, or that gathering the information has to be a painful and intrusive process.

Many advisors employ an abbreviated data sheet initially, which is completed by a potential client and submitted prior to the first meeting or brought to the first meeting. Initial data is a "first cut" used to get a sense of whether the advisor and the client have a basis for a long-term, mutually satisfactory relationship. The objective is to gather enough information to determine the scope of the prospective relationship, as well as to have the opportunity to define the *process*, whether it is investment management consulting and/or a more comprehensive wealth management and financial planning process.

Patience is required during the data aggregation stage of the process, especially if the client's business, financial, and personal affairs are complex. Contact must be made with their CPA, insurance counselor, business or tax attorney, and other professionals to bring all assets into view. "Scattered assets" are the norm and it may take more time to gather this data than it does to do actual planning and execution.

Basic data gathering will encompass at least the following:

1. Family census: names; residential and business addresses; contact data (phone, fax, e-mail); names of children; ages and dates of birth for all family members; Social Security numbers; citizenship status. Are children married? Grandchildren? Health status? Special needs?

2. Net worth statement: determine ownership for all assets, i.e. ownership by client, spouse or partner; joint ownership; trust; a business entity; other (define, such as accounts held for minors). Request copies of the following statements.

    a. Checking; savings; money market; CDs (show maturity date).

    b. Stocks; bonds; mutual funds; (list or provide brokerage or custodial statement). Include data on U.S. savings bonds. Obtain tax basis for all securities.

    c. Annuities (fixed and variable). Obtain copy of policy and recent quarterly and annual reports. Determine owner; annuitant; primary and contingent beneficiaries; tax basis.

    d. Life insurance. Request copy of policy; original proposal; last annual report. Determine type of policy; face amount; the insured; owner; beneficiary (primary and contingent); premium payments; adequacy of payments (how long will the policy carry given current assumptions?); purpose of the coverage; cash values if applicable (current value, surrender value, loans outstanding). Include data on group insurance and any coverage tied to employer benefits or business arrangements such as buy/sell agreements. Determine all sources of death benefits.

    e. Real estate, including residence; vacation home; rental properties; location (city, state, or country). Identify owner; purchase price; current value; mortgage terms and current balance; cash flow from rental properties.

f. Partnership investments (obtain copy of recent quarterly or annual report). Determine cash flow; tax benefits; estimated values; liquidity, if any.

g. Business interests: name; type of business; form of ownership; percentage of ownership; value of interest; buy/sell agreement or succession plan.

h. Personal assets: description (car, boat, aircraft); value; debt. List value of other assets such as jewelry; household furnishings.

i. Retirement plans: obtain statements for all pension/profit sharing plans; IRAs; 401(k); 403(b); 457 plans; deferred compensation plans, etc. Specify primary and contingent beneficiaries.

j. Stock option plans: obtain complete description; type of options; number of shares; exercise price; current stock price; vesting.

k. Education planning: Section 529 Plans; Education IRAs; other.

l. Tangibles: type of asset (precious metals, gems, coins); date of purchase; original investment; current value.

m. Other insurance: copies of homeowner, rental, auto, umbrella liability policies; personal and group disability policies; long term care.

n. Copies of legal documents and other key documents: will(s); trusts (including revocable or irrevocable living trusts, charitable trusts); durable powers of attorney for assets and health care; divorce decrees, alimony and child support agreements; prenuptial agreements; stock purchase agreements; business buy/sell agreements; family limited partnerships; most recent tax return(s).

o. The advisory team. Name, address, and contact information for other key advisors such as a CPA or other tax advisor; attorney; banker; trustees; insurance agents; brokers; etc.

p. Anything else the client(s) thinks is important to his and/or her life and future.

What are some ways to gather these facts and figures? A written form or workbook is helpful and asking outright can work, too, but it's also possible to overwhelm a client with too much interrogation. Financial relationships are built through a deeper, more personal discussion with clients about more than their assets. The basic questionnaire does not always give an advisor a true understanding of a client's dreams and aspirations.

Probing Deeper

As a trusted advisor you need to know what the client may want beyond financial peace of mind: a second career, spiritual goals, charitable interests, legacies for survivors and the continuing family line. They may wish to fund trusts, endow causes, build cultural edifices, create foundations, educate, enlighten and inspire.

These are the "soft issues" regarding their life and their assets. What is needed are questions that go beyond basic data gathering forms and other paperwork, probing deeper areas beyond surface simplicities that will set advisors apart from their competition. These are "psychographic" questions that explore a client's life goals, family, charitable interests, leisure and recreation desires, and legacy concerns.

The World of Money Management

Psychographic questions often serve as an icebreaker at the first client meeting and let the clients know that the advisor is interested in them as people, and not just in the money they may have to invest. If an advisor is meeting with a married couple, ask how they met. Ask about where they went to college. Ask about family, hobbies and what they like to do for fun. The answers to these and other less cut-and-dried questions will help an advisor undercover their "drivers," what motivates them and steers them through life. Understanding a client's personal philosophies and lifestyle can help the advisor glean insight into such financial factors as their risk tolerance and/or their propensity toward contributing to charities or other causes.

An advisor also needs to take into account a client's particular life phase, such as whether they are in a "wealth accumulation" phase or retirement distribution phase. It's important to "get the client's story." This is the advice of Mitch Anthony, a life planning coach and force behind the Financial Life Planning Institute. Anthony suggests advisors must look at four areas of a client's life: life history and background; current life transitions; goals; and principles that guide their life and money.

Similarly, in formulating an investment policy statement (IPS) for a client, the advisor recognizes the three phases in the "money life" of a person: accumulation; preservation; distribution. Each category requires an advisor to help determine which types of investment vehicles and asset classes are most appropriate.

The Three "Money Life" Phases

- *Accumulation:* The phase in which the client, generally in his or her 20s to 50s, is working to accumulate wealth. In the early stages, however, this person is also thinking about buying a home, raising a family, etc. Insurance needs are higher. Risk tolerance is usually higher. Time frames are longer.

- *Preservation:* The client (mid-50s to mid-70s) is working to preserve a current or desired lifestyle, personal freedom and independence as long as possible. For example, the client does not want to be a burden to his or her children. Women, in particular, worry about being widows, running short of money, and having to lean on or live with their children, a circumstance to be avoided. Risk tolerance is lower.

- *Distribution:* The client (usually age 65 or older) has accumulated enough wealth so that there is little to no fear of outliving assets. The client is pondering how to allocate wealth, Whether by contributing to charities, placing funds in trusts, or setting money aside for children or grandchildren. The reduction, or elimination, of estate taxes is a consideration. This phase is strongly influenced by a person's emotional, philosophical, and religious attitudes.

A Holistic Plan

Clients want an integrated wealth and asset management process. The key word is *process*. It is the advisors process that will set them apart; how they blend the precepts of estate, tax, investment, and financial life planning into a strategic overlay. It is the *process* that distinguishes the advisor's client presentation, fact-finding and data mining, formulation of a plan and actionable recommendations, plan execution, and monitoring.

The advisors mission should be to enhance the client's probability of achieving defined goals and objectives — both the quantifiable and un-quantifiable, what might be called "interior" or "emotional finance," and "exterior finance," the numbers. "Money life" phases will be affected by transitions, for example, having children, education, key religious and cultural events, caring for aging parents, job or career changes, divorce, accidents and illness, handling life's other "emergencies" and curve balls. Life phases and transitions may overlap. A client may keep accumulating wealth in the "preservation" phase, for example, and transitions may occur at any time. "Positive transitions," like marriage and children, tend to occur early in life; "negative transitions" such as degenerative illness, often occur later in life as a function of the aging process.

Changing Demographics

Populations in the United States and most advanced countries are aging, with profound financial planning implications relating to elder care, concierge, trust, and other services. Improvements in healthcare, nutrition, education and living standards are extending planning assumptions as to longevity. Statistics show that by 2030, almost 20 percent of the U.S. population will be 65 or older. In 2000, 12.4 percent were 65 or older. In advising older clients, different factors should be considered. As people age, they naturally grow more contemplative, and are searching for more answers about the meaning of life and what will "be left of them" as a legacy when they pass into the afterlife. The new generation of retirees is interested in staying active, healthy and more committed to giving back to society. Many people no longer want to retire "for life" and opt to continue working with short retirements in between.

A client's view of retirement is important for an advisor to discern. Even people with the same financial profile can have completely diverse views on what they want to do with their assets in that distribution phase. As Mitch Anthony states in his book, "The New Retire-mentality," retirement "is about living rich, not dying rich."

The Financial Life Planning Institute has created worksheets that provide questions to help an advisor get a better understanding of their clients' priorities when it comes to life and financial matters. For example, one question posed is: "What observations have you made and lessons have you learned from watching others retire?" Another sheet suggests that a client write down their "ideal week" in retirement. The client is asked what he or she might do, morning, afternoon, and evening, in a typical seven-day retirement week.

The exercise is an eye-opener. Most realize that they cannot write, golf, fish, play bridge, visit, travel, etc, in every square. Perhaps they want to continue to work, but at a slower pace, or change careers, or do charitable or community work. The point is to get them to think through what retirement really means over a potentially longer lifespan.

Mitch Anthony's concept, "Maslow Meets Retirement," offers a unique perspective on the development of the investment policy and asset allocation plan designed to minimize the risk of running out of money in retirement. He puts a retirement twist on Abraham Maslow's "Hierarchy of Needs," breaking the pyramid into five levels from base to point. Survival money secures the base of the pyramid, meaning the following needs must be satisfied first:

- *Survival money*— What the client needs to make ends meet, pay the bills, and fund a basic standard of living

- *"What if?" money*— For unexpected expenses and emergencies

- *Freedom money*— For enjoyment and fulfillment, travel, a higher standard of living

- *Gift money*— For people and causes; gifts to children and grandchildren

- *Dream money*— The actualization of dreams, once-in-a-lifetime experiences, adventure

The Maslow hierarchy is an example of how advisors can learn more about their clients, helping them to make informed decisions about investment strategies. Base survival money and emergency capital could be kept in no-risk to low-risk asset classes to satisfy conservative survival instincts. Risk/reward characteristics could be increased for portions of the portfolio aimed at self-actualization, i.e., freedom, gift, and dream money.

The Bottom Line

Gathering information is one of the most critical facets of an advisor's job. If not done correctly, faulty or incomplete information can put a client's financial future in jeopardy, and create liability and regulatory issues. Advisors who move too quickly into the "solution phase" without first considering how to build a relationship with a client, will not find long-term success in an increasingly fee-based world with fiduciary obligations.

Wealth management starts with building trust. It's a matter of understanding how a client's upbringing formed their beliefs about saving, spending and giving away money. If an advisor knows a client's risk tolerance is low, the advisor should also know why. Are we dealing with interior and emotional finance, or are we dealing with external issues?

Advisors also need to understand how the aging process affects people – particularly their clients. Historical events, such as 9/11, bear market episodes, market volatility, and financial services industry scandals, impact how people view their assets. This does not mean that advisors have to be part psychologist and/or psychotherapist, but they do need to take the time to get to know clients on a more personal level.

The soft approach to the client questionnaire and the subsequent data mining will, in the long run, help to uncover hidden assets and unarticulated needs. An advisor who truly follows the "know your client" philosophy, will find himself or herself with a long list of referrals and a secure future.

❖ ❖ ❖

8

EFFECTIVE RISK MANAGEMENT
INCREASING THE PROBABILITY OF INVESTOR SUCCESS

John Nersesian, CFP®, CIMA, CIS
Managing Director
Frances L. Potter, CFP®
Vice President
Wealth Management Services
Nuveen Investments, Inc.

"You cannot manage outcomes, you can only manage risk."

—*Peter Bernstein*[1]

In the late 1990s, many investors conveniently ignored some of the fundamental tenets of investment management. The concepts of asset allocation, diversification, a disciplined process, rebalancing, policy statement development, and the value of professional advice were lost in a frenzied environment of double-digit returns and active trading.

Equally ignored was the fact that in order to obtain better returns, investors were inadvertently exposing themselves to risk that, in hindsight, was greater than their personal risk tolerance.

During this time period—from 1995 through the second quarter of 2000—the immutable risk/return law of investing was seemingly turned on its head. Market returns were almost twice the long-term average and were accompanied by risk characteristics that were perceived to be significantly lower than the norm. Investors came to believe that increasing their risk profile was not problematic because, in a sense, big gains in their portfolios somehow "protected" them. This experience led investors to draw precarious conclusions about the market and the risks of investing. Their behavior suggested they believed the historical concept of assuming increased risk to achieve greater returns did not apply to them. Instead, they viewed risk as missing the obvious opportunity to create significant short-term wealth by being out of the market or in the wrong stocks.

The dramatic bear market from 2000 to 2002 changed all that. By late March 2001, near the bottom of the market, investors had lost between $4 trillion and $5 trillion[2] and exited the market in droves; many advisors lost clients and left the business, and the industry lost considerable public trust.

Not all the news was negative, however. One of the positive aspects that emerged from the turmoil was that investors "rediscovered" the importance of investing fundamentals they had previously ignored. They now understood more clearly the dual nature of financial decisions—reward *and* risk—and began paying more attention to historical returns and to the risk associated with those returns. In many ways, investors learned an expensive, but important, financial lesson— risk cannot be ignored.

In this new environment, imagine the power of an approach that offers a more advanced method of describing risk to clients and prospects; an approach that educates them about risk and helps them view it not as something to be feared or avoided, but as something to be embraced, understood, and managed. With that objective in mind, this chapter will:

- Review the various ways advisors and investors define and describe risk
- Examine the "human element" in managing risk; how investors feel about volatility and loss and how those feelings influence their behavior
- Introduce portfolio risk management tools and illustrate how advisors can use them to communicate risk and manage client expectations

Readers will understand how the ability of the advisor to communicate the concept of risk is critical and can be one of the most useful tools in establishing trust, managing expectations, and demonstrating the power of professional advice.

Risk: What Does It Mean?

Too often, investors sidestep the risk aspect and focus only on one-half of the investment equation. They ask, "What is the historical return?" believing that's all they need to know to make critical investment decisions. As advisors, we must move investors away from such an isolated discussion, because the approach is flawed. In its place we need to adopt a better approach that examines all the aspects of risk—positive and negative. This begins with understanding how risk is defined.

Risk is defined in many different ways by different audiences. To those working within the investment community, risk is typically viewed in terms of variability or inconsistency of returns. However, any definition that is used to explain the variables of risk to a client must also take into consideration the client's point of view about risk. Here are four viewpoints of risk:

1. *Risk as Loss*: Investors don't want to experience losses, so they will typically define risk in one narrow way: *losing money*. Using this definition, risk has nothing to do with relative return, beating inflation, or achieving objectives. Investors may feel that if they don't lose money on an investment—even if the return is substandard—there is no risk involved in the equation.

2. *Risk as Variability:* Advisers want to know how consistently an investment manager produced the annual returns that led to the average return. They define risk as *variability*: how much will the investment's actual return differ (or vary) from the expected return.

3. *Risk as Uncertainty:* Investors often base their investment decisions on a historical investment return but may experience a result less than their expectation. For example, the historical return is 12%, but the actual return is something lower. This outcome can create doubts and fears that are validated through disappointment and anxiety.

4. *Risk as the Failure to Achieve Specific Financial Goals*: The greatest risk for many investors is not losing money in a specific period, underperforming a stated benchmark or an inconsistent portfolio return pattern. The most meaningful risk an individual investor can experience is the failure to achieve their personal financial objectives.

Consider a couple with $1 million of assets whose objective is to accumulate $2 million over a 10-year period to provide sufficient income during retirement, support for the surviving spouse, and residual capital to leave to children or charitable organizations. Assume they need a 7.5% return to achieve these objectives. The couple tells the advisor that although they intellectually appreciate the planning work, the recommendations are outside their emotional "comfort zone." What they want to do instead is invest everything in Treasury Bills, given their perceived stability and guaranteed nature. In this case the couple may think they are taking less risk with this type of investment. What they fail to understand is the consequence (risk) to which they are exposed, since this investment is unlikely to produce the return necessary to achieve the stated goal.

Although portfolio return is a straightforward concept and one that investors readily understand, risk is much more complex and challenging for investors to comprehend. That's why the advisor's role in the investment process is a crucial one. Advisors not only help clients manage their investment risk by selecting the right tools, but also communicating *how risk impacts them.*

Adding the "Human Element" to the Risk Management Equation

Much of economic and financial theory is based on the premise that when individuals make decisions they act rationally and consider all available information. Evidence compiled by researchers in the field of Behavioral Finance indicates this is often not the case. Numerous academic studies have documented how emotion and cognitive biases influence investors and the decision-making process.

To be effective, advisors, managers, and consultants must be able to address not only the technical side of investing, but also acknowledge and understand the equally important human element involved in the process. While some advisors may find the psychological part of the equation somewhat abstract, the growing body of evidence suggests it cannot be ignored as a major contributor toward investment success or failure.

Consider these two examples of investor behavior in the past 20 years:

During the period 1986 through the end of 2002, there were five significant declines in the Dow greater than 20%. Each of these five declines provided investors an opportunity to purchase equities at discounted levels. What is unfortunate about the events of this period is that investors not only did not capitalize on the market "pull back," they also did not stay their charted course. Instead, as the chart on page 50 (top) illustrates (using mutual fund flows as a proxy for investor action), they used all five of their opportunities to *get out* of the market.

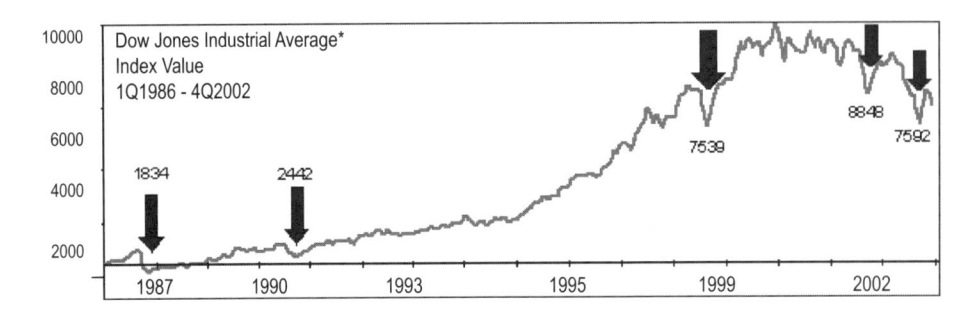

The World of Money Management

Dow Jones Industrial Average*
Index Value
1Q1986 - 4Q2002

Sources: *Bloomberg and ** Strategic Insight. Past performance is no guarantee of future results.

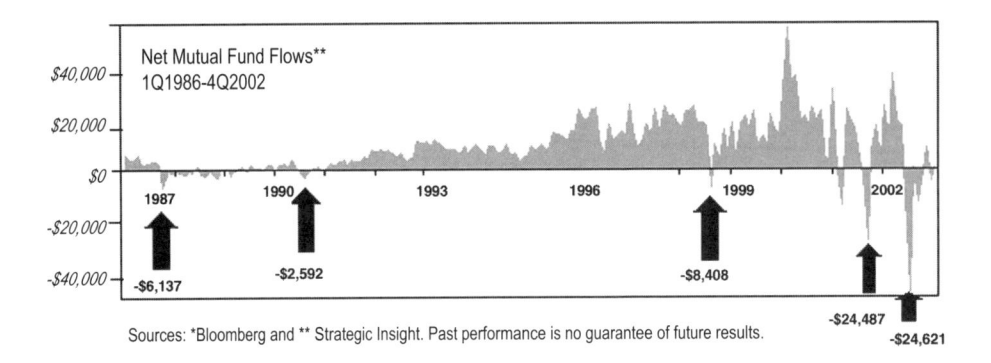

Net Mutual Fund Flows**
1Q1986-4Q2002

Sources: *Bloomberg and ** Strategic Insight. Past performance is no guarantee of future results.

A second example (right) illustrates the effect emotional decision-making can have on investment results.

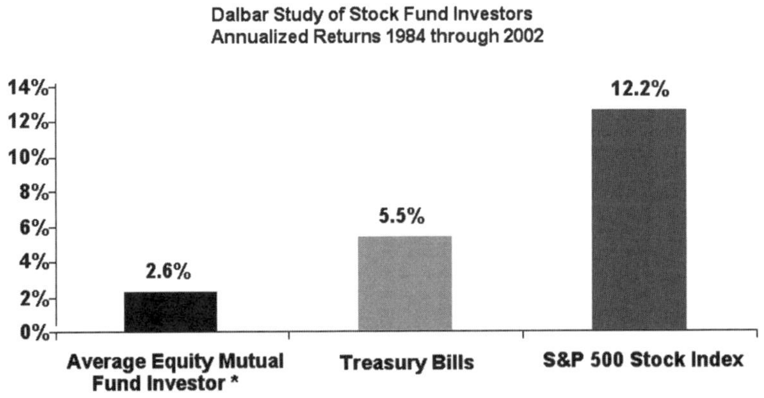

According to a Dalbar survey that covered the period 1984 through 2002, investors experienced a much lower annualized return than the S&P 500 or Treasury Bills for the period 1984 through 2002.[3]

Dalbar Study of Stock Fund Investors
Annualized Returns 1984 through 2002

- Average Equity Mutual Fund Investor*: 2.6%
- Treasury Bills: 5.5%
- S&P 500 Stock Index: 12.2%

Source: DALBAR Inc. "Quantitative Analysis of Investor Behavior," July 2003
DALBAR Inc. is a Boston-based financial research firm. Data based on cash inflows/outflows and performance of over 6,000 mutual funds representing over 95% of all funds. Past performance is no guarantee of future results. All indices are unmanaged and unavailable for direct investment.

This relative poor performance can be partially attributed to shifting from one "hot" fund to another rather than staying the course. In this example, investors on average held mutual funds for only two and a half years. Their decisions reflect our all-too-human tendency to think short-term performance represents a long-term trend and to make investment decisions based on that judgment.

As these examples demonstrate, it is critical that advisors and consultants fully understand the impact of *investor emotion* on the success or failure to reach financial goals. Earlier, "losing money" was identified as an investor definition of risk. Now look further at what loss means to an investor and how they react. This insight will help advisors frame their discussions of risk with investors.

Behavioral finance experts tell us that most human beings operate with an "aversion to loss." This loss aversion can be a meaningful ingredient in a client's willingness to either accept or reject the solutions an advisor recommends.

The late Amos Tversky, frequently recognized as the father of Behavioral Finance Theory and Princeton University's Daniel Kahneman, the Nobel Price recipient in Economics in 2002, conducted studies that enabled them to quantify the magnitude of feeling people have about loss. They found that losing one dollar makes people feel two to two-and-one-half times as bad as winning one dollar makes them feel good. Or, as basketball great Larry Bird put it "Losing hurts worse than winning feels good."

The extent to which an investor might go to avoid a loss can be seen in a psychological experiment conducted by Tversky and Kahneman whose famous work, "Prospect Theory: An Analysis of Decision-Making Under Risk" (*Econometrica*, 1979), launched a wave of behavioral research.

Kahneman and Tversky presented groups of subjects with a number of problems.

The first group was presented with the following dilemma:

In addition to whatever you own, you have been given $1,000. You are asked to choose between:

  A. A sure gain of $500.

  B. A 50% change to gain $1,000 and a 50% chance to gain nothing.

The second group of subjects was presented with a different problem:

In addition to whatever you own, you have been given $2,000. You are asked to choose between:

  A. A sure loss of $500.

  B. A 50% chance to lose $1,000 and a 50% chance to lose nothing.

While the two problems offer identical net cash to the subject, the selections by each group were different and illustrate the effect that the phrasing of the questions had on their answer. In the first group, 84% chose A, the *sure gain*, which provides $1,500. In the second group, 69% chose B, which would provide either $1,000 or the original $2,000. Rather than opting for the *sure loss*, which would have provided the same $1,500 net result as chosen overwhelming by the first group, they chose to take a chance (a risk) they would lose nothing.

Discussing this experiment can be an eye-opening experience for advisors and clients. It could help make clients more aware of their own psychological blind spots as well as providing the advisor with a clearer understanding of how much his or her client is willing to "risk" to avoid a loss.

Clear Discussions of Risk Help Manage Client Expectations

Armed with an understanding of the human side of the risk management equation, advisors can make better use of its technical aspects in their work with clients — communicating important concepts to them, educating them to a fuller understanding of risk and showing them how this can improve their decision-making.

Standard Deviation—Standard Deviation is a statistical measure of the spread or *variation* of investment returns around the average expected return. It is a valuable tool in helping to communicate risk in terms of the range of potential returns.

This chart illustrates an investment with an average return of 10%, and a standard deviation of 15%. From statistics we know a 1-standard deviation range of returns encompasses 68% of all outcomes. In this example, 1 standard deviation on either side of the average return is -5% and +25%, meaning that 68% of the time the investor's return is going to fall between -5% and +25%. A 2-standard deviation range of returns encompasses 95% of all outcomes or, in this example, returns between -20% and +40%.

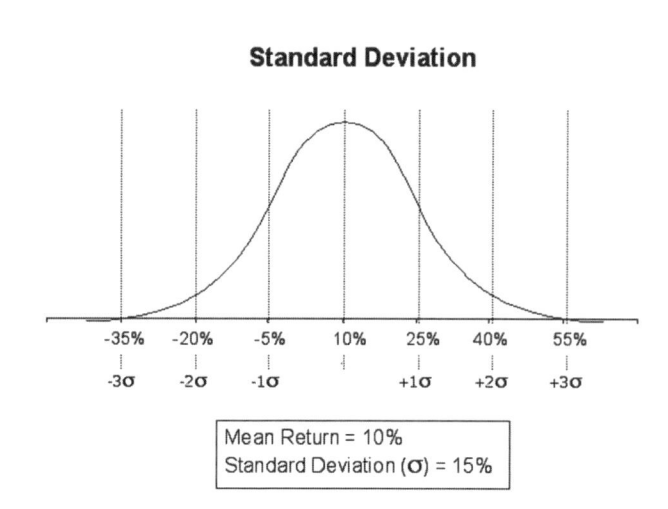

Standard Deviation

Mean Return = 10%
Standard Deviation (σ) = 15%

Using standard deviation to communicate risk to clients can help manage their expectations. The client understands there are a "range of potential returns" for the investment rather than expecting the investment to produce the historical average return exactly each year. Standard deviation can also help an investor understand the "consistency" of those returns. If the investment has a low standard deviation (or range of returns), then it is likely that the investor will experience annual results very close to the average return. If, however, the return comes with a high standard deviation, the average return will be produced but the annual experiences may vary widely.

A clearer understanding that returns will fall in a range can help improve the odds of investor success. Managing expectations in this way, by discussing the full extent of possible scenarios, prepares clients in advance to deal with possible outcomes. The investor will be less likely to succumb to their emotions and act irrationally during periods of volatility, making an imprudent decision at precisely the wrong time which may ultimately result in a lower return and reduce the probability of investor success.

Value at Risk—As useful as standard deviation is in helping to illustrate consistency, it fails to communicate risk in a client-centric manner. If an advisor looks at a client's $10 million portfolio and notes the standard deviation of the portfolio is 15%, what does this observation say about actual dollars at risk in the portfolio? For this reason, Value at Risk, a tool used primarily in the institutional arena, is being embraced more and more by advisors to high net worth investors.

Value at Risk (VaR) communicates risk in a manner that is meaningful to individual investors. It *quantifies the maximum downside loss in dollar terms* during periods of market stress with a certain level of statistical confidence, usually 95% or 99%, of occurring. This calculation of the dollar value at risk within a certain confidence interval can be used to manage expectations during the portfolio construction process to give the client a more practical and personal picture of what risks they face.

Effective Risk Management

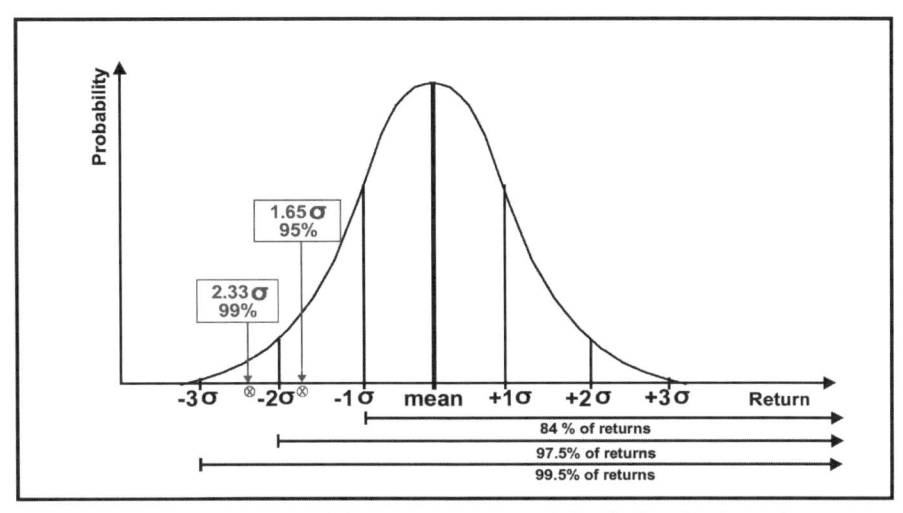

This graphic illustrates standard deivations in a normal distribution. We know from statistics that with normal distributions, 50% of returns will lie on each side of the mean. As shown here, a 95% confidence level is at -1.65 standard deviations and 99% at -2.33 standard deviations.

There are several ways of calculating Value at Risk, some of which are proprietary. This is the formula for calculating Value at Risk using the Parametric, or Delta Normal method which uses the known properties of standard deviation to help determine maximum downside risk. It assumes a normal distribution of returns and a linear relationship to the various risk factors, making the tool simple but somewhat limited.

$$\text{VaR @ 95\%} = \text{PV\$} \times \frac{(\overline{X} - 1.65\sigma)}{\sqrt{N}} \qquad \text{VaR @ 99\%} = \text{PV\$} \times \frac{(\overline{X} - 2.33\sigma)}{\sqrt{N}}$$

PV\$ = Portfolio Value In Dollar terms
$\overline{X}$ = Mean return of the portfolio for holding period
σ = Standard deviation of the portfolio
N = Number of years in projected holding period

Using the return and standard deviation from the standard deviation example mentioned earlier to calculate VAR for a $1 million portfolio:

$$\text{VaR @ 95\%} = \$1{,}000{,}000 \times \frac{[.10 - 1.65*.15]}{\sqrt{1}} = -14.75 \text{ or } \$147{,}500$$

In this example, there is a 95% probability the client's largest potential loss in the one year holding period would have been no more than $147,500.

As useful as VaR is, it also has its limitations. It is not the worst case scenario that reflects the maximum potential loss a client can expect to endure, nor does it intend to estimate potential losses under particular market conditions. Used in concert with other risk metrics, Value at Risk can be useful in educating clients and managing expectations.

Monte Carlo Simulation—Monte Carlo Simulation offers another view of investment risk in terms a client can understand: the likely success or failure in achieving specific financial goals (for example desired retirement income or target value of a portfolio). It can help prepare the investor for the possibility that their returns might deviate from expected returns in a meaningful way.

More specifically, Monte Carlo Simulation is a non-linear forecasting tool that utilizes randomly generated returns based on a portfolio's risk and return profile (i.e., historical or estimated standard deviation and expected return) or random sequencing of historical risk and return data. The returns are used to calculate thousands of different, potential portfolio values over a given time period.

Financial advisors who incorporate it into their practice enhance their ability to:

- Manage client expectations more effectively
- Construct portfolio strategies that are more likely to achieve the client's financial goals
- Present recommendations in a more compelling manner

The following hypothetical example utilizes Monte Carlo Simulation to compare and contrast the potential outcomes of a concentrated portfolio with those of a diversified portfolio. In this example, a 60-year-old client with a $3 million portfolio has the following financial goals over the next 30 years:

- Generate $100,000 per year for living expenses, before taxes
- Leave the current portfolio assets of $3 million, adjusted for inflation, to his estate

The client's current portfolio has 75% of the value concentrated in a single large-cap equity position. The remaining 25% of the portfolio is invested in the S&P 500 index. Based on historical data, the portfolio has a standard deviation of 44% and an average return of 12%.

The client is also considering a more diversified portfolio. The alternative portfolio would have 55% allocated to the S&P 500 index, 35% allocated to the Russell 2000 index and the remaining 10% in cash.[4] This portfolio, based on historical data, has a standard deviation of 19% and an average return of 13%. The diversified portfolio has an additional consideration; capital gains tax must be paid to diversify the portfolio out of the concentrated large cap position. The concentrated position of $2,250,000 has a basis of $583,333 generating a capital gain of $1,666,667. The $250,000 capital gains tax is assumed to be paid immediately at the current rate of 15%.

A Monte Carlo Simulation demonstrates how the inefficiency of the concentrated portfolio impacts the probability of the client achieving their stated goals. Based on 1,000 different models of the 30-year time period calculated for the Monte Carlo Simulation, the concentrated portfolio was successful in achieving the client's goals ($100,000 per year living expense and leaving $3 million adjusted for inflation) *only* 31% of the time. The diversified portfolio was successful in achieving the client's goals *84%* of the time. Clearly, the higher vola-

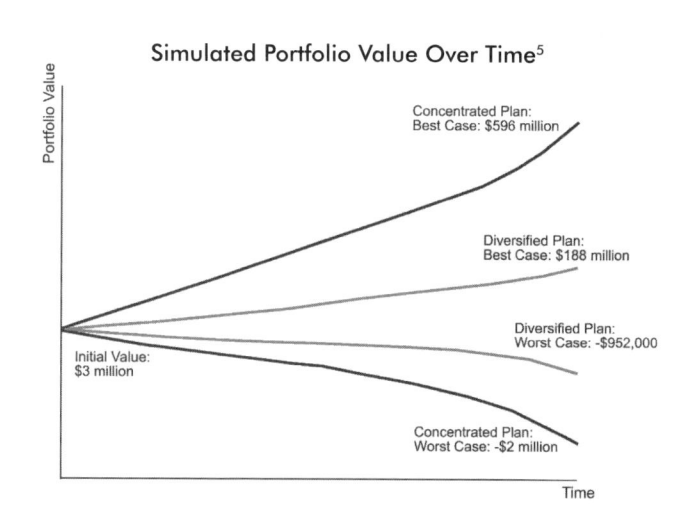

Effective Risk Management

tility of the concentrated portfolio has a direct, negative impact on the client's ability to achieve their goals.

The graph on page 54 shows the simulated value of the concentrated and diversified portfolio over time for both the best and worst case scenarios. The variability of outcomes is much narrower for the diversified portfolio than the concentrated portfolio. This narrower range of outcomes increases the probability of achieving the client's goals. Even though the best case scenario for the concentrated plan has a much higher terminal value than the diversified plan, the probability of achieving that value is very small. Using illustrations of this type to communicate risk to clients can be very beneficial.

Monte Carlo Simulation is clearly beneficial when compared to linear forecasting due to the variety of outcomes that are generated. However, it does have its limitations. Some simulations assume investment returns are normally distributed. Also, simulations typically rely on historical data, which is not indicative of future results. It should be viewed as a statistical tool for illustrative purposes only and not relied on solely for any investment decisions.

Managing Risk Through Portfolio Rebalancing

Many advisors appreciate the importance of setting an appropriate asset allocation strategy for their clients and find it is critical to managing risk. According to the work done by Brinson, Hood, and Beebower[6] in 1986, asset allocation accounts for approximately 90% of the *variability* in portfolio returns.

As advisors discuss diversification and asset allocation with their clients, some may unintentionally fall short in their explanation of the specific benefits in terms of what the investor will actually experience.

For example, an advisor makes representative investments in various asset classes — stocks, bonds and cash — and allocates money among styles and sectors, thus further diversifying the client allocation. Many investors may not realize that if asset allocation works as intended, the one thing that *almost always happens* is that one of these investments is not going to perform particularly well during any given market cycle.

Advisors need to explain more carefully to clients that the asset classes don't move in tandem because the correlation between them is different. If all the asset classes did similarly well during a certain period of time then, conversely, they may all perform poorly during similar periods of time. Non-correlated moves are to be expected.

While the preponderance of academic evidence indicates that the actual asset allocation plays a primary role in determining portfolio returns, this is not the case. The most important determinant is, instead, the ability to adhere to the long-term, target asset allocation, otherwise known as the investment policy.[7]

A good illustration of the importance of having a long-term plan is a study conducted by University of California at Berkeley Associate Professor Terrance Odean and University of California at Davis Professor of Finance Brad Barber. Their results found that individual investors trading stocks with no plan in place and no established asset allocation significantly underperformed the market. Moreover, the more they traded, the worse they performed, which led the researchers to conclude that "trading is hazardous to your wealth."[8]

While establishing an initial asset allocation is helpful in achieving investor objectives, by itself it may not be sufficient. Active portfolio rebalancing, the process of reallocating portfolio assets back to a policy target, helps advisors go further by providing a number of benefits:

- The potential for increased returns — many studies have identified a "rebalancing bonus" derived from an active rebalancing methodology.[9]

- A more consistent (i.e., lower risk) portfolio experience – active rebalancing, by definition, requires the reduction of portfolio sectors that have become over-weighted through market volatility, contributions, and differing returns, which helps to moderate risk.

- A disciplined process to making difficult financial choices – a formal rebalancing process requires investors to reduce their exposure to assets that have performed well recently, and add to assets that have underperformed or are currently out of favor. This process, despite the obvious rationale is, by its very nature, counterintuitive and difficult for investors to adopt.

The chart below illustrates the periodic rebalancing method, an approach which specifies regularly scheduled adjustments to bring the portfolio back to the targeted allocation. Most studies suggest a very minor difference between quarterly, semi-annual or annual rebalancing, and many advisors have adopted the less-frequent annual rebalancing approach in order to minimize transaction costs and tax recognition.

The chart shows a hypothetical $1 million portfolio including the initial allocation amounts to each of the asset classes[10], the returns produced in the first year (using calendar year 2002 returns in our example), the resulting asset class values at the end of the first year, the new allocation targets, and the necessary portfolio adjustments.

Without a formal rebalancing process many investors would have been reluctant to add money to equity investments and take money out of municipal bond investments at the end of 2002 to bring their portfolio back into "balance." Practically speaking, rebalancing an investment portfolio *forces us to do what is emotionally uncomfortable.*

A further example of the benefits rebalancing can provide is illustrated in a study conducted by Nuveen Investments Wealth Management Group. This study examined the results of annual rebal-

Annual Rebalancing —A Hypothetical Example
Returns for year ending December 2002

	Lehman Muni 40%	Russell 1000G 30%	Russell 1000V 30%	Total Value of Portfolio
Start of Year	$400,000	$300,000	$300,000	$1,000,000
Return in 1 Year	9.60%	-27.89%	-15.53%	-9.19%
Value at end of Year 1	$438,400	$216,330	$253,410	$908,140
Rebalance to	$363,256	$272, 442	$272,442	$908,140
Rebalancing at end of Year 1	Withdraw $75,144	Deposit $56,112	Deposit $19,032	

Benefits of Rebalancing
$1 million portfolio: 40% Lehman Muni; 30% Russell 1000 Growth; 30% Russell 1000 Value

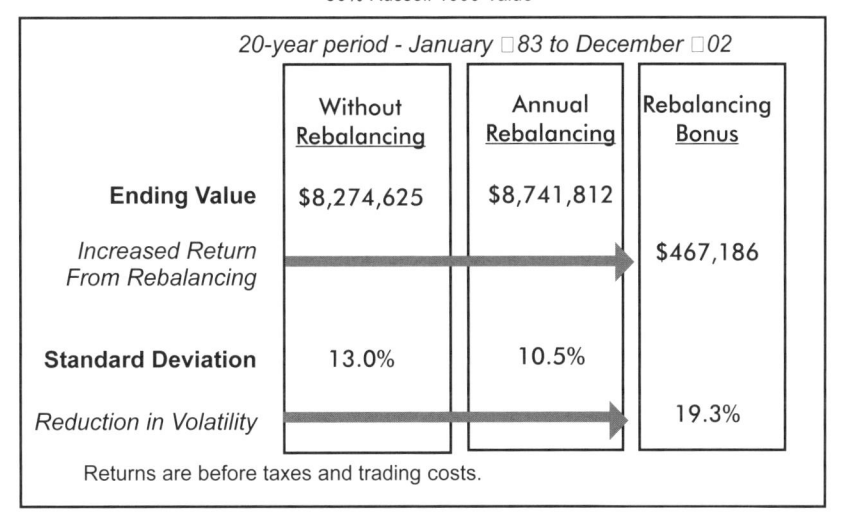

20-year period - January '83 to December '02

	Without Rebalancing	Annual Rebalancing	Rebalancing Bonus
Ending Value	$8,274,625	$8,741,812	
Increased Return From Rebalancing			$467,186
Standard Deviation	13.0%	10.5%	
Reduction in Volatility			19.3%

Returns are before taxes and trading costs.

ancing and its positive impact on client success over a 20-year period, from 1983 to 2002. Two $1 million portfolios were tracked using indices to represent portfolio investments in growth, value and municipal bonds. The first portfolio remained "static." The $1 million grew to approximately $8.2 million at the end of the 20-year experience, with a standard deviation of 13%.

The second portfolio was rebalanced annually, and its return increased from $8.2 million to $8.7 million or $500,000 worth of incremental returns. The far greater benefit to the investor, however, was the reduction of risk from rebalancing—a decline in the standard deviation of the portfolio by over 19% to 10.5%.

Get to Know the Client by Asking the Right Questions

With so many behavioral elements and personal biases to be considered, advisors are challenged to fully understand their clients' attitudes and tolerance for risk.

In a 1998 study conducted by psychological testing firm Elsayed and Martin, investors completed a questionnaire measuring financial risk tolerance. Results revealed that advisors' estimates of the risk tolerance of their clients were accurate in less than one-half of the cases; were slightly accurate in one-in-three cases; and were significantly inaccurate in one-in-six cases. There was a tendency among advisers to *overestimate* when the risk tolerance of clients was low. On the other hand, advisors *underestimated* when risk tolerance was high.[11]

This study indicates that it is often not easy for advisors to estimate the risk tolerance of their clients. There exists a level of overconfidence among some advisors, possibly reinforced by their misplaced belief in the effectiveness and accuracy of their personal measures of risk tolerance. This overconfident seems to lead these advisors to believe their estimates are more accurate than they actually are. Advisors should be aware of this challenge, and take advantage of the many educational resources available on the subject of behavioral finance to better understand the nuances of individual investor psychology. The more advisors know about their client's "emotional" attitudes about risk, the more successful their relationship will be.

It may also be naïve to think that any one mathematical "model" or standard client questionnaire can adequately measure risk tolerance. Many advisors who have used these questionnaires to determine how their clients would "feel and act" in certain market conditions can attest to a phenomenon that behavioral finance experts called "dynamic inconsistency." This term describes the difference between how investors *say* they will act in a particular instance (for example, when the market declines 10 %) and how they actually *do* act. An investor filling out a questionnaire may say they can tolerate a loss of 10% of their portfolio but, when it actually happens, may find that is not the case and they abandon their strategy.

There is a significant opportunity for advisors to bring value to their relationships with clients by helping them understand their tolerance for risk through guided self-discovery. This is one facet of the investment process that investors are often ill-equipped to do on their own. This discovery process goes deeper than the typical profiling forms, making liberal use of open-ended questions which are designed to learn how clients feel and suggest what they will do in certain circumstances. Examples of questions that can be used in developing a dialogue with clients follow. Using questions of this type can serve to clarify expectations from the beginning of a new client relationship and contribute to an enhanced understanding of current clients' situations and thinking.

Questions designed to uncover general attitudes about risk:

1. Describe situations in life or activities you think are risky.

2. If you won a $1,000 wager and had the opportunity to double it or lose it all by betting again, would you keep the $1,000 or bet again?

3. If you lost a $1,000 wager and had the opportunity to get it back, or double your loss by betting again, would you bet again?

4. When you think of the word "risk," what comes to mind? (Examples that could be used if needed to prompt the client might include: Loss, Uncertainty, Opportunity, or Excitement.)

5. How would your best friends describe your attitudes about risk? (Examples that could be used to prompt the client might include: "you are a gambler" or "willing to take risks after much consideration" or "very cautious" or "you avoid risk when possible".)

6. Please react to the statement . . ."When I make decisions, immediately knowing the outcome is not important to me."

7. How would you describe your philosophy about life? (Examples which could be used to prompt the client might include: "Nothing ventured, nothing gained," "Everything in moderation," "Slow and steady wins the race.")

Questions designed to understand how individuals feel about investments and the experience of investing:

1. Tell me about your best investment. What made it the "best"?

2. Tell me about your worst investment. What made it the "worst"?

3. If, at the end of the year, the market was up 20% and your portfolio was up 10 %, a return that would enable you to achieve your objective, how would you feel about your results?

4. Imagine you buy shares of a stock fund and three months later the price increases by 35%. What would you do?

5. Imagine you buy shares of the same stock fund and three months later the price falls by 35%. What would you do?

6. Imagine you buy shares of the same fund and the price falls by 35%. The fund is part of an investment portfolio that you won't need until retirement in 20 years. What would you do?

7. Tell me about your time frame for meeting your goals.

8. What are the long term effects if your investment program fails to achieve its goal? (Examples of type of answers clients might give could include: "Child does not go to college," "Retirement is delayed,, "Purchase of vacation home is delayed.") How do you think you would feel about that outcome?

9. Please complete this sentence: "It is most important to me that this investment _____." (Examples of answers might be "beats the benchmark," "doesn't lose any money," "meets my investment objective," "outperforms my neighbors' (friends') investments.")

10. Tell me how you felt during the recent bear market. Did it keep you awake at night?

11. Tell me what you did during the recent bear market. Did you sell because the prospect of continuing to lose money was too stressful? Did you see it as a buying opportunity for quality investments?

12. What dollar amount of your total net worth could you bear to lose?

13. Tell me about the provisions you've made (emergency fund, stable income) that would enable you to ride out market ups and downs.

Advanced Approach to Risk Management Benefits Investors and Advisors

The natural temptation for many investors is to ignore risk and focus on what they consider to be the more pleasurable aspects of investing – the potential returns. Risk is, however, an inherent part of the investing equation and leading financial advisors are helping their clients develop a greater understanding of what it is and how it can be managed. These advisors want to:

- Educate clients about the several ways that risk can be defined
- Help them understand the human element of investing and how their emotions can influence their behavior
- Use appropriate risk measures to manage risk and communicate with clients in ways that are meaningful to them

This enhanced perspective contributes to a more satisfying investor experience and an increased probability of success. From the advisors' point of view, by educating clients as to why risk is relevant, and clarifying the two-sided nature of financial decisions, they earn the position of trusted professional and the privilege of managing more assets.

❖❖❖

---

[1] Bernstein, Peter L. "Against the Gods: The Remarkable Story of Risk, "Chichester: Wiley, 1996. 383 p.
[2] Dreman, David, Stephen Johnson, Donald MacGregor, and Paul Slovic, "A Report on the March 2001 Investor Sentiment Survey." *The Journal of Psychology and Financial Markets*, 2001, Vol. 2, No. 3: pp. 126-127.
[3] Treasury Bills are short-term, debt instruments backed by the full faith and credit of the U.S. Government. Returns do not reflect fees and expenses.
The Dow Jones Industrial Average is a price-weighted average of 30 significant stocks traded on the New York Stock Exchange and the Nasdaq.
S&P 500 Index measures the performance of large capitalization U.S. stocks. The S&P 500 is a market weighted

index of 500 stocks that are traded on the NYSE, AMEX, and NASDAQ.

[4] S&P 500 Index measures the performance of large capitalization U.S. stocks. The S&P 500 is a market weighted index of 500 stocks that are traded on the NYSE, AMEX, and NASDAQ.

Russell 2000 Index measures the performance of the 2,000 smallest companies in the Russell 3000 Index, which represents approximately 8% of the total market capitalization of the Russell 3000 Index.

[5] Monte Carlo Simulation results generated with Financeware.com software. Historical data is based on averaging rolling historical periods (total of 888 ten-year periods). Other programs could produce different results.

[6] Brinson, Gary P., L. Randolph Hood, and Gilbert L. Beebower, "Determinants of Portfolio Performance," *Financial Analysts Journal*, Vol. 42, No. 2, July-Aug. 1986, 39-44.

[7] Surz, Ronald J., Dale Stevens, and Mark Wimer, "Investment Policy Explains All," *The Journal of Performance Measurement*, Summer 1999, 43-47.

[8] Barber, Brad M. and Terrance Odean, "Trading is Hazardous to Your Wealth: The Common Stock Investment Performance of Individual Investors", *Journal of Finance*, Vol. LV, No. 2, April 2000, 773-806.

[9] "10 Reasons to Rebalance Clients' Portfolios", Horsesmouth, October 28, 2002

[10] Russell 1000 Growth Index (Large-Cap Growth) measures the performance of those Russell 1000 companies with higher price-to-book ratios and higher forecasted growth values.

Russell 1000 Value Index (Large-Cap Value) measures the performance of those Russell 1000 companies with lower price-to-book ratios and lower forecasted growth values.

Lehman 7-Year Municipal Bond Index (Municipals) is the 7 Year (6-8) component of the Lehman Brothers Municipal Bond index which is a market-value-weighted index engineered for the long-term tax-exempt bond market.

[11] Elsayed, H., & Martin, J. (1998). Survey of financial risk tolerance: Australian technical report. Sydney: Chandler & Macleod

---

Disclosures: This material is provided for informational and educational purposes only. The statements contained herein are the opinions of Nuveen Investments Wealth Management Services and are subject to change without notice.

Hypothetical examples are shown for illustrative and educational purposes only and do not reflect actual portfolio performance results. It is not possible to invest directly in an index. Index returns include reinvestment of dividends and do not reflect taxes, investment advisory and other fees that would reduce performance in an actual client portfolio. Individual investor results will vary. Different benchmarks and economic periods will produce different results.

The results of the hypothetical Monte Carlo Simulation example are based on results from Financeware.com software. Monte Carlo Simulation is a method to compute a possible statistical outcome. Historical investment performance data is summarized in statistical quantities using a lognormal distribution and the quantities are inserted into assumed probability distributions. Then samples are drawn from these assumed distributions for each year in the planning horizon to arrive at an outcome. This is replicated many times (e.g., 1,000) and these outcomes are summarized into probability results. The probabilities from Monte Carlo Simulations are not guaranteed or assured in any respect, and should not be relied upon solely for any investment decision. Monte Carlo Simulation is a tool for illustrative purposes and is designed to be used in concert with other risk measures. Other tools may produce substantially different success and failure outcomes.

This report contains no investment recommendations and should not be construed as specific tax, legal, financial planning or investment advice. Clients should consult their professional advisors before making any tax or investment decisions. Investing entails risk including the loss of principal and there is no assurance that an investment will provide positive performance over any period of time. It is important to review investment objectives, risk tolerance, tax objectives and liquidity needs before choosing an investment style or manager. Information was obtained from third party sources, which we believe to be reliable but not guaranteed. Past performance is no guarantee of future results.

Nuveen Investments Wealth Management Services group has sponsored in part the publication of this book by purchasing copies for distribution, a requirement for participation.

INVESTMENT POLICY STATEMENT
A BLUEPRINT FOR GUIDING THE INVESTMENT PROCESS

Gus Fleites, CFA®
Senior Principal
State Street Global Advisors

A well-developed Investment Policy Statement (IPS) is a written document that clearly establishes an investor's long-term financial objectives and provides a disciplined decision-making process for achieving those objectives. A blueprint for managing a client's assets, the IPS should plainly articulate the client's investment philosophy, objectives and risk tolerance over a relevant time horizon—taking into consideration the investor's financial obligations, liquidity needs, and tax status.

A first critical step to creating an effective IPS is to take the time to understand clients' unique circumstances and financial needs: Do they have expected future obligations such as college tuition? Do they plan to purchase a new home? Would they like to own a second home? When do they plan to retire? What will they need to retire comfortably?

A carefully crafted IPS links a client's objectives to the investment strategies the advisor employs, thereby providing the framework for all future investment decisions. Additionally, a comprehensive IPS should include parameters by which to monitor and measure how well the investor's portfolio is performing against the established goals.

The Importance of an Investment Policy Statement

A properly developed IPS promotes adherence to objectives, instills focus and discipline, and acts as a compass to guide investors through periods of heightened market volatility. The IPS will help protect against an investor's natural inclination to make decisions based on short-term market performance.

A systematic, disciplined approach toward investing can stave off panicky moves to quickly sell assets that might be underperforming in a market downturn, or to invest too heavily in one specific "hot" asset class when the market is booming. An investment policy statement guards against this type of risky emotional investing and keeps investors focused on long-term financial goals—a very difficult, but critical, thing to do during times of market volatility.

A Collaborative Process

Creating the IPS is a collaborative process between the advisor and the client. Working together, the advisor and investor evaluate the client's current positions and—based on unique requirements, risk tolerance levels, and long-term objectives—define an effective asset allocation strategy.

Close collaboration enables the advisor and client to mutually establish the rules of their working relationship. While typically written by the advisor, the IPS is signed by both the advisor and the client and represents an agreement and commitment on the part of both to abide by the objectives, procedures and benchmarks as stated in the written document.

It is important to note that the IPS is not a legal contract, but rather a directive from the client to the advisor. It provides a framework for an advisor's decisions and recommendations and sets forth client expectations regarding communications. Additionally, while not a legally binding contract, the IPS could provide some safeguard for fiduciaries in that it provides a record of the client's outlook at the beginning of the process and establishes agreement as to the responsibilities of both parties.

A Prudent Investment Process

The Prudent Investor Rule, or some version thereof, is a standard adopted by most U.S. states to guide those with responsibility for investing the money of others. The rule stipulates that fiduciaries or trustees must act as a prudent man or woman would be expected to act, with discretion and intelligence, to seek reasonable income, preserve capital, and, in general, avoid speculative investments. The Prudent Investor Rule has its roots in the "Prudent Man Rule," the standard adopted by most trustees prior to the creation of the Prudent Investor Rule in 1992, and the Employee Retirement Income Security Act (ERISA) of 1974.

The Prudent Man Rule originated in 1830 when Judge Samuel Putnam in ruling on the case of "Harvard College v. Armory, 26 Mass. (9 Pick.) 446 (1830)" decreed that: "Those with responsibility to invest money for others should act with prudence, discretion, intelligence, and regard for the safety of capital as well as income."[1] The Prudent Man Rule did not prohibit any specific investment practices, thereby giving trustees the flexibility to best respond to varying investor and market circumstances. Subsequent legislation did, in fact, specify imprudent practices and "speculative techniques," and thereby diminished the usefulness of the formerly established Prudent Man Rule. Trustees developed a fear of liability that prevented them from pursuing investment strategies aimed at generating wealth that could be deemed speculative or imprudent under the evolving Prudent Man Rule standard.[2]

Gradually, the Prudent Man Rule came to be viewed as potentially detrimental to long-term investment interests. In 1974, ERISA was passed primarily to help ensure sufficient investment returns for defined benefit plan participants. ERISA established a standard of prudence by which to govern pension investments that gave less consideration to specific rules prohibiting investment techniques and strategies and focused more on ensuring that trustees adhered to an investment process that gave "appropriate consideration" to the facts and circumstances of the investment as it relates to the objectives and needs of the portfolio, or pension plan, overall. ERISA established a more modern, process-oriented standard that enabled trustees to have greater flexibility in utilizing specific investment techniques and strategies that best served the long-term interests of the plan participants.[3]

The American Law Institute's 1992 Restatement (Third) of Trusts, from which the Prudent Investor Rule is derived, established a standard for prudent investment of trusts that leverages the innovations of ERISA. The Prudent Investor Rule, too, established a process-oriented approach to prudent investing that emphasizes the portfolio as a whole rather than any specific investment. There are no categorical restrictions, but instead the rule demands that trustees adhere to an investment process that carefully considers the risk/reward tradeoff within the context of the overall portfolio and its goals.[4]

While the Prudent Investor Rule and a subsequently developed model state statute called the Uniform Prudent Investor Act apply to professional trustees only, they do serve as models for financial intermediaries who provide professional advice as well. Advisors have a responsibility to put their clients' interests first. Advisors, plan sponsors and money managers must provide investment advice and make investment decisions in a prudent manner, always with an eye on maximizing returns for an accepted level of risk. Primary obligations and responsibilities of fiduciaries under the "Prudent Investor Rule" include:

- To understand the investor's current positions
- To diversify in order to minimize risk of large losses – unless not advantageous
- To seek the highest returns for acceptable amount of risk
- To control costs and minimize fees where possible
- To invest both for income and capital appreciation
- To closely monitor the suitability of investments

Understanding the Client

It is important to understand, before embarking on the process of creating an IPS, the different requirements of various investor types. When discussing an investment policy statement with clients, an advisor must recognize that the risk/return objectives of individual clients will differ greatly from those of institutional clients.

For individual investors, remember that risk alone is not the sum of all fears. These clients are highly loss-averse, not risk-averse. For example, many individuals will define risk by how much they could lose, whereas institutions are more concerned with the risk associated with not being able to fund their liabilities. An individual's preferences also are much more likely to change over time depending on what life stage they are in, as opposed to an institution that is governed by a set of policies that most likely will not change dramatically over the course of a very long time horizon.

Individual Investor Traits	• Subjective in defining risk, i.e., "How much can I lose?" • Characterized by psychological factors • Defined by stage in life • May invest in whatever they want

Institutional Investor Traits
- Concerned with taxes
- Objective in defining risk
- Characterized by beneficiaries
- Comply with corporate and fiduciary responsibilities
- Governed by policy constraints
- May not be constrained by taxes

Designing a sound IPS hinges on a clear understanding of a client's tolerance for risk. The initial discussions with clients should include assessing their ability to handle near- and long-term losses, what the maximum acceptable loss for a given year or longer would be and the implication if wealth accumulation targets are not met. Having this discussion will help the advisor not only to define an investment strategy that is consistent with the client's unique life stage and circumstances, but also to provide the advisor with clear direction when creating and implementing the asset allocation strategy.

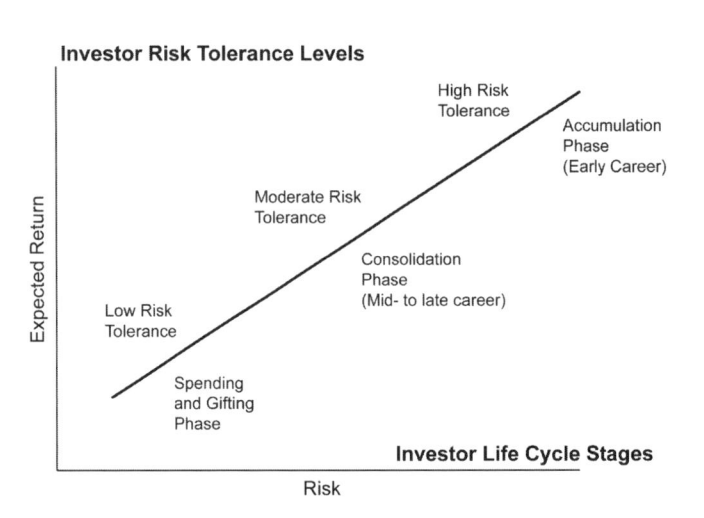

Investor Risk Tolerance Levels

- High Risk Tolerance — Accumulation Phase (Early Career)
- Moderate Risk Tolerance — Consolidation Phase (Mid- to late career)
- Low Risk Tolerance — Spending and Gifting Phase

Expected Return vs. Risk — **Investor Life Cycle Stages**

Key Components of the Investment Policy Statement

Before discussing in detail the process of creating and implementing an investment policy statement, let's first establish the elements that constitute an effective IPS:

Objectives & Goals—Based on the advisor's discussions with the client, this section outlines what the client is trying to accomplish and the investment time horizon within which to achieve those goals. This section should also prioritize those goals.

Investment Philosophy—The section of the IPS describes the investment theories and practices to which advisor and client will subscribe in seeking to achieve the long-term goals already established.

Preferences & Constraints—The client's preferences and constraints should be as specific as possible and should encompass: tolerance for risk; return expectations; liquidity requirements; and asset class preferences and limits.

▸ Risk Tolerance: Given an established investment time horizon, this section should consider the client's ability to afford short term market fluctuations. Essentially, what is his or her tolerance for risk? Perhaps the client can't afford to take any more than a 15% loss over a three-year period.

▸ Return Expectations & Liquidity Requirements: And what are the client's performance expectations? Does he or she want to achieve a certain percentage of real returns, or excess return relative to a benchmark? What are the income requirements over a given time period? This section should also describe in detail the client's tax situation. Will significant capital gains be realized? How might these be mitigated?

▶ Asset Class Preferences & Limits: This section should set forth the client's asset class preference. In seeking a diversified portfolio, does the client want to include bonds and cash in addition to stocks? Does the client want to use large-cap growth stocks *and* large-cap value stocks? Does the client prefer not to use international equity stocks? And how much volatility in asset classes is the client willing to tolerate? Given that every asset class has an associated level of risk and expected return, what are the client's asset allocation limits? Does the client wish to employ active or passive management? Will the active versus passive decision vary by asset class, market cap or style preference?

Investment Selection Performance Standards—This section will help steer the investment selection process. Here, advisor and client establish standards or criteria by which to include or exclude certain investment options. Criteria include the following:

▶ Performance record: The investment should typically have a minimum performance record by which to judge its consistency in returns. Typically, minimums are set at no less than three years.

▶ Consistency in returns: The investment should deliver consistent return performance over an extended period.

▶ Rate of return relative to peers: The investment option also should generally have a high performance record relative to its peers over lagging periods of performance.

▶ Consistency in style: Style purity of an investment option is necessary to ensure that the portfolio adheres to its diversification goals and standards.

▶ Relative risk: Investors may want to establish that the risk of the investment relative to peer offerings be lower, while having achieved similar rates of return as those peer offerings.

▶ Expenses & Taxes: Investment options should not have exorbitantly high expenses. When investing over the long-term, high tax costs and expenses can erode portfolio wealth.

Process for Monitoring & Reviewing Performance—This last section establishes rebalancing rules and limits for the client's portfolio as well as performance standards by which the portfolio and its managers will be evaluated. Criteria could include whether the allocation limits set in "Preferences and Constraints" have been exceeded. Did the portfolio meet its return targets? Did losses exceed the permissible loss limit?

Developing the Asset Allocation Strategy

Developing a sound asset allocation strategy is a critical component of the IPS—and the success of the client's portfolio depends upon it. According to a popular 1991 study by Gary Brinson, Randolph Hood, and Gilbert Beebower, the asset allocation decision accounts for 93% of the *variance* in portfolio returns.[5] As a result, it is the asset allocation decision that should drive the investment process—not when or in which stocks to invest.

Understand the Client's Goals and Constraints—In order to develop an effective asset allocation strategy, advisors must first understand their clients' financial goals and constraints. An investor's risk tolerance and life circumstances will guide advisors in constructing allocations that best pursue the client's objectives.

The World of Money Management

Avoid the Perils of Market Timing—A well-defined asset allocation strategy acts as a compass for clients to navigate through periods of market volatility. In up or down markets, investors too easily can become overconfident or panicked. Sticking to the investment strategy as dictated by their own needs and objectives helps investors avoid the perils of market timing.

Asset classes react differently under varying market conditions. Timing these market cycles is extremely difficult and rarely successful. If one looks at compounded annual returns over the last 10 years, the S&P 500 returned 11.07%. However, if one were out of the market for the best 10 days, the return drops by approximately 45% to 5.94%. If one missed the 30 best days, the return drops even further to under 1.00% and below. The investor would have missed out on over 95% of the return generated over the last 10 years.

Compound Annual Returns*
December 1993 to December 2003 (2,520 business days)

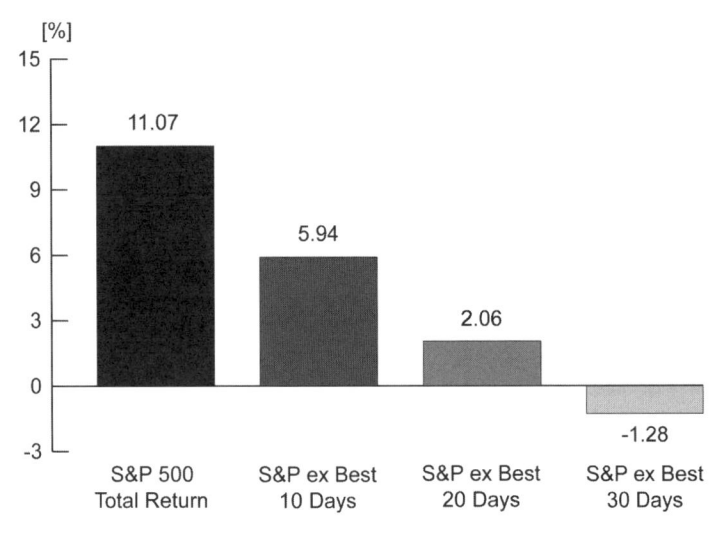

Period	Return [%]
S&P 500 Total Return	11.07
S&P ex Best 10 Days	5.94
S&P ex Best 20 Days	2.06
S&P ex Best 30 Days	-1.28

* Source: SSgA Advisor Strategies-Advisor Consulting Services Research. For Illustrative purposes only. Past performance is not indicative of future results.

Additionally, in terms of asset classes, what performs well one year may not perform the next. For example, large cap growth was the top performer in 1998 and 1999, but the worst performer in 2000. International equities was the worst performer in 1992, but the best in 1993 and 1994.

Diversify Assets—Diversification across multiple asset classes, then, is paramount to a prudent asset allocation strategy. Based on the client's risk/return preferences, owning a broad range of

Diversification: Which Asset Class is Next?

For purposes of illustration only. Past performance is not indicative of future results. Risk and return will vary with each asset class.
Source: Zephyr Style Advisor

investments can help to generate a more efficient, optimal portfolio over the long term. The allocation of assets across a broad range of investments—such as equities, fixed income, alternative investments and cash—may, in fact, be the most important step when constructing the client's portfolio.

Each asset class has an associated level of risk and expected return. In order to develop the most appropriate mix of asset classes, each asset class must be analyzed relative to other asset classes to determine the value that can be added via a broad portfolio allocation. Historical and global market correlations are useful in analyzing potential returns for different asset classes in distinct market environments. Forward-looking analysis should be performed and should be based on forecasts for each asset class return over multiple time periods.

Once projections for asset class returns, standard deviations and correlations have been calculated and assigned, the advisor can apply that information against both the client's objectives and risk tolerance to develop multiple allocation scenarios that hold the potential to deliver the highest level of return for a given level of risk. The development of optimal allocation scenarios can be achieved using mean variance optimization, a process that uses the mean returns (either historical or projected), standard deviations (variance), and correlations to analyze the interrelationship between various asset classes to calculate optimal asset allocations. This collection of optimal allocation mixes along the risk spectrum is called the "efficient frontier."

The Efficient Frontier of Diversified Assets

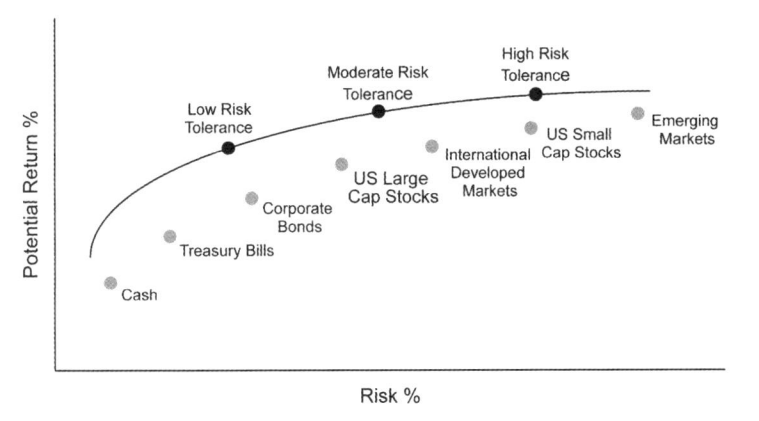

Typically, advisors will present a client with three potential portfolio options with varying levels of risk (e.g., aggressive, moderate, and conservative).

* Source: SSgA Advisor Strategies-Advisor Consulting Services Research. For Illustrative Purposes only. Past performance is not indicative of future results. Risk/return will vary for each asset class.

Validate the Asset Allocation Mix—Being able to validate whether clients will be able to reach their stated objectives given the portfolio options presented is a critical component of the asset allocation process. The advisor needs to determine what the probability is that the client will be able to achieve his objective within a defined time horizon, given his stated tolerance for risk. Probabilities are just that—not certainties. But they do provide guidance as to "best" and "worst" case scenarios and help validate the chosen asset allocation strategy.

Once the advisor has developed a client's portfolio options, or various asset allocation mixes, these should be "stress tested" to understand the range of possible outcomes for a given mix. Forecasting techniques such as Monte Carlo analysis use projected returns and standard deviations to calculate hundreds to thousands of possible return combinations. Factors such as cash flows and spending rates can also be factored in to provide more realistic monitoring.

The output of Monte Carlo analysis provides statistical probabilities of certain outcomes. It is critical to stress test portfolio options through multiple market cycles. The broader the time period tested, the more capable and prepared the advisor will be to present to the client the probability each portfolio option holds for meeting the client's goals. The client can then decide, given the return probabilities presented and given how much risk of not meeting the objectives he or she is willing to tolerate, which portfolio option is right for them.

Portfolio Implementation

Once the asset allocation has been validated and the client has chosen the portfolio option with which he or she is most comfortable, the next step is implementation. Implementing the asset allocation is just as important as defining it. Careful consideration must be given to the choice of investment strategies that will fill the various asset class buckets and to hiring best-fit managers to execute on those strategies.

Active versus Passive Investment Approach—The "active versus passive" debate is an ongoing one, and each side has its proponents and detractors. Each of these investment approaches enables a manager to take advantage of asset class efficiencies or inefficiencies. Certain asset classes, such as fixed income and U.S. large-cap equity are generally efficient. Therefore, it is much more difficult for active managers in aggregate to add value. Other asset classes such as small-cap and international are much less efficient. Active managers have typically been able to add more value in less efficient asset classes.

It follows, then, that the best investment methodology may be a blended strategy that incorporates both active and passive approaches. Utilize passive management for efficient asset classes and active management for the less efficient asset classes. By employing a blended approach investors can better manage the amount of risk they take and ensure that they are being compensated where they do take risk. The result? A much more efficient portfolio.

Style Diversification—Style diversification is also important. The investment universe is often split up into growth and value styles. Growth investing typically uses revenue and earnings growth to identify rising companies. Investing in growth stocks makes the assumption that organizations with strong earnings and revenue growth will also experience an increase in stock price. Growth companies generally have high price-to-earning ratios. Alternatively, value investing typically selects those companies with lower price-to-earning or price-to-book ratios. Value investors seek to invest in those companies with sound financials that the market has undervalued. Again, as illustrated previously, markets are cyclical and investment styles move in and out of favor quickly. Value companies tend to outperform in bear markets and growth typically outperforms in a bullish market. Diversification, then, is crucial for generating long-term returns. To guard against being "out of favor" in the short term, allocations should include representation from multiple styles within each asset class.

Selecting a Manager—A critical part of the implementation process is manager selection. Once decisions have been made as to the asset mix to be pursued, and the management styles warranted, it is the advisor's responsibility to match the styles of money managers to the needs and objectives of the investor. With thousands of money managers to choose from, selecting the right money manager for a client is not an easy task. It is important to note, too, that for many consultants and investment advisors, due diligence and manager selection is coordinated through the analytical resources of the sponsor organization, typically a brokerage firm or bank.

It is critical to evaluate whether a money manager's investment philosophy complements the investor's philosophy as set forth in the IPS. Does the money manager's decision-making process complement the investor's unique needs? Managers must be able to meet the criteria set forth by the advisor/consultant in order to receive recommendations for client investment. Selecting the right manager requires that the advisor do everything possible to ensure that manager's integrity. Advisors should be certain before hiring a manager that there have been no breaches of regulatory compliance laws and standards.

Additional criteria against which to evaluate a manager's fit for the strategy include:

▸ Background and Experience: How many years in the business? Is performance really his or hers and is it accurate? Check references.

▸ Firm stability and compensation structure for key professionals: High turnover can result in inconsistencies in management styles, performance and investment philosophies.

▸ Consistent process: Do they do what they say they will do? Admit when they're wrong? Read past correspondences. Will they allow the advisors to look at their own portfolios (or at least the top positions)? Most managers will. Do the positions mirror the stated strategy?

▸ Longer term evaluation horizon: A manager who turns over his or her portfolio frequently may have little conviction in his investing and is trading clients' money tax inefficiently.

▸ Check manager performance relative to indices and peers

Managing the Asset Mix—Determining how to manage the asset allocation mix is a key component of the implementation phase. One method is to manage the asset weights tactically based on the manager's evaluation of current markets and opportunities. This is called Tactical Asset Allocation. With this approach, the manager adjusts the weightings of assets based on his or her evaluation of market opportunities. For example, a manager may sell stocks when they appear poised to fall and increase equity exposure when they begin rising. However, the manager should always keep the asset weights within the ranges established in the IPS and should determine how cash flows are invested.

The other option is to keep the asset mix consistently in line with the asset allocation benchmarks regardless of the manager's or client's evaluation of the market. This is called Strategic Asset Allocation. In this approach, the manager needs to decide how frequently to rebalance the strategic allocations and how to manage cash flows as the holdings deviate from the target allocations due to investment performance.

Most prudent investors agree that the strategic allocation will be the most important factor responsible for long-term results of the portfolio. Any reallocation activity should be limited to preserving the integrity of the strategic policy. This does leave some room for flexibility in implementation. For example, a blended risk approach may be okay, even in conservative portfolios—as long as the risk tolerance level of the portfolio overall is met. A portfolio that contains some percentage of "higher risk" investments does not necessarily violate the parameters of the original IPS—unless, of course, the IPS specifically forbids certain asset classes or investment vehicles.

Monitoring & Reviewing Performance—Again, as stated previously, it is the fiduciary's responsibility to regularly monitor the performance of the selected investments and of the portfolio overall against the IPS to ensure that all portfolio decisions being made are working in the best interest of the client. Again, as with the manager selection process, for some consultants and advisors, tracking of and reporting on portfolio performance are facilitated by the sponsor organization.

Rebalancing—Rebalancing is an important part of the monitoring and review process. It is the key to preserving the asset allocation strategy of the client and to keeping the portfolio's performance on target. Rebalancing can be performed on a periodic basis—such as monthly, quarterly or annually—or can be done in response to set limits or trigger points. Rebalancing limits should be set as dictated by the amount of volatility the investor can tolerate. Rebalancing limits, then, are defined by both the asset allocation plan as established in the IPS and the unique risk/return tolerance of the investor.

Rebalancing, whether periodic or based on target levels, is important because it provides a disciplined and systematic process for managing the portfolio on an ongoing basis. It effectively takes the emotion out of investing, making it possible for the client to buy low and sell high. By periodically rebalancing, advisors can trim the winners and add to the laggards. Historically, quarterly and annual balancing significantly outperforms the buy and hold strategy. Without rebalancing, as in a buy and hold strategy, investment portfolios can become over-concentrated in certain areas, exposing an investor to significant risks.

The Benefits of Rebalancing

The impact of rebalancing a client's $1 million portfolio over a five year period.
Asset Allocation: 40% Large Cap Stocks; 10% Small Cap Stocks; 10% International Equities; 40% Bonds.

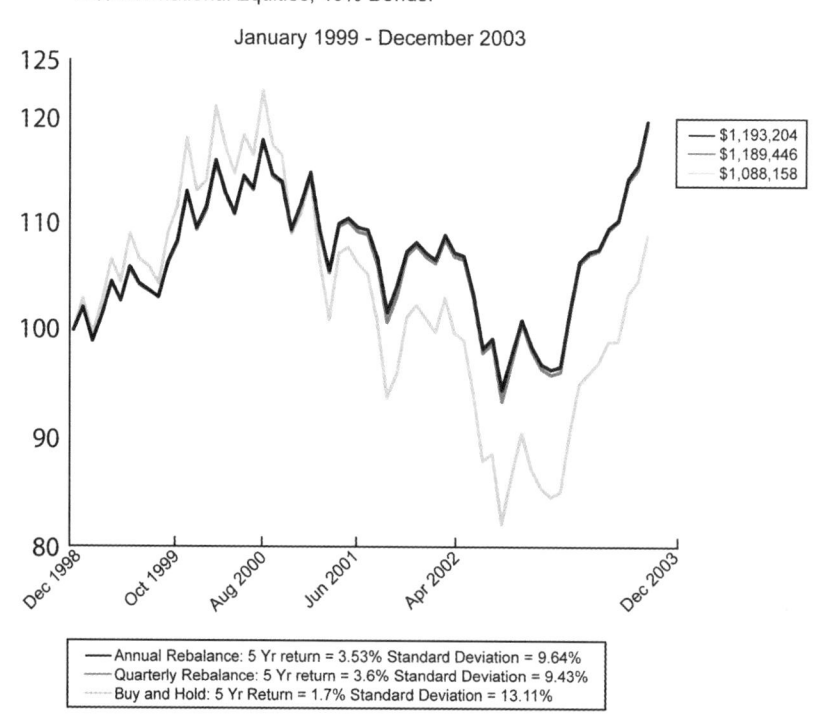

January 1999 - December 2003

- $1,193,204
- $1,189,446
- $1,088,158

—— Annual Rebalance: 5 Yr return = 3.53% Standard Deviation = 9.64%
—— Quarterly Rebalance: 5 Yr return = 3.6% Standard Deviation = 9.43%
······ Buy and Hold: 5 Yr Return = 1.7% Standard Deviation = 13.11%

Source: SSgA Advisor Consulting Services Research. The following indexes were used as a proxies: S&P 500, Russell 2000, MSCI EAFE and Lehman Aggregate Bond Index.

Both annual and quarterly rebalancing of the portfolio not only delivered higher returns over a 5-year period, but lowered the overall risk of the portfolio relative to a "buy and hold" strategy.

Investment Policy Statement

What, then, are some of the tactics used to rebalance a portfolio that has fallen under or exceeded the rebalancing limits established in the IPS?

- Sell off a portion of the asset class that has increased in value to reinvest in asset classes that are lagging.
- Change policy for future allocations, investing more in lagging asset classes until asset allocation across the portfolio is balanced again.
- Add new investments to the portfolio in the lagging asset classes and funnel contributions to those assets

Controlling Expenses

Advisors have the responsibility to keep a close eye on expenses and costs. Advisors need to ask themselves the following:

- Is the client's wealth being maximized?
- Are the selected investments performing as well as they look – after taxes?
- Have I taken into consideration commissions and market impact?

Taxes can quickly erode portfolio wealth, so it is crucial that every investment decision made on behalf of the client take into consideration the impact of taxes. Too often, portfolios that appear to perform well on a pre-tax basis actually underperform on an after-tax basis. A prudent IPS should carefully evaluate the client's tax status and outline tax-efficient management strategies for mitigating the impact of those taxes on long-term portfolio performance.

There are multiple tax-efficient investment solutions available to investors today. For taxable investors, allocating a percentage of their portfolios to a tax-aware strategy or investment solution that employs aggressive tax loss harvesting may be an excellent way to lessen the consequences of high capital gains taxes and ultimately create more wealth

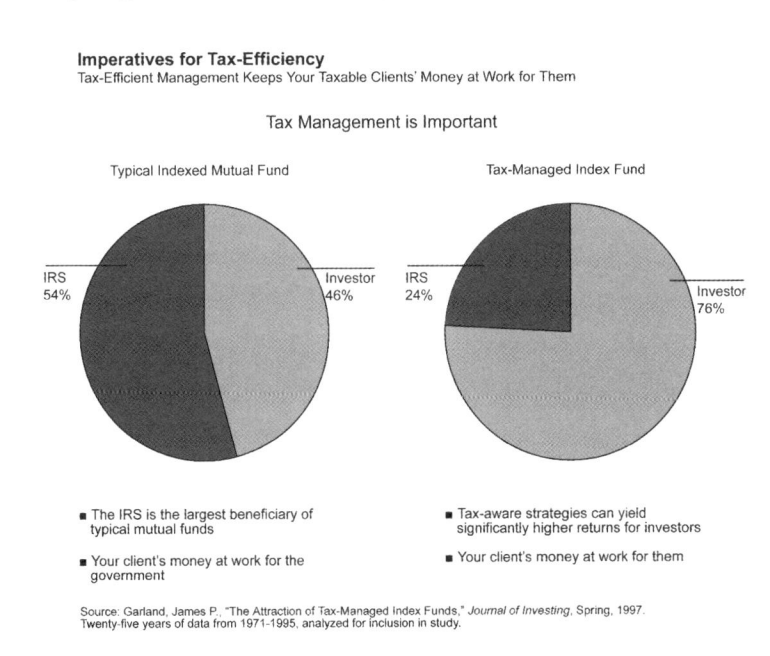

Imperatives for Tax-Efficiency
Tax-Efficient Management Keeps Your Taxable Clients' Money at Work for Them

Tax Management is Important

Typical Indexed Mutual Fund: IRS 54%, Investor 46%
Tax-Managed Index Fund: IRS 24%, Investor 76%

- The IRS is the largest beneficiary of typical mutual funds
- Your client's money at work for the government
- Tax-aware strategies can yield significantly higher returns for investors
- Your client's money at work for them

Source: Garland, James P., "The Attraction of Tax-Managed Index Funds," *Journal of Investing*, Spring, 1997. Twenty-five years of data from 1971-1995, analyzed for inclusion in study.

Likewise, high fees, commissions and market impact can severely affect long-term portfolio results. At all times, advisors should seek to mitigate operating expenses, transaction costs and fees in order to maximize client wealth.

Monitoring Manager Performance

It is the advisor's responsibility, often in tandem with a platform sponsor, to regularly monitor and review the performance of the portfolio manager against the objectives and benchmarks as established by the IPS.

There are a number of criteria against which one can measure a manager's performance:

Consistency in Performance – Relative & Absolute—Does performance align with stated strategies? Style drift is a leading cause of poor performance. Past performance has no value whatsoever if the investment philosophy, process and personnel of a firm do not remain consistent over the period within which the track record was established.

Additional questions that may be helpful in evaluating a manager's individual performance include:

- How did the manager perform relative to a passive benchmark or index?
- What risk did he or she take to achieve returns, i.e., what were the absolute returns?
- Were the securities chosen consistent with the mandate of the IPS?
- Did the manager deliver sufficient excess returns to cover fees of active management?
- What factors drove portfolio performance?
- How did the manager perform relative to peers with the same investment styles? Compare absolute performance after adjusting for risk.

Accessibility—During stressful periods, is the money manager or another top manager avaiable to address the advisor's concerns and answer questions?

Focus—Is there a continued focus on growing the client's assets, even in the wake of very positive performance? Or has the manager grown complacent? Does the manager's attention wane over time?

Communications—The manager should maintain consistency in communications. Quarterly reports and other correspondence should be sent on time.

Managers are serving clients on the basis of the advisor's or sponsor's recommendation. Therefore, it is crucial that the sponsoring organization and the advisor maintain control over the relationship and closely monitor the money manager's performance. Due diligence is an ongoing process. If, in the process of reviewing a portfolio or an IPS, an advisor or sponsor determines that the manager is stepping outside of the IPS and is not adhering to established benchmarks and guidelines, then it is the advisor's or sponsor's responsibility to recommend termination of the investor-manager relationship and to quickly identify an alternative manager for the investor.

Making Changes to the Investment Policy Statement

The IPS is the basis for prudent investing. Therefore, it is fundamental to evaluate the statement on a regular basis to ensure that all objectives, guidelines, and benchmarks are being followed. It is recommended that a formal review of the IPS be conducted, at a minimum, once every three years for institutional investors and once a year for individual investors. A review does not necessarily require a change in strategy, but may simply serve to reaffirm that the chosen investment approach is appropriate.

More frequent reviews of the portfolio and of the IPS can be triggered by such things as a change in funding status for an institutional client or a change in status, such as an inheritance, for individual investors. In sum, major life changes—and not market changes—should prompt re-examination of the IPS. Upon review, the advisor may determine that revisions to the IPS are necessary.

Investment Policy Statement

The following events can trigger the need to make changes to the IPS:

For Individual Investors
- Significant change in financial situation
- Maturing to another life stage
- Changing needs as a result of significant life events—a new baby, a new home, higher education costs, etc.
- Performance evaluation guidelines, investment manager selection or risk and return parameters change
- Significant event in the economic or business world warrants a substantial change in investment direction

For Institutional Investors
- The plan's investment funding status, asset allocation strategy or investment objectives change
- Change to plan's risk profile or liquidity need
- Change in service providers or a company's administrative procedures are revised
- Company acquires another firm or disgorges a subsidiary or other entity
- Performance evaluation guidelines, investment manager selection or risk and return parameters change
- Significant event in the economic or business world warrants a substantial change in investment direction
- A new qualified or non-qualified plan is adopted

Conclusion

An IPS, when prudently constructed and implemented, can be an invaluable tool for both advisors and clients. Below are several concluding guidelines for successfully creating and implementing an IPS:

Spend time to understand the client's needs and objectives. Invest a significant amount of time in discussions and meetings with the client to understand where that client is coming from and where he or she wants to go. This will help the advisor to draft a tailored, comprehensive IPS.

Educate the client as to the value of asset allocation. Be as thorough as possible in educating the client as to the importance of asset allocation to a portfolio's performance. Be sure the client understands that markets cycle. Illustrate for the client the inability to predict which asset class or style will be in favor at any given time.

Use facts to set realistic return expectations up front. Validate the asset allocation strategy and communicate those results in order to set appropriate expectations.

Communicate, communicate, communicate—and do it proactively! A carefully created IPS inspires discipline and consistency in decision-making and performance. Clients will feel more connected to the investment process, more empowered, and at the same time less likely to make rash, emotional decisions about their investments.

Development of a comprehensive IPS is an imperative for all fiduciaries. Simply put, the IPS is the foundation upon which the success of the client's portfolio is built.

❖❖❖

---

1 Source: InvestorWords.com
2 Maloney, Eugene F. "The Investment Process Required by the Uniform Prudent Investor Act". *Journal of Financial Planning*. November 1999. Article 14.
3 Ibid.
4 Ibid.
5 Source: Determinants of Portfolio Performance, Brinson, Hood and Beebower, Financial Analysts Journal, July/August 1986; Explanation of Total Return Variation, Brinson, Hood and Beebower, Financial Analysts Journal, May/June 1991

Disclosure: The information contained herein does not constitute investment advice and it should not be relied on as such. It should not be considered a solicitation to buy, or an offer to sell, a security. It does not take into account any investor's particular investment objectives, strategies, tax status or investment horizon. Past performance is not indicative of future results. We encourage you to consult your tax or financial advisor. The views expressed are the views of Gus Fleites only through the period ended January 27, 2004, and are subject to change based on market and other conditions.

10

THE ART AND IMPORTANCE OF ASSET ALLOCATION

Larry Sinsimer, J.D.
Senior Vice President and Managing Director
Managed Accounts, Eaton Vance Distributors, Inc.

If a person turns on their computer, goes to their favorite search engine and types in asset allocation, 36-pages of articles, books, software descriptions and professional services pop up. However, that shouldn't discourage anyone from learning about this important concept. Asset allocation is fairly easy to understand and to put into practice, particularly with the help of a financial advisor or consultant.

Asset allocation is the process of dividing investment dollars into different categories that tend to behave differently in market cycles. Whether consciously planned or not, *where an investor puts their money* is their asset allocation. If they decide the safest place for their money is in a coffee can in the back yard, they have allocated their investment dollars to cash. Perhaps they have done so on the theory that they are preserving capital at the risk of loss of purchasing power due to the long-term effects of inflation.

Many people confuse asset allocation with diversification. While they work hand-in-hand, asset allocation generally refers to which investment categories capital is invested in, and diversification usually applies to how many holdings the investor has in each category.

There are several theories on the best way to achieve investment success. The concept behind diversification is "Don't put all your eggs in one basket." The contrary theory is "Put all your eggs in one basket and watch that basket carefully." Everyone has heard of the investor who struck it rich investing in

Client application

Microsoft at its initial public offering. Anyone would love to discover the next Cisco or Intel. While the likelihood of finding such an opportunity is small, the rewards are great. The risk, however, is even greater. The "big bets" approach is used by gamblers, and like gambling, is unlikely to achieve any long-term success. Asset allocation, on the other hand, used in conjunction with diversification can prove to be a successful long-term strategy for the investor.

How important is asset allocation? Early studies by Brinson, Hood and Beebower (*Financial Analysts Journal* July/August 1986) determined that more than 91% of the variability of portfolio returns (how one portfolio performs versus another) came from its asset allocation. In other words, where the capital is invested (stock, bonds, cash, etc.) is more important than which specific stock or bond is selected.

This study was immediately challenged by other academics. In 1991, Brinson, Beebower and another associate, Bryan Singer again studied portfolio returns and determined that 93% of the variability of portfolio returns came from asset allocation (*Financial Analysts Journal* May/June 1991). This report created so much controversy that brilliant academics like Harry Markowitz, William Sharpe and Roger Ibbotson responded with studies of their own, coming to various conclusions about how much of the portfolio's return could be attributed to the asset classes in which it is invested and the amount allocated (anywhere from 60% to 88%). While the debate continues — including an attack on asset allocation by investment pioneer William Jahnke[1], it is clear that how investment dollars are divided will be a major determinant of investment success.

The reason that asset allocation is so important is that the performance of asset classes is unpredictable and can vary widely. Last year's winner may be this year's loser and vice versa. Or last year's winner may be this year's winner again. It is totally unpredictable in the short run. In addition, the more asset classes an investor adds, the less predictable the short-term outcome. The goal of asset allocation is to blend different asset classes to achieve investment goals in a manner that will keep investors comfortable so they don't panic and bail out at the wrong time. Asset allocation should not be viewed as a magic potion or panacea. It is no guarantee of investment success. It is at best a road map to be used by investors to help them reach their investment goals while attempting to minimize risk, keeping in mind that there is no permanent safe haven for capital.

In its simplest form, an asset allocation model may include stocks, bonds and cash. In order to determine the proper mix of these asset classes, investors must look at their goals, time horizon and risk tolerance. Many investors start out by saying they want to get the highest rate of return with zero risk. This investment exists. It is called a 90-day Treasury bill. In 90 days, the government returns the invested money with a small amount of interest. The risk of loss of capital is minimal since the government can print the money to make good on its obligation. The problem with investing in treasury bills is that, after taxes and inflation, investors historically end up with less money in terms of real purchasing power than they started with. In other words, this is a great way to grow poor safely. On the other hand, as stated earlier, investing in a single stock or riskier asset class such as emerging markets may provide great rewards, but also entails great risk. Most investors' assets belong somewhere between 90-day Treasury bills and emerging markets. Where those assets are placed determines an investor's asset allocation.

Think of investing as a journey. If people don't know where they're going, any road will take them there. But if they have some idea of what they are trying to accomplish, they can begin to construct a road map to get them from where they are to where they want to be. The problem with the investment journey is that like any real journey, the road can be filled with potholes and delays. If travelers want to go from New York to Boston, chances are they would take Interstate 95. If they were going from San Diego to Los Angeles, they would take the 405; or Tampa to Orlando, they would take Interstate 4. In any event, the freeway would be the means to their goals. The problem is, the freeway has bumper-to-bumper traffic and sometimes a traveler is in the lane that's not moving very fast, if at all, while the lane next to them is whistling by. What happens the minute they change lanes? It stops dead! What happened to the lane they were just in? It takes off like a rocket. If the freeway is the means to reach the investment goal, then asset allocation would suggest that investors put a car in every lane— a lane called growth stocks, value stocks, international stocks, and bonds taxable or tax-free. Having a car in every lane means that something is always moving toward their investment goal. If something is always moving forward, investors are less likely to change lanes at the wrong time. In fact, it is this behavior of chasing yesterday's performance that often leaves investors frustrated and depressed and even believing that the system is somehow rigged against them.

Goal Setting

In his book, *The Seven Habits of Highly Effective People*, Stephen R. Covey indicated that one of the most important things that effective people do is to begin with the end in mind. This is especially important with investing. What is the purpose of this money? Is it for children's education? Retirement? Family security? How many years will this money be invested before it's required to meet the goal? And most importantly, how much risk can one tolerate during the period between now and when the money is required?

By setting goals at the outset, advisors can help investors determine not only which road is most appropriate, but into which lanes their assets should be invested by utilizing another tool called Modern Portfolio Theory (MPT).

MPT looks at the detailed historical behavior of different asset classes. In a given market cycle, some asset classes will outperform while others will under perform. MPT uses complex mathematical formulas to evaluate different combinations of asset classes to determine the best return for the amount of risk over a specific time horizon. Risk itself can be quantified into a statistically accurate prediction of the range of future performance. The uncertainty of performance decreases as the time horizon increases.

MPT has been applied by institutional investors for years. Most large pension plans and endowments employ this theory to help them determine the right mix of asset classes and the proper allocation in order to meet their objectives.

While MPT is an excellent tool, it is not fool proof. Part of the problem is that it assumes that performance of asset classes historically will continue into the future. In other words, the future is an average of the past. The flaw in this thinking can be seen when one reviews how asset classes have performed in periods of hyperinflation as opposed to periods of low inflation. Small-cap stocks for example, significantly outperformed large-cap stocks during the mid-1970s to the early 1980s. However, as inflation came into line, the small-cap advantage began to disappear. Similarly during the 1980s, international stocks as measured by the MSCI EAFE [2] index added significant performance to domestic stocks while reducing portfolio risk. In hindsight, it is clear that most of this was attributed to the Japanese market. With the collapse of the Nikkei Index beginning in 1989, the risk reduction and performance enhancement of international stocks has largely disappeared.

Despite its flaws, MPT is still an excellent tool for investors to use in constructing an asset allocation designed to meet their goals within their risk tolerance. The next problem is determining which asset allocation is right for them.

The World of Money Management

There is no shortage of asset allocation models available through financial planners, insurance professionals and brokerage firms each touting the benefits, features and fundamental science that makes the program the very best for each investor. Asset allocation models run the gamut from the very simple to the highly complex. One of the simplest asset allocation models suggests that investors take their age, subtract it from 100 to determine their equity allocation. Ten percent of their assets should always be in cash and the balance should be invested in bonds. In other words, at age 30 they should have 70% of their assets invested in stocks; 10% in cash and 20% in bonds. At age 70, they would have 30% in stocks, 10% in cash and 60% in bonds. The problem with the simplified allocation is that it assumes that the 30-year-old will always be comfortable being heavily invested in stocks while the 70-year-old has more of an immediate need for capital preservation or income and no need for growth. Clearly, for the 30-year-old who cannot stand to see his or her assets drop in value, this allocation would prove disastrous. Likewise, for the financially secure 70-year-old who understands risk and may even be investing for the next generation, the 60% bond allocation is totally inappropriate.

Many software programs available today have tried to quantify the investor's risk tolerance by asking pointed questions regarding the investor's attitudes toward market volatility and short-term loss. In its simplest form, risk tolerance can be defined as: "How far does something have to drop before I wish I had never heard of it?" "How much pain can I stand before I bail out of the program?" An understanding of human nature makes it clear that this is less than a scientific measure. Research shows that investors tend to be more confident than perhaps they should be in up market cycles and probably too cautious and pessimistic in down market cycles. Despite their shortcomings, software programs are very good starting points for most investors.

While stocks provide the greatest opportunity and small stocks generally offer a better opportunity than large stocks, the volatility of the stock market can scare an investor into doing the wrong thing — such as selling out in a down market. The following chart demonstrates the lack of predictability for stock market returns. It shows that 2003 was a great year for small growth stocks, which returned more than 48%. However, 2002 saw small growth stocks lose more than 30% of their value. For many investors, the loss of 30% would be devastating and cause them to miss the year that stocks rose over 48%. The other dynamic of the chart is that it shows the lack of predictability for any stock

Eaton Vance Distributors, Inc.
Annual Total Returns of Key Asset Classes 1979-2003

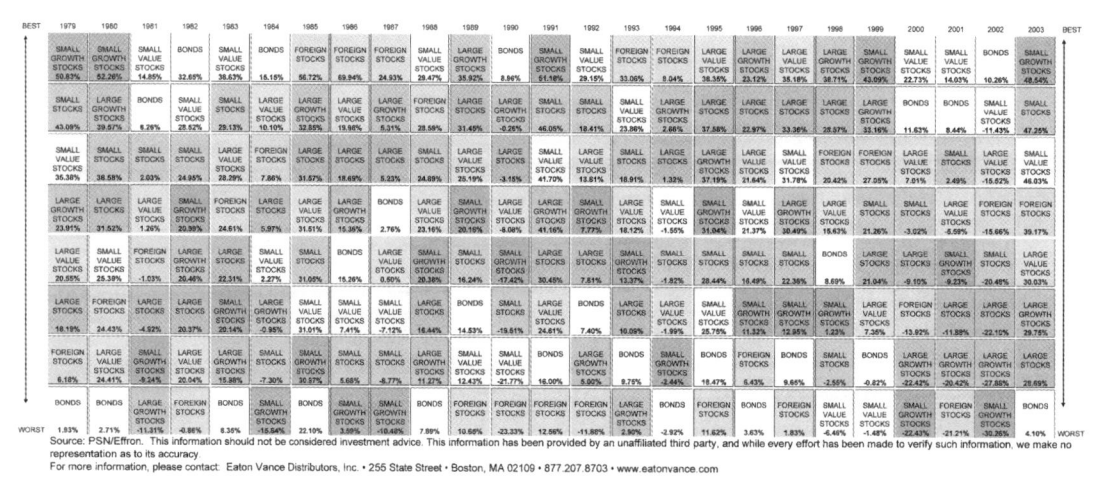

The Art and Importance of Asset Allocation

or bond asset class. Last year's loser is not necessarily this year's winner, and there are periods of time when a single asset class may be the best place to be for several years in a row. So what's an investor to do? The answer is, if they keep their end-objective in hand and understand the market volatility of asset classes, an advisor can put together an asset allocation to help them achieve their goals while maintaining peace of mind. One of the best ways to do this is to mix complementary asset classes that tend to move with differing amounts of velocity so that the combination provides superior rates of return while diminishing risk.

Chart 1 demonstrates what would have happened had an investor hired a traditional growth manager for the 10 years ending December 31, 2003. This growth manager has about a median rate of return for his or her peer group. As seen, the manager has returned 11.99% versus 11.07% for the S&P 500 during the period. In addition, the manager's portfolio had a higher standard deviation (variability of rate of return). The manager captured 104% of the upside of the market and 99.6% of the downside. So, while he/she provided superior rates of return, he/she also provided a little more volatility. If one takes 50% (Chart 2 - page 80) of the money from that growth manager and gives it to a value manager with median rates of return compared to his/her peer group, the 10-year return rises to 12.46 versus 11.07 for the Standard & Poor's 500, but the standard deviation drops from 18.58 to 16.18. In other words, by combining the two asset classes of large growth and large value, rate of return increases significantly and volatility is reduced.

Chart #1

TOTAL RISK REWARD ANALYSIS
CURRENT UNIVERSE
10 YEAR PERIOD ENDING DECEMBER 31, 2003

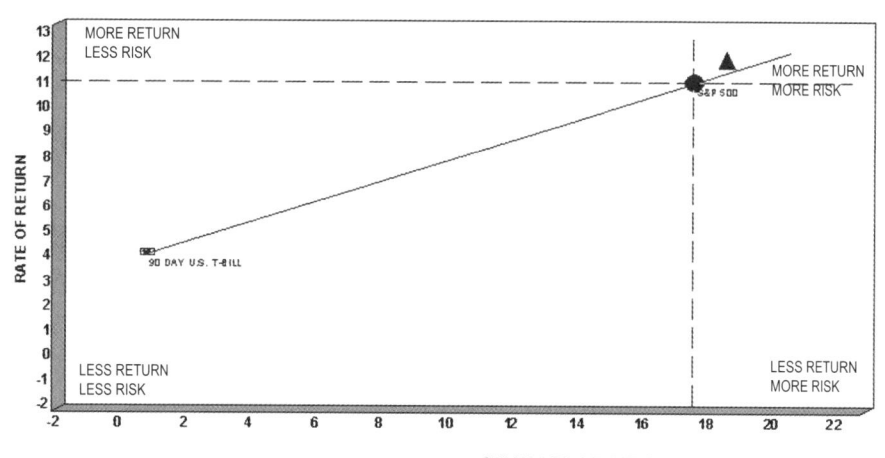

	ROR	STD DEV	ALPHA	BETA	R-SQUARED	OWN CAP RATIO	UP CAP RATIO	WORST QT RS
LARGE CAP GROWTH	11.99	18.58	0.81	1.83	0.96	99.63	104.49	-26.86
S&P 500	11.07	17.55	0.00	1.00	1.00	100.00	100.00	-26.62

Risk benchmark used for this analysis = S&P 500
This information contained herein was from Effron Enterprises, Inc. and is believed to be correct, but has not been independently verified and is not guaranteed by Eaton Vance.

The World of Money Management

Chart #2 — TOTAL RISK REWARD ANALYSIS
CURRENT UNIVERSE
10 YEAR PERIOD ENDING DECEMBER 31, 2003

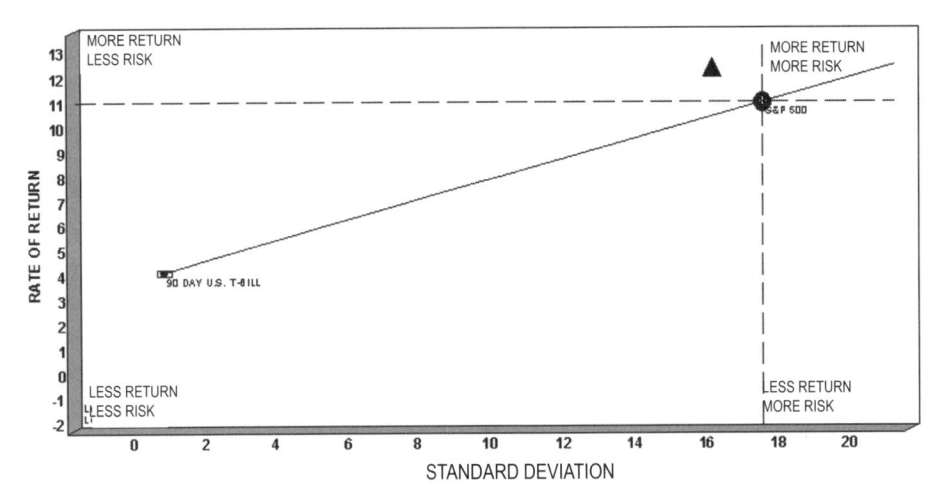

	ROR	STD DEV	ALPHA	BETA	R-SQUARED	OWN CAP RATIO	UP CAP RATIO	WORST QT RS
50/50	12.46	16.18	1.90	0.89	0.96	81.46	95.38	-23.43
S&P 500	11.07	17.56	0.00	1.00	1.00	100.00	100.00	-26.62

Risk benchmark used for this analysis = S&P 500
This information contained herein was from Effron Enterprises, Inc. and is believed to be correct, but has not been independently verified and is not guaranteed by Eaton Vance.

Chart #3 — TOTAL RISK REWARD ANALYSIS
CURRENT UNIVERSE
10 YEAR PERIOD ENDING DECEMBER 31, 2003

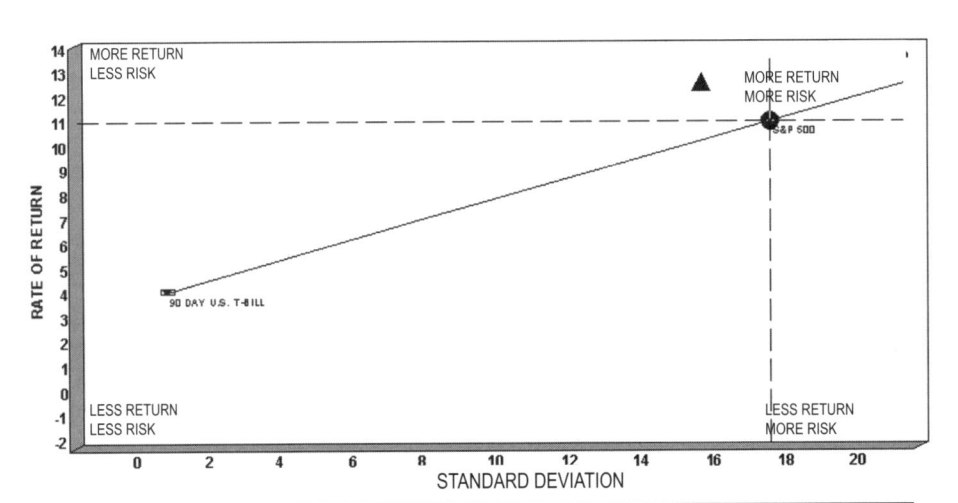

	ROR	STD DEV	ALPHA	BETA	R-SQUARED	OWN CAP RATIO	UP CAP RATIO	WORST QT RS
35/35/30	12.67	15.6	2.1	0.85	0.90	74.28	92.12	-21.91
S&P 500	11.07	17.56	0.00	1.00	1.00	100.00	100.00	-26.62

Risk benchmark used for this analysis = S&P 500
This information contained herein was from Effron Enterprises, Inc. and is believed to be correct, but has not been independently verified and is not guaranteed by Eaton Vance.

The Art and Importance of Asset Allocation

Chart #4

TOTAL RISK REWARD ANALYSIS
CURRENT UNIVERSE
10 YEAR PERIOD ENDING DECEMBER 31, 2003

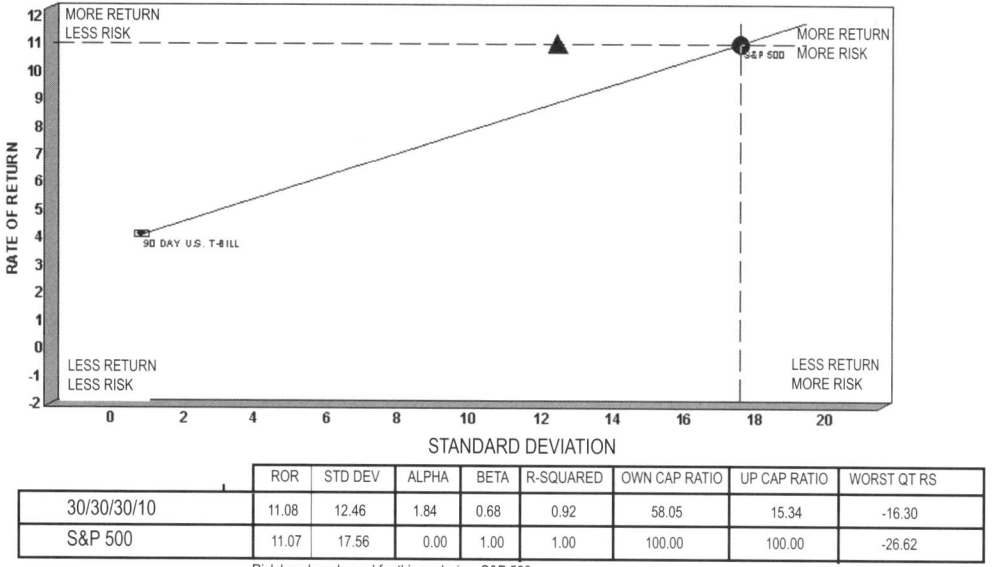

	ROR	STD DEV	ALPHA	BETA	R-SQUARED	OWN CAP RATIO	UP CAP RATIO	WORST QT RS
30/30/30/10	11.08	12.46	1.84	0.68	0.92	58.05	15.34	-16.30
S&P 500	11.07	17.56	0.00	1.00	1.00	100.00	100.00	-26.62

Risk benchmark used for this analysis = S&P 500
This information contained herein was from Effron Enterprises, Inc. and is believed to be correct, but has not been independently verified and is not guaranteed by Eaton Vance.

Chart 3 (page 80), demonstrates the benefit of putting different asset classes together. In this instance, large growth and large value allocations have been reduced to 35% each and the other 30% is in a core portfolio of small cap stocks. As seen, once again the rate of return has increased, this time from 12.46 to 12.67; surprisingly the standard deviation has dropped from 16.18 to 15.68. Even though small stocks are more volatile, historically, than large stocks, adding them to an existing portfolio of large stocks reduces risk while enhancing portfolio return. Similarly, when bonds are included, as in the next example (Chart 4), risk is decreased, and yet a respectable rate of return is achieved. The one thing that is assumed, however, is that the allocation percentage remains the same over the entire time frame. That is why it is so important to rebalance the portfolio periodically.

The following are several suggested asset mixes for investors at various stages of their investment lives or with varying risk tolerances. As seen, the more risk an investor is willing to take, the better the opportunity for higher investment results. However, there is a greater chance of significant losses in the short run. It is also important to keep in mind that there is no permanent safe haven for capital. Therefore, assets have to be actively managed and periodically rebalanced to achieve goals.

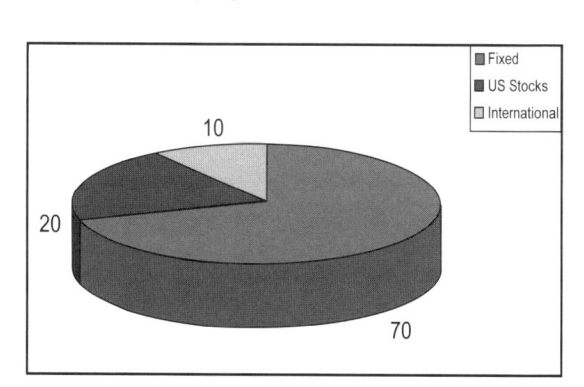

Allocation No. 1: 70% fixed income, 20% large-cap U.S. stocks and 10% international equity. This would be suitable for some-

Allocation-1

one who is approaching their goal of retirement or funding children's education. This allocation might also be suitable for someone who is risk-averse or with little understanding of stock market volatility and is just beginning the investment experience. This allocation might be defined as capital preservation with some growth potential.

Allocation No. 2: 55% fixed income, 25% U.S. large-cap stocks, 10% international equity and 10% small cap. U.S. equities would be appropriate for investors with a little longer time between now and when the capital is required, but still has an aversion to risk and whose primary goal is capital preservation.

Allocation No. 3: 35% fixed income, 45% U.S. large-cap stocks, 10% small cap and 10% international. This mix would be appropriate for investors with a longer time horizon with little need for immediate income. The investor in this category should have an understanding of market volatility and realize there could be periods of negative returns.

Allocation No. 4: 20% fixed income, 50% U.S. large cap stocks, 15% U.S. small cap stocks and 15% international equities. This allocation would be appropriate for investors with a long-term time horizon and no immediate need for income. They need to realize there could be prolonged periods of negative returns.

Allocation No. 5: No fixed income; 70% in U.S. large-cap stocks, 15% in U.S. small stocks and 15% international equities. This aggressive allocation is suitable for investors with a long time horizon and a sophisticated attitude and understanding of risk and reward. While this allocation provides the best opportunity for long-term investment results, it also has the greatest risk of short-term losses.

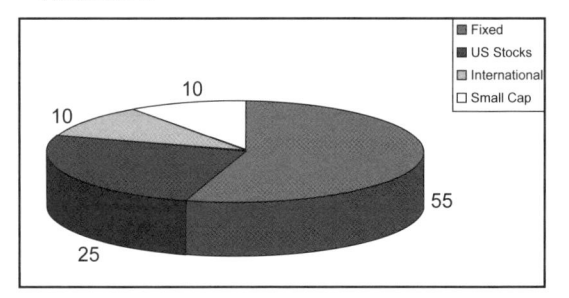

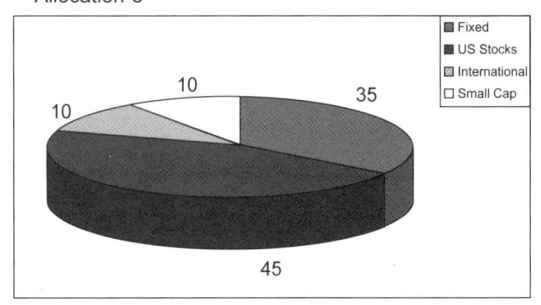

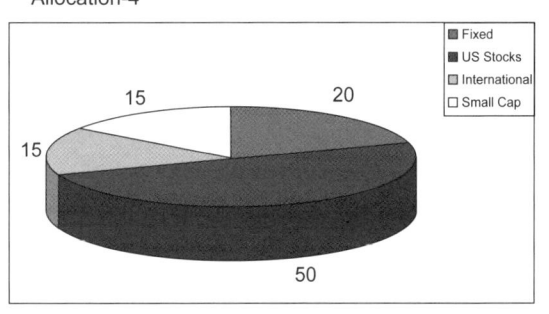

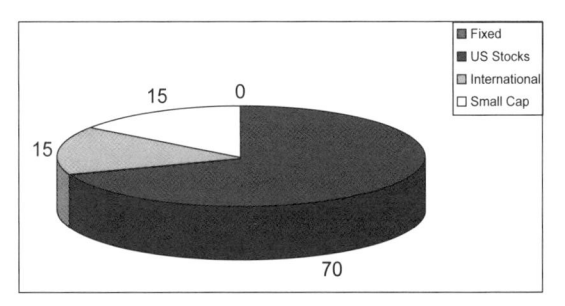

An investor, over their life, may begin with Allocation No. 5 (page 82), but as time goes on and the need for the invested capital increases, that investor may shift to allocations No. 4, then No. 3, No. 2 and eventually Allocation No. 1.

Likewise, a less experienced investor might start with Allocation No. 1, but increase allocation to equities over time as he/she becomes more comfortable with the stock market. One of the most important factors in any asset allocation plan is the understanding that it can be modified to accommodate changes in goals, time horizon and most importantly, risk tolerance.

Asset Allocation and the Taxable Investor

Tax ramifications are important to consider in any financial plan, which is why it is important to differentiate an asset allocation plan for a tax-deferred entity such as a pension plan or endowment and the taxable investor. Taxes can be the single biggest drain on investment returns. Short-term capital gain and non-qualifying dividends are taxed at a 35% rate at the federal level and in most instances are subject to state taxes. This means that portfolio returns of 10% could return as little as 6.5% on an after-tax basis. It is estimated that taxes actually cost the investor 17% over a 10-year period. Recognizing the impact of taxes, some firms, including ours, have begun offering tax-managed funds and separate accounts. Under the new tax bill, qualifying dividends are taxed at 15%, as long as the underlying security is held for 60 days around the ex dividend date. Most money managers investing primarily tax-deferred money are not prepared to customize the taxable individual's portfolio to make sure that stocks are held for the qualifying period.

Conclusion

Whether 90% or 65% of a portfolio's return comes from its asset allocation, it is clear that asset allocation is the major determinant of portfolio performance. Asset allocation is not, however, a magic potion or a panacea. Asset allocation, combined with MPT, is a useful tool to help investors manage risk while attempting to reach their goals. To get the full benefits of asset allocation, investors should have clearly stated goals for their assets, an understanding of their ability to accept risk and a clear time horizon in which to achieve their goals.

❖❖❖

---

1 William Jahnke, "The Asset Allocation Hoax," *Journal of Financial Planning*,
This landmark 1997 article by William Jahnke, president of the financial consulting firm Jahnke & Associates, asserted that there are several flaws with the study – not only in how it was conducted, but the conclusions it reached. For the 10-year period covered in the BHB study, Jahnke concluded that the asset allocation policy explained only 14.6% of the range in actual portfolio returns, not 93.6%.
2 The Europe, Australia, and Far East Index from Morgan Stanley Capital International. An unmanaged, market-value weighted index designed to measure the overall condition of overseas markets.

Disclosure: The information contained herein does not constitute investment advice and it should not be relied on as such. It should not be considered a solicitation to buy, or an offer to sell, a security. It does not take into account any investor's particular investment objectives, strategies, tax status or investment horizon. Past performance is not indicative of future results.

Editor's note: This article is an extremely valuable pass-along tool for advisors or consultants to give to their clients. For reprints, go to http://www.fisherleblanc.com. Important: Before distributing to investors, please have materials approved by compliance and/or management.

11

MANAGER SEARCH AND EVALUATION A MAGIC FORMULA?

Richard M. Todd, CIMC
Co-founder
Innovest Portfolio Solutions

"Many people think they are smarter than others in the stock market and that the market itself has no intrinsic intelligence as if it's inert. Many people think they are smarter than others in baseball and that the game on the field is simply what they think it is through their set of images/beliefs. Actual data from the market means more than individual perception/belief. The same is true in baseball."

- E-mail from Red Sox owner John Henry,
quoted in Moneyball by Michael Lewis

This is a quote from *Moneyball*, a wildly entertaining book by Michael Lewis on the story of the reconstruction of the Oakland A's and their general manager, Billy Beane. In a nutshell, the A's took on conventional baseball wisdom and began playing under a different set of rules than everyone else. They used historical statistics that no other franchise cared about and consequently, with the second-lowest payroll in the major leagues, the A's managed to become one of the winningest franchises.

The A's flouted the traditional approach to player evaluation and building a team. They focused more on the amateur draft and tossed aside the old tools used to judge players. Traditional baseball experts focus on the ability to hit, field, throw and run. The A's focused instead, almost exclusively, on seldom-evaluated statistics. They liked college players who had high on-base percentages, got deep into counts (wears out the pitcher) and few strikeouts.

By being fiercely independent, the A's focused on process instead of outcomes. By focusing on process, the A's could accept some short-term pain, but could drastically enhance their odds for long-term success.

As an investment consulting firm, we have spent considerable time and money searching for the Holy Grail of manager search and selection —specifically, a few historical quantitative factors that will lead to the identification of future superior managers. We thought perhaps rolling relative Sharpe Ratio or rolling Alpha or 12-month consistency screens relative to a benchmark or peer group— maybe it's all three?

Money managers have been successful at identifying attractive stocks by purely quantitative measures, but are there factors that will also lead us to superior managed products across all styles? Can we be the Billy Bean of the consultant community?

Unfortunately, we believe the answer is "no."

Although we find evaluating past performance interesting—and it can certainly indicate past success—we are convinced there is no successful black box approach to evaluating or selecting investment managers, including mutual funds, separate account managers, and hedge funds. It would be easier (and certainly less expensive) if there was a magic Oakland A's style quantitative formula, but there is not.

This is What We Believe

We have structured our own investment philosophy based on the following assumptions, and one that may suit the core beliefs of fellow consultants:

- Portfolio design (or asset allocation) determines the majority of performance variability
- Market inefficiencies exist and can be exploited by active management, but passive management can make sense in certain situations and environments
- Consistent managers perform better in the long run and gradually rise to the top of their peer group
- Expenses and taxes directly impact long-term performance

Slicing and dicing historical performance can validate historical success, but evaluation must have an emphasis on looking forward. A manager may produce a positive alpha, but we *must* be convinced that their "edge" will be sustained in the future. We believe there is no substitute for hard work.

As investment management consultants, our own manager research process is driven by three primary goals: 1) Identify managers with a proven ability to produce alpha (that's the easy one); 2) Understand a manager's risk exposure and sources of return in a manager's investment strategy (does a manager's philosophy, process and performance attribution align properly?); and, 3) Determine if that alpha generation is sustainable. Are there outside factors, in particular, that would disrupt this success? (This is the hard one!)

By and large, the following questions can identify key facts that explain past performance (positive or negative) and, more importantly, can help provide a sense of whether a manager will be able to add value going forward. A complete organizational analysis must be completed as well.

Here are five key factors to successfully evaluating managers:

1) *Does the manager (or team) have exceptional insight, work experience, and/or academic success?* There is absolutely no substitute for solid, long- term experience in managing money. Academics can be important, but, generally, we believe it will not lend to any special insight. There is an abundance of interesting academic research on successful stock market strategies written by students and their professors. At times, it can even be the genesis of a product or idea, but there is a big difference between academic research and real-world implementation.

2) *Does the manager employ a unique strategy that can capitalize on market inefficiencies (perhaps as a result of their intellectual edge)?* We like unique, complicated, and difficult-to-replicate strategies. When the strategies become popular or duplicatable, the edge is lost. Some firms produce excellent research, and they may even sell it. But they, typically, will use it themselves before others do.

3) *Does the manager have more firepower in terms of total experience, number of professionals, or systems?* Today, money management firms seem to lean toward teams to protect themselves from a "star" manager departure. Teams do not always work though, and "group think" can lead to mediocrity. On the other hand, complete dependence on one key individual can be a major negative.

4) *Does the manager have better access to information than do their peers?* Regulation FD (Full Disclosure) definitely has impacted a firm's ability to get information from public companies that they previously could easily obtain. But some money managers go deeper than others – interviewing competition, customers, suppliers. Others do a better job in digging deep into a company's financial characteristics, perhaps focusing on the quality of the data, and not taking it at face value.

5) *Does the manager have superior trading skills or systems that can enhance performance?* We have seen many of cases of how poor trading costs a manager significant performance, quarter in and quarter out. The reverse is also true at some trading desks. Particularly, some hedge funds are exceptionally adept at consistently adding value through quality trading.

Firms with superior back office capabilities, low personnel turnover, independent firms with few conflicts of interest, firms with plenty of "skin in the game," as well as those with a specific specialty attract our attention, and are ones we believe other consultants should pay attention to.

About Style

Consultants have the bad habit of putting every manager in a style box, and if they don't fit well in that box, they won't fit well with any client. Certainly, some clients need managers with low tracking error relative to a particular style and there are excellent managers that have been able to squeeze out consistent alpha relative to a benchmark.

But for other investors, there are talented managers who search for alpha wherever they can find it; unconstrained by strategy, style, sectors, market cap, or direction (long/short). Of course, evaluation of these two types of managers requires very different approaches.

Good performance by a manager due to security selection gets a thumbs-up from us. What was the most common reason for out-performance in the late '90s? Over-allocation to technology stocks, and most everyone paid for that concentration from 2000-02. The beauty of the last 10 years for investors and their consultants is that the markets have taken us through incredibly different environments – *great* times for small growth stocks, as well as *terrible* times for small growth stocks—and the same for small value, large growth and large value. It has been a pretty good test of the times, but not a perfect one.

Since we've been in a dramatically falling interest rate environment, non-U.S. investments significantly have lagged domestic investments over that time period. Some managers have passed this test of time successfully; many have not.

About Passive Management and Hedge Funds

Passive management certainly can be a component in an investor's portfolio if they are looking for pure exposure to a certain opportunity set. In addition, particularly for a taxable investor, index funds can generate deferred growth through low turnover that is difficult for most active managers to beat on an after-tax basis.

Can active managers beat passive products? Sure, some of them can some of the time; but none of them all of the time. Can an average manager beat the relevant index? Perhaps not, but we believe there are certain high-quality active managers who will beat the market over time. But in some areas, like non-U.S. equity, even mediocre managers have out-performed the EAFE benchmark.

For those who believe that successful active managers are just lucky, hedge funds prove them wrong. There are certainly talented managers who have added value on both the short and the long side fairly consistently. Because the market, typically, is taken out of the equation with these alternative strategies, it is the ultimate proof of talent in the investment business. It's no wonder why so much talent has migrated to hedge funds. Higher fees have had an impact as well.

A Few Words About Portfolio Construction

Before conducting a manager search, it is imperative to understand the role of each manager in a portfolio. It is certainly possible for an investor to have an array of very talented managers, but if the fit is awkward, total portfolio performance can be mediocre. For instance, deep value complemented by aggressive growth. We saw many large stock portfolios in the late 1990s comprised of an aggressive growth manager and a relative value manager. As the market tumbled in 2000 to 2002, the value manager was not nearly as defensive as the investor had hoped, and the portfolio was punished.

As mentioned earlier, a variety of combinations of multi-manager portfolios regressed over the last 10 years or so, will provide a fairly accurate indication of style and market cap biases in addition to performance characteristics in a variety of market scenarios.

Conclusion

Many professionals in the investment business are searching for that magic Billy Bean style quantitative formula to find great managers and products. Typically, though, their formula leads them only to managers and products that have done well historically and offers little insight as to whether future success is likely. There is no magic formula.

We believe that the only meaningful way to judge a manager's future success is to:

- Intimately understand strategies and apply them to future scenarios. An opinion about the future markets and economy is imperative.

Manager Search and Evaluation

- Have a firm grasp of the talent pool in the money management firm, their motivation, leadership, and firm ownership
- Understand the impact of growth issues such as portfolio size and constraints
- Evaluate outside forces such as taxes and regulation
- Completely understand how each strategy in a portfolio relates to another

Anyone can crunch numbers but, although quantitative analysis is useful, ultimately the multi-manager portfolios that will be successful in the long run are those that are "powered by people."

❖❖❖

12

EVALUATING INVESTMENT MANAGER PERFORMANCE

Barry Mendelson, CIMA, Managing Partner
Richard Iwanski, CFA®, Partner
Jennifer Arnold, Partner
Capital Market Consultants, LLC

If the process of selecting, monitoring and evaluating investment managers was like constructing a house, it would be built with the bricks and mortar of science, but would rest firmly on a foundation of professional judgment. The strength and quality of the decisions regarding engaging or retaining a money manager are dramatically enhanced by employing a sensible and repeatable review process – no different than following an architecturally sound process when building a house and maintaining the structure once completed. Employing and retaining investment managers, like any investment discipline targeted for success, requires great initial care and ongoing decision-making.

To the surprise of many advisors (often, unfortunately, after the fact) evaluating investment manager performance does not lend itself to isolated and purely quantitative decisions (especially a cursory review of past performance). Caveat Emptor: for advisors who hope to reduce manager searches and performance evaluation to quick screening exercises conducted on user-friendly commercial databases, or a quick review of side-by-side historical performance, we believe those approaches increase the likelihood of:

- Unintended investment mistakes from selecting managers not well-suited for particular clients (and loss of business reputation and momentum)
- Causing unnecessary higher-maintenance client relationships (and the

ensuing revenue reduction) through poor investment suitability screening

- The inevitable investment surprises that could have been avoided through careful evaluation at the front end, coupled with regularly refreshing one's performance evaluation perspective

(These types of errors caused by erroneous performance evaluation processes or judgments will be discussed later in this chapter.)

Rather, performance evaluation should be carefully done within a larger context that considers and balances a variety of manager factors (often called the "Four P's" see Table 1) as well as client factors (e.g., are the client's goals, objectives and risk tolerance still the same and the manager's performance still appropriate for their needs?):

Table 1: The Four P's

Factor	Performance Evaluation Questions
The **people** side of the management organization	Is the organization **stable** and will it likely continue to be while they are managing your clients' money?
The investment **philosophy** of the management company	Do they possess **sound, fundamental investment beliefs** that are being shaped into a consistently applied process?
The investment **process** of the management company	Are the data and decision-making processes and people responsible for them **reliable and intact**?
The **performance** of the management company	Does the historical record of investment performance demonstrate a **consistency of style and persistence of skill** that produces an economic value added?

Careful ongoing investment manager evaluation, therefore, has immediate benefits to advisors, not the least of which is the protection of their practice, its reputation and brand name value in the marketplace.

This chapter is organized in a way to give advisors both perspective and practical tools to improve their own performance evaluation processes when hiring, retaining, or terminating an investment manager on behalf of their clients. For advisors newer to the separately managed account (SMA) world, primary guidance is provided here for an evaluation process that can be used right away. For more advanced practitioners, additional ideas are provided for those who have the tools to pursue further research.

The Perspective of Experience

As veteran consultants, we have been performing manager evaluations for nearly a quarter of a century through some pretty glorious and ugly markets. Our careers date back to the early days of separately managed accounts, and we have learned many practical lessons worth sharing to help shortcut the advisor's path to functional expertise.

First, readers of this text are either independent advisors, consultants, or advisors working within a larger firm. It is, therefore, more likely than not that their firm—or the platform they use as an independent—provides them with a manager program or platform within which to work. It also is likely that their firm, or the platform they use, has research staff evaluating various manager options, or has outsourced that research effort.

How do managers get on a firm's recommended list? The answer to this question will reveal that not all "recommended" managers are created equal and have equivalent skill. In our experience, we have found there are two primary reasons why managers get on a recommended or preferred list: one is based upon perceived value-added of the researchers at the investment management firm (e.g., superior skill determined by an evaluation of past performance and the organization supporting that performance) and the other reason is largely based on the practical business needs of the sponsor firm. The latter factors include advisor education, marketing resources and capabilities, and the trust and comfort factor with local and regional sales and marketing managers. The "bricks and mortar" aspect of sales and marketing efforts can have a very beneficial effect. The former factors are driven by the talent, skill and resources of the investment management firm's research staff.

In any event, it is important to understand that some of the managers on the advisor's list or the platform are there largely due to their ability to meet the business needs of a sponsor firm, and not due strictly to the outstanding performance or skill of the manager. Knowing this beforehand should help advisors organize their own preferred manager sub-lists and maintain ongoing performance evaluation routines relating to client preferences and the development of their investment consulting brand in the marketplace.

Second, manager selection and performance evaluation, while important, pale in importance to the asset allocation decisions advisors must make for clients. Recent research has shown that manager and fund selection and the related ongoing evaluation of performance represent important, but, relatively minor factors in overall portfolio performance[1]. While performance evaluation is a "sexy" part of the business, it is not as important as the strategic risk-return tradeoff decision between various asset classes. Clients need to know that.

Third, there are limits to what even the most rigorous performance evaluation analysis can reveal about future performance. This is because the analysis is based upon historical data and an overlay assessment or judgment about how much of that process-driven skill can be transferred into the future. Ultimately, the world of money management is a people business, and the manager's behavior and performance will vary from what we expect or predict it will be. On a related note, for a full performance evaluation, it is critical to get to know the key individuals responsible for the performance. Quantitative performance evaluation is best seen from the human context.

Fourth, the term "style consistency" is greatly misunderstood. Consistency should not be confused with rigidity. The natural by-product of the ebb and flow of the capital markets will cause security and, hence, portfolio characteristics to change (e.g., in bull markets P/Es rise asymmetrically across sectors). Even consistent managers will vary and, generally, can be seen to function well and normally within a certain band of change we refer to as their operating domain (See Chart 1- page 92).

Variation within that operating domain is to be expected as a consequence of market behavior along with the disciplined investment process employed by the manager as they search for investment opportunity.

Fifth, as a by-product of the scandal-ridden times in which we now live, the devastating bear market of 2000-2003, and the more competitive SMA market, it is more likely than ever before that clients will expect the advisor to stay on top of the investments made on their behalf.

Chart 1: Operating Domain

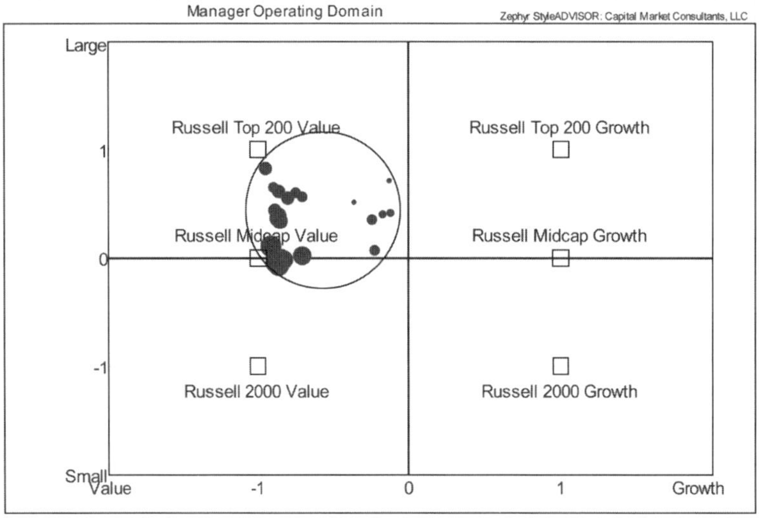

Sixth, client accounts that fall under the jurisdiction of the Employee Retirement Income Security Act (ERISA)–qualified plans, the Uniform Prudent Investor Act (UPIA) – trust accounts, or Uniform Management of Public Employee Retirement Systems Act (UMPERS) – municipal employee retirement plans, will require higher standards of professional service as a matter of best practices. These standards will include a prudent process by which managers and investment products in these portfolios are evaluated. The performance bar for advisors is higher with larger pools of money to manage.

Lastly, performance evaluation is too frequently viewed from the perspective of the manager only. Often, advisors fail to keep the close link between the client and the manager's performance behavior (not percentage return results!). By this we mean the suitability of a manager for the client's financial needs. If an optimizer indicates large value is required to diversify the portfolio, who is going to determine which type of large value manager is most appropriate for this unique client given their circumstances, and also taking into consideration the remainder of the holdings that will be in the final portfolio?

This chapter, then, will attempt to illustrate the importance of manager suitability, quarterly manager monitoring and manager sub-style analysis, and their relevance to client management and retention. A lack of awareness of important behavioral differences between similarly styled managers (e.g., a large cap relative value manager versus a large cap deep value manager) will have a confusing and confounding impact on client management. It is always best to avoid this mishap by selecting the right manager—or manager combinations—in the first place.

The Concept of Suitability

Like it or not, clients have unique assumptions and expectations about their investments. Understanding those expectations – and communicating the limitations and risks involved – is the responsibility of each financial advisor, money manager, or consultant. Proper standards of care require advisors to work with their clients to develop an appropriate asset allocation and investment policy statement (IPS). However, even the best policy is worthless unless the client stays the course; to win, they must feel comfortable with their investments and stick to the long-range plan.

Proper manager selection can have a substantial impact on the success of the client relationship. This is the concept of suitability: the awareness that specific investment manager-client combinations have a greater certainty to meet client goals based on an optimal blend of investment manager skill and client preferences.

All too often, clients face "moments of peril" over the course of their investment horizon that can jeopardize their plan and their relationship with the advisor. Many of these moments can be avoided with proper manager selection. If an investment goal can be defined as the desired ending value, a client objective is defined as the path to get there. Objectives are based on an investor's (perhaps limited) understanding of equity market behavior and their own proprietary definition of risk. Common client objectives include:

- Absolute Return: The client is more interested in absolute returns regardless of the benchmark return.

- Out-performance: The client desires to beat the market in positive market cycles and acknowledges there is risk on the downside.

- Risk Avoidance: The client understands the portfolio will lag in up markets, but is willing to forego upside to preserve wealth during market declines.

- Low Tracking Error: The client desires managers that meet or beat the market over the long-term, as long as they don't "blow up" (lag the benchmark significantly).

- Story-Focused: The client has a preference for certain types of investing that he or she perceives to be of value, such as high dividend-paying stocks or aggressive growth stocks.

- Opportunity Loss: The client feels he or she is "missing out" by not participating in the hottest market segments.

Initial Manager Selection for Clients

Investment managers, like all marketable "products" or solutions, come in an exceptionally wide variety of models, shapes, sizes, and colors. The industry has made significant advances to organize this manager diversity by incorporating the "style box" system of manager identification. This concept is now considered to be an accepted industry practice, resulting in the potential for more thoroughly diversified investor portfolios.

Unfortunately, a concurrent trend is also taking place as managers are identified solely by their style box (e.g., a large cap growth manager) instead of through a deeper understanding of their unique investment approach. This is an understandable oversimplification given the necessity to process in-

Chart 2 - STYLE BOX
Distinguishing Domestic Equity Investment Styles

Value	Core	Growth
Barra Large Cap Value	S&P 500	Barra Large Cap Growth
Russell® 1000 Value	Russell® 1000	Russell® 1000 Growth
Russell® Mid Cap Value	Russell® Mid Cap	Russell® Mid Cap Growth
Russell® 2000 Value	Russell® 2000	Russell® 2000 Growth

← Style →

↑ Capitalization ↓

Index: Unmanaged group of securities representing a portion of the economy, capital market structure or investment style
Value: A portfolio with stocks trading below their estimated intrinsic worth
Growth: A portfolio with stocks with earnings growing faster than the market
Core: A market-oriented portfolio with both value and growth characteristics

formation quickly, but what is lost in the generalization is the reality that managers *within* each style box can vary significantly from one another in their approach and performance behavior. These differences are intentionally structural and independent of cyclical investment returns. This is a direct result of their investment process and, with proper research, can be identified and categorized in groups within a style called "sub-styles."

Grouping and evaluating managers by process driven sub-style has significant benefits to advisors and their clients. With a deeper understanding of the manager's investment process, advisors can better ascertain *the pattern* of investment performance over time. The result is an improved risk profile and an enhanced ability to properly match client expectations with their investment managers.

Within the large cap growth space, for example, managers employ a variety of investment processes that produce very different return patterns such as Momentum, Stable Growth, or Growth at a Reasonable Price (GARP). Each sub-style has different return and risk patterns that make them suitable for different clients. *We recommend a practical approach for most advisors – assign managers a suitability category of either conservative, moderate, or aggressive within their style box.* Think of a client in a similar manner. Are they conservative, moderate or aggressive? Recommend managers that match the client's preferences and tolerance for risk.

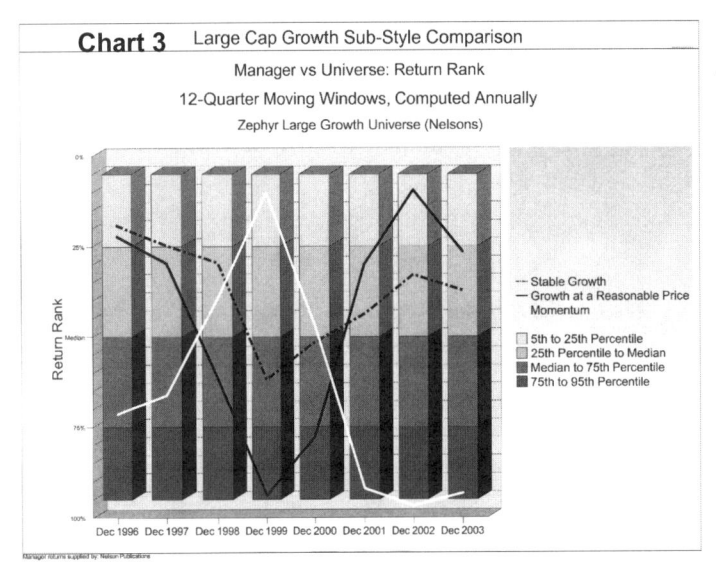

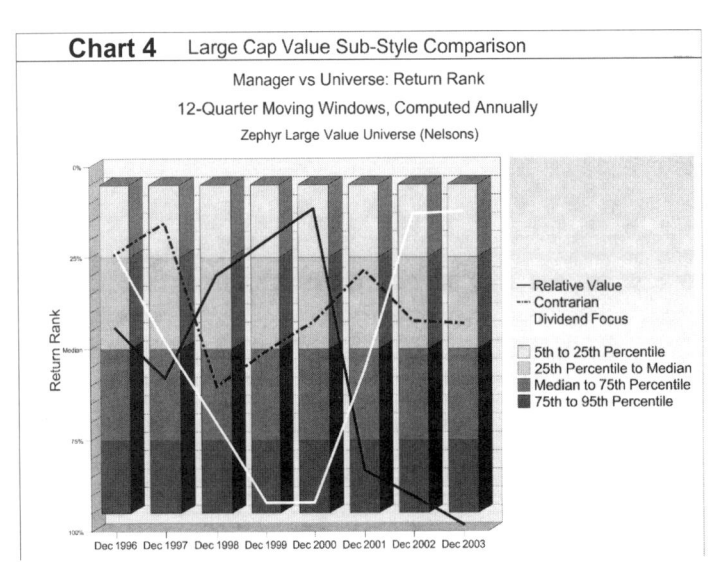

Using this approach also applies when assembling multi-manager portfolios, although additional analysis is required to better understand how the managers complement one another within the overall portfolio. For example, managers who do not correlate highly with each other are preferable to those who are highly correlated. Such examinations require adequate technology to execute; ideally this work is performed by an organization's due diligence group, or is outsourced. While this is an important extra step, it does not undermine the primary objective–to provide a guide to pair clients with suitable managers.

These charts display the relative performance of three managers with distinctive sub-styles within their respective universe. The first, displaying Large Cap Growth (Chart 3) includes a Momentum manager, a Stable Growth manager, and a Growth at a Reasonable Price (GARP) manager. The second, displaying Large Cap Value (Chart 4) includes a Dividend Focused manager, a Contrarian manager, and a Low Price-to-Earnings Ratio manager. On each chart, the vertical bars indicate the range of returns in the peer universe over rolling three-year performance periods.

The charts on the previous page illustrate the impact sub-styles can have on relative performance as they go in and out of favor in the market. Note how the Momentum manager and GARP manager have rotated since 1999 near the market peak. *More importantly, this reversal is consistent with other managers within the two sub-styles.* Certainly, individual manager skill is always a factor, but so is an understanding of the marketplace they invest in.

In conclusion, when selecting a manager, advisors should have a general awareness of their sub-style; as a general rule of thumb, aggressive clients should be matched with aggressive managers and so on. Advisors should discuss with new clients their understanding of the market and whether they have particular preferences. Remember that the client is not in control of manager selection; the objective is to ascertain what their biases are, and to best match suitable managers that meet their goals. A best-effort attempt is made to develop an investment policy that both meets their investment objective *and keeps them on that path*; in essence, a custom fit in an ordinarily off-the-rack world.

Manager Reviews and Ongoing Performance Evaluation

A critical part of any advisory business practice is the ongoing monitoring of managers used in client portfolios. As previously stated, clients expect advisors to perform ongoing reviews of their investments. Although most organizations have due diligence departments at the home office, we believe it is important that advisors conduct their own basic level of quarterly monitoring. The most useful manager reviews should be proactive, rather than reactive. Advisors who know their managers have strategic advantages beyond singularly meeting their responsibility to the client. A deeper understanding is evident in the following ways:

- Provides a suitable match from the onset
- Ensures that suitability is ongoing
- Contributes significantly to client communication in volatile markets
- Enhances client satisfaction
- Leads to more meaningful referrals and better business for the advisor

> *Can't manager selection be accomplished by picking the best-performing manager in each asset class?*
>
> A common mistake made by advisors is the over-reliance on performance in the selection process. This is understandable: focusing solely on performance is a draw to both advisor and client. After all, isn't it likely that excellent performance will continue–that the manager has real skill? Perhaps. But everyone has read the studies showing top-performing managers rarely stay on top. What is just as likely, especially in regard to short-term performance, is that the manager's sub-style of investing is in favor. In other words, the broad stock market currently favors those particular securities that the manager typically owns in the portfolio. It is a cyclical factor that does not persist. There is no better example of this than momentum growth investing during the late 1990s. After all, how difficult was it in 1999 to assemble a portfolio of Internet stocks with excellent past performance?

So what responsibilities do advisors have in this process, what tools are available to them, what records do they keep, and—an always difficult question—at what point do they terminate a manager?

The review process begins by getting organized. Advisors need to review the roster of managers available to them (or their own developed list). They need to examine any material produced by the manager, their firm's due diligence group supporting the platform they use, or an outsourced solution that specializes in manager research. Comprehensive due diligence efforts require tools, as well as an interpretation of the available information so that insightful conclusions can be made for effective client management. However, regardless of who provides the research, ensure that they are contacting the portfolio managers of the management organization (not merely the marketing staff) quarterly to review this information.

Manager Review Routines

Now that we have discussed the materials and a basic review of their components, what are the critical elements to review each quarter, and what is the best way to develop a routine? Begin with a reflection of why the manager was initially hired. What – exactly – was this manager hired to do? Keep this perspective in mind throughout the evaluation, and critically examine whether the performance analysis continues to support the original objective. For example, an advisor determines that a conservative, dividend-focused manager with the objective of low-risk and preservation of capital is most suitable for the client. Over the course of the quarter, the market accelerates and the manager lags behind. Should the underperformance be of critical concern? Based on the framework previously described, the simple answer is no; underperformance in a strong up market is expected. Moreover, given the manager's preservation of capital approach, it is likely that they have lagged in past markets, too.

Manager examination can be done more effectively with better organization and established routines. We all know that marketing and sales information is everywhere, but no one has enough time to read it all (assuming they want to). Advisors can develop an organized series of quarterly routines to perform. *Here's* a *simple tip*– create a checklist to initial, date, and file when completed. List all elements required for a manager examination, and include text boxes for personal commentary. Attach all supporting information and keep a manager file. These records demonstrate an advisor's consistency and thoroughness.

The following section examines procedures for a manager review. The elements covered are ideal for inclusion in the checklist, although advisors may not have access to all the tools to produce them. In that instance, make do with what is available, but understand that the lack of information will increase the likelihood that the analysis may be incomplete or inconclusive. Outlined are the four vital steps in the analysis:

Step 1: Communicate With the Manager

First, examine how the manager performed during the quarter compared to their benchmark:

Large Cap Value Manager	4.05%
Russell 1000 Value Index	5.50%

So far, so good. The challenge is to determine whether this difference is meaningful. Clearly, more information is needed; it's not feasible to draw conclusions on a manager with data from only one quarter.

Start by reviewing the manager's most recent quarterly commentary. Many managers produce commentaries that can be received via e-mail or obtained from their web site. At the very least, the quarterly commentary gives advisors the manager's opinion of the portfolio and the market. It's just a starting point – but never forget the author's imbedded bias.

After reading the manager's story, ask the question – does the explanation ring true? Verify its accuracy and draw an independent conclusion. All manager evaluations rest on a foundation of three core analytical elements:

- Returns-based analysis – examines performance only
- Holdings-based analysis – examines performance and verifies process
- Qualitative analysis – examines people, philosophy, process, and organization

Each element, discussed below, has a distinctive advantage and level of usefulness.

Step 2: Returns-Based Analysis

Returns-based style analysis was pioneered by Nobel Laureate William F. Sharpe, whose goal was to determine and evaluate a portfolio's investment style without portfolio holdings. His methodology compared the returns of a manager to the returns of a set of indices to determine investment style. This was a radical concept in its day. His work, coupled with today's computing power, has enabled analysts to examine a portfolio in much greater detail than was previously possible. Most importantly for the advisor, the process is quick and easy.

Once again, managers should never be evaluated on one quarter alone. Ideally, long-term performance data should be viewed in the context of manager philosophy and process. In other words, does the performance track record support the manager's objective? Clearly, if a manager's goal is to beat the S&P 500 index with less risk over a full market cycle, one would want the performance track record to support this objective, at least most of the time. On the other hand, if preserving value in down markets is the goal, one would want to verify their past success from that perspective.

Use this time to review the manager's long-term trends over three, five and 10 years. Look at performance versus the index benchmark, performance over rolling periods, check for style drift, and learn to use helpful ratios like Sharpe, information, and downside risk. Since examinations will be quarterly, changes tend to be gradual. This procedure also gives an advisor some insight into the portfolio's return pattern over time, and helps with determining client suitability.

Don't neglect to review the benchmark itself. Often, unique characteristics within the benchmark will drive its performance and impact sub-styles differently. A timely example of this is the performance of low-quality stocks within the S&P 500 index during 2003. During the year, low-quality stocks ("C" and "D" rated, as defined by S&P) significantly outperformed stocks of higher quality. Managers who, typically, would not own such securities were likely to lag during the year. Benchmark analysis can be produced by a firm's due diligence group, investment managers, and obtained through professional publications. The more that knowledgeable advisors understand about the dynamics of manager benchmarks, the more accurate their analysis will be.

While returns-based style analysis is exceptionally useful, it has its drawbacks. Chief among them is the nature of performance itself. The phrase "past performance is no guarantee of future results" rings resoundingly true. An examination of returns does not give us a deep insight into the organization itself, nor does it provide any evidence that the historic alpha the manager may have produced will persist. Was the manager skillful or lucky? With returns-based analysis, no one knows.

A. Review Historic Investment Results—An advisor should examine manager historic returns like the large cap value manager below (Manager A), and make some relevant observations on his or her performance. Begin by reviewing the historic investment results, including current quarter, one-, three-, five-, and 10-year history, if available. Also review calendar year returns to identify any significant period of excess return.

Trailing Year Returns	Qtr	YTD	1Yr	3Yr	5Yr	10Yr
Manager A	2.58	12.44	18.96	1.06	4.94	10.49
Russell 1000 Value Index	2.06	13.87	24.37	-2.01	4.00	10.37
Excess Return	0.52	-1.44	-5.41	3.08	0.94	0.12

Calendar Returns	2002	2001	2000	1999	1998	1997
Manager A	-15.26	0.81	5.85	9.59	13.21	27.62
Russell 1000 Value Index	-15.52	-5.59	7.01	7.35	15.63	35.18
Excess Return	0.26	6.40	-1.16	2.24	-2.42	-7.56

Observations—From the data above, note that Manager A has exceeded its benchmark (the Russell 1000 Value Index) during the most recent quarter and over three-, five-, and 10-year periods. Performance lagged significantly in 2001. Understanding the cause of underperformance or performance variations is an important next step. Overall, it appears that this manager tracks the benchmark fairly closely.

B. Review Historic Performance Statistics—Next review an array of performance statistics over the same time periods to drill down the analysis further. There is a sizable number of tracking, risk, risk-adjusted, consistency, and volatility measures available. Each has meaning on its own, but considered together and over varying time periods, these measures provide a more complete story of actual performance behavior. Which are the most important? *Our recommendation: start with a few to get a feel for their usefulness and relationship to each other.* This is the "art" portion of manager evaluation.

Index Relative Statistics*	3 Yr	5Yr	10Yr
R-squared	96.56	94.42	92.94
Batting Avg	75.00	65.00	55.00
Beta	0.94	0.90	0.89
Tracking Error	3.76	4.53	4.25
Alpha	2.81	0.88	0.70
Info Ratio	0.78	0.13	-0.04

Observations—There is a number of performance observations that can be made about Manager A:

Risk & RAR Statistics	3 Yr			5Yr			10Yr		
	Manager	Index	Excess	Manager	Index	Excess	Manager	Index	Excess
Standard Deviation	19.24	19.98	-0.74	17.32	18.77	-1.45	14.65	15.91	-1.26
Downside Deviation	14.76	17.13	-2.37	11.73	12.73	-1.00	8.40	8.65	-0.25
Sharpe	-0.09	-0.23	0.14	0.07	0.02	0.05	0.41	0.37	0.04
Upside Down Ration	0.35	0.25	0.10	0.55	0.53	0.02	0.96	0.99	-0.03
Omega Excess Return	-2.15	0.04	-21.9	-0.88	-0.16	-0.72	-0.26	-0.14	-0.13

*RAR = Risk Adjusted Return

Evaluating Investment Manager Performance

- Manager R-squared to the benchmark is high and tracking error is particularly low, indicating that the Russell 1000 Index is a good benchmark. Generally an R-squared over 80 indicates an acceptable level.
- Standard deviation is consistently less than the benchmark; excess returns have been achieved with less volatility.
- Excess Sharpe ratio is positive in each period as is Alpha; the manager has added economic value on a risk-adjusted basis.
- Downside deviation is significantly less, especially over the last three years; the manager appears to have weathered the bear market fairly well.
- A high batting average over the last three years indicates there is a consistency to the outperformance; it did not occur during an odd quarter or year.

C. Returns-Based Graphics: A Picture is Worth a Thousand Words—A great advantage of returns-based analysis is the ability to graphically view the information. The benefits are clear to the eye. With the right technology, charts are easy to produce, provide visual clues, and display performance results dynamically over time. The following charts are useful to further interpret how a manager has performed.

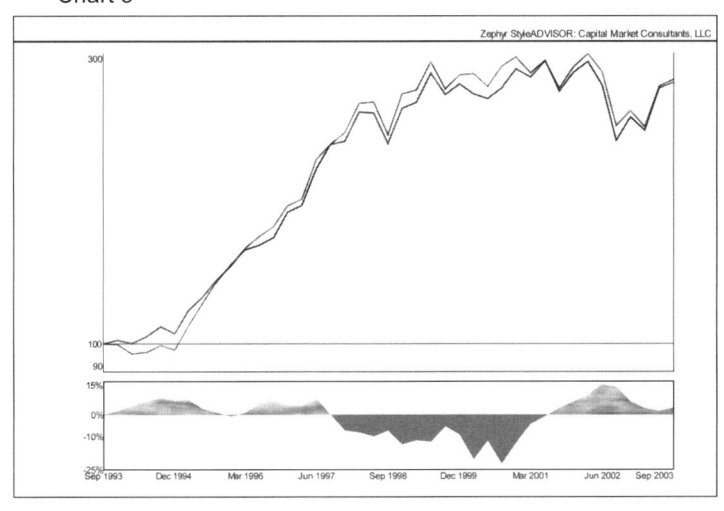

Chart 5

GROWTH of INVESTMENT

The top portion of the graph compares the growth of a $100,000 investment in this manager versus its performance index over time. The bottom portion indicates the cumulative excess return. Gray = Manager   Black = Benchmark

Observations—The manager tracks its benchmark fairly closely. There was a performance lag from late 1997 through 2001, the peak of the bull market. This should be examined more closely. Outperformance has since resumed.

Chart 6

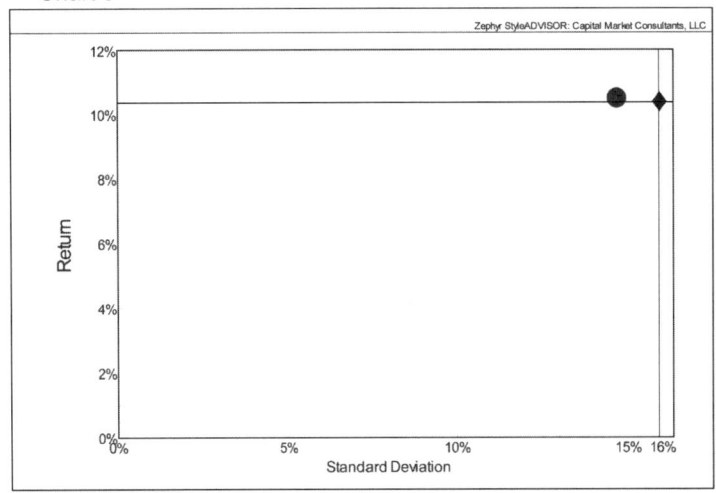

RISK vs. RETURN

The graph compares the risk & return tradeoff of the portfolio (as measured by standard deviation of returns) versus the index over a 10- year period.

Observations—The manager has slightly outperformed its benchmark with less risk on a 10-year basis. This chart also should be viewed over shorter time increments.

Chart 7

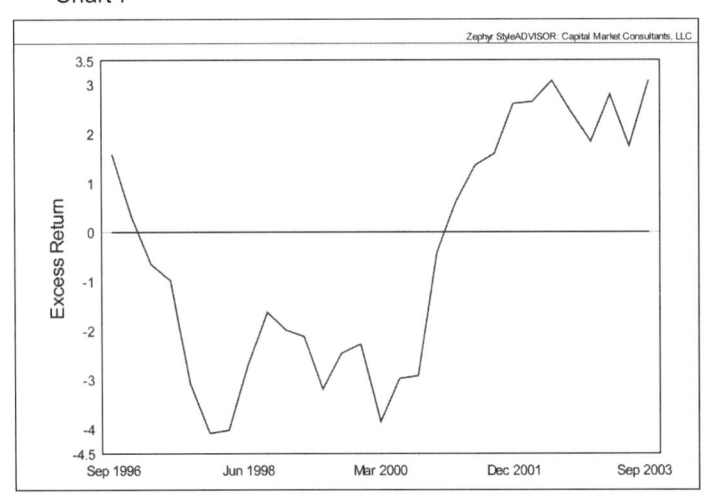

ROLLING EXCESS RETURN

This graph illustrates the consistency of the manager's 3-year excess return versus its benchmark over time. Manager returns above the horizontal line are desired.

Observations—As Chart 5 also indicates, performance lagged over the 1997 to 2001 period. Excess returns have since been greater than the benchmark.

Chart 8

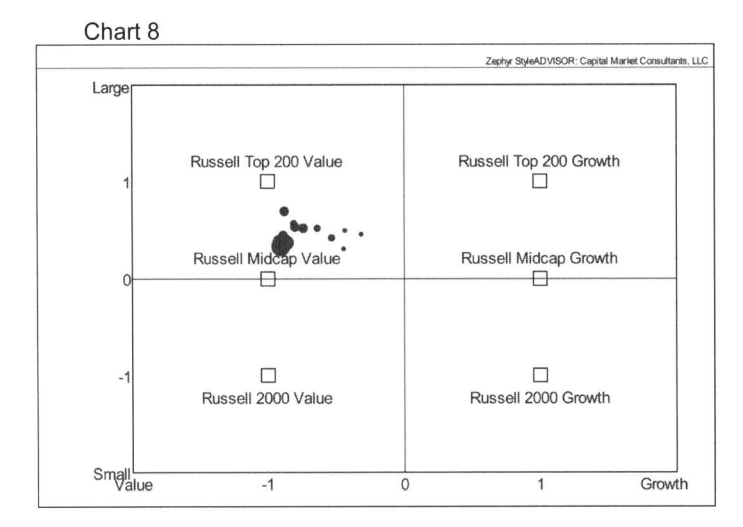

ROLLING STYLE

This graph illustrates consistency of manager style over time. Style measurements are determined by evaluating the statistical similarity between the behavior of the managed product with various style indices. Larger circles represent more recent time periods.

Observations—The manager has some mid cap exposure that requires further investigation. There is some consistency to this exposure – it may be process-driven.

Chart 9

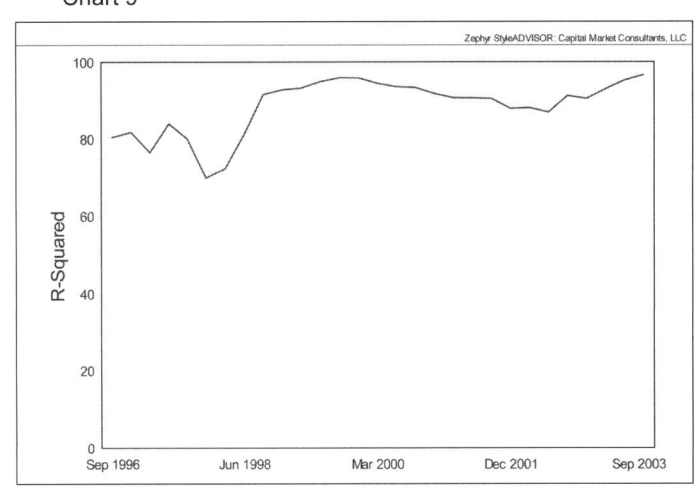

ROLLING R-SQUARED

This chart examines R-Squared over rolling 3-year periods. The R-Squared statistic measures the degree to which manager performance can be explained by the performance of the index. R-Squared values range between 0 and 1. Values near 1 indicate that manager performance is explainable by movements in the benchmark.

Observations – Three-year rolling R-squared has been high since 1998, although prior to 1998 it was below 80, the threshold for a proper benchmark. This requires further examination.

Returns-Based Style Analysis Conclusions

Given the information presented in this example regarding Manager A, one should be able to draw some meaningful conclusions and be better able to tell the manager's performance story, such as:

- Performance has generally exceeded the Russell 1000 Value Index over the time periods measured.

- The portfolio did lag modestly from 1998 through 2001, the peak of the bull market.
- The portfolio was less risky as measured by standard deviation and downside risk over every period measured, including the recent bear market.
- The manager also appears to be style-consistent, tracking the benchmark closely.
- Style analysis indicates some exposure to mid cap stocks.

Within this framework, a clearer picture is provided as to what type of client this manager is most suitable for. In this case, the positive Sharpe ratio, low standard deviation and downside risk, and low manager tracking error indicate that Manager A would be most suitable for a conservative client who is concerned about consistent performance and preservation of capital.

Step 3: Holdings-Based Analysis

The process of evaluating a portfolio by its holdings is as old as security analysis itself. However, it generally is not a part of most research procedures. The reasons holdings-based style analysis isn't widely employed include:

- Holdings may not be available or are difficult to obtain.
- Sophisticated software is needed to conduct the research[2].
- Correct interpretation requires skillful analysis.

With the proper holdings, software, and knowledge, the advantages of holdings-based style analysis are significant and the results much more powerful than returns-based analysis. Evaluating historic results and past performance alone does not allow us to actually see what's going on right now in a portfolio. Nor does it do a good job of ascertaining whether performance results were achieved skillfully or with luck. For example, was a poor quarter due to a high concentration in a particular sector (e.g., industrials)? Was this management decision unique in the period, or a persistent theme? Or was the problem poor stock selection? To answer these types of questions, a holdings-based review is required.

To perform the review, portfolio holdings and their weightings (number of shares or portfolio percentage) are required. We usually recommend at least five years of data for evaluation. For a one-quarter review, holdings-based attribution analysis is the only option. Review the exposures to economic sectors and market capitalization. Review contributions due to stock selection, sector weightings, and timing. The best managers add alpha with good stock selection over time.

A sample one-quarter review is shown on Chart 10:

Observations—The table provides an executive summary of a holdings-based review. The upper left panel breaks out overall performance into three main contributors: market, style, and skill. These three contributors to return sum to the fund's return for the quarter. Skill is further segmented into sector allocation, stock selection, and trading activity skill. In this example, the market return (all companies in the database) was relatively flat (+0.38%), although the benchmark performed quite well (+9.27%). Since the portfolio return was greater (+12.25%), the difference (+2.60%) is considered skill. More importantly, this skill is further divided into three components: sector allocation skill (-0.07%), stock selection skill (+5.80%), and trading activity skill (-3.13%).

Evaluating Investment Manager Performance

Attribution Analysis for Domestic Fund
Quarter Ending 9/30/00
Russell Mid Value

Chart 10

Components of Return

Market*	0.38	
Benchmark	9.27	Mid/Val
Skill	2.60	
SECTOR Allocation	-0.07	
STOCK Selection	5.80	
Activity	-3.13	
Total	12.25	
Ranks:		
Total	5	
Within Style	35	

Important Factors

What Helped		What Hurt	
Style Benchmark	9.27	Style Bets	-5.94
Energy Selection	2.19	Activity	-3.13
Finance Selection	1.88	Tchnlgy Allocation	-1.14

Style Effects

	Large			Mid			Small			
	Value	Core	Growth	Value	Core	Growth	Value	Core	Growth	Total
A) Benchmark Allocation	13.70	0.00	0.00	56.20	30.10	0.00	0.00	0.00	0.00	
B) Market* Allocation	19.12	17.34	23.63	12.61	8.10	14.20	2.05	1.18	1.76	(m)
C) Market* Return	6.66	-5.94	-8.37	13.01	4.73	0.66	7.87	2.23	-10.91	0.38
Style Effects										
(A - B) * (C - m)	-0.34	1.10	2.07	5.51	0.96	-0.04	-0.15	-0.02	0.20	9.27
D) Fund Allocation	11.39	13.00	11.71	25.89	26.53	10.85	0.00	0.00	0.00	
Style Bets										
(D - A) * (C - m)	-0.15	-0.82	-1.02	-3.83	-0.16	0.03	0.00	0.00	0.00	-5.94

* Market = Entire Compustat database - all companies.
Source: Ron Surz, PPCA Inc.

StokTrib – Stock-Based Attribution

The upper right panel lists the important factors that drove manager performance. In our example, what helped in the quarter includes style benchmark, stock selection in the energy sector, and stock selection in the finance sector. What hurt performance included style bets, trading activity, and an overweight in the technology sector.

The bottom panel details the performance effects of style during the quarter. Each row will be discussed individually:

A. The first row displays the effective style profile of the Russell Midcap Value Index. Not surprisingly, this index is dominantly midcap value (56%) with a sizable portion in midcap core (30%).

B. The second row displays the style composition of the entire market. In this example, the market consists of large cap stocks with smaller mid cap and small cap allocations.

C. The third row shows the returns in the quarter for each style. In our example, mid cap value stocks performed exceptionally well in the quarter.

D. The final row calculates additional incremental return derived from deviation from the benchmark, using the portfolio's actual style allocation. In this example, negative returns indicate that the style bets negatively impacted performance.

Conclusions—The analysis indicates that the portfolio has added value in the quarter, primarily through good stock selection. Performance would have been higher if the portfolio was more concentrated in mid cap value stocks, since this segment of the market outperformed the broad market. Stock selection in the energy and finance sectors also added value. The portfolio has overweighted large cap stocks relative to the index, and has some growth stock exposure.

The World of Money Management

PEOPLE
Their Credentials

Experience
A firm whose PMs have moderate to extensive experience should be rated higher than a firm whose PMs have moderate to limited investment experience.

Credentials
A firm whose PMs or analysts with CFA designations and/or MBA from highly ranked schools should be scored higher than a firm with individuals who back advanced degrees or designations.

Turnover/Retention
A firm with little or no PM/analysts turnover should be scored higher than a firm with moderate to above average employed turnover.

Motivation/Morale
A firm with PMs and analysts who enjoy what they do, who are excited to talk about the stocks they buy and who strive to excel at what they do, should be scored higher than one whose PMs and analysts lack motivation and morale.

Compensation/Contribution
A firm that provides an attractive and effective compensation package (salary and benefits) should be rated higher than other firms.

Staffing Adequacy
A firm that has an adequate number of PMs, analysts, traders and other related personnel should be rated higher than a firm that is slow to fill positions.

Retirement/Age
A firm that has key PMs or analysts who are nearing retirement should be scored lower than other firms, since this raises the possibility of a change in the firm's people component or investment process

Ethics
PMs or analysts who do not have high ethical standards pose additional risks to the firm (lawsuits, morale and turnover) as a result. A firm that does note advocate high ethical standards should receive a lower score than a firm that requires high ethical standards.

PHILOSOPHY
Their Beliefs

Ownership
A firm with ownership that is disseminated among key employees should be rated higher than a firm with concentrated ownership in individuals who may or may not be involved in the portfolio management of the product. A firm with ownership by a parent company with significant resources should receive a relatively high rating.

Management Succession
When applicable, firms with an adequate management succession plan should be rated higher than firms without such plans.

Asset Size
Firms with a limited number of assets (e.g. less than $500 million) should have a lower score than firms with a higher level of assets.

Asset Distribution/Concentration
Firms with a concentration of assets with one party or client should be scored lower than firms with no concentrations.

Client Service
Firms with good advisor and client service and communication should be rated higher than other firms as they are better able to retain assets when performance lags.

PROCESS
The Discipline of Their Process

Consistency/Flexibility of Process
A consistently applied process leads to consistent style (relative to the flexibility of the process) and this should be scored higher than a firm whose process has changed.

Team vs. Star
A team approach to buying and selling stocks should be scored higher than a star system, as a team approach poses lower risk to continuity of the investment process if one person leaves the firm.

Quantitative vs. Qualitative
In general an approach that is more quantitative than qualitative experiences less disruption when a PM or analyst departs. As a result a firm that has a process that is more quantitative than qualitative may need to receive a slightly higher score.

Performance, the fourth "P" has previously been discussed.

PM= Portfolio Managers

Step 4: Qualitative Analysis

As indicated earlier, manager analysis focuses on the "4 P's" – Performance, People, Philosophy and Process. Qualitative (non-performance) analysis is an investigation of the last three. An examination of qualitative factors provides:

- An insight into the stability of the organization
- A deeper confidence that historic alpha will persist
- Reassurance in the firms' ability to service advisors and their clients

Returns and holdings-based reviews focus on performance. Neither allows a look "into" the investment management firm. Think of them as a manager's resume before an interview; they are helpful, but not as helpful as the interview. Never forget separate account management is a "people" business. Portfolio decisions are always made by teams within the investment process that they develop; for this reason, qualitative factors are important in manager evaluation. In the end, an investment team should validate and support their track record. A list of qualitative elements for review is listed on page 104.

Conclusion—Qualitative factors are often overlooked when performing a basic level of manager evaluation, primarily because there is no quick way to evaluate them and it takes practical experience to know whether the information is significant. Always remember that changes within the organization may have an impact on future performance, and properly identifying these changes can help manage client expectations.

When to Terminate a Manager

The most difficult decision to make in the manager review process is determining what factors lead to the termination of a relationship. A sound manager review process utilizes a "weight of the evidence" approach, balancing all known information. It is impossible to know all the information that could be known. The question is: when is there enough information to make a decision? What is the cost of waiting?

There is no simple or quick quantitative solution for termination; multiple factors usually come into play. What is needed is a comfort level that termination makes sense given the information that is available. There never will be perfect knowledge or a perfect time. Advisors should make a commitment to avoid "paralysis by analysis" – the all-too-common condition in which an advisor delays a decision due to a "let's wait and see" attitude.

To provide perspective, factors that lead to manager termination can originate from either the client or the manager. A change in a client's investment objective, risk tolerance or financial circumstances may very well necessitate a need to reallocate assets and change investment managers.

More commonly, events leading to termination come from changes by the manager. Again, these changes can be organized into the "Four P's" – Philosophy, Process, People, and Performance. What factors can lead to termination and at what point are they insignificant? These factors are discussed on the following page, along with possible "trigger points" that can act as a catalyst for termination. In each case, there has been a change in the manager's original value proposition. With each change, the manager's value has been altered and the original rationale for hiring the manager is no longer valid. Therefore, a replacement must be found to meet the client objective.

Philosophy—A significant change in stated firm philosophy is a likely catalyst for termination. An example would be a firm changing its investment objective to maximum growth of capital from the original mandate of preservation of capital in order to increase returns and capture new client assets. In this case, the decision to terminate is straightforward; the original investment premise for the client *as well as* the historic track record are no longer valid. Because this type of change is significant, it is relatively uncommon among established firms.

Process—Changes in process are more subtle than changes in philosophy. Procedural changes deal with day-to-day portfolio management. In one sense, procedural changes can, and should, be a natural business evolution. After all, the marketplace is constantly evolving; managers must change and improve as well. There may come a point, however, when a procedural change invalidates the original manager premise. Significant change in process can also reflect underlying conflict within the organization.

To make the evaluation process more difficult, in most cases managers will not notify advisors of a modification in their investment process. Consistency of process should be revisited quarterly in direct discussions with investment managers. Sometimes asking is the only way to find out. So when does a process change become a termination issue? Only when it calls into question the original premise by which the manager was hired. Usually, process changes are the response to other more problematic issues; it represents firm "damage control." The challenge in this case is determining whether the solution is sufficient.

People—People are the heart of an investment firm, and the departure of key people can have an immediate, substantial and lasting impact. Determining whether termination is necessary requires a solid understanding of the rationale for departure as well as a level of comfort with their eventual replacement. First, determine the contribution level of the departing staff. To a great extent this should already be known. The departure of "star" decision makers (all or majority influence on the portfolio) will more likely lead to termination than non-key members. In the event that responsibilities are broadly shared, the decision is less clear and can be a judgment call. Next, examine the rationale for the departure. For example, did they leave for a one-of-a-kind opportunity or was it due to internal friction? Third, evaluate the replacements. Are they adequate or superior? If not adequate, what changes will be made to the organization to fill in the gaps? An advisor should feel very comfortable with the outcome. Uncertainty with any of these issues raises the likelihood of termination.

Organization—There are several factors that can impact the stability of the management organization. Sale of a firm would be the most significant factor, and events of the last decade show that independent managers were most likely to be acquired by a larger financial institution. The key in this instance is to conclude that the acquisition was in the best interest of the acquired firm, that key decision-makers remain in place with either substantial equity stakes in the new firm, or meaningful and lengthy employment contracts, access to research is either unchanged or improved, and that level of service remains unaltered. Other significant organizational developments include the loss of accounts and assets that place the financial viability of the firm in jeopardy.

Performance—Termination due to underperformance is always the most challenging factor to analyze. First, using the steps outlined earlier, identify the sources of underperformance using returns-based, holdings-based, and qualitative analysis. Determine whether the performance lag is cyclical (a result of sub-style) or structural (poor stock selection). If cyclical, re-examine the appropriateness for the client. If the premise still holds, it may be prudent to retain them. Persistent underperformance due to manager specific issues violates the original purpose for hiring them. In this case, termination is in the client's best interest.

What To Do When a Manager is Terminated

The decision to terminate a manager is never easy. Always revisit the rationale made at the time of hire and consider whether that premise is still valid. If not, a change is warranted. When a manager is terminated, it is critical to consider the following:

- Discuss the matter with a client in a manner they can relate to.
- Reinforce to the client that an advisor is an objective consultant working in the client's best interest.
- Do not pass up the opportunity to revisit their long-term objectives, discuss asset allocation, and why the change improves their overall picture.
- Always provide suitable alternatives.
- Consider the tax consequences for taxable accounts.

Conclusion

An integral part of an advisor's job is evaluating investment manager performance throughout the hiring, reviewing and terminating processes. For their benefit and that of their clients, every advisor should perform ongoing performance evaluation. There are limits to what an advisor can analyze without more sophisticated tools in hand, including returns-based and holdings-based analysis. Remember that manager evaluations are neither all quantitative nor all qualitative, but an ideal combination of both that helps to convey the story of how well a manager has done, how they did it, and how likely they are to do it in the future.

❖ ❖ ❖

---

1 "The Importance of Investment Policy: A Simple Answer To A Contentious Question" 1999 Ronald J. Surz, Dale Stevens and Mark Wimer
2 CMC uses Stoktrib by PPCA, Inc.

Common Performance Statistics

Alpha - Measures non-systematic return, or the return that cannot be attributed to market performance. Thus, it can be thought of as how the manager performed if the market has had no gain or loss.

Batting Average - A measure of a manager's ability to beat the market consistently. It is calculated by dividing the number of quarters (or months) in which the manager beat the index by the total number of quarters (or months) in the period.

Beta - Beta measures the systematic risk, or the relative volatility of a manager to a benchmark.

Downside Deviation - An alternate measure of risk to standard deviation, downside risk measures deviations below some minimum acceptable return (MAR). Unlike standard deviation, the MAR is not always the mean, and deviations above the MAR are omitted.

Excess Return - Measures the difference between the manager's return for a period and that of the index.

Information Ratio - A measure of economic value added by the manager. It is the ratio of (annualized) excess return above the benchmark to (annualized) tracking error.

Omega Excess Return - Indicates the excess return the manager achieved after adjusting for the manager's style and downside risk.

R-squared - A statistic that measures the degree to which manager performance is explained by market performance.

Sharpe Ratio - Measures excess return per unit of risk. The Sharpe Ratio relates the difference between the portfolio's return and the return of the risk free rate to the standard deviation of the differences for the same period.

Standard Deviation - A gauge of risk that measures the spread of the difference of returns from their average.

Tracking Error - A measure of how closely a manager's returns track the returns of a benchmark. The tracking error is the annualized standard deviation of the excess returns.

Upside Potential Ratio - A measure of the ability to exceed an investor's minimal acceptable return (MAR) relative to the amount of downside risk he or she is taking. It is the ratio of Upside Potential to Downside Risk.

Risk - The variability of return as measured by annualized standard deviation of investment returns

13

PERFORMANCE REPORTING AND CLIENT MEETINGS

Barry Mendelson, CIMA, Managing Partner
Richard Iwanski, CFA®, Partner
Jennifer Arnold, Partner
Capital Markets Consulting, LLC

Periodic reporting to clients on the performance of their managed account(s) is a critical and even required component of an advisor's client servicing and communication routine (see Chart #1). The phrase "managed money" or "managed account" not only refers to the investment manager making portfolio construction and maintenance decisions but, just as important, it also refers to the advisor who has chosen to use professional money management as part of their total approach to portfolio care and client servicing.

The world of money management is not merely the marketing and selling of a separately managed account; a better description is that it is a process through which a client's circumstances are evaluated, and then their capital is allocated, professionally managed, and reviewed over time. Effective performance reporting to clients is a vital part of fulfilling the promise of a managed account to the investor. Further, prudent portfolio monitoring and supervision practices often are based on both regulatory code and case law for retirement plans (ERISA), trusts (UPIA) and public retirement funds.[1]

In addition to complying with legal and regulatory standards of care, and delivering the important service the client pays for through recurring fees, there is good reason for advisors to take performance reporting meetings very seriously: Effective performance reporting routines *create value* in the minds of clients that accrue to the reputation, brand, and business development efforts of the advisor. How so?

The Managed Money Client Service Process

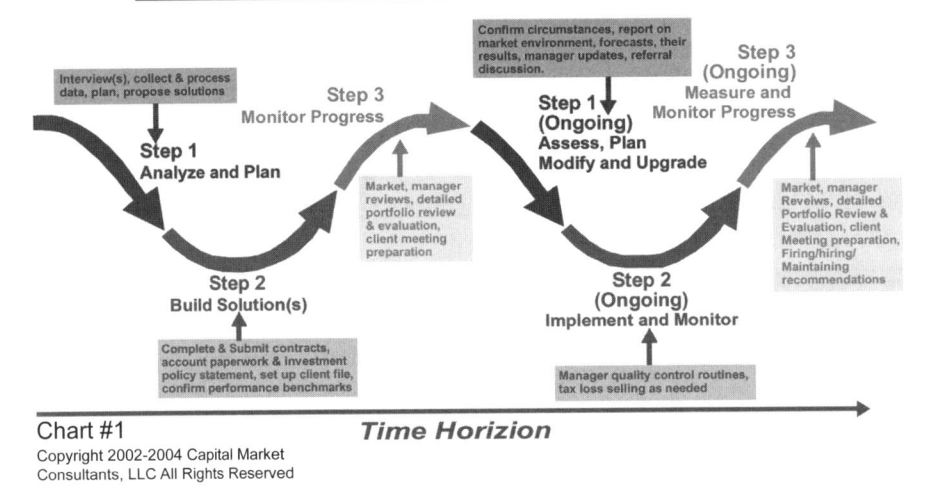

Step 1 — Interview(s), collect & process data, plan, propose solutions
Step 1 Analyze and Plan

Step 2 Build Solution(s) — Complete & Submit contracts, account paperwork & investment policy statement, set up client file, confirm performance benchmarks

Step 3 Monitor Progress — Market, manager reviews, detailed portfolio review & evaluation, client meeting preparation

Step 1 (Ongoing) Assess, Plan Modify and Upgrade — Confirm circumstances, report on market environment, forecasts, their results, manager updates, referral discussion.

Step 2 (Ongoing) Implement and Monitor — Manager quality control routines, tax loss selling as needed

Step 3 (Ongoing) Measure and Monitor Progress — Market, manager Reveiws, detailed Portfolio Review & Evaluation, client Meeting preparation, Firing/hiring/ Maintaining recommendations

Time Horizon

Chart #1
Copyright 2002-2004 Capital Market Consultants, LLC All Rights Reserved

- It is proof to the client that the advisor is proactively being accountable for recommendations – arguably, professional accountability is an attribute worth acquiring.

- It is proof, if positioned properly to the client, that the advisor is objectively measuring and assessing the investment products in their portfolio as *third-party providers*. The advisor is serving as a client advocate and not an agent for the investment manager–this approach positions the advisor on "the same side of the table" as the client.

- It is proof to the client that the advisor is progressively measuring progress toward the client's life goals.

- In well-orchestrated client review meetings, the advisor's overall organization and preparation communicate a brand that is polished with confidence.

In short, it is helpful to think of performance reporting as a crucial ongoing standard for client retention activity.

Guidelines for Performance Reporting and Client Meetings

Before providing detailed recommendations on the kind of practice procedures advisors should consider regarding performance reporting, a bit of perspective is in order so as not to lose sight of the "forest for the trees."

Performance reporting, in many ways, is the nexus of data in managed accounts. It is all too easy for advisors to get consumed by the numbers and charts and forget that the point of the exercise primarily is to inform the client about how he or she is doing. Keep the focus on *total portfolio performance*. This is not the time to provide clients with a crash course in finance and get into subject matter that should be reserved for another date and time. Try to keep reporting at a level of detail and sophistication that is appropriate for the client's needs. This will vary from client to client – be sensitive to their needs. Remember, the advisor is there to communicate, not pontificate. Generally, performance reporting should be in a summary form unless circumstances about an individual manager or market conditions require further detail.

Performance Reporting and Client Meetings

Customarily, performance reporting should be part of a client meeting during which other items are discussed as well. Keep the typical performance reporting segment to no more than about 30 minutes. Avoid overdoing the detail; a performance reporting meeting does not mean advisors should cover, line-by-line, every schedule provided. To avoid this trap, it is best to construct an executive summary document that summarizes, on a single piece of paper (or screen), the key data that the client should understand about the measurement the advisor has been doing. Examples are provided in Charts #2, #3 (private investor) and Chart #4 (institutional client). Stick to the executive summary and go into further detail only as the need arises.

Before advisors place themselves and their clients on a stringent routine of regular quarterly performance reporting they should be sure about the frequency with which clients want to be served. Don't assume that institutional investment management consulting standards for frequency of reporting need apply to every retail investor. Be careful not to inundate clients with data implying, unwittingly, that decisions hang in the balance and quarter-to-quarter changes carry significant meaning. Give them what they need to be well-informed and do not treat the delivery of a performance report as a heartless commodity that is ground out every quarter. Advisors should use this time as yet another opportunity to get to know and re-affirm their value to clients by demonstrating interest and concern.

Meetings should be orderly and follow a preset agenda. This agenda can be sent to the client in advance or presented to them at the review meeting (if that is soon enough for the client). They should be told well in advance how long the meeting will take so they can plan their time accordingly. They should know what the advisor intends to cover. If the client has items they want to discuss, the advisor should capture these in the agenda as well, so the meeting becomes a collabora-

---

Chart #2

Client Name
Quarterly Portfolio Review
by
Your name here
Senior Vice President – Investments

ABC & Co., Inc.
123 Main Street
Anywhere, USA Zip
Phone #

Investment Objectives: Portfolio growth and income (to be taken from questionnaire)

Economy: Key indicators and interpretation: growth, interest rates, employment, inflation data, etc. (this is an overview)

Market: Overview, valuations, perspective, opportunities (this is an overview)

Portfolio Appraisal:

Beginning Balance	$
Contributions	$
Withdrawals	$
Ending Balance	$
Net gain/loss	$

Portfolio Performance:

Year-to-date	%
2003	%
2002	%
2001	%
2000	%

PM Issues: Enter your plans and specific points you want to discuss (e.g. rebalancing needs, consolidation of accounts, etc.)

Client Issues: Concerns, needs, changes, (ask for introductions, referrals, attorney/accountant data, capital additions)

The World of Money Management

Chart #3 — Capital Market Performance - Domestic Equity

← Capitalization →

Barra/S&P Value		St. Dev	S&P 500 Composite		St. Dev	Barra/S&P Growth		St. Dev
1 Year	31.80%	14.64%	1 Year	28.69%	11.39%	1 Year	25.68%	8.61%
3 Year	-2.71%	19.09%	3 Year	-4.05%	18.32%	3 Year	-5.72%	18.67%
5 Year	1.95%	17.61%	5 Year	-0.57%	17.15%	5 Year	-3.48%	19.23%

Russell 1000 Value		St. Dev	Russell 1000		St. Dev	Russell 1000 Growth		St. Dev
1 Year	30.03%	12.98%	1 Year	29.90%	11.24%	1 Year	29.76%	9.88%
3 Year	1.22%	16.22%	3 Year	-3.78%	18.32%	3 Year	-9.37%	22.98%
5 Year	3.56%	15.93%	5 Year	-0.14%	17.24%	5 Year	-5.11%	22.75%

Russell Midcap Value		St. Dev	Russell Midcap		St. Dev	Russell Midcap Growth		St. Dev
1 Year	38.06%	13.08%	1 Year	40.08%	12.76%	1 Year	42.72%	12.93%
3 Year	8.47%	15.94%	3 Year	3.48%	18.77%	3 Year	-6.13%	27.88%
5 Year	8.73%	15.85%	5 Year	7.23%	18.06%	5 Year	2.01%	29.93%

Russell 2000 Value		St. Dev	Russell 2000		St. Dev	Russell 2000 Growth		St. Dev
1 Year	46.02%	15.58%	1 Year	47.25%	16.21%	1 Year	48.53%	17.20%
3 Year	13.83%	18.68%	3 Year	6.27%	21.95%	3 Year	-2.04%	27.38%
5 Year	12.28%	16.90%	5 Year	7.13%	22.48%	5 Year	0.86%	30.24%

← STYLE →

Lehman US Aggregate Bond Index		St. Dev	MSCI EAFE Index		St. Dev	CSFB High Yield Index		St. Dev
1 Year	4.11%	5.26%	1 Year	39.16%	14.63%	1 Year	27.93%	4.84%
3 Year	7.57%	4.26%	3 Year	-2.57%	18.08%	3 Year	11.74%	8.49%
5 Year	6.62%	3.86%	5 Year	0.26%	16.49%	5 Year	6.43%	7.54%

Nareit Mortgage-Reits		St. Dev	MSCI World Ex. US Index		St. Dev	MSCI World Index		St. Dev
1 Year	57.39%	14.10%	1 Year	40.03%	14.17%	1 Year	33.76%	12.33%
3 Year	57.10%	16.34%	3 Year	-2.29%	18.02%	3 Year	-3.52%	17.72%
5 Year	24.59%	20.98%	5 Year	0.77%	16.53%	5 Year	-0.40%	16.28%

Lehman US Gov/Credit Intermediate		St. Dev
1 Year	4.30%	4.74%
3 Year	7.67%	3.87%
5 Year	6.65%	3.44%

LB= Lehman Brothers
CSFB= Credit Suisse First Boston

Chart #4 — Sample Client Portfolio
Investment Performance and Asset Allocation
Quarterly Progress Report as of Sept. 30, 1999

Investment Policy	Manager	Market Value As of 9/30/99	Third Quarter 1999 Manager	Benchmark	1999 Year to Date Manager	Benchmark	Fiscal Year to Date Manager	Benchmark
Fixed Income	Manager 1	$ 3,918,490	-1.86%	-0.39%	-1.41%	-0.58%	-2.35%	-0.29%
Large Cap Value	Manager 2	$ 7,427,441	9.16%	10.80%	9.54%	13.96%	27.25%	33.82%
Large Cap Growth	Manager 3	$ 2,834,928	0.04%	3.83%	1.68%	6.27%	46.69%	47.47%
Aggressive Growth	Manager 4	$ 2,390,536	7.11%	10.42%	13.98%	14.19%	47.51%	44.42%
Small Cap	Manager 5	$ 2,721,395	13.39%	16.56%	6.84%	5.26%	33.03%	14.81%
International	Manager 6	$ 3,564,892	15.92%	2.61%	25.01%	4.11%	52.65%	25.71%
Total		$ 22,857,782	6.96%	7.13%	10.22%	8.45%	29.82%	25.28%

Investment Policy Allocation	9/30/1999 Allocation	Policy Range
Fixed Income	17%	15 - 20%
Large Cap Value	32%	30 - 40%
Large Cap Growth	12%	10 - 20%
Aggressive Growth	10%	10 - 20%
Small Cap	12%	10 - 20%
International	16%	10 - 20%
Total	100%	

Portfolio Asset Allocation
- International 16%
- Fixed Income 17%
- Small Cap 12%
- Aggressive Growth 10%
- Large Cap Growth 12%
- Large Cap Value 33%

Fiscal year to date performance uses a beginning date of 9/30/98 rather than 10/01/98.
Benchmarks include: Lehman Brothers Intermediate Government/Corporate index, S&P 500 Barra Value index, S&P 500 Barra Growth index, Russell Midcap Growth index, Russell 2000 Value index, and the MSCI EAFE index.

tive effort. The goal is for advisors to stay in control of the meeting process.

Never forget the admonition that "proper preparation prevents poor performance." Reports need to be in order and without errors (take the time and make the effort for perfection). If possible, personalize reports for each client. Be prepared to answer questions regarding their portfolio results and the performance of the individual managers. This requires prep time (well in advance!) with a regular due diligence routine (like the one described in Chapter 12). Advisors should use the same kind of preparation to get a view on the economy and the capital markets as a whole. This is not an admonition to forecast or predict, but clients will expect their advisors to have a point of view about what is going on.

Finally, remember that reporting performance should be done as quickly after the quarter as possible. Timely and fresh feedback to a client is important in the Internet age. Granted, sometimes it can take weeks to gather reports, depending on who is in control of the reporting process. But, if advisors cannot get a full performance report until weeks after the calendar quarter is over, they should consider trying to get data from either their firm, or the manager on their composite performance number or, at least, their preliminary composite number. In addition, they should ask for some commentary on the market from the manager so they know quickly after the quarter is over how the manager fared (but not how their client did). This sense for how they performed can be conveyed to clients in conversation with the appropriate caveats within the first 10 to 20 days after the calendar quarter. Weeks should not pass before an advisor gets in touch with clients, regardless of when the formal review meeting is scheduled.

Time management is an important skill. It takes time to prepare and personally deliver performance reports at client meetings. Advisors should be proactive in scheduling, and do so with the entire staff.

"Performance Reporting Season"

Depending on the size of the advisor's managed account business, and certainly as it becomes more successful, performance reporting and the client meetings during which these reports are delivered will generally occur throughout a time period spanning roughly the first two months of each new calendar quarter (with activity typically falling off toward the end of the period). For effective time management and pacing, it is helpful to think of performance reporting "season" in three phases: preparation, client meetings and follow-up. The special challenge of performance reporting season is that it invariably requires an advisor to integrate this period of intense routines with new business development, other client services, and business administration activities.

Preparation Routines for Performance Reporting and Client Meetings

Preparation routines can vary from firm to firm, depending on the type of performance reporting schedules available. The more detailed and extensive the schedules, the more preparation time is required.

1. Schedule appointments by phone and confirm them by mail with a card. Once the review meeting process begins, subsequent appointments can be made immediately after each review meeting by giving that client an appointment card. The day before the next review meeting, staff should call to confirm with the client.

2. Staff should compile recent manager, economic, and market data for review by the advisor. Staff should store this information in labeled folders or a tabbed three-ring binder for ease of organization and storage. Chart #3 represents an example of how staff could consolidate market

Chart #5

Month 1						
1	2	3	4	5	6	7
8	9	10	11	12	13	14
15	16	17	18	19	20	21
22	23	24	25	26	27	28
29	30					

Month 2						
		1	2	3	4	5
6	7	8	9	10	11	12
13	14	15	16	17	18	18
20	21	22	23	24	25	26
28	29	30	31			

Preparation time
Client Meetings
Follow up

information into a simple spreadsheet. This data should be available from the advisor's firm and is certainly available on commercial databases and on the Internet for independent practitioners.

3. Review data from step 2 and prepare a one-page personal summary posting to the file or binder.

4. Call key clients with preliminary numbers and manager outlook (if necessary).

5. Prepare and review client performance reports – keep the focus on the longer term – how is the client's portfolio performing vis-à-vis expectations, goals, and the market?

6. Revise or edit, as needed.

7. Complete executive summaries (Chart #2, page 111) for all clients and collate to beginning of performance report. (Chart #4, page 112)

8. Have staff prepare meeting agendas for each client.

Preparation Routines for Client Meetings

Client meetings should be controlled by the advisor. They should be relatively modest in length – generally, no more than one hour. To control the time and flow of events, the advisor needs to be prepared. Preparation will take some time: it is recommend that the client case/file, meeting agenda and performance report be reviewed one to two days before the client meeting.

As mentioned earlier, in the meeting both the client and the advisor should know what is going to be discussed and approximately how long the meeting will last. The advisor should either send an agenda to the client in advance or provide one to them at the meeting.

When the client meets at the advisor's office, the advisor must make every effort to ensure that there will be no distractions while the meeting is taking place. In that regard, phone calls should be forwarded to staff or voice mail; cell phones, radios and TV's should be turned off. The performance reporting meeting is a time when the advisor must give a client undivided attention. If an advisor's office is not large enough or tidy enough, the meeting should be held in a conference room; the office

Performance Reporting and Client Meetings

should not be a distraction. Clients need to walk away from that meeting feeling certain that the advisor showed them the ultimate in respect and professionalism.

Performance review meetings should follow a logical path moving from "macro to micro," from general to specific. The below agenda order works well for private and institutional investors alike.

Preparation Routines for Performance Reporting Follow-Up

Follow-up activity (actually, follow-*through* activity) to client meetings is the most frequently overlooked aspect of performance reporting. Remember, while the *advisor* may be discussing the *manager's* performance as being the most important element, the client also is evaluating the *advisor's* ongoing performance. Advisors who represent their service offering as a (continuous) process must realize that client meetings cannot be the only occasions for meaningful client contact.

Sequence of Topics	Rationale
1. Review and confirm of client investment objectives and goals	Confirm appropriateness of investment policy, identify new opportunities and upcoming issues
2. Review of the economy	Explore the general environment in which investments were being made — favorable or unfavorable?
3. Review of market performance	Details the response of market segments to the business, political and regulatory environment
4. Portfolio appraisal	Cover the basics how much money client started with, how much was added, how much withdrawn, and how much the client ended with
5. Portfolio performance	Cover year-to-date numbers, rolling time periods and calendar years. Subject to availability both returns and risk characteristics should be reviewed. Compare to client goals and policy or benchmark references.
6. Portfolio management issues	Review relevant detail, issues and concerns such as need for re-balancing, further diversification, manager performance issues, tax and or estate planning issues, etc.
7. Client issues	Provide open forum for client to discuss any needs, concerns or issues
8. Review of action steps	Public agreement with client about what course of action is next
9. Schedule next performance reporting meeting	Provide appointment card

Client meetings should be followed up with a *written* communication covering:

- The main points discussed at the meeting
- Any action steps agreed upon, and who is responsible for them
- The timeframe in which the action(s) are to be completed
- A reference to any follow-up contact required
- Encouragement for the client to respond to meeting notes by editing and returning them so there is complete agreement between advisor and client

Any actions that need attention as a result of the performance reporting meeting should immediately be attended to.

The Annual Review

The annual review is a variation of the normal performance reporting meeting. The primary differences are: the annual review should reconsider the appropriateness of the recommended investment policy for the client and provide a more extensive historical review—and analysis of—individual manager performance.

In reconsidering the client's investment policy each year, the principal questions the advisor should be exploring include:

- Does the risk-return tradeoff imbedded in the portfolio asset allocation still accurately reflect the client's financial needs, objectives, time horizons, and tolerance for risk?
- Does the implementation approach still match the client's level of sophistication, asset level, tax needs, cost sensitivities, and need for transparency?
- Does the existing portfolio have optimal sub-styles that best manage client expectations and overall portfolio risk?

Putting manager performance in historical, longer-term context allows the advisor to explore trends in return and risk patterns, style variation, and performance attribution to help the client-advisor team determine just how well the manager has performed with the client's money. The principal questions that should be explored for continued engagement are:

- Has the manager's style stayed true to form?
- Has the manager performed as expected (though not necessarily hoped for)?
- Are there any reasons to be concerned about the stability of the organization?
- Are there any reasons to be concerned about changes to the manager's methodology?

Conclusion

Performance reporting and client meetings represent an important part of the delivery of a professionally managed portfolio service. This aspect of the world of money management offers multiple opportunities for advisors to serve and protect the wealth of their clients. Educating and informing clients is a crucial value-addition advisors can excel at to grow their businesses. Remember, the client cares not only about how the manager performs, but how the advisor performs as well.

❖ ❖ ❖

---

[1] "Prudent Investment Practices: A Handbook for Investment Fiduciaries," by the Foundation for Fiduciary Studies

14

CONSULTANTS AND MANAGERS
MAINTAINING THE SYMBIOTIC RELATIONSHIP

Drew Washburn, CIMC, CIMA, CFP®
VP, Regional Marketing Director
The Roosevelt Investment Group
CIMC Course Trainer, ICIMC, 1998-2003

Symbiotic Relationship: a relationship between two entities which is mutually beneficial for the participants of the relationship. A positive-sum gain from cooperation.

The Miriam-Webster Collegiate Dictionary

All successful consultants and the managers working with them can use this term to best describe their associations with one other. Add the elements of trust and respect to the equation, and the bond strengthens. Other terms used to describe this affiliation are "strategic alliance" and "strategic partnership."

Because the money management and investment consulting processes increasingly are migrating from a transactional to a relationship-driven business, the consultant/manager relationship has become a win-win proposition for both parties. In the past, managers spent much of their time presenting and closing on their "product" to advisors and consultants. Now, with the emphasis on value-added and relationship-building, most of the money manager's time is spent identifying needs and delivering value. Consultants, in turn, remain loyal to managers who not only perform in line with the client's policy statement and consistent with their disciplines, but also provide practice management and development solutions.

Two basic types of relationships exist: One is between the financial consultant and either the money manager or the money management representative (i.e., wholesaler, regional vice presidents, sales and marketing reps, etc.). The other is between the consultant and the firm offering a third-party investment management platform.

Some consultants who choose to have a direct relationship with a manager develop their own "boutique" stable of money managers and do their own due diligence work; others work with managers already on their firm's preferred list. The association is two-pronged: The relationship a consultant has with the marketing executive (or investment management rep) at the money management firm tends to be more qualitative and can add value to the consultant's practice in terms of business development and continuing education, whereas the money manager's actual value to the relationship is more quantitative and evaluated in terms of staying true to their discipline.

The Four Keys to a Symbiotic Relationship

No matter whether the relationship between the financial consultant and money manager evolves from a direct connection with a manager or from an investment consulting platform, several elements must be in place to establish and maintain a symbiotic relationship. (For purposes of this chapter, we'll focus on the direct connection. See Chapter 33 for more information on platforms and technology.)

The essential elements are: Service, Delivery, Practice Development, and Relationship Maintenance. Here's a brief look at each one:

Service: Everybody is a Client

A key differentiation factor in a strong professional relationship is the commitment to "client" service. The money manager's client is the consultant. The consultant's client is the investor. "Client" service is one of the most important pieces of the process a money manager's representative can offer a consultant or advisor. It solidifies the relationship, and both parties work together toward the common goal of meeting the investors' needs.

Consultants should expect the money manager to develop a system for this service, and anticipate and make any changes to the system as the relationship grows. Additional expectations of all parties should be discussed on the front end, agreed upon, and maintained throughout the relationship. A few critical items within the service process that should be on both the consultants' and managers' agendas are:

- Number/frequency of phone and/or office contacts
- Objectives and goals for each contact
- How to keep communication channels open
- Follow-up procedures/action items

While both parties are getting to know each other through e-mails, phone calls, office visits, and at industry conferences, here are some important attributes both managers and consultants should seek in the relationship:

- Be passionate about the business
- Have relationship-building skills

- Go the extra mile
- Be available; respond quickly
- Help develop business/refer business
- Admit mistakes; implement appropriate action immediately
- Show respect
- Understand points-of-view
- Be willing to help each other

Delivery is a Two-Way Street

As mentioned above, managing expectations on the parts of both the manager and the consultant is an essential aspect of "delivery." Each should be direct and upfront and *ask* what to expect. This way, everything is clear from the beginning. There is no such thing as over-communication. The goal is to go the extra mile in the relationship. The relationship then becomes a two-way street between the money manager and the consultant.

Consistent delivery also is pertinent because the consultant should continue to strive for a high level of confidence with the manager, i.e., no surprises on the investment discipline side of the equation. Extreme stress is created if managers deviate from their discipline, (i.e., excessive over- or underweighting an area, creating volatility and potential losses.) This type of action creates an unwanted surprise in the relationship, causing confidence in the manager to decline.

The following elements should be integrated into the working system between money managers and consultants to improve delivery:

- Manager: Understand the consultant's business
- Consultant: Understand the manager's process
- Manager: Understand what the consultant expects
- Consultant: Let the manager know what is needed
- Manager: Help the consultant build his/her business
- Consultant: Refer business to manager when applicable

Both parties should uphold the vital elements of honesty, integrity, and trust coupled with expertise and knowledge of their respective areas. Investors deserve to have their consultants (and their money managers) work together as an ethical team and keep checks and balances on each other, thus avoiding potential transgressions, no matter how slight.

Practice Development

A symbiotic relationship in this area will blossom into tangible, value-added benefits for consultants and advisors. They can leverage their relationships with money managers to help develop new business. Money managers are happy to provide resources that will help consultants capture assets and build their practices. Managers often provide marketing tools, educational materials for clients, event sponsorship and participation, reference pieces and white papers on their web sites, training, professional designation assistance, and other such assistance. These services are offered to consultants as a thank-you for doing business with them and to encourage business referrals. Advisors or consultants simply need to inquire about the resources available to them.

Relationship Maintenance

There are a few simple rules to follow in maintaining a symbiotic working relationship:

- Remember that thank-you's are important
- Show appreciation and excitement about forming a long-term association
- Be respectful of the partnership
- Set parameters and boundaries
- Remember that consistency is paramount
- Asking for referrals works both ways

In Summary

The successful symbiotic relationships that currently exist between the consultant and money manager quickly are becoming a vital part of a consultant's practice. Increasingly, managers are providing crucial assistance in helping the consultant manage and educate clients on risk expectations, volatility, and the market in general.

Money managers continually need to articulate their particular skill or process and its uniqueness. The consultant, in turn, must grasp what the disciplined process is, and how it adds value for the client. When all parties exhibit professionalism, integrity, respect, honesty, diligence, teamwork, passion and trust on behalf of the investor, then all parties win.

❖❖❖

Consultants Speak Out

Following are veteran consultants' comments about the manager/consultant relationship, and what is important to them in maintaining the alliance:

"The consultant should be comfortable with their key contact, and when that person is unavailable, the qualifications of the 'support' contacts are crucial. It is very important that a qualified person answers each call from the consultant.

The money manager should provide training and materials covering, not only its own firm, but those of the industry as a whole. Educational and informative materials on specific topics can help service existing clients and attract new ones. Other helpful services are analyses of prospective clients' existing portfolios, a study on the potential impact of the alternative minimum tax (AMT), or other issues specific to clients. The objective is to assist the consultant in finding new assets, not just to move clients from the current manager to another."

—Ken Certain, CIMA

"Money managers and their reps should deliver 'event-triggers' with white papers, charts, and comments to consultants. These tools can be exceptional support in helping the consultant communicate with his or her clients."

—Thomas J. Barbatti, CIMC, RIA

"Consultants and advisors need more 'hands-on' education about alternative investments—especially hedge funds—from the actual hedge fund money managers that can be passed on to clients in terms they can clearly understand. The true understanding of alternative investments requires a special skill that many consultants are not yet accustomed to within their own consulting process.

Also needed are better aids such as attribution tools, performance reports, regular investment updates, special reports, hot lines, web site capabilities, and quality presentation materials."

—Gene Krinn, CFA

"The consultant needs to understand with clarity the money manager's process and philosophy. Is it passive or active? What is the defined style diversification within the portfolio? If after studying and evaluating the information, the consultant does not see a good fit, they should be honest and just admit it. The consultant should not string the money manager along."

—Joe Garner, CIMC

"Provide new information; no 'noise' or irrelevant information. Use technology to communicate; but don't send useless e-mails. Keep the consultants informed of the consulting industry and how it is evolving. Offer to introduce consultants to their peers for networking. Encourage advisors and consultants to attain professional designations within the industry."

—Don Hagan, CFA, CIMC

"The eventual selection of specific managers is influenced greatly by the quality of the relationship the money manager has developed with the consultant. This added value goes beyond the objective analysis already in place in the selection process. The consultant is looking for exceptional service, clear communication, and sincere desire from the money manager to support the total investment process outlined by the consultant. The money manager must provide educational support using seminars to help build the consultant's business and strengthen the consultant's credibility.

The money manager must have the ability to relate to the consultant and understand his or her business and how it operates. To help this effort, the consultant needs to convey its business and demonstrate it. The relationship between the money manager and the consultant is like a linked chain. The money manager needs to understand the consultant's clients (types) and the objectives and goals of the practice. Money managers must recognize where they can help the consultant's practice management and take action to implement it. If any of these factors break a link in the chain, then the relationship will negatively be impacted or fail."

—Thomas W. Bodensteiner, CIMC

"The money managers who add value to client relationships are the ones who keep consultants informed about what is going on in the portfolio, at their firm, and in the market. Top money managers understand that the consultant is their conduit to the mutual clients, and that they are partners with the same goal: to keep clients happy and to meet their needs.

Being proactive is a big plus. If the manager is underperforming, they should acknowledge that fact and explain why and what they are doing to get things to improve. It may just be that his or her style is out of favor for the time being. The key is to keep the consultant informed. The consultant will be better prepared to talk to clients, the clients will be better served, and the account is more likely to stay put through those periods of underperformance that all managers experience at some point in time.

Consistency is something else important to look for in a money manager. Consistency in service, style, personnel, and investment performance are what clients and consultants expect, and what top money managers provide."

—Leon G. Spheeris, CIMC, former president, ICIMC

15

THE VALUE OF ADVICE
IS IT WORTH THE FEE?

Stephen Winks, Chairman
Portfolio Technologies
Publisher, *Senior Consultant*

It is the rare investor indeed who does not see the benefit and/or understand the wisdom of engaging professional investment and administrative counsel in making investment decisions. Investors can either be too close to their investments and succumb to their emotions, or so busy they fail to exercise their discretion.

The knowledge, judgment, and dispassionate attention brought by professional investment and administrative counsel to their financial affairs are well worth its cost—even if the investor is financially astute. This is why physicians engage other physicians when it comes to their own health. Many investors are limited not only by their professional investment knowledge, but also by their sense of trust and/or control that obscures, or even precludes, sound reasoning.

Even though investors would like value to be added and advisors want to add value, unless the financial advisor takes the personal initiative to (1) gain access to the processes and technology necessary to add value (2) create a division of labor within their practice to facilitate high level counsel and (3) acknowledge fiduciary responsibility; it is simply not possible for them to address and manage a broad range of investment and administrative values as required by regulatory mandate.

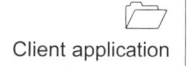

Client application

Value and Compensation: The Big Issue

There is a disconnect between selling financial products and adding value. Financial products in their own right add no value. *It is what an advisor does with the financial product, or process, that adds value.* Presuming the advisor is capable of adding value, the question then becomes, "Is the value added worth the fee required to engage the professional investment and administrative counsel of the advisor?"

Industry researcher and ratings provider, Dalbar, suggests that the average return achieved by investors acting on their own behalf is nearly five percent, while the return realized by utilizing transaction-based advisors is just 50 basis points (one-half of one percent) better. So, for those advisors or consultants using a processes, and have the technology, and division of labor necessary within their practice, there is considerable value they can add relative to the poor returns achieved by investors who have to rely on their own limited counsel.

But there is no question the cost of professional counsel does offset somewhat the value the advisor adds. So, how does one compensate a highly skilled advisor? Should these advisors (investment management consultants) earn half of the returns realized in excess of that which the client can achieve on their own? No, because the absence of professional counsel creates far too low of a threshold for performance. This would exaggerate the value-added attributed to the consultant. The client could always invest in an index fund or an ETF and use that as a threshold for performance.

As an alternative then, should these highly skilled advisors/consultants be compensated on a share of the return they achieve in excess of a custom index-based benchmark developed for each investor? No, because it would minimize the value the consultant adds and does not take into consideration important aspects of counsel that are not return related (tax efficiency, risk, cost structure and liquidity).

If the emphasis is placed solely on the return, in order to beat the benchmark the advisor would be motivated to take more risk than implied by the benchmark, as the advisor is not being measured based on risk. Or, if the benchmark return becomes particularly challenging to achieve, the advisor may seek other forms of compensation from other sources such as mutual funds, which offer ongoing 12(b)1 compensation.

This is why Congress and state legislatures have created public policy in the form of UPIA, ERISA, UMIFA, UMPERS[1] which establishes the parameters within which an advisor must work in order to fulfill their fiduciary responsibility. Fiduciary responsibility requires full disclosure of all forms of compensation of all relationships and of all potential conflicts. Insurance agents would have to disclose that they earn hundreds of thousands of dollars after arranging for large employers to switch defined contribution plan providers without any material change in plan or participant services. Commissioned brokers would have to disclose that popular mutual funds are more expensive than managed accounts. Asset management firms would have to voluntarily disclose that they are not performing well relative to their investment mandate and their appropriate peer group.

The role of the advisor should always be to act in the clients' best interest without conflicts of interest. Again, the only way to achieve this is through full disclosure and the acknowledgement of fiduciary responsibility. As a consequence, the best means of compensation is to engage an advisor for an ongoing advisory fee that entails full disclosure. This requires the advisor to address and manage a broad range of investment and administrative values as required by regulatory mandate set forth in investment policy statement (IPS).

Time, Talent and Resources

The seldom disclosed secret of senior investment management consultants is that they have limited time, and that the continuous, comprehensive counsel is very labor-intensive. If an advisor is to offer this type of counsel there is a limit as to how many clients it would be possible for the advisor to serve. Typically, the financial services industry's top advisors provide continuous comprehensive counsel to 100 clients or less. Depending upon the division of labor within the advisor's practice, more clients can be served—or a higher level of custom service can be provided—to a smaller number of clients. Yet, because this type of counsel is so demanding on time, talent and resources, regardless of whether a client has $10,000 or $10 billion, the advisor gravitates toward those with larger assets who have the greatest needs, who view fiduciary responsibility more seriously, and who have a greater appreciation of high-level counsel.

Consequently, it is not uncommon for advisors offering high-level counsel to have an account minimum of $250,000 to $1 million or more. Some senior consultants only entertain new client relationships of $10 million or more, and in the institutional market, $100 million minimums are common. This assures the high-level of counsel is both economically viable for the advisor/senior consultant to provide and that their counsel is responsive to the unique needs of each client, typically entailing highly customized client support.

Cost for High-Level Counsel

Describing high-level counsel and its six financial services investment process is a topic unto itself. The cost of this counsel *averages* around 1.9 percent or 190 basis points for individuals. Larger institutions and individual investors who have substantial assets, command a lower fee based on the size of assets which will be placed under the consultant's advisement. The 190 basis point fee for individual investors includes (1) best-in-class, objectively selected, third-party asset management at 50 basis points, (2) best-in-class custody, clearing, trade execution at 5 to 20 basis points (3) advisory support services, either structured within the advisors practice, outsourced to their supporting broker/dealer, or to outside supporting firms at 60 to 70 basis points and (4) 60 to 70 basis points for the advisor's continuous comprehensive counsel to fulfill their regulatory responsibilities.

An advisor has to spend 60 to 70 basis points for the advisory support technology and the technical support staff within their practice that makes high-level counsel possible. Custody, clearing and trade execution cost is the actual wholesale cost incurred in holding, monitoring and trading (buying and selling) assets. Similarly, in asset management, the actual wholesale cost incurred in engaging money managers to manage a very specific investment mandate defined and monitored by the advisor/senior consultant is 50 basis points. The fee-based advisor does not receive any compensation from the money managers they engage on their client's behalf in order to avoid any potential conflict of interest. The cost of the high-level counsel is 190 basis points, but the advisor actually only earns about 60 to 70 basis points.

Everyone would agree that at 190 basis points, continuous comprehensive counsel is an extraordinarily compelling value proposition considering a mutual fund costs, on average, 150 basis points, not including trading and clearing cost which can easily run another 100 basis points. By prospectus, a mutual fund is run according to its stated purpose at the discretion of its manager. By definition, a mutual fund cannot be sensitive to individual investors' needs and circumstances. It does not have tax lot accounting and does not allow direct ownership of its underlying securities, so in mutual funds, a high-level of customized portfolio detail can not be managed for each investor.. Thus, mutual funds can not come as close to addressing and managing a broad range of investment and administrative values as an accomplished senior consultant can.

And most importantly, the advisor/consultant can do so far less expensively than a mutual fund. But, therein lies the problem. Though everyone wants high-level counsel, most often it is only within the reach of investors who have at least $250,000 in investable assets. Even at $250,000 minimum, there are far more investors who want high-level counsel than there are advisors capable of providing it. High-level counsel has not yet been institutionalized.

So, is continuous, comprehensive advice valuable and worth the fee? Of course it is, for all of the reasons stated above, and more. The industry simply needs more advisors who are willing to complete rigorous professional and educational programs, expend time and capital on their practices, and devote themselves to providing comprehensive investment and administrative counsel to each client, large and small.

❖ ❖ ❖

---

[1] UPIA: Uniform Prudent Investor Act; ERISA: Employee Retirement Income Security Act; UMIFA: Unified Management of Institutional Funds Act; UMPERS:

Editor's note: This article is an extremely valuable pass-along tool for advisors or consultants to give to their clients. For reprints, go to http://www.fisherleblanc.com. Important: Before distributing to investors, please have materials approved by compliance and/or management.

PART III

A Discussion Of Various Investment Strategies And Disciplines

16

BALANCED PORTFOLIO MANAGEMENT

Dianne Pagano Anthony, CFA®
Principal, Director of Fixed Income
Rorer Asset Management, LLC

The Efficient Frontier Theory reminds us of the risk-return tradeoff inherent in investing. And for good reason. On an annual basis since 1973, the stock market[1] has outperformed the bond market[2] 18 times, while bonds have bested stocks 13 times. The often-negative interrelationship between these two asset classes makes the primary case for a balanced portfolio management style. The case does not stop here, however. The need for diversification is only one of the many benefits that balanced management satisfies. This chapter will explore how this style further lends itself to a sound investment strategy.

The Risk–Reward Tradeoff

Identifying a client's risk-reward profile is, of course, the first and most important step in creating an appropriate asset allocation mix. Maintaining that allocation is equally important, and this is where the balanced management style adds value. A balanced manager rebalances the portfolios with a level of regularity that continues to meet the strategic allocation deemed best by the client's investment advisor to meet their needs. By maintaining that target, the balanced money manager is able to keep volatility to a minimum by preventing one asset class from becoming too over- or underweighted at what may be precisely the wrong time. The negative correlation (-0.24)[3] between stocks and bonds, as well as the volatility in each of the markets as shown in the accompanying grid of annual performance figures, illustrates this very concept. If a balanced portfolio had begun in 1994 with an allocation of 60 percent stocks and 40 percent bonds and had allowed its equity position to continue to grow without being rebalanced, it would have embarked on the year 2000 with a 73 percent equity weighting. The relative underperformance of stocks versus bonds for the three years that followed had not been witnessed since the early 1930s.

Annual Performance Returns, 1973-2003

	S&P 500	Lehman Bros. Gov't/Credit Index		S&P 500	Lehman Bros. Gov't/Credit Index
1973	-14.5%	1.1%	1989	31.2%	17.5%
1974	-26.0%	-6.3%	1990	-3.1%	6.5%
1975	36.9%	16.4%	1991	30.0%	19.5%
1976	23.6%	20.5%	1992	7.4%	8.5%
1977	-7.2%	2.5%	1993	9.9%	16.2%
1978	6.4%	-0.3%	1994	1.3%	-7.1%
1979	18.2%	-3.3%	1995	37.1%	30.0%
1980	31.5%	-2.7%	1996	22.7%	0.1%
1981	-4.8%	0.1%	1997	33.1%	14.5%
1982	20.4%	43.7%	1998	28.3%	11.8%
1983	22.3%	6.1%	1999	20.9%	-7.7%
1984	6.0%	16.4%	2000	-9.3%	16.2%
1985	31.6%	29.8%	2001	-11.9%	7.3%
1986	18.5%	21.4%	2002	-22.1%	14.8%
1987	5.7%	-0.8%	2003	28.9%	4.7%
1988	16.3%	9.7%			

Sources: Standard & Poors and Lehman Brothers

Risks abound in the investment arena, though they often affect each asset class differently. An unbalanced portfolio can become too risky and no longer reflect the client's tolerance. By taking a collective view of the portfolio, the stock and bond portions complement each other, and disciplined rebalancing can prevent asset allocation drift when unforeseen risks permeate the markets.

Some of the more common risks include:

- *Political and Geopolitical Risk*: Both domestically and globally, these risks often have an inverse effect on stocks and bonds. A higher level of uncertainty often reflects positively on bonds to the detriment of stocks, as an example.

- *Interest Rate Risk*: Movements in interest rates have a differing effect on stocks and bonds because they are often an interpretation of the business cycle. With rising rates, bond prices recede. Although they also translate into higher financing costs for companies, rising rates are usually indicative of an improving economy which generally bodes well for stocks.

- *Business Cycle and Economic Risk*: Differing stages of the economic cycle, and its attendant indicators such as growth and inflation, often have an inverse impact on stocks and bonds. Bonds tend to thrive during an economic slowdown, while stocks do so during an expansion, all else being equal.

- *Company and Credit Risk*: A company's balance sheet and corporate management will affect its asset prices differently. For instance, one that grows aggressively, possibly through leveraged acquisitions, may increase shareholder value, but the lower interest coverage will likely cause its corporate bonds to be less coveted in the marketplace.
- *Correlation Risk*: The common bond among all of the above-mentioned risks in today's marketplace is that they affect each asset class in different ways. A balanced portfolio allows the advisor to reduce the correlation risks that may occur when the primary asset classes are managed separately. Viewing the portfolio as an integrated whole and maintaining a disciplined rebalancing policy optimizes the low-correlation benefits and is key to minimizing the volatility caused by a whole host of uncertainties.

Timing Market Movements

A client's temptation to time the market and chase the hot money is one that the money management industry strongly dissuades. It is human nature, however, to compartmentalize many things in life, particularly investment choices. By falling prey to this, a client will tend to isolate each of his or her money managers and penalize the one whose asset class may be out of favor at the moment. Though few certainties exist in our industry, we know of one: market timing often results in increased risk and missed opportunities.

It is tempting to assume that a particular trend will continue. Risk aversion tends to diminish when an otherwise riskier asset class is surging. Those portfolios whose allocations were left to drift into higher and higher stock positions would have done well during the latter half of the 1990s. But the negative stock market returns that ensued for the next three years were surely a shock. Did the strict rebalancer know that this would be the case? Certainly not. However, the rebalanced portfolio would not have been unduly overweighted in an asset class that was negatively affected from 2000 to 2002 by many of the risks mentioned earlier, such as business cycle risk, interest rate risk, correlation risk, and not the least of which, geopolitical risk. If one were to compare two $100,000 portfolios beginning in 1994 with an allocation of 60 percent stocks and 40 percent bonds, the ending market values by 2003 are quite different using the index performance shown in the aforementioned grid. A portfolio that is rebalanced each year to maintain the original 60/40 allocation would have finished the time period with $272,712. The unbalanced portfolio would have ended with a dollar value of $259,368 – fully 5 percent lower and having taken on much more risk along the way. The bottom line is that an unbalanced portfolio exposes clients to a level of volatility that no longer reflects the risk-reward tradeoff deemed suitable for their tolerance level. By removing the emotion that can overtake a sound strategy, a disciplined rebalancing keeps the portfolio positioned for the long run.

Fiduciary Responsibility

The Forward of this book notes, "the perfect equation for any successful client-advisor-money manager relationship is that of trust, responsibility, and accountability." It is that fiduciary responsibility that binds us in this alliance. A balanced approach provides the advisor with the knowledge that the client's risk tolerance will be adhered to and that any allocation drift will be kept to a disciplined minimum. Many balanced managers have two distinct teams of investment specialists who concentrate on the management of the equity and fixed income styles, offering clients and advisors the benefit of two professionally managed asset classes under one umbrella. In this way, the client enjoys the expertise in both stocks and bonds that are actively managed to take advantage of the best possible relative value within each asset class. In addition, the equity and fixed income specialists can act as a single team in assessing the economic and market landscapes, preventing the client from being overexposed to any one industry, company, or sector of the economy that may occur when bonds and stocks are managed separately. Active and disciplined rebalancing allows consultants and managers to maintain the client's risk-reward target, reduce the portfolio's volatility, and satisfy the fiduciary responsibility inherent in this triage relationship.

Summary

The recurring theme that characterizes the many aspects of balanced account management is *reduced volatility* for the portfolio. Creating an appropriate asset allocation for a client is one that the advisor does not take lightly. This mix reflects that which best satisfies the client's desire for return within a tolerance level for risk. The ups and downs of the markets can be tempting for clients to let their mix drift, often with the unwelcome outcome of higher portfolio risk. A disciplined approach to rebalancing within balanced money management eliminates the emotional roller coaster of outsized highs and lows by maintaining the allocation target created by the client and advisor. In the long run, such a portfolio can grow and benefit from having professionally managed asset classes within an actively rebalanced portfolio that seeks to reduce volatility from the many unforeseen risks that permeate the markets. Finally, the money manager and advisor are able to work jointly in satisfying the fiduciary responsibility that each party to the relationship holds in creating and maintaining an appropriate risk-return tradeoff composition for the client.

❖❖❖

---

1 As measured by the S&P 500 Index
2 As measured by the Lehman Brothers Government/Credit Index
3 Correlation coefficient between the S&P500 Index and the Lehman Brothers Government/Credit Index, 1994 — 2003. Source: Mobius.

Disclaimer: Rorer Asset Management, LLC, an investment management firm founded in 1978, is based in Pennsylvania and manages accounts for institutions and individuals. The views expressed throughout this chapter represent the opinions of Rorer.

17

CORE EQUITY MANAGEMENT

The Madison Core Equity Team
Madison Equity Group

Mankind appears to have a deep need to classify the world around us. In investing, this trait inspires us to sort assets and investors into classes, and then subdivide within, until, at the extreme, the man-made world of stocks looks like classical taxonomy.

In many ways, these financial categories have been great positives for investors and investment professionals, promoting understanding of differences in securities and performance attributes and facilitating needed diversification. On the other hand, there is always the danger that we'll fall into the trap of over-zealous zoologists of the past, whose eagerness for new species exceeded the evidence.

The idea of "core equity" investing comes out of this need for classification. For many years a stock was a stock, fairly or unfairly priced as it might be. Much later evolved the notion of value and growth stocks: on one side, under-appreciated, "beaten-up" issues; on the other, seemingly high-priced stocks of companies with exceptional business momentum, or even just rapidly rising stock prices.

In the extreme, value and growth investors were seen as deeply divided disciplines, confronting each other like the white-hatted and black-hatted gun-slingers in old Westerns. It was once common to believe that splitting an equity portfolio between growth and value managers covered the market. In fact, one strand of core management follows this route: building portfolios that are 50 percent value and 50 percent growth. But this approach is not what most modern consultants consider core management, since similar results could be obtained by splitting the investment between pure value and growth managers. In actuality, a great many companies fall into the gap between, and the results of these companies are not simply the average of the extremes. Just as these companies possess multiple dimensions, most core managers use diverse strategies that employ both growth and value disciplines.

The history of style-specific management is intimately connected to modern portfolio theory. However, the concept of core management was one of the later developments in style description, and although the actual point of origin is obscure, we can see evidence of its roots. In the 1970s, consultants were already using the term "core" in connection with real estate investments, applying it to the higher-quality real estate trusts. By the mid-1980s, pension fund managers and consultants were using the term "core equity" to describe the foundation of an equity portfolio, often associating it with S&P 500 indexing.

By the early 1990s, George Russell Jr. of Frank Russell Co. was able to cite that his firm had tracked, in 1986, "268 equity managers in a core equity universe."[1] In many ways, core managers initially were defined by what they weren't: managers whose discipline kept them clearly at either the value or growth end of the spectrum.

Many managers of different ilk place their roots in the Graham-Dodd school of investing. Some of the most famous of Benjamin Graham's students added a layer of qualitative analysis to Graham's pure quantitative analysis. Among the areas that these investors began looking at were such factors as the skill of the management team, the competitive position of the company, and the value of brand. Once these factors were considered, companies that might not look attractive to a pure Graham disciple appeared to be great opportunities.

It was this sort of blending of strategies that lent a need to find a way of describing investment managers who were not purists in terms of a growth or value approach. This is not to suggest that core managers are less disciplined or have the latitude to wander freely into any investments that might have appeal, but rather that the discipline itself is multi-faceted. Another term that has gained popularity for this general approach is "Growth at a Reasonable Price" or GARP.

This combination of growth and valuation disciplines can be traced back many years. In the mid-1950s, investment and risk management guru Peter Bernstein wrote a paper for the *Harvard Business Review* titled, "Growth Companies vs. Growth Stocks."[2] In this article, he attempts to define growth companies both by what they are (companies whose growth is organic and comes from within) and what they are not (companies whose growth comes from acquisitions or from the benefits of serving a growing market). He writes that "the ability to create its own market is the strategic, the dominating, and the single most distinguishing characteristic of a true growth company." He concludes with the observation that the term "growth stock" is meaningless—it can only be identified in hindsight after its price has increased. However, a "growth company" has real characteristics that can be studied and identified. He is quick to add that simply identifying growth companies is not enough. "No amount of study [in the identification of growth companies] can minimize the important of trying to buy at a fair price…"

Here's a current definition of core equity management, as provided by Mobius:

"A type of equity management that invests in diversified portfolios, typically using a broad index such as the S&P 500 Index as their benchmark. Usually these managers are expected to achieve returns that are comparable to general market performance, at the least. In a typical scenario, a core equity manager acts as the central base of an active equity portfolio, on which other specialized, more dynamic managers build."

With this definition in mind, and the caveats about over-exacting classifications, the best way to understand a core equity manager is to take a deep look at a particular practitioner, which we will present in an upcoming section.

The Difference between Active and Passive Core Management

"What we used to have was three closet indexers," explained Keith Harding, investment manager of the Rolls Royce pension fund. "If you're going to have closet indexers, you might as well have an explicit index fund and pay lower fees." This exchange, referring to the core equity portion of a pension fund, quoted in the British Journal *Financial Director*[3] in May of 1987 sums up a good deal of the tension that exists around the topic of active and passive approaches to core investing.

To the extent that a core manager looks like the index, either by intent or by style, this argument has validity. In fact, one emerging trend has been "core plus" managers, who actively track their index. In brief, these are managers who don't seek differentiation from their benchmark, but attempt to outperform it with small, often quantitatively driven adjustments. This enhanced indexing approach has been utilized by a number of money managers over the years. The downside to both indexed and index-related core approaches was seen in 1999 and early 2000, when the S&P 500, the most common index used for these approaches, became dominated by a narrow list of high-priced technology companies, whose value plummeted in the ensuing years. By definition, indexing, or near-indexing, captures virtually all of the market's downside. Even non-indexed, active core managers were not immune from this same risk since many gravitated toward the higher risk side of the market during the 1999-2000 bubble in an attempt to capture the rise and pace of their benchmarks.

However, it would be a mistake to assume that all core managers mimic the broader market. Many have disciplines that consistently demonstrate a low R-squared, setting themselves apart from their benchmarks. Other core managers stayed more centrist in their equity choices, and concentrated on the out-of-favor, more modestly growing companies that eventually came back in favor during the bear market of 2000-2002. These firms are not likely to be characterized as "closet indexers."

Fitting Core Equity into the Overall Portfolio Strategy

If an investor had to allocate long-term equity dollars to a single strategy, core equity would be the choice of most consultants. The decision of active or passive would hinge on the consultant's background and bias and the client's needs. The benefit of an active, and adept, core manager is the ability to range among a wide number of stocks with both growth and value characteristics, and not be locked into one category. This allows for contrarian impulses, as in 1999, when it was possible for a core manager to shift away from high-priced stocks, while still participating in the growth stock-dominated market of the 1990s.

Another reason that core, as its names suggests, makes a good foundation for a diversified equity portfolio is in the area of risk management. As we've learned from bear markets past, investors, even those who profess to be risk averse, do not handle losses well. The relatively new science of behavioral economics has come to the same conclusion: the pain of a loss is much greater than the joy of a gain.

It's often said that clients have an asymmetrical view of risk. They want relative returns in a bull market, yet absolute returns in a bear market. Core managers, by sticking with the proven, steady companies, have the potential to outperform in down markets, while participating in up markets. When push comes to shove, experience shows this matches most client's needs and profiles. Other style managers can then be successfully added around this core position for both additional diversification as well as attempts to enhance portfolio alpha.

Year after year, different styles lead the market. Yet over time, it is striking how often the winning style is close to the market's center. The following chart illustrates the historic results.

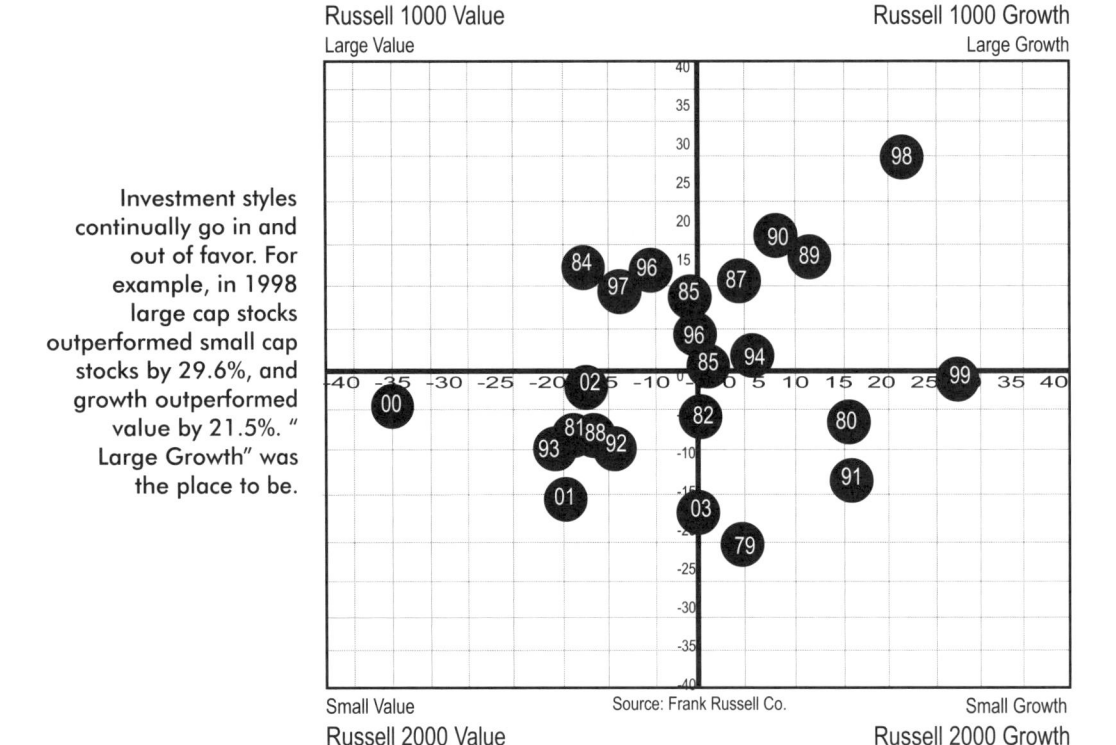

Investment styles continually go in and out of favor. For example, in 1998 large cap stocks outperformed small cap stocks by 29.6%, and growth outperformed value by 21.5%. " Large Growth" was the place to be.

Source: Frank Russell Co.

"Participate and Protect"— A Specific Approach to Core

The foundation of this equity approach is the simple notion that the key to success over time comes from owning great, high-quality companies. Add to this an aversion to losing money that can be summarized in an oft-repeated saying: "The key to making money over time is not to lose it." Great companies are defined as ones that can produce steady, reliable growth. The sense is that these are the kinds of companies that participate in the long-term upward trend of the stock market. Buying these companies when their prices are "reasonable" is the optimal way to protect capital in down markets. For example, we like to summarize this approach as "participate and protect." The emphasis on downside protection has led us to a slight revision of the descriptor "Growth at a Reasonable Price": *"Growth at a Reasonable Risk."* This is also a concise way to explain core equity investing to clients. "Participate and Protect" translates into less volatility and potential market-beating returns for them, and a concept readily accepted.

Stock Screening Process

While some managers are looking for deep-value turnarounds, and others are riding the rocket of go-go growth firms, like other core managers, this approach tracks firms in the middle, looking at companies one at a time, in a bottom-up process designed to identify companies growing faster than the market (growth), yet selling at below market valuation (value).

In order to come under consideration, the first basic screen for companies in the firm's capitalization range (generally $1 billion and up) is steady growth. The preference is for corporations capable of growing top and bottom lines at 10-15 percent, as opposed to emerging companies with higher growth rates that are not viewed as sustainable. Predictability of earnings is given a premium, and this eliminates many of the companies in more cyclical industries.

Analysts examine the company's business model, and a preference is given to firms with a protectable franchise—a large moat around their businesses. This sustainable competitive advantage could involve barriers for competition, proprietary product or strength of brand. The management team is also evaluated, looking for high-quality, stable teams whose interest is aligned with shareholders. The ideal scenario is to find management teams who have a record of allocating capital wisely, whether for expansion, acquisitions, co-share buy-backs or otherwise. Straightforward accounting is another requirement.

This process narrows the list, depending on the environment, to a few hundred prospects. Investment is only made when the valuation parameters are met. Companies are valued by a number of quantifiable measures, as well as examining historic pricing for the stock. The goal is to purchase at prices which provide a margin of safety to downside risk. The ideal projection will show a best-case, worst-case ratio of three to one. In other words, the stock has three times the upside potential to downside risk. In the end, prospects are whittled down to a focused portfolio of some 25-35 companies. In aggregate, it is expected that this portfolio will have lower than market Price/Earnings ratios, better than average growth, and stronger balance sheets. Due largely to earnings predictability, these companies tend to fall into five broad market sectors: Financial, Technology, Consumer, Health Care and Industrial.

Stocks are sold for three reasons: when the company appears fully priced, when more attractive alternatives become available, or when fundamentals deteriorate. The end result is a portfolio of companies that show solid growth, yet have reasonable valuations.

Thesis Reports and Sell Strategy

One component of our own research process is the generation of thesis reports. Unlike many analysts who write lengthy, detailed reports, less is more in our opinion. We suspect that long industry and stock reports probably involve more energy in the writing than in thinking about the investment or understanding it. Boiling the information down to a one-page report, highlighting the key reasons and rationale for buying a stock, is an excellent way to remain objective.

Each buy involves the preparation of a short thesis report, which becomes a touchstone throughout the holding period. These reports allow us to get our hands around the reasons we bought and own a stock. If these reasons are no longer intact, we sell. It helps take the emotion out of the sell decision, which is consistently the toughest call for money managers, who can easily become over-enamored with an idea.

Another aspect of the thesis reports is the analyst's confidence level for a stock on a one-to-five scale, with five being the best (and rarest) of prospects. Only stocks rated three to five are eligible for purchase, and lower-rated stocks are kept on a shorter lease. In other words, if a three-rated stock approaches its target valuation, it is sold, whereas a five-rated stock would probably only be trimmed.

Summary

A last word on the value versus growth issue is summed up in a Warren Buffett citation, and makes a good case for the black-and-white-hatted gunslingers to 'shake hands and put their guns away.' In his 1992 Berkshire Hathaway Annual Report, Buffett states: "Most analysts feel they must choose between two approaches, customarily thought to be in opposition: 'value' and 'growth.' Indeed, many investment professionals see any mixing of the two terms as a form of intellectual cross-dressing. We view that as fuzzy thinking (in which, it must be confessed, I myself engaged some years ago). In our opinion, the two approaches are joined at the hip: Growth is always a component in the calculation of value, constituting a variable whose importance can range from negligible to enormous and whose impact can be negative as well as positive."

In conclusion, core equity encompasses a wide variety of managerial styles that attempt to give investors a solid foundation of stock ownership. While not all core managers utilize qualitative analysis, the consultant attempting to match clients and manager will need to apply qualitative analysis of a different sort to look behind the numbers. Understanding the benefits and potential drawbacks of each of these various approaches is essential to manager selection. In doing so, it is possible to fulfill Mobius's definition: "In a typical scenario, a core equity manager acts as the central base of an active equity portfolio, on which other specialized… managers build."

❖ ❖ ❖

---

1 April 15, 1991 interview with the *Minneapolis Star Tribune*.
2 "Growth Companies vs. Growth Stocks," Peter L. Bernstein, *Harvard Business Review*, Harvard Business School Publishing (September 1956), pp. 87-98
3 32-34 Broadwick Street, London W1A 2HG, UK; www.financialdirector.co.uk

18

BONDS FOR ALL SEASONS

Richard Duff, Managing Director
Private Client Group
BlackRock

While many investors may feel most at home investing in equities, bonds are an exceedingly important asset class both in terms of total returns and risk management. Knowledge of the bond market may significantly help an investor improve the performance of his or her portfolio, while also potentially reducing risk versus a pure equity strategy. Likewise, expertise in this area can potentially improve an investment advisor's ability to effectively advise his or her clients. This chapter will discuss the essential elements of individual bonds and the broader bond market, and will offer some perspective on how bonds can be used to help optimize both portfolio risk and total returns.

Individual Bonds

Generally speaking, a bond is a security issued by a private company or government body that pays a stated interest rate and offers the return of principal at a given time. For example, a 10-year U.S. Treasury bond may offer a 5 % annual interest rate and guarantee the return of principal in 10 years. Interest payments are typically made on a semi-annual basis to the investor. Investors who purchased a $1000 10-year Treasury bond with a 5% annual interest rate, for example, would receive 2.5% (or $25) every six months. Given that bonds offer a fixed stream of income to the investor, they are often referred to as "fixed income" securities.

In purchasing a bond, an investor is essentially loaning money to the issuer.

Unlike equity ownership, bond ownership does not represent partial ownership of the issuing body. Instead, a bond owner is a creditor of the issuer. As such, bonds may also be referred to as "credits."

The Essential Elements of a Bond

Typically, a bond has three essential elements: the principal amount, the coupon, and the maturity date. The principal is the amount that the investor will receive when the bond comes due or "matures." The coupon is the rate of interest the bond will pay the investor. For example, a five-year Ford Motor Company bond might be purchased for $900 and pay a coupon of 7%. A bond's maturity date is the point in time at which the investor will receive the principal amount, as well as the bond's final interest payment.

How Bonds are Sold

Bonds may be sold by any company or government body that wishes to raise capital. Both private and government bonds are typically sold in units of $1000. This is referred to as "par value." In the open market, bonds may trade above or below par. Bonds purchased above par are said to trade at a premium, while bonds purchased below par are said to trade at a discount. Whether a bond is purchased at a premium or a discount, the investor will still receive par at maturity. Under certain circumstances, investors may be willing to purchase a bond at a premium in order to be assured of receiving a favorable coupon rate. Under other circumstances, investors may seek to improve their total return by purchasing bonds at a discount. The return that an investor will earn by purchasing a bond at a premium or discount is referred to as its "yield to maturity."

Understanding Yield

A bond's yield is the percent return that an investor will receive given a bond's price, its coupon rate, and time to maturity. A bond trading at par will have a yield equal to its coupon. Given that bonds may trade above or below par, a bond's yield may be greater or less than its coupon. If a bond is purchased at a premium to par, its yield will be less than its coupon. For example, a 10-year General Motors bond with a 5% coupon purchased at $1100 will yield 3.79% if held to maturity. Conversely, if a bond is purchased at a discount to par, its yield will be greater than its coupon. For example, a 10-year General Motors bond with a 5% coupon purchased at $900 will yield 6.37% if held to maturity. Accordingly, one can establish the general rule that price and yield move in opposite directions. As the price of a bond increases, its yield decreases. Likewise, as the price of a bond decreases, its yield increases.

Fixed Income Mutual Funds

While investors may purchase a wide variety of individual bonds, it is important to note that bonds may also be purchased through fixed income mutual funds. Many types of fixed income funds exist, each of which offers unique portfolio holdings and a distinct risk profile. Generally speaking, the diversification offered by fixed income funds may help offset the risks encountered by owning individual bonds. These may include credit quality risk, interest rate risk, and liquidity risk.

Types of Risk in Fixed Income Investing

While fixed income investing is typically thought of as "conservative" or as a "safe haven" for liquid assets, it is important to note that investing in the bond market involves risk, including the loss of principal. Investors and their financial advisors should be aware of the various types of risk

Bonds for all Seasons

they may encounter in the fixed income market and plan their asset allocation strategy accordingly.

Credit Quality—Each issuer of fixed income securities has a unique financial condition. Some issuers, like the U.S. Government, may have an extraordinary ability to make timely payments of interest and principal on the bonds they issue. Other issuers, such as emerging companies, may be less likely to make timely payments, or to make the appropriate payments at all. The "credit quality" of a bond is essentially a measure of the likelihood that the issuer will make timely payments of interest and principal. Two major ratings organizations, Moody's and Standard & Poor's (S&P), have established ratings systems in order to compare the credit qualities of various bonds.

Using S&P ratings, a 10-year Treasury bond would be rated AAA or better, because there is virtually no risk that the U.S. Government will not make timely payments of principal and interest on its bonds. The bonds of a well-known, financially stable corporation would likely be highly rated as well, since it is unlikely that such a corporation would fail to meet its obligations to its bondholders. Bonds of a less-established or financially distressed company, however, might receive a lower rating, as it is more likely that such a company would fail to make timely payments or principal and interest. The risk that an issuer will fail to meet its obligations to its bondholders is known as "default risk."

All bonds rated BBB or above by S&P and Baa or above by Moody's are considered "investment-grade." All bonds rated BB or below by S&P and Ba or below by Moody's are considered below-investment-grade bonds. These issues may also be referred to as "high yield" bonds.

Generally speaking, lower quality bonds will trade at a discount to par. Given their higher default risk, investors will usually be unwilling to pay par value for these bonds. Expressed another way, investors will want to be compensated for the greater risk they are taking in purchasing these bonds by receiving a higher return. As alluded to previously, the lower prices of these bonds will generally create a higher overall yield for the investor.

Interest Rate Risk—We have established the idea that a bond offers a certain yield based on its price and coupon rate. It is important to note, however, that the prices of existing bonds will be significantly impacted by changes in interest rates. These changes in price will, in turn, affect a bond's yield.

A Changing Rate Environment—Let's assume that an investor purchased a 10-year IBM bond with a 7% coupon for $1000. If interest rates were to rise, IBM might offer 10-year bonds with 8% coupons in order to attract investors in the rising rate environment. At this point, the price of the bond with the 7% coupon would likely decline, because it would be less attractive to investors relative to the 8% bond. Investors who needed to liquidate these 7% bonds prior to maturity might suffer a partial loss of principal. Mathematically, the present value of the cash flows in the 7% bond would be worth less than those in the now-par 8% bond, and would, therefore, trade at a discount.

Broadly speaking, when interest rates rise, the prices of existing bonds tend to fall. Conversely, when interest rates fall, the prices of existing bonds tend to rise.

Assessing Interest Rate Risk: Duration and Convexity—One of the most useful tools for assessing the interest rate risk of a bond is its duration. Still, the concept can be elusive for both investors and their advisors.

Duration can help predict the likely change in the price of a bond given a change in interest rates. As a general rule, for every 1% increase or decrease in interest rates, a bond's price will change approximately 1% in the opposite direction for every year of duration. For example, if a bond has a duration of five years, and interest rates increase by 1%, the bond's price will decline by approximately 5%. Conversely, if a bond has a duration of five years and interest rates fall by 1%, the bond's price will increase by approximately 5%.

Duration	Interest Rate Change	Approximate Price Change
5 years	+1.0%	-5%
5 years	-1.0%	+5%

Calculating Duration—Duration is defined as the average time to receipt of all the cash flows of a bond, weighted by the present value of each of the cash flows. Essentially, it is the payment-weighted point in time at which an investor can expect to recoup his or her original investment. (Graphic A)

Given its relative ability to predict price changes based on changes in interest rates, duration allows for the effective comparison of bonds with different maturities and coupon rates. By comparing the bonds' durations, investors may be able to anticipate the degree of price change in each bond assuming a given change in interest rates. Accordingly, duration calculations may help investors more precisely structure their portfolios against the backdrop of their overall investment objectives and risk tolerance.

Rules of Duration—When thinking about duration, a few general rules apply. With everything else being equal:

- The duration of any bond that pays a coupon will be *less* than its maturity, because some amount of coupon payments will be received before the maturity date.

- The lower a bond's coupon, the *longer* its duration, because proportionately less payment is received before final maturity. The higher a bond's coupon, the *shorter* its duration, because proportionately more payment is received before final maturity.

- The longer a bond's maturity, the longer its duration, because it takes *more* time to receive full payment. The shorter a bond's maturity, the shorter its duration, because it takes *less* time to receive full payment.

Considering Duration and Convexity—Duration assumes a linear relationship between bond prices and changes in interest rates. (Graphic B)

In actuality, however, prices rise at an increasing rate as interest rates fall; similarly, prices decline at a decreasing rate as interest rates rise. This disparity implies that duration will consistently *overestimate* the amount of price

Graphic A   Source: BlackRock

For example, for a two-year bond with a $1000 face value and one coupon payment every six months of $50, the duration (calculated in years) is:

$$0.5\,y\left(\frac{50}{1200}\right) + 1\,y\left(\frac{50}{1200}\right) + 1.5\,y\left(\frac{50}{1200}\right) + 2\,y\left(\frac{50}{1200}\right) + 2\,y\left(\frac{1000}{1200}\right) = 1.87 \text{ years}$$

Where: y = Years
  50 = Interest paid every six months
  1000 = Principal payment
  1200 = Total of all payments received, including principal

As illustrated below, duration can be intuitively understood as the point along a time spectrum at which a bond's total payments roughly balance:

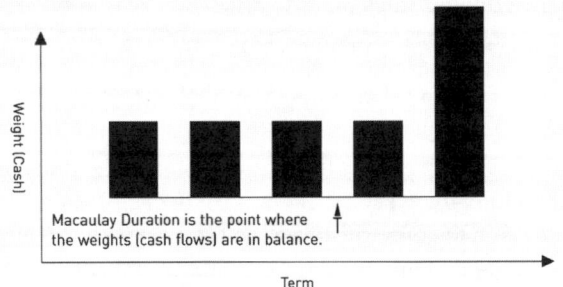

Macaulay Duration is the point where the weights (cash flows) are in balance.

Graphic B

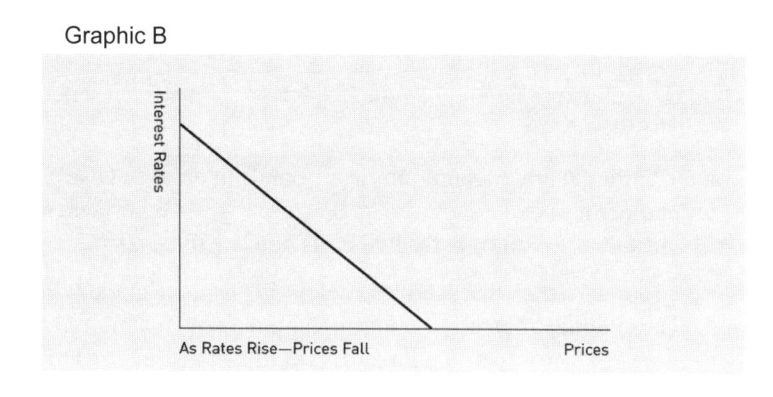

[Graph showing downward-sloping line: Interest Rates (y-axis) vs Prices (x-axis), labeled "As Rates Rise—Prices Fall"]

decline associated with a large upward move in interest rates. Conversely, duration will consistently *underestimate* the amount of price increase associated with a large drop in interest rates.

In order to compensate for this disparity, the concept of "convexity" was developed. Convexity corrects for the error that duration produces in anticipating price changes given large movements in interest rates. As such, convexity also measures the rate of change in duration, thereby fully accounting for the dynamic relationship between prices and rates. (Graphic C)

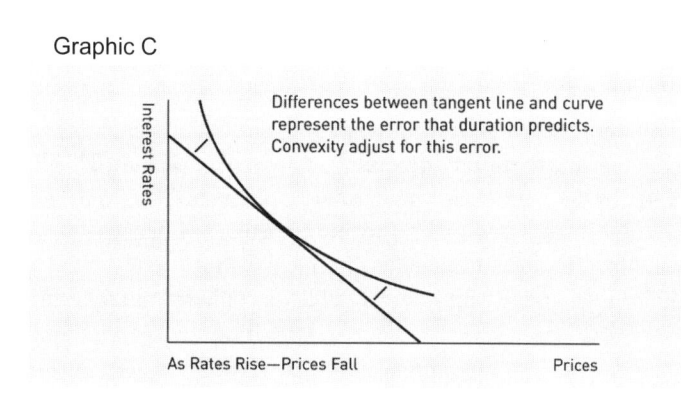

Graphic C

[Graph showing a convex curve with a tangent line. Annotation: "Differences between tangent line and curve represent the error that duration predicts. Convexity adjust for this error." Axes: Interest Rates (y-axis), Prices (x-axis), labeled "As Rates Rise—Prices Fall"]

Convexity can help investors anticipate how quickly the prices of their bonds are likely to change given a change in interest rates. Everything else being equal, investors may find issues with greater convexity more attractive, as greater convexity may translate to greater price gains as interest rates fall and lessened price declines as interest rates rise. Certain bonds may have embedded features (such as call options) which can reduce or even negate the convexity of the bond.

By understanding duration, financial advisors can help their clients better structure the interest rate sensitivity of their portfolios as it relates to their overall investment objectives and risk tolerance.

- *Liquidity Risk*—Unlike many equities, bonds are not traded on centralized exchanges. Instead, they are traded between dealers in the over-the-counter (OTC) market. At any given time, there may be a wealth or a lack of buyers or sellers for any given bond. In this case, the bond may be difficult to purchase or sell and may, therefore, be "illiquid." This may affect the purchase or sale price an investor will receive.

The Bond Market

Like the equity market, the bond market consists of various sectors. These sectors in turn consist of numerous sub-sectors, each of which offers unique investment opportunities.

The Treasury Market—Perhaps the best-known bonds in the world are those issued directly by the U.S. Government. These issues are collectively known as Treasury securities. While many types of Treasuries exist, the most commonly recognized are the three-month, six-month, two-year, five-year, and 10-year Treasury issues. Given their exceptional credit quality, Treasuries are generally considered to be the safest bonds in the world. They are also among the most liquid securities in the world, trading many billions of dollars on a daily basis.

Income earned on Treasury bonds is subject to federal income tax, but is exempt from state and local taxes.

The Corporate Market—As noted earlier, many corporations issue bonds in order to raise capital. A given corporation may have numerous bond issues outstanding at any given time. Generally speaking, the greater the financial health of a company, the higher its bonds will be rated.

As previously discussed, those corporate issues that are rated below investment-grade will be considered "high yield" issues. These bonds typically offer coupon payments that are greater than those of higher-rated issues in order to compensate investors for this increased credit risk. High yield bonds are generally issued by companies seeking to finance business expansion or to meet operating cash flow requirements.

Given their higher coupons, high yield bonds may offer greater levels of current income than investment-grade bonds. Due to their higher degree of credit risk and potential price volatility, high yield issues may also offer increased total returns to investors willing to accept a higher degree of risk exposure. Additionally, high yield bonds may improve the diversification of a traditional fixed income or equity portfolio.

High yield securities are predominantly speculative with respect to the issuer's capacity to pay interest and repay principal when due, and therefore involve a greater risk of default. The market for high yield bonds is not as liquid as the markets for higher rated securities. The prices of high yield bonds are generally more volatile and sensitive to actual or perceived negative developments, such as a decline in the issuer's revenue or a general economic downturn, than are the prices of higher-grade securities. In addition, the market for high yield bonds could be hurt by future tax or other legal changes.

Income earned on corporate bonds is subject to federal, state, and local taxes.

The Mortgage Market—The mortgage sector is one of the largest and most complex sectors of the fixed income market. Mortgage-backed securities (MBS) may be issued by the U.S. Government or by private corporations.

Generally speaking, MBS are bonds representing an ownership interest in a pool of residential mortgage loans. Residential homeowners make mortgage payments that are ultimately pooled each month; these pooled payments are then "passed through" to MBS holders in the form of principal and interest cash flows.

To create a MBS, a lending bank first pools together a group of mortgage loans that it has issued. The bank then presents this pool of mortgages to a government-sponsored agency designated to issue and guarantee MBS. These agencies may include the Government National Mortgage Association (GNMA or "Ginnie Mae"), the Federal National Mortgage Association (FNMA or "Fannie Mae"), or the Federal Home Loan Mortgage Corporation (FHLMC or "Freddie Mac"). Alternatively, private issuers may assemble pools, with credit enhancement arising from a combination of insurance and senior/subordinate structuring.

The agency issuing the MBS guarantees the timely payment of principal and interest to MBS investors. The principal and interest payments the mortgage borrowers pay to the bank are "passed through" to MBS investors each month. Investors can purchase individual MBS securities, or mutual funds comprised of MBS holdings.

Bonds for all Seasons

In order to facilitate the flow of funds to the housing industry, the U.S. Government created three major housing agencies to support the mortgage market:

Ginnie Mae—The first MBS was issued in 1970 by the Government National Mortgage Association (GNMA). Ginnie Mae is a government-owned corporation that issues MBS backed by the full faith and credit of the U.S. Government. As a *direct* obligation, the timely payment of principal and interest is guaranteed, regardless of mortgage payments or default.

Fannie Mae—The Federal National Mortgage Association (FNMA) is a stockholder-owned, government-sponsored corporation subject to Treasury regulations. While FNMA has a line-of-credit with the U.S. Government, Fannie Mae MBS are currently considered a *moral* obligation of the U.S. Government, providing federal agency credit quality.

Freddie Mac—The Federal Home Loan Mortgage Association (FHLMC) is a stockholder-owned, government-sponsored corporation established to increase mortgage credit and provide liquidity. Like Fannie Mae MBS, Freddie Mac MBS have an as-yet undrawn line-of-credit with the U.S. Government and are currently considered a *moral* obligation of the U.S. Government, offering federal agency credit quality.

Both Fannie Maes and Freddie Macs generally offer higher current yields than Ginnie Maes in order to compensate for their slightly lower perceived credit quality. Together, these agencies help to effectively lower lending rates on residential mortgage loans. They also facilitate the flow of funds to the U.S. housing industry by providing lending institutions with the money they need to offer additional mortgages.

Unlike other fixed income investments, which typically pay periodic interest and return principal in one lump sum at maturity, MBS make interest and principal payments to investors on a monthly basis. As such, MBS investors receive their principal back over the life of the investment, instead of only at maturity. This occurs as the monthly loan payments made by homeowners (which consist of both interest and principal) are passed through to MBS holders.

Because homeowners can prepay their mortgage loans in advance, the size of MBS monthly payments and the bond's maturities are only estimated and can vary. In exchange for their estimated payment and maturity characteristics, MBS generally offer a yield advantage over other comparable quality fixed income securities.

Principal prepayments can affect both the monthly income stream and the maturity of a MBS. In theory, if every homeowner in a pool of mortgages made their monthly payments on time and held their mortgages for the full term (for example, 30 years), MBS investors could expect to receive equal monthly payments of principal and interest for 30 years. However, homeowners can choose to prepay all or part of their mortgages prior to maturity. This is known as "principal prepayment."

One type of prepayment is known as refinancing. Refinancing typically occurs when interest rates decline, providing mortgage borrowers with the opportunity to take advantage of lower mortgage rates. When this refinancing occurs, the prepaid principal is returned to the lending bank, and then passed through to MBS investors. (Graphic D)

Prepayments also occur through home sales. When homeowners relocate or simply want to buy another home, the sale results in the prepayment of the principal amount due on the existing mortgage. Again, this principal prepayment is then passed through to MBS investors.

Another type of prepayment occurs when mortgage borrowers add to the minimum principal amount due each month on their mortgage statements. In this way, they accelerate the payment of principal, effectively paying off the loan before it's due. When MBS are prepaid during periods of declining interest rates, investors will generally be forced to reinvest the proceeds at a lower rate of return.

Income earned from MBS is subject to federal, state, and local taxes.

The Municipal Market—Like the U.S. Government, states and municipalities may issue bonds in order to meet budget requirements or to finance new projects. Municipal bonds are typically of high credit quality, given that they are backed by government entities with the power to raise capital through taxation and revenue generation.

Two important types of municipal bonds are general obligation bonds and revenue bonds. General obligation bonds are typically issued by a state or municipality to finance ongoing budget needs. Interest and principal payments are derived from the state or municipality's tax revenues. Revenue bonds are typically issued in order to raise capital for new development projects, such as highways or hospitals. Interest and principal payments are derived from the revenues of the project.

The income earned on municipal bonds is exempt from federal taxes, and is normally tax-free to residents of the issuing state. This may be of particular significance for higher-income investors wishing to offset their taxable income obligations. Investors who own municipal bonds from states in which they are not residents may be required to pay state taxes on those holdings. Investors and their financial advisors with tax questions regarding municipal bonds should consult a tax specialist.

The International Market— As in the United States, many foreign governments and corporations issue bonds in order to raise capital and finance ongoing operations. Two of the more noteworthy bonds issued by foreign governments are the 10-year Japanese Government Bond (JGB) and the 10-year German Bund. Just as the 10-year Treasury Bond serves as a benchmark for interest rates in the United States, these issues are considered broad reflections of the interest rate environment in Japan and the Eurozone.

U.S. investors purchasing international bonds should be aware of the special risk that currency fluctuations may pose to their investments. As in the equity markets, investors holding bonds denominated in foreign currencies may benefit or suffer as those currencies appreciate or depreciate versus the U.S. dollar. This is especially true of so-called "emerging markets" issues, or bonds issued by governments or corporations of developing nations. These securities may exhibit a much greater degree of price volatility and currency sensitivity than their counterparts in more developed economies.

Graphic D   Source: BlackRock

What are the Effects of Interest Rate Changes on MBS?

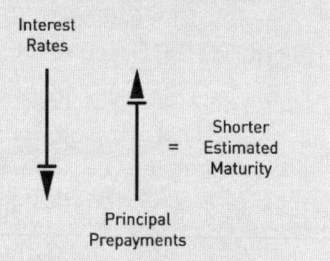

Interest Rates ↓ / Principal Prepayments ↑ = Shorter Estimated Maturity

When interest rates fall, principal prepayments typically accelerate, due to increased refinancing and new home buying. As a result, the size of the principal prepayments to MBS investors increases and the estimated maturity of the MBS shortens. This occurs as principal is paid back sooner than expected.

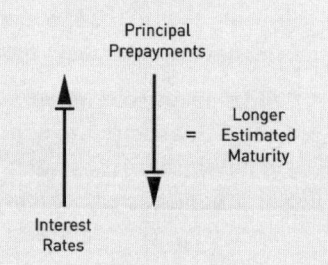

Principal Prepayments ↓ / Interest Rates ↑ = Longer Estimated Maturity

When interest rates rise, principal prepayments tend to decelerate, as refinancing and home buying typically decrease in a higher interest rate environment. Typically, the size of principal prepayments lessens and the estimated maturity of the MBS lengthens. Given these possibilities, MBS investors must rely on statistical information to anticipate the rate of principal prepayments, as well as the estimated maturity of the security.

Bonds for all Seasons

Managing Risk with Fixed Income Investments

Aside from the obvious benefits of providing relative safety of principal and regular income, fixed income investments can also serve to diversify an investor's portfolio and improve risk control.

Portfolio diversification has protected investors during periods of significant market volatility. For example, during periods of substantial equity market declines over the past 20 years, a diversified portfolio of 50% equities and 50% bonds offered investors considerable downside protection when compared to a non-diversified portfolio of 100% equities. (Graphic E)

Graphic E

Diversification Cushions the Impact of a Market Downturn

	100% Equity	50% Stocks/50% Bonds
October 1987 (8/31/87-11/30/87)	-29.6%	-18.5%
Gulf War (12/31/89-10/31/90)	-11.5%	-5.7%
Russian Crisis (6/30/98-8/31/98)	-15.4%	-9.3%
Tech Bubble (2/29/00-10/31/02)	-35.2%	-4.0%

Source: Ibbotson Associates, Inc.

Investors should review their portfolio with their financial advisor to determine an optimal asset allocation strategy, and maintain this balance through changing markets. Over relatively short periods, volatile markets can substantially skew a portfolio away from its intended asset allocation targets. It is important for investors to periodically rebalance their portfolios in order to avoid unintended exposure to any single asset class.

For example, consider a portfolio originally intended to maintain a balanced allocation of 50% equities and 50% fixed income as of 1983. If left unmanaged, by August 31, 2003, the growth rate of equities would have skewed the portfolio towards much greater equity market exposure than originally intended[1]. (Graphic F)

Accordingly, investors may be best served by maintaining a balanced mix of equity and fixed income assets. By doing so, investors may achieve an optimal balance between realizing strong absolute returns and managing portfolio risk.

Graphic F

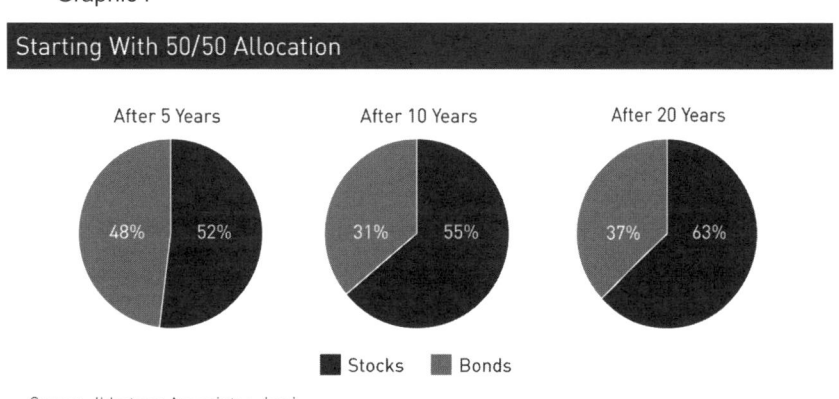

Starting With 50/50 Allocation

After 5 Years	After 10 Years	After 20 Years
48% / 52%	31% / 55%	37% / 63%

■ Stocks ■ Bonds

Source: Ibbotson Associates, Inc.[1]

Actively Managed Fixed Income Strategies—One of the means by which investors can potentially achieve strong absolute returns and effective risk control is through active portfolio management. In active portfolio management, a professional fixed income manager structures a portfolio of fixed income investments with the objective of outperforming an established benchmark over the long term. To this end, the manager actively selects securities for the portfolio based on a range of risk and return parameters. In doing so, the manager relies on his or her knowledge of the market and experience of the historical trends that form the portfolio's investment backdrop. Active managers charge fees for their services; these typically vary by fund and fund company.

Active portfolio management directly contrasts with passive portfolio management. In passive portfolio management, a manager seeks to mirror the returns of a given benchmark. Unlike an active manager, a passive manager does not actively select securities for their portfolios and does not seek to outperform a given benchmark. Passive managers also charge fees for their services, but they are typically significantly lower than those of active managers.

While some investors may appreciate the lower fees typically associated with passive portfolio management, active portfolio management may offer several potential advantages in terms of total returns and risk control. These include:

Security Selection—An active manager may be able to select securities for their portfolios that will offer an average yield that is higher than that of the benchmark. Importantly, they may also be able to avoid holding securities that would represent serious credit risks to the portfolio.

Duration and Convexity Positioning—Based on a manager's interest rate outlook, they may be able to structure a portfolio with more favorable duration and convexity characteristics than those of the index. This may aid the portfolio's performance in an environment of rapidly rising or falling interest rates.

Sector Allocations—Based on a manager's analysis of the relative value of a fixed income sector at a given time, they may be able to hold a greater or lesser position in that sector versus the portfolio's benchmark. This is referred to as "overweighting" or "underweighting" a portfolio's sector allocations. Effectively over- or underweighting sector holdings may result in greater overall returns to the investor.

Tax Efficiency—Given active managers' greater relative flexibility in buying and selling securities for their portfolios, they may be able to realize tax benefits for investors in a broad range of income brackets. These may include harvesting losses at opportune times during the year or purchasing securities with favorable tax profiles, such as municipal bonds.

Both active and passive management can offer distinct benefits to investors depending on one's particular investment needs. Whether an investor prefers active or passive management may depend on a number of variables, including risk tolerance, return objectives, and overall portfolio structure.

Managed Accounts

One of the means by which an investor may best realize the benefits of active portfolio management is by establishing a managed account. A managed account is an individual investment account offered by financial consultants in conjunction with a select group of asset managers. The financial consultant's role is to provide analysis of the client's financial needs, set investment objectives, and then select and monitor the appropriate asset managers based on the client's identified objectives. These may include managers for fixed income, equity, money market, and alternative investments. Typically, the client is charged a single asset-based fee for services rendered through the managed account.

While managed accounts have historically been the province of the super wealthy, by the close of 2003, assets under management in managed account programs were estimated to have increased to more than half a trillion dollars[2]. Investors from a variety of financial backgrounds may benefit from the advantages of a managed account.

These include:

- Access to institutional-quality investment management previously available only to large institutions and the ultra rich.
- A customized investment approach that is geared to meet the investor's specific investment objectives.
- A single asset-based fee structure. This fee typically includes investment counseling, portfolio management, brokerage fees, and ongoing account administration.
- The flexibility to manage assets for tax efficiency.
- The ability to structure a socially conscious portfolio, i.e., a portfolio that avoids holdings in industries such as alcohol, tobacco, and gaming.

As clients continue to demand increasingly sophisticated investment solutions, many consultants and asset managers have developed more flexible programs for attracting a greater variety of managed account investors. Given the substantial growth in managed account assets over the past several years, this dynamic approach appears likely to continue.

Conclusion

Fixed income investing has traditionally been viewed as a conservative strategy for preserving principal and earning steady income. As the preceding chapter has alluded to, however, fixed income investing can offer a much wider range of potential benefits to investors who pursue their investment strategies with care and precision. As always, investors should consult their financial advisors to determine which fixed income strategies are optimal for their investment objectives.

❖ ❖ ❖

---

1 Source: Ibbotson Associates, Inc. Past performance is no guarantee of future results. Fixed income returns are based on the Lehman Brothers Aggregate Bond Index. The Lehman Brothers Aggregate Bond Index is a market-capitalization weighted index of investment-grade fixed-rate debt issues, including government, corporate, asset-backed, and mortgage-backed securities, with maturities of at least one year. Equity returns are based on the S&P 500 Index. The S&P 500 is a widely recognized, unmanaged index of common stocks. An investor cannot directly invest in either index.
2 Source: Money Management Institute. Estimate based on observations of other proprietary databases and projections from MMI sources.

BlackRock's contribution to this book is solely limited to the content of this chapter, entitled Bonds For All Seasons. BlackRock takes no responsibility for the content of any other chapter included in this book. The information contained in this chapter is not to be construed as a solicitation or an offer to buy or sell securities. The views contained herein are those of BlackRock and are based on information obtained by BlackRock from sources that are believed to be reliable. This material should not be considered tax, investment, legal or other professional advice.

19

GROWTH INVESTING
THE HUNT FOR OUTSIZED RETURNS

David C. Kahn, Managing Director
Portfolio Manager - Large Cap Growth
Roxbury Capital Management, LLC

Patience, skill, and recognition of opportunity are their own rewards. This is true on the plains of Africa, and equally true when it comes to growth investing. It is the hungry lion that chases anything that moves, whether or not it has any hope of catching its prey. The seasoned hunter, however, knows better, biding his time, surrounded and hidden by the tall grass until the exact moment its ideal target comes within striking distance.

Warren Buffett, arguably the world's greatest investor, takes to heart the lesson of the lion patiently stalking its prey. He is highly selective of his targets and very patiently waits for his prey to come within reach. He has achieved a remarkable record of success by recognizing unique opportunity and knowing when to move and when to remain still.

Today, Buffett's firm Berkshire Hathaway is a major stockholder of some of the most recognizable companies on the planet, including Amazon, Disney, Coke, and American Express. Paradoxically, Buffett is known as the consummate value investor, but his major public holdings represent some of the most recognizable growth success stories of the past 30 years. Well, which is he, a growth manager or a value manager? We believe he represents the best of both styles, understanding the compounding power of a great growth company and appreciating the margin of safety that comes from buying stocks at good prices.

For example, when Buffett purchased Coca-Cola in 1988, many value investors considered the company to be too expensive. Yet after a year of little movement, the stock doubled in price in 1989. A subsequent purchase in 1992 sat for two-and-a-half years before Coke started its meteoric ascent in the second half of 1994. What ultimately drove the share price performance were the market's gradual understanding of the power of Coke's global brand, its 15-year record of compounding earnings at an average of 15 percent, and a dramatic increase in its returns on capital. Buffett generated huge profits in Coke because he bought the stock before all these growth factors were reflected in the stock price. Buffett's purchase of Coke returned close to 800 percent over the subsequent period while a similar type investment in Interpublic Group in 1973 secured returns of more than 900 percent in 11 years.

Why were these stocks such good investments? As Buffett has communicated in various essays, a high margin of safety and the uniqueness of a company's products or business model are paramount to him. He's looking for stocks when the market is underestimating the staying power of the company's earnings trajectory. Valuation protection lowers risk, but it is the growth and the consistent compounding of that growth that drive returns over the years.

	Annual Growth Rate	10-yr Cumulative Growth Rate	Warranted P/E
Company A	7.5%	106%	18x
Company B	10%	160%	28x
Company C	15%	305%	40x

[1]This is an illustration using theoretical data. The scenario presumes growth rates are sustained for 10 years and then revert to the mean over the next five years. Market multiples and discount rates are used for all 3 scenarios.

While Company C's growth rate is double the growth rate of Company A, it generates three times the wealth over a 10-year period. This is the power of compounding and the allure of growth investing. If we assume that Company A represents the market average and assign an arbitrary price/earnings (P/E) multiple of 18 to the market, an investor could pay a P/E multiple of up to 40x for Company C and still outperform the market. If an investor is savvy enough to identify the unique companies that can generate this kind of growth on a consistent basis, they can be willing to pay fairly high P/E multiples and still generate outsized returns.

Warren Buffett has been just this kind of investor. By waiting until the time was right, he has been able to achieve returns that most investors and financial professionals only dream about. Without a doubt, Warren Buffett is the king of the investing jungle.

Growth – Investing in Three Dimensions

According to New York University's Leonard N. Stern School of Business, growth investing is defined as "investing in companies where the price paid is less than the value of that growth."[1] At first glance, it seems simple enough, but this straightforward definition implies that growth investors must evaluate two distinct factors. First, a growth investor must assess the growth opportunity for various companies. Second, a successful growth investor must find securities where these growth characteristics are not reflected in stock prices ("the value of that growth").

This definition provides a construct to start defining growth investing. We know we need to ex-

Growth Investing

pand on the dimensions of growth, incorporating both degree (how much) and duration (how long) for measuring the growth of a company. But what about space? The stock market is fairly efficient, implying that what has already happened is fairly accurately reflected in securities prices. Consequently, a growth manager must assess the variable of growth *in the future*.

Simply put, growth investors are forward-looking. They choose to look at "what will be," rather than focus on the past. A growth company is then one that can exploit business advantages to grow at above-average rates going forward, while an attractive growth stock is a growth company where all these growth opportunities are not yet reflected in the stock price.

After Graham & Dodd Came Price

A look back can help provide a construct for evaluating the dimensions of a company's growth potential. Fortunately, growth investing has been around the block. T. Rowe Price, the founder of the mutual fund company that bears his name, first pioneered it in the 1930s. Slowly taking a foothold within the investing community, its development had been sufficiently established in the 1940s and 1950s whereby investors began using growth investing to take advantage of the industrial boom following World War II.

Price developed six basic characteristics that he believed were representative of growth companies. Businesses that successfully demonstrated these qualities, hopefully, would create a corresponding rise in their stock prices. According to Price, any growth company needed the following to become successful:

- The company should conduct high-quality research and development.

- Growth companies should have an early competitive advantage that would be defensible over time. These factors could include patents (or today's intellectual property), low cost production techniques, or cutting-edge products with customers inclined to stay with their supplier.

- There should be few government regulations in the company's area of business. Price believed that the more regulations a company had to contend with, the more the likelihood that growth would be hindered.

- The company should pay its employees well, yet keep its unit labor costs low through higher productivity.

- It should have a strong probability of high returns on capital. A company's return on capital indicates how well that company invests its money.

- Target companies should exhibit exceptional earnings per share growth.

Price was something of a pioneer, because he was willing to challenge the depression-era mindset that was skeptical of business and reticent to look to the future with optimism. For those investors willing to implement growth investing tools, the post-war period proved to be very rewarding indeed. Equally remarkable has been the staying power of his six criteria for evaluating growth companies, which are as applicable today as they were over 70 years ago.

The order of Price's desired attributes is meaningful. Exceptional earnings-per-share growth, which is a starting point for many investors, was actually a by-product of a variety of other factors endemic to a company. His first four factors could be summarized as "what characteristics make this company unique?" Productive research and development, barriers to entry, little government regulation, and low unit labor costs are all factors that can drive sustainable, high levels of profits. High returns on capital are the proof statement, which will be discussed later in this chapter. Finally, outstanding earnings-per-share growth is the piece of the puzzle that propels stock price appreciation. More than anything else, it is the characteristic of uniqueness that defines growth investing. While it may be manifest in a variety of forms, it is this quest for "one of a kind" companies that is the ultimate goal of growth investors.

The Many Faces of Growth Stocks

Corporate and investor success stories over the years suggest growth-oriented companies belong in most serious investor portfolios. For advisors and clients to successfully navigate the jungle of growth investing, they need to understand differences in defining growth stocks and select managers with whose criteria they agree.

When delving into sub-styles of growth investing, the unit of measurement becomes a critical determinant. In other words, above-average growth sounds great, but growth of what? Does growth mean expanding sales, profits, margins, cash flow, or dividends?

The unit(s) of measurement a manager analyzes is often indicative of the investment style they implement. Aggressive growth styles have a heavy reliance on sales, because many of these companies are early stage with minimal or no profits. Profits, or earnings per share, are probably the most common tool used by the middle ground of growth investors because it is these profits that can be used to reinvest in growth opportunities or make acquisitions. More conservative growth managers (sometimes called Growth at a Reasonable Price, or "GARP") use earnings, as well as cash flow and dividends, and tend to incorporate more valuation tools than some other growth styles.

Is one more appropriate than the other? It comes down to an investor's risk tolerance.

Aggressive growth investing is based upon the speed of a company's growth, or its progression in the business cycle. Typically, start-up or early stage companies fit this definition because their growth curve is quite steep, and larger growth percentages are easier to achieve when a company is small. Such young companies are capable of producing gains of several thousand percent over a 10-year time frame. With this potential for higher return comes higher risk, because these companies face much higher risk of business failure or competitive incursions from larger companies.

Momentum investing is another sub-sector of growth investing and it can cross all capitalization ranges. Essentially, these investors try to "catch" a company's accelerating growth cycle. The strategy implies that an object in motion tends to stay in motion and accelerating earnings or price movement (momentum strategies generally imply they will move in tandem) is a signal that future returns can be attractive. Price multiples are less important to momentum managers. When the positive momentum stops, these types of investors tend to sell, causing these strategies to have higher-than-average turnover rates in general. The return opportunity for momentum strategies can be large, but so is the risk. Higher turnover rates make these strategies most appropriate for tax-exempt accounts.

Growth strategies that gravitate toward larger companies, on the other hand, tend to see lower growth rates due to the laws of large numbers, the maturity of end markets, as well as the influence of the economic business cycle. With maturity comes stability, however, and larger growth companies face much less bankruptcy risk and often have entrenched products and customers. More stable and predictable profit opportunities are often the result. Yet even established growth companies should return several times the original investment over the span of a decade.[2]

Despite personal differences in opinions, the fundamental problem with many of these classifications is that the managers themselves define them. Growth is a large family with some disparate siblings. While all members of the family have the same last name, the investment approaches can differ meaningfully, as can the risk and return profile of each sub-style. Investors considering a manager or style must look behind the labels and explore variables like the unit of measurement(s) a manager employs, their approach to defining attractive growth parameters, and the methodology the manager uses to implement these tools.

Putting Theory to Practice

Once a path toward a growth allocation is charted, however, portfolio managers/analysts, as well as investment consultants and their clients, are still faced with a challenge: benchmarking.

As discussed earlier, there are a variety of ways to measure and define growth, and differences in methods lead to inevitable differences in identifying growth stocks. This also applies to the purveyors of market indices. For example, Standard and Poors' growth indexes use market-driven price multiples exclusively (using BARRA price-to-book calculations) to divide the market capitalization into equal weightings of growth and value stocks.[3] The logic goes something like this. The market is willing to pay a high multiple of book value for a company today, so it must believe that this company can grow faster than average in the future. Consequently, higher than average price-to-book companies must be growth companies.

Frank Russell Company's (Russell) methodology, on the other hand, interprets higher price-to-book calculations *and* faster five-year growth estimates by analysts as indicative of growth stocks. However, Russell can and does put stocks in both growth and value benchmarks, blurring the distinction between styles.

Turnover in these style benchmarks is rather high, as they are rebalanced every six months to one year. A company that was considered a growth stock six months ago may now be viewed as a value stock, only to return to its status as a growth stock in less than a year. In addition, accounting book measures such as price-to-book value can lead to distortions. For example, a company with a low price-to-book value could become a growth stock by writing off half its book value. Such adjustments could mean the difference between being considered a growth or value stock, even though the company fundamentals have not changed.

Another important challenge facing the current state of growth investing is the evolution of the economy, which is vastly different from the one Price faced when he pioneered growth investing in the 1930s. We have transitioned from a hard-asset (inventory, plant, equipment, etc.), industrial-based economy to a soft-asset, service-based economy, and this has a dramatic impact on a company's book value. Today, a good portion of a company's book value may consist of intellectual property and intangible assets, such as patents or brands. This is particularly true for companies in growth-oriented sectors like healthcare, media, technology, and consumer products. This has the practical impact of depressing book value and earnings for many companies in these industries because many of the investments these companies make to build value (R&D, marketing) are expensed through the income statement rather than capitalized on the balance sheet and depreciated, like a physical plant would. Consequently, price-to-book and price-to-earnings multiples today should be higher, all things being equal, and comparisons versus hard-asset and soft-asset companies using price value multiples are misleading at best. The end result is that growth-oriented market benchmarks may be inappropriately skewed toward soft-asset companies.

Style benchmarks can help investors understand the stocks generally considered to be style specific and, thus, the appropriateness of the investments their managers are buying. Style benchmarks are also a useful tool for performance measurement, but must be used in concert with other tools like peer group analysis. Given their shortcomings, however, style benchmarks should be used as guideposts, not straightjackets.

Pitfalls of Growth Investing

A discussion of growth investing would not be complete without a discussion of both the benefits and the shortcomings of the discipline. When it comes to growth investing, the rewards of significant returns are alluring. But as with any reward, there are potential pitfalls, as well as ways to avoid them.

For most growth investments, the opportunity for high returns is coupled with the potential for high risk in terms of both volatility and capital loss. When growth investing fails, it is most often a failure to properly assess growth opportunities. For an example of this, you need look no further than the dot-com boom of the late 1990s. Price multiples were high for these companies for several years, but the stocks did not come unglued until the growth stopped or the profit windfall did not materialize.

Pioneering work in investor behavior by academics like Daniel Kahneman, 2002 Nobel Prize-winner in Economics, help shed some light on this topic.[4] These behavioral psychologists discovered that investors demonstrate some consistent biases in their investment practices. They tend to "anchor," extrapolating recent invents into the future. They overestimate their ability to forecast accurately and they tend to be unreasonably optimistic in their growth forecasts. Taken together, growth investors may have a propensity toward unrealistically high growth expectations. In fact, we believe that this is the Achilles heel of growth investing. Even growth stocks with very high price multiples ultimately "grow into" their valuation – a sideways trending stock price in the worst case. On the other hand, a high multiple stock that fails to deliver on growth forecasts is often met with a steep price decline.

These biases can be measured empirically, allowing us to prove the point and suggest some remedies. Let's start with investors' expectations for growth. Since 1982, stock market analysts have maintained an expectation of 14 percent for profit growth for large (S&P 500) companies.[5] As Kahneman et al would opine, they have proven to be too optimistic. From a period of 1951-1998, a sample of over 2,900 public companies generated the following results, on average:

Growth of Income		Dividend Yield		Inflation		Real GDP
10%	=	2.5%	+	4.0%	+	3.5%

The data suggests that companies, in aggregate, only grow their earnings, after dividends, at the rate of nominal GDP (real GDP plus inflation).[6] In the face of the power of this data, why do securities analysts overestimate growth by 40 percent? While agency bias (fluffing numbers for investment banking clients) may explain part of it, over-exuberance in growth expectations is probably the primary culprit.

This analysis gives us a framework for evaluating growth going forward. In a low inflation world, economists are hard-pressed to forecast nominal GDP growth rates beyond 5 to 6 percent. This suggests a relatively modest expectation for average earnings growth, with dividends adding another 2 percent. Investors should be suspect of high double-digit growth forecasts for all but the best aggressive growth stocks. We suggest that investors adopt a more reasonable threshold for defining a successful growth stock at 10 percent, which amounts to roughly double the rate of nominal GDP.[7]

We've seen that investors' earnings expectations are too high on average, but what about persistence? Historically, by far the most powerful factor for predicting future earnings performance has been recent earnings results. This is an example of anchoring, where investors base their expectations for the future upon events in the recent past. Sounds reasonable enough, but data suggests this bias does not pay off.

Likelihood of Company Maintaining Growth Stock Status[8]						
1980-2003	All Sectors	Tech	Health Care	Consumer Staples	Consumer Cyclicals	Finance
3 Years	51%	55%	57%	57%	55%	41%
5 Years	37%	35%	37%	45%	39%	23%
10 Years	12%	10%	19%	27%	16%	8%
20 Years	2%	2%	4%	5%	1%	1%

This study focused on those companies that have cumulatively outperformed the market for at least 10 years, and have outperformed at least in 7 out of the 10 years.

The data suggests that of the companies that establish themselves as successful growth companies, only about 50 percent keep the above-average growth going for three years. Looking out five years, only about one-third still make the cut, and only about 10 percent maintain their growth status for 10 years. This data, as well as other studies suggest strong earnings growth is tough to come by and growth companies don't tend to keep that status for long.[9]

There are some lessons here that are very applicable for growth investors. Investors tend to be overly bullish in their forecasts, put too high an emphasis on the accuracy of these forecasts, and believe recent growers will continue this growth well into the future.

Obviously, being on the wrong side of these decisions can be dangerous to an investment portfolio.

An Alternative Approach to Growth Investing

Can these biases be overcome? We believe investors consistently underestimate the power of mean reversion in a competitive economy. High profits are a magnet for competition, and few competitive advantages aren't competed away over the course of only a few years. Competition doesn't mean disaster; it just causes profits or growth to revert to the mean. There have been exceptions over the years, however, in the names of sustainable growth franchises like Coca Cola, Johnson & Johnson, McDonalds, Procter & Gamble, and Cisco Systems.

While no tool is perfect, our firm employs a multi-faceted technique to help compensate for some of these pitfalls. We think of a business as an empty box. Money goes into the box in terms of capital – equity and debt capital, retained earnings, capital investments, and acquisitions. There are more, but this is a good start. Hopefully, money comes out of the box in terms of cash flow. By cash flow, we mean real economic earnings, stripping out accounting-oriented, non-cash factors like depreciation, pension expense, and others. It is not that these accounting figures are not meaningful, they are just estimates of reality. Cash is not. It is hard to manipulate and easier to count. We call it "measuring what matters."

This simple box metaphor allows an investor to answer the two most important questions one can have about a company: How much capital has management deployed in this business, and, how much cash has the company generated from these investments? Only companies that generate higher cash returns than the cost of their capital generate any wealth for shareholders. And it is the growth of the difference between cash returns and a company's cost of capital that generates wealth over time.[10]

This methodology allows an investor to capture the three drivers a company has at their disposal to increase profits: sales growth, margin expansion, and capital deployment. Stronger sales and/or higher margins can increase cash profits: this is the numerator. Capital deployment reflects management's investment decisions in their business: this is the denominator. The ratio, called return on invested capital (ROIC) is a quick, handy report card to measure whether or not a company is creating value for its shareholders.

Wal-Mart provides an excellent working example. For years since its founding, Wal-Mart was an earnings juggernaut and a homerun for investors. Then, in the mid-1990s, the retail giant exhibited continued earnings per share growth, yet the company's cash returns on capital declined, as the company was in the process of building out its SuperCenters nationwide. While the ROIC numerator went up, the denominator went up even more. After initially being fooled by the continued growth in earnings, investors gradually reduced the price multiple they were willing to pay for Wal-Mart's earnings, prompting a multi-year period of underperformance. Once the SuperCenter build-out matured in the late 1990s and Wal-Mart continued to execute its low price strategy, the ROIC trend turned and the stock price again outperformed.

This methodology is conceptually simple and sound, but, more importantly, helps tilt the tough odds of identifying sustainable growth companies in an investor's favor. While finding the next Wal-Mart is not easy, there are several characteristics that have led to long-term outperformance. Fortunately, most if not all can be captured in a well-thought-out ROIC calculation.

Long-Term Outperformance Versus Market[11]

	Distinguishing Factors			No Correlation to Outperformance		
Time Period	ROE	Gross Margins	Share Repurchase	5-Yr Sales Growth	Price/Book	P/E
1952-1969	3.1%	6.6%	-8.1%	0.7%	1.04	.95
1970-1989	3.3%	3.4%	-9.9%	0.3%	1.02	1.03
1990-2003	7.8%	9.1%	-10.0%	-0.1%	1.03	1.00

This study focused on those companies that have cumulatively outperformed the market for at least 10 years, and have outperformed at least in 7 out of the 10 years

The data is remarkably consistent and tells an interesting story. Sustainable growth and long-term outperformance are tied to superior returns on equity (or capital), high gross margins (which suggests pricing power), and capital discipline (using either capital investment to sales or share repurchase). Five-year sales growth or valuation added no value when trying to identify successful growth companies.

Successful growth companies are those that generate high returns on their investments, have the pricing power necessary to maintain high gross margins, and both generate free cash flow and have the discipline to invest it prudently. When they don't have high return investment opportunities, they use excess cash to repurchase their own stock. We believe companies that generate these characteristics will continue to be outperformers and ROIC analysis helps an investor measure the key attributes for success.

Tying it all Together for Growth Investors

In order to navigate the complexities of investing in growth stocks, advisors and investors need to not only understand the concepts behind growth investing, but also the variations in defining what a growth stock is and how growth stocks are valued. In doing so, they will be able to select managers with whose criteria they agree, and effectively manage the risk associated with growth investing.

From T. Rowe Price to Warren Buffett, successful growth investors have provided the blueprints to profitable growth investing. If an investor keeps it simple and pays close attention to what is real, i.e., cash on cash returns, the uniqueness of a company's product or service, and the ability to defend their franchise, investors in these growth stocks can be handsomely rewarded. These kinds of companies do not come around all the time, if they did, investing would be easy. But like the lion laying in wait, investors who possess the right combination of patience, skill, and recognition of opportunity can pounce and achieve outsized returns, becoming the king of their own investing jungle.

❖❖❖

---

[1] This is an illustration using theoretical data. The scenario presumes growth rates are sustained for 10 years and then revert to the mean over the next 5 years. Market multiples and discount rates are used for all 3 scenarios.
[2] "Growth Investing," New York University Leonard N. Stern School of Business. http://pages.stern.nyu.edu/~adamodar/New_Home_Page/invphillectures/growth.html
[3] "Common Stocks and Uncommon Profits and Other Writings," by Philip A. Fisher, p. 57, John Wiley and Sons, May 1996.
[4] "Growth or Value? Yes!" author, Roxbury Capital Management, LLC, 2003.
[5] *Journal of Portfolio Management*, Summer 1998.
[6] Source: IBES
[7] "The Level and Persistence of Growth Rates", *Journal of Finance*, April 2003
[8] "What Makes a Growth Company", Roxbury Capital Management, LLC, 2003
[9] "Equity Portfolio Strategy Update", by Vadim Zlotnikov, Sanford C. Bernstein & Co., LLC, February 26, 2004
[10] "The Level and Persistence of Growth Rates", Journal of Finance, April 2003
[11] For more information on this topic please reference, "The Quest for Value", by G. Bennett Stewart, III
[12] "Equity Portfolio Strategy Update", by Vadim Zlotnikov, Sanford C. Bernstein & Co., LLC, February 26, 2004

This material is provided for informational and educational purposes only. The statements contained herein are the opinions of Roxbury Capital Management, LLC and are subject to change without notice.
This report contains no investment recommendations and should not be construed as specific tax, legal, financial planning, or investment advice. Clients should consult their professional advisors before making any tax or investment decisions. Investing entails risk including the loss of principal and there is no assurance that an investment will provide positive performance over any period of time. It is important to review investment objectives, risk tolerance, tax objectives, and liquidity needs before choosing an investment style or manager. Information was obtained from third party sources, which we believe to be reliable but not guaranteed. Past performance is no guarantee of future results.

20

INTERNATIONAL EQUITY

Patrick J. McCall, CFA®
Executive Vice President, Portfolio Manager
Templeton Private Client Group
Bill Deakyne, CFA®
Vice President, Director of Product Management
Franklin Templeton Private Client Group

Americans are often faulted for being a self-centered people, with little awareness or appreciation for the cultures of other nations. If their investment portfolios are any indication, there is plenty of truth to the stereotype: although U.S. stocks account for fully half of the total value in global equity markets, U.S. pension plans held only about 13 percent of their equities in international stocks in 2002, according to Greenwich Associates. Individual U.S. investors are focused on their home market as well: the Investment Company Institute reports that assets in mutual funds with international objectives hold just 13 percent of all U.S. equity mutual funds assets.

The choice of investing at home or overseas, however, is more than just an abstract allocation among capital markets. Economies and stock markets of individual countries are increasingly linked, led by large corporations that operate worldwide. Investors who anchor themselves to the U.S. market forfeit significant potential benefits of an international perspective – reduction of volatility in portfolio returns, a broader set of quality investment opportunities, and participation in the highest-growth regions of the global economy. International investing presents additional challenges as well: to complement the traditional stock-picking skills required for domestic portfolios (consider that not all managers are stock pickers, some are more country allocators), successful international managers must be experts in their knowledge of foreign currencies, economies and financial structures, and integrating those insights into a portfolio that meets a client's risk appetite.

Episodic Returns

U.S. investors actually can be forgiven for not placing more in the overseas markets in the 1990s, due to a long stretch of disappointing returns. During the mid-1990s, returns from U.S. and international stocks were comparable, but the U.S. market was far stronger early in the decade, and in the run-up of technology and telecom stocks in the late 1990s. Figure 1 compares the long-term return history of the Morgan Stanley Capital International EAFE (Europe, Asia and Far East) index, priced in U.S. dollars, to the MSCI US market index. The graph illustrates gross rolling three-year returns, annualized, from 1980 to 2003. What is not apparent from the three-year returns, however, is that international's outperformance tends to come in bursts of six or 12 months duration: to benefit from the international markets, investors probably need to maintain long-term investment commitments.

Looking back to the 1980s, however, investing in international equities provided a sustained period of higher returns than the U.S. market. The favorable translation effects of a falling dollar created some of the advantage, as did dramatic appreciation in the Japanese market of the late 1980s. In general, though, the international markets for years offered an embedded extra return, which became part of the conventional wisdom surrounding international investing.

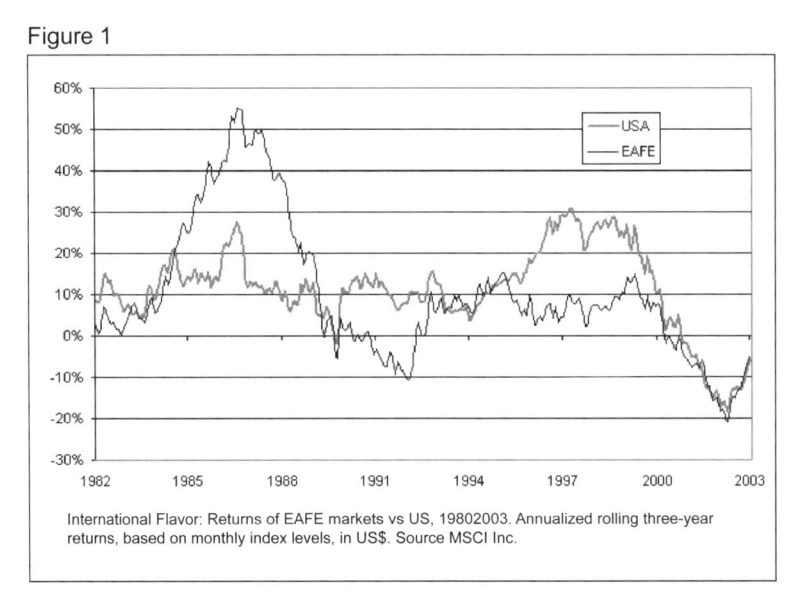

Figure 1

International Flavor: Returns of EAFE markets vs US, 19802003. Annualized rolling three-year returns, based on monthly index levels, in US$. Source MSCI Inc.

The bigger benefit for U.S. investors, however, has lain in the interplay of the United States and international markets. Through the 1980s and until the middle 1990s, the biggest influence on overseas markets tended to be their domestic economies. The independent trajectories of individual countries' growth, plus the large number of markets that make up the EAFE index, yielded a pattern of returns for international equities as a whole that little resembled that of the United State. On average, the correlation between the MSCI US and EAFE indexes was about 0.5, varying from 0.4 to 0.6, depending on the time period under study. The low correlation between the broad U.S. market and MSCI EAFE index offered significant reduction in the volatility of returns to a portfolio owning both assets. Correlation between two variables measures the degree to which they fluctuate together over time: two series that move in the same direction, in the same proportion, at the same time, show a correlation coefficient of 1.0, while series that move in exactly opposite directions have a negative correlation (and a coefficient of –1.0.) Series that have no relationship in their movements would be uncorrelated (and a coefficient of zero).

Figure 2 plots the efficient frontiers of the S&P 500 and EAFE for the 1980s and 1990s, showing the impact on volatility of returns from adding the modest correlation of international stocks to U.S.

portfolios. The circled points on each line represent a portfolio comprised of 70 percent U.S. stocks and 30 percent international. During the 1980s, adding 30 percent international stocks cut standard deviation of returns to 14.6 percent from 16.3 percent for an S&P 500 portfolio. The 1970s, not pictured, produced a return enhancement and risk reduction through an allocation to international investing similar to the 1980s.

Figure 2

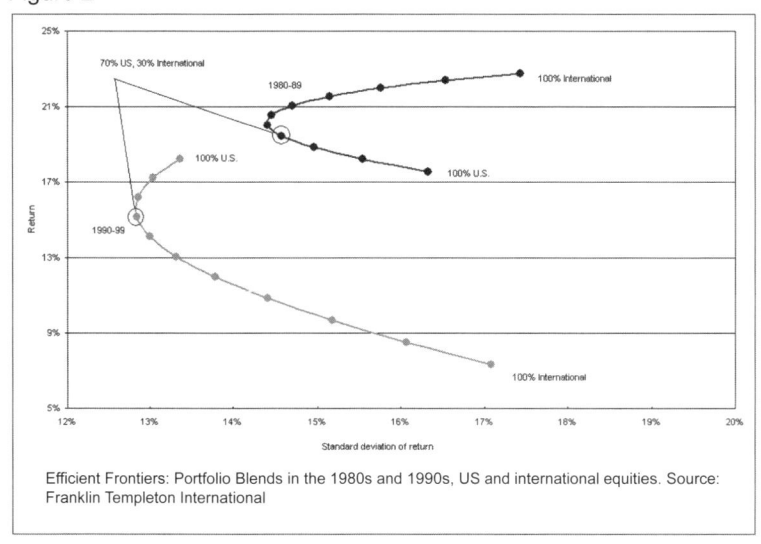

Efficient Frontiers: Portfolio Blends in the 1980s and 1990s, US and international equities. Source: Franklin Templeton International

International investing in the 1990s was less compelling in two respects, delivering lower returns than the United States, and with less diversification benefit. In mid-decade the United States started to dominate the global investment scene, due in part to its unprecedented economic expansion and claim to much of the information technology innovation, so world markets appear to have reacted less to their own domestic fundamentals than what happened on Wall Street. A surging U.S. tech sector pulled along its international counterparts, and their market-cap momentum gained, correlations among markets shot up, at least temporarily. Correlations rose, leaving international stocks with only a marginal diversification benefit to U.S. portfolios in the 1990s; adding 30 percent EAFE to an S&P 500 portfolio cut standard deviation of return by just one-half of a percent, to 12.8 percent.

Globalization

The free lunch of systematically higher returns that international investors came to expect in the 1970s and 1980s has probably disappeared for good. Correlations among the U.S. and international markets may not return to the low levels of the 1970s and 1980s, but they have fallen from the unusual highs of the late 1990s. Correlation among markets is cyclical, so it is reasonable to expect a return to the lower correlations of more normal market periods. International investing, nevertheless, still offers compelling benefits to U.S.-based investors, in particular valuations: in early 2004, international markets were more reasonably priced than the U.S. markets on measures of earnings and cash flow, even after outperforming the U.S. markets by 700 basis points in each of 2002 and 2003.

More enduring, though, are the changes in the equity markets from the evolving competitive environment and balance of power among sectors and companies in the global economy of the 21st century. Corporations have doubled their international production over the last 20 years; as an example, consider auto production, much of which has been shifted close to the end markets. Mergers and acquisitions across borders have sharply increased, so that even product brands traditionally thought to be "American," like Q-Tips, Green Giant, Frigidaire and Gerber, now have non-U.S. owners.[1]

At the same time, companies, industries and economies are changing their fundamental structures. German banks and insurance companies are unwinding their controlling stakes in industrial businesses, and privatization continues across Europe. The Japanese banking system has undergone a consolidation and recapitalization, and monolithic industrial corporations across Asia are adopting more shareholder-focused philosophies. The result of this corporate evolution is streamlined, concentrated industries on a global scale, where many of the biggest companies operating in the United States, and competing with S&P 500 companies, are based in Europe or Asia.

By looking for investment ideas across the global economy, U.S. investors in international markets have a far broader opportunity set for finding mispriced stocks than those restricting their purchases to the home market. About 15,000 companies are listed in the U.S. markets, but with 50,000 more listed around the world, global investors can choose from a greater number of potentially undervalued stocks. "If you search worldwide," says international investing pioneer Sir John Templeton, "you will find more and better bargains than by studying only one nation. You will also gain the safety of diversification." A wider choice is especially important when U.S. investors face the paradox of an uncertain economic picture combined with a domestic market already discounting strong growth. The benefit of a wider range of choices is intuitive, but confirmed by investment theory: the broader the universe of independent choices, the greater the potential value added, according to Richard Grinold's Fundamental Law of Active Management. [2]

Emerging Markets

The reasoning in favor of international stocks applies equally to the 30 developing economies around the world defined as "emerging markets." They offer similar attractions as stocks in their larger international counterparts: a broad opportunity set, even lower correlation with the U.S market than developed market foreign stocks and appealing valuations. The emerging economies are growing rapidly, both in their export sectors and domestic economies, and corporate governance and minority shareholder representation is improving. (It is interesting to note that Japan was characterized as an emerging market prior to its major bull market during the 1980s.) The knowledge and skill required for successful emerging market investing is even more specialized than what is needed for the developed markets, but it is possible for astute managers to regularly beat their benchmarks. Nonetheless, investments in emerging markets carry considerable political and currency risk, returns can be volatile, and trading is often illiquid. That said, returns in emerging markets have been excellent for several years, and offer excellent prospects as the emerging markets leverage the ongoing global economic expansion.

New Investment Signals

As the markets evolved in a global dimension the 1990s, the investment signals required for successful international investing – the second driver of value-added postulated in Grinold's Fundamental Law – appear to have changed dramatically as well. In the 1970s and 1980s, the focus of international investing was on countries – selecting country stock markets for their economic growth and potential currency appreciation against the dollar. Business operations were predominantly local, and cross-border investing was less prevalent, so that reaction to growth in a country's economy was confined to its own stock market.

Industry and Sector

Researchers at the Atlanta Federal Reserve looking at the world stock markets conclude that for the share prices of globally diversified companies, global economic developments have become a far bigger influence than country-specific events. They also find, logically, that these effects are amplified where the home countries have open financial systems that foster foreign investment.[3] Other financial researchers have extended this analysis beyond global factors to the sectors and industries where companies operate. They find that sector and industry effects have become more meaningful than country factors, but especially so for large firms. Mid- and small-sized companies in international markets are more likely to serve their domestic or adjacent regional markets, exposing their earnings to a diversified set of economic fundamentals, and creating the potential for greater diversification and risk reduction versus a U.S.-based portfolio.

The emergence of these influences requires a greater research effort by international investors to know many companies intimately, but provides a benefit as well. Many sectors and industries, examples being retail, banking and insurance, telecoms and utilities, exhibit low correlations, which should allow an additional layer of diversification to an international portfolio.[4] This is due in part to the fact that some industries are more globally oriented. For example, the supply and demand for electricity in Switzerland has very little to do with that of the United States.

Managers have reacted accordingly, reports InterSec Research, a firm that has followed U.S. investing overseas since the 1970s: about 70 percent of actively-managed international equities owned by U.S. institutions are today invested with managers who invest from the bottom up.

Country and Currency

The main reason for the diffusion of country and currency effects is the influence on global economic structures, built to foster world trade. One example is the World Trade Organization; another is the adoption of a single currency across the European Union. But currencies and political developments within individual countries still bear on investment results, adding volatility and uncertainty.

Figure 3 illustrates annualized three-year rolling returns of the MSCI EAFE index, measured in U.S. dollars and in local currencies from 1990 through 2003. There is no obvious pattern to the behavior of currencies: the dollar-denominated index has both won and lost against the local currency version, in both strong and weak markets. Since the 1970s there have been four major moves in the dollar, for and against U.S. investors, lasting an average of seven to eight years. In 2002 and 2003 the weak dollar was a decided strength for international investors, when dollar-based portfolios earned an incremental nine percent and 18 percent, respectively.

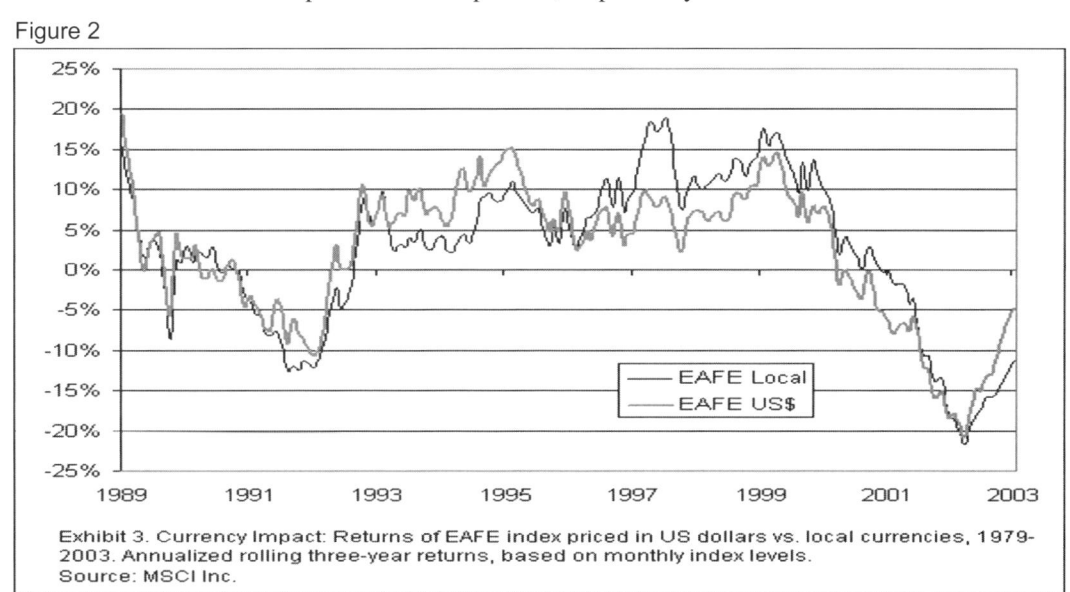

Figure 2

Exhibit 3. Currency Impact: Returns of EAFE index priced in US dollars vs. local currencies, 1979-2003. Annualized rolling three-year returns, based on monthly index levels.
Source: MSCI Inc.

Currency hedging was more prevalent for top-down international strategies of a decade ago, when investors made a few choices of countries rather than many decisions on individual stocks. Today's bottom-up managers do take currencies into account, however, as a part of their fundamental company research, and focus on selecting the right companies over trying to outguess the currency markets.

Although currencies have moved to the background, international investors are still acutely aware of the political risks of their target countries. Concerns are not confined to the risk of a political *coup d'etat* in developing nations; even large ostensibly stable countries present political risk as well. German GDP, for instance, has been stagnant, and investors need to weigh the political consequences of the incumbent government's choice of fiscal and monetary tools to right the economy. In addition, many large developed economies are facing public pension system crises over the coming 20 years, requiring difficult political and economic choices.

Equity Style

The early generations of international investors sought out the most attractive countries, and did not directly address the question of style, along the lines of growth versus value, or large cap versus small. Most of them probably fit the middle-of-the-road category now known as "Growth at a Reasonable Price" or GARP. Over time, however, as U.S. consultants focused on recommending international managers to their institutional clients, they assigned style designations as a means to fitting managers into client portfolios.

Style as a means of evaluating and choosing international managers became a necessity in the 1990s. Growth and value styles went through typical episodes of strong and weak performance early in the decade, but as the tech bubble inflated growth portfolios significantly outperformed value, for a time at least. In the following collapse of tech stocks, value strategies excelled, and investors and consultants were obliged to focus on the distinction. In response to growing interest, index providers have created and refined style measures within their broad international indexes; these measures call for going beyond classifying stocks as growth or value on reported financial data, to apply universal accounting and valuation criteria to all companies. Managers and consultants disagree on how the concepts should be applied, and how valuable the distinctions are to evaluating performance, but style is likely a permanent part of the international investing framework.

Financial researchers have studied the performance differences between international growth and value equity styles for about 10 years. The conclusions tend to significantly favor value over growth and smaller firms over large; researchers assert that investing with managers who closely track a broad international index of large capitalization names typically provides little diversification to U.S.-based portfolios.[5] This finding is intuitively logical: growth companies and larger companies are more visible in the markets and get more investor attention, and thus, are the most global and efficiently priced; smaller, less exciting names are likely to be under-followed by analysts and under-appreciated by the markets. Importantly, out-of-the-way stocks also are likely to exhibit return correlations below that of large cap names, and provide greater diversification. Moreover, the returns of international growth and equity styles tend to be uncorrelated (i.e., showing correlation close to zero) with each other, allowing investors one more degree of diversification through combining managers exploiting different styles.

International in Action: Value Added from Active Management

In keeping with the greater complexity of investing overseas, international managers execute their portfolio strategies in many different ways, offering investors a variety of risk profiles that can yield quite different results.

- At one end of the spectrum of international manager value-added are index funds that replicate the returns of a broad international index of markets in developed economies, like the MSCI EAFE. Investable indexes are also available for the emerging markets, and for the developed and emerging markets together. This option is seldom, if ever, used in the separately managed account world.

- Active management begins with "enhanced" index funds that, like the index, invest in more than one thousand stocks, but make subtle over- and underweighting decisions on individual issues, typically relying on quantitative models. These funds produce modest, but persistent, returns above the index, targeting perhaps 100 basis points per year while keeping tracking error against the index modest as well, to about two percent. Enhanced index funds typically are offered by very large managers – those who possess the requisite investment scale to operate index funds efficiently, and the resources for effective research that covers all the world's markets. This option is seldom, if ever, used in the separately managed account world.

- The next step is to "passive/active" (or "active/passive") portfolios. In these strategies the manager sticks to the benchmark weights for allocations to countries (or to sectors), but expresses his or her point of view in the sector and industry weights (or country weights) of the portfolios. Some managers vary this style by actively managing both country and sector allocations, but staying with preset limits with respect to the weights of the benchmark. In order to stay close to the benchmark, these strategies generally need to hold between 800 and 1200 stocks.

- Fully active managers construct their portfolios from an aggregation of individual stock selections, without regard for index weights. Those managers expressing a strong preference for growth, value or small cap need this level of freedom from benchmark constraints to carry out their styles; accordingly, these portfolios create greater benchmark tracking error. Some managers add opportunistic allocations of emerging market stocks to their strategies, although these holdings are often limited to 20 percent or so of the account. These strategies typically hold 50 to 100 securities at one time, although "concentrated" versions are also available with just 40 to 60 positions.

All of these strategies can be carried out for the developed international markets, on a global basis including the U.S. market, or restricted to specific regions. The choice of strategy depends on the investor's appetite for volatility, how closely he or she wishes to follow a benchmark, whether there is a need to balance an overexposure somewhere else in the portfolio, and the investor's preference to avoid certain countries or industries.

Many international stocks are listed in the U.S. markets or traded in as American Depository Receipts (ADRs), eliminating the costs and complex trading, settlement and custody in overseas markets that international investors had to contend with 20 years ago. Actively managed global or international separate accounts with proper diversification can be created with an investment of $100,000.

International managers often have been successful in exploiting the many dimensions of investing overseas. Consultants report that, as a group, international managers have turned in better relative recent performance versus their benchmark more often than their counterpart U.S. managers. The investment manager database of Callan Associates shows that for the five years ended December 2003, the median manager of a U.S.-based core portfolio returned 0.31 percent annually, versus –0.57 percent for the S&P 500, while the median core EAFE manager earned 2.87 percent annually over the same period, against –0.06 percent for their benchmark. Moreover, international managers ranking as low as the third quartile managed to beat the index in those five years. Thus, the Fundamental Law of Active Management holds for international equities: At any one time, the valuation of markets around the world varies widely, and talented international managers are able to find cheap countries and companies. More opportunities and more ways to apply skill should add more value.

International Should Not Be Foreign

Most of the world's stocks and markets are based outside the United States, meaning that opportunities for excess return are widespread and, as a group, international managers have tended to add value more consistently overseas than managers restricted to the U.S. markets. The correlation of international markets' returns with the United States has risen in the evolving global economy, but adding an international allocation should still provide significant diversification to U.S.-based equity portfolios. International equity products are available to meet the risk appetites of any investor, and international value and growth equity styles can be combined in one portfolio to generate even more diversification. International investing is not for opportunists; however, the best returns typically come from short, and unannounced, periods of strong performance, so that international equities deserve a permanent place in the portfolio of most investors.

❖ ❖ ❖

---

[1] Brooks, Robin, and Marco Del Negro. September 2002. "The Rise in Comovement across National Stock Markets: Market Integration or IT Bubble?" Working paper, Federal Reserve Bank of Atlanta.
[2] Grinold, Richard C. 1989. "The Fundamental Law of Active Management." *Journal of Portfolio Management*, vol 15 no 3 (Spring): 30-37
[3] Brooks, Robin, and Marco Del Negro. September 2002.
[4] "Strategies for International Investing," Franklin Templeton Institutional, November 2002.
[5] Sinquefield, Rex. 1994. "Where are the Gains from International Diversification?" *Financial Analysts Journal*, January/February 1996. Conclusions in the article were reiterated in recent interviews.

Disclaimer: The views expressed herein are the views of the authors, and not necessarily the views of Franklin Templeton Investments.

21

THE VALUE OF VALUE INVESTING

ING Investment Management

"Success in investing doesn't correlate with I.Q. once you're above the level of 25. Once you have ordinary intelligence, what you need is the temperament to control the urges that get other people into trouble in investing."

—Warren Buffett

As the bloom began falling off growth stocks in April of 2000, value investing once again entered the limelight. Or was it, rather, that the hare, thinking he had enough of a lead on the tortoise, took a nap and the tortoise just kept right on going?

To formulate the question from the advisor or consultant point of view, is value investing something that will treat investors well through good times and bad? The answer is a resounding "yes." However, that "yes" requires a certain type of investor mindset. We know that, typically, most individuals buy stocks that are hot, then sell them when they are out of favor. So they generally end up buying high and selling low. They trade in and out with value managers and in and out with growth managers—precisely at the wrong time. Value investing requires patience, a virtue not often found in today's investors.

But value investing has a place in most portfolios. Instead of taking a random walk down Wall Street, the value investor's objective is to take advantage of the inefficiencies of the market by accurately valuing companies that the market has mispriced. Fostering a comprehensive understanding of the benefits of value investing and its place in investors' portfolios is the objective of this chapter.

Value According to the Masters

Value investing is most closely associated with Benjamin Graham and David Dodd, who literally wrote the book on value investing, "Security Analysis." This book is a staple of many securities analysis courses. The work stresses looking at company fundamentals and the relationship of the stock price to those underlying fundamentals. Those ratios—price to earnings, price to cash flow, price to sales—are what tell much of the real story.

Today, there are three different camps in the value world. Traditional managers follow the classical Graham and Dodd methodology. They buy good businesses that are well-financed and, thus, have lower risk. The second camp consists of managers who buy what are commonly called "toxic waste" whose future is difficult to determine. Those managers who buy them can be very successful, but this represents a riskier style of value investing.

Relative value, the newest approach, looks at the entire market and picks the best value within each sector or industry. For example, if the semiconductor industry is selling at high multiples, a relative value manager will look for the cheapest stock within that sector according to his or her definition of cheap. A traditional or classic value manager would not consider the semiconductor sector at those multiples. Relative value managers can invest in practically anything because they will have a unique definition of cheap and will be able to justify anything that is purchased. (See chapter 22 for more information on Relative Value.) The classic value manager operates on an entirely different level.

In Graham and Dodd's "Security Analysis," which quickly became the bible of all value security analysts and spawned such famous investors as Warren Buffett, John Templeton, William Ruane, Marshall Weinberg, and others, the authors present entirely different answers to the questions posed by most analysts—even some value analysts—of which stock to buy and at what price. Graham and Dodd viewed investing as a commitment of funds. They proposed asking the questions, "To what enterprise [should the investor commit funds]?" and "On what terms is the commitment proposed?" These questions take into consideration not just the security and its price, but also the fundamental condition of the company relative to the market conditions of the time.[1]

Graham and Dodd based their analysis on four fundamental elements:

- The security
- The time
- The price
- The person

The personal element, or what is commonly known in the investment world as suitability, is the most important consideration. A security investment that might be appropriate for a $20 million net worth business entrepreneur may not be appropriate for a $500,000 net worth widow with a fixed income. Of course, the sophistication and experience of the investor is the second part of the suitability equation.

The time, or state of a company's condition during which a security is analyzed, may affect the conclusions drawn. Changes in a company's outlook may influence an analyst's view of the stock. If a company's balance sheet is not solid, yet the market price is only $8, an analyst may not consider the stock a real value, even though the price seems to be low. If that same company improves its balance sheet, however, and the market is not yet assigning a price that reflects that change in condition, the analyst is much more likely to consider the stock of that same company a real value. Hence, the conditions of the company have a bearing on the analyst's view of the stock at the time.[2]

The price should be analyzed according to the company's intrinsic value, which is based on the fundamental factors found on the company's balance sheet.

Ideally, a stock's market price would be 50 percent of the company's intrinsic value. This type of valuation would be attractive to any value manager. A stock like Exxon selling at $30 with earnings of $2—a P/E of 15—that goes to $60 a share is a prime example. But reaching that $60 price with a 30 P/E requires patience for the market to recognize the value represented when the multiple is 15. Legendary portfolio manager Peter Lynch made considerable profits on companies that went up 10- or 12-fold. He did that by not limiting his upside, by not having a target return of 20 or 30 percent. He believed having such a target puts a price limit on the stock. Analysts who put such profit limits on stocks rarely look at the underlying earnings or fundamentals which, then, limits the upside. This doesn't mean the stock price should be ignored; the stock price should be evaluated on the basis of the value of the business as a whole, and the potential that business may have for the future.

Value in the Eyes of the Institutional Consultant

The institutional consulting world generally splits the equity markets down the middle, calling one side value and the other side growth. But, not all stocks fit clearly into the value or growth labeling slots. Case in point: the Russell 1000 Value Index and the Russell 1000 Growth Index each have 328 companies. But there is duplication of companies in each index because these particular companies fit both the growth and value criteria Russell uses. The stocks that do not clearly fit either of these categories are called either core or relative value.

One would think that if a stock is not a value stock, then it must be a growth stock. However, the two styles are not mirror images of each other. The criteria of a value manager versus the criteria of a growth manager are not symmetrical. Therefore, a more precise definition of value stocks would be, "companies that are selling at low price to earnings, low price to book, low price to sales, low price to cash flow, low price to free cash flow." These are the fundamental factors of value stocks. When examining the financial statements of a company whose stock is considered "value," the appropriate price of the stock will most often be the price reached by applying an analysis based upon the measures just mentioned.

Growth stock managers generally look at income statements rather than balance sheets. They look at top and bottom line growth and sometimes dividend growth. Some growth managers will look only at the profit and loss statements and may completely ignore the market price. A few growth managers will see a company they like, and if the earnings and revenue are growing, they will buy the stock regardless of the price.

Institutional consultants also tend to slice and dice value and growth into style boxes. Compare this to a tic-tac-toe board: value, growth, mid cap, small cap, and large cap with core being at the center. Some managers say they don't fit into a style box and, therefore, these consultants won't hire them. Or, a consultant will put that manager into some kind of style box, whether or not the manager agrees.

Advice from Graham and Dodd for the 21st Century

In 1999 and 2000, many value managers abandoned the traditional or classic value stocks and justified their drift into stocks like Cisco Systems, America Online, and Global Crossing by saying those stocks were cheap within their sector. The problem was this: if investors hired XYZ value manager and ABC growth manager in 2000, they ended up with far more exposure to growth than they realized. The XYZ value manager held that, "Cisco is value, Lucent is value, Nortel is value." As a result, the investors had an overlap of positions with the growth manager, and the client ended up with twice as much Cisco, Lucent, and Nortel. It was exactly the opposite in the 1980s. The growth managers were coming into the value side of the equation, and some growth managers were even adding the word "value" in the names of their firms.

The advice Graham and Dodd would give us today would be to look for the companies that have staying power, that have a competitive edge, and whose value the market has not yet realized. They would warn us to not chase the hot dot or justify purchases in order to get in on what's attracting the most attention from the general investing public. Of course, since 2000, there haven't been many hot dots.

So how would this apply to today's environment?

The market of today is difficult for most investors—as well as for many advisors and consultants. The investing public has looked upon value and growth as seasonal investment venues. When growth is in season, value is out. When value is in season, growth is out. The classic philosophy behind value, however, is to buy companies that have good solid fundamentals and exceptional earnings potential which have not been recognized by the market. It also emphasizes looking at the company in a much broader sense. "Graham developed a framework for making people think through what those numbers really mean," says manager William Ruane in Janet C. Lowe's book, "Benjamin Graham on Value Investing: Lessons from the Dean of Wall Street."[3] He did not uncompromisingly follow an investment formula. Instead, he thought about what the fundamentals told the investor about the company as a whole.

Warren Buffett took this concept and ran with it. Every stock Buffett has ever purchased has been analyzed from the standpoint of the company as a whole. He has "transformed what long had been a sideline of Berkshire—the acquisition of entire companies—into the main event."[4] Buffet has adhered to that practice with every stock or company he's ever purchased. What counts is the presence of a competitive advantage, says Buffett. "You want a business that's a big castle with a moat around it and you want that moat to widen over time… We want an economic castle."[5]

Graham would also caution today's advisors and investors about the necessity of putting all managers into a style box, as mentioned earlier. The whole style-box phenomenon came from a focus on performance—a focus not included in the criteria of traditional value analysts. Some style boxes don't match up with a manager's practices. Many times, the style boxes don't match up with the underlying index. Most advisors use the Russell 1000, which represents value, core and growth stocks, but there is significant overlap from large to mid cap and even to small cap within these indexes. Trying to clearly distinguish between large, mid, and small cap introduces a lot of contradiction in the definitions of value, growth, and core.

These distinctions are qualified by different characteristics and their boundaries are not clear. Therefore, it is the job of the investment management consultant or advisor to guide the client in concentrating on the benefits of buying sound companies with excellent prospects for the future rather than focusing on trying to force-fit a manager into a style box. This deeper understanding of value investing should form the basis for the consultant's discussions of value investing with the client. Advisors and consultants must teach clients the comprehensive benefits that value investing holds for their portfolios.

Guiding Investors onto a Low-Risk Path to Investment Success

In educating the client, the consultant must first understand the misconceptions investors may have about value. Ask the average investor to define value investing and we'll hear such statements as, "the opposite of growth" and "buying stocks on the cheap." It is clear that these definitions limit the true meaning of value investing.

By thinking of value as buying cheap stocks, investors mistakenly focus on market price drops without taking into consideration the cause of those price drops. On the other side, investors will use stop losses and sell a company if the stock price drops 10 percent, 20 percent, or whatever downside limit the investor has set. Again, that limits the opportunity for the investor to gain. If the company is sound and the correct analysis has been done, then price drops are, in actuality, opportunities to add to a position rather than a reason to sell a good company.

For example, Warren Buffett's purchase of Washington Post Company stock illustrates this point.[6] In 1973, Buffett purchased a significant portion of Washington Post shares. The economy was horrible, but traditional value investors were in their element. Washington Post's market capitalization had declined to $80 million. Buffett asked himself if the market cap dropped again by half, to $40 million, would that make a purchase of the shares riskier?

An answer based on traditional value according to Buffett would have been, "not at all." Buffett viewed the company already as having a good margin of safety—a nice moat around the castle, so to speak. Another 50 percent drop only would have increased that moat or margin of safety and made the investment that much more attractive. This margin of safety, or moat as Buffett would call it, has absolutely nothing to do with a company's volatility.

With the market backdrop of the Internet Bubble followed by the bear market, investors may be more inclined to appreciate the benefits that classical value investing can offer their portfolios. It is not that investors should never invest in growth stocks; but rather, that value can provide a long-term anchor for their portfolios regardless of what is happening in the market.

The Emotional Side of Value

By understanding investors' misconceptions of value and educating them on a truer method of approaching value, the consultant will be able to better guide the investor in reaching his or her investment objectives. Does that mean each investor's portfolio should include value shares? That depends on the investor's propensity for patient, long-term investing and the consultant's confidence in the particular value portfolio manager.

Clients tend to be emotional. It is those emotional reactions that provide value investors the opportunity to pick up good companies at less than their intrinsic value. Buffet once described the effects of emotions and the psychology of the market this way, "If you think about [the markets] you get these huge swings in valuations. It is the ideal business arrangement as long as you don't go crazy. Human nature has not changed. People will always behave in a manic-depressive way over time. They will offer great values to you."[7]

Emotional responses must be viewed in two ways by the consultant. The emotional responses of investors are the instigators of opportunity for the institutional value investor. On the other hand, individual emotional reactions of clients require the consultant to keep the client on track with his or her investment plan. A value portfolio is a wonderful tool for helping direct the client's emotions toward investment success.

Many firms have taught their advisors not to focus on the emotional side of investing—to encourage investors to stick to a long-term investment discipline that will keep emotions out of the equation. However, emotions should be considered in the same manner as risk. The goal is not to eliminate risk (or emotions); the goal is to manage risk to ensure the greatest probability of success. Avoiding a client's emotions will make them feel that the consultant does not care about their concerns.

It is quite easy for advisors to avoid clients' emotions during a market downturn that is providing opportunity for value investors—they simply don't call their clients! It is difficult to call a client when a portfolio is down 20 or 30 percent. But those who do call send the right message and create the opportunity to educate clients on what value investing can do for their portfolios. Value investing teaches patience. It changes focus from the gyrations of the market to an idea rarely acted upon—that of purchasing a good company at a sale price.

This focus also helps the consultant keep the client on track to achieving the investment objectives that have been outlined for the portfolio. It is much easier to call a client with a down portfolio when the consultant has properly educated that client about the reason value investing works and why taking a long-term investment view is important. We cannot know when the market will recognize a company's true value. We do know, however, that having the patience to buy a good company at the right time, and not before, can pay off richly for the investors.

Value Investing and Academia

There are few investment factors that academically have been demonstrated to work. Historical studies in the value context highlight two such factors. A 1992 paper by Ken French and Eugene Fama,[8] published in *The Journal of Finance*, shows that markets are fairly efficient, except that low P/E and price-to-book value stocks can outperform high multiple stocks over time.

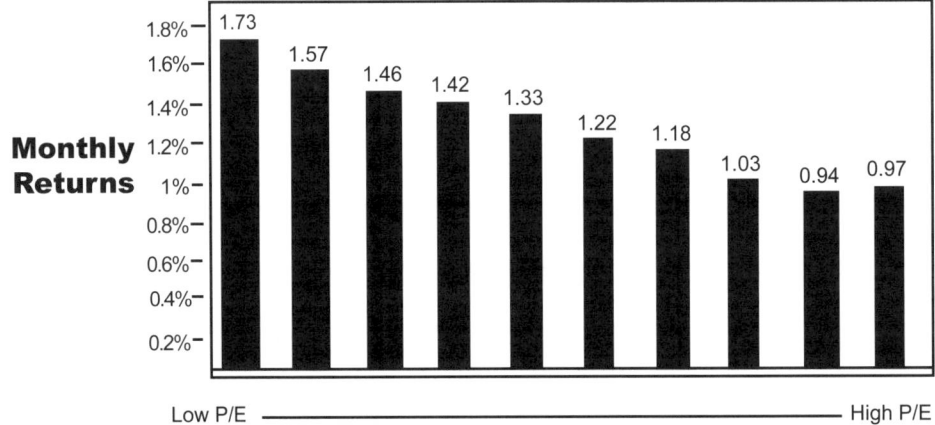

by Price/Earnings Ratio
1963 -1990

Monthly Returns:
- 1.73
- 1.57
- 1.46
- 1.42
- 1.33
- 1.22
- 1.18
- 1.03
- 0.94
- 0.97

Low P/E ————————————————— High P/E

E. Fama & K. French
Journal of Finance, June 1992

One exception is the growth manager who consistently can pick good companies and outperform the indexes over time. There are managers who can do that, but they are few in number. Most people think that go-go growth stocks outperform the slow, dull stocks that are trading at low multiples. That works from time to time, but, typically they experience a bear market like 1973-1974 or 2000-2003 and it wipes them out. By investing in value, investors are playing on much more fertile ground. They don't have to hope they've picked one of the limited number of successful growth managers. And they develop an entirely different view of the inevitable fire sale.

So in looking at academic literature on what works in investing in U.S. equities, there are two factors to consider: P/E and price-to-book. Over the years, the effectiveness of using those two factors has been demonstrated as a follow-up to Graham and Dodd's fundamental tenets of investing.

Large Cap Versus Small Cap

Large cap stocks do not fare better over time than small caps. Small cap stocks inherently carry more risk, and their performance tends to be concentrated in "bunches" of years. These companies are small because they have not established their viability and cannot be evaluated on the same basis as large companies. It is easy to think that a small company might outperform a large company, but there is a flip side to that equation. Take the example of the small hardware store versus Home Depot, or the Kress store versus Wal-Mart. These companies have come into cities and simply annihilated small businesses.

Large value companies provide the margin of safety that offers clients "sleep tight" portfolios. Value investing creates loyalty in clients. The major markets have a long-term upward bias and large cap stocks make up the major markets. Since this long-term bias exists, it is dangerous for an investor not to be fully invested. When good companies are selected for the right reasons and purchased at the right times, a slice in the market price of those companies simply creates more opportunity for investors. That's exactly how Warren Buffett built his fortune, by buying good companies with good prospects at the right time and adding to his position when opportunities arose. Buffet looks for companies that have a sustainable competitive edge. Sustainable means a 20- to 25-year time frame. This time frame corresponds with that most often cited by long-term investment proponents—20 years. Many investors would likely accept that what's good enough for Buffett would be good enough for them.

The Process

There are about 1,350 companies in the United States above the $1 billion market cap. P/E ratio analysis cuts this list in half so that growth stocks like Cisco Systems and Microsoft—classic growth stocks—are excluded.

We use 12 fundamental value measures such as price to sales, price to book, etc., and rank the remaining universe accordingly. Some managers will look at the entire universe and rank order it without eliminating any stocks. To take advantage of the academic work that's been done on value investing, which basically says, "the lower the P/E, the better," we use the proprietary computer screening process only to a certain point. The computer screening is used as a preliminary tool to identify the best companies, then the computers are turned off. At that point, the fundamentals of the company are evaluated as outlined by Graham and Dodd.

By the time the computers are turned off, there are some 125 companies on the focus list. These companies are examined very closely. We attempt to expand upon the analyst's vision of what will go on in each business. Diversification is a critical element since it is impossible for any analyst to know a business completely. Diversification widens the safety moat. Companies are identified as being "out of favor" by evaluating the fundamentals in this manner and by looking at the value the market currently is placing on the company.

"Out of favor" means no hot dots. It emphasizes going against the crowd or being a contrarian. This may not be appealing to a lot of investors, because there is no sex appeal to being out of favor and not knowing when a company might come into favor.

But value investing helps clients manage risk. It helps them sleep at night. And if the consultant does a good job of educating clients about the benefits of value investing have for their portfolios, the consultant can sleep well at night, too.

❖ ❖ ❖

---

1 "Benjamin Graham on Value Investing: Lessons from the Dean of Wall Street," by Janet C. Lowe, Dearborn Trade Publishing, October 1994.

2 "Security Analysis," by Benjamin Graham and David Dodd, McGraw-Hill Trade, Second Edition, October 10, 2002.

3 "Benjamin Graham on Value Investing: Lessons from the Dean of Wall Street," by Janet C. Lowe, Dearborn Trade Publishing, October 1994.

4 "The Warren Buffet You Don☐t KnowAce Stockpicker, of course, and Now Empire Builder," by Anthony Bianco, *Business Week*, July 5, 1999. http://www.businessweek.com/1999/99_27/b3636001.htm

5 "Homespun Wisdom from the Oracle of Omaha," by Anthony Bianco, *Business Week*, July 5, 1999. http://www.businessweek.com/1999/99_27/b3636001.htm

6 Information cited in this example is taken from "Value Investing from Graham to Buffett and Beyond," by Bruce C.N. Greenwald, pp. 11 and 12, John Wiley & Sons, May 31, 2001.

7 "Homespun Wisdom from the Oracle of Omaha," by Anthony Bianco, *Business Week*, July 5, 1999. http://www.businessweek.com/1999/99_27/b3636001.htm

8 Fama, Eugene F., and Kenneth R. French. 1992. "The Cross-Section of Expected Stock Returns." *Journal of Finance*, Vol 47, No 2 (June): pp 427-465.

22

RELATIVE VALUE
EVERYTHING IS RELATIVE

Edward C. Rorer, Chairman and CIO
Clifford B. Storms, Jr., CFA®, Director of Research
Rorer Asset Management, LLC

Dramatic events unfolded in the fall of 1982, shortly after the summer launch of what would become the greatest bull market in history. On Chicago's West Side, seven people mysteriously died within a short time. At first, the deaths seemed unrelated, but as detectives pieced together the horrifying evidence, panic ensued, starting at first in Illinois and soon spreading across a terrified nation. Police took to the streets with bullhorns. Bulletins interrupted regularly scheduled newscasts. A killer was on the loose, and no one knew who would be the next victim.

As more evidence was gathered, it became apparent that the victims had been poisoned with cyanide. Further investigation revealed that they had all taken Extra Strength Tylenol within hours of their deaths. The manufacturer of Tylenol, a subsidiary of Johnson & Johnson, moved swiftly to recall the product from drugstore and supermarket shelves across the nation. Until that moment, Tylenol had been a highly successful drug and represented an important source of revenue and earnings for Johnson & Johnson.

As this tragedy was unfolding, Johnson & Johnson was one of the most respected companies in America. Known for its high-quality medical, surgical, and pharmaceutical products, it had compiled an enviable record of uninterrupted growth in sales and earnings over the years. Its balance sheet was strong and its prospects were bright. Investors had recognized its outstanding potential, and its stock consistently had been one of the best performers on the New York Stock Exchange. Indeed, the stock regularly traded at a "premium" to the average company in the S&P 500 Index. Accordingly, it sported higher financial ratios in terms of earnings, book value, cash flow, and return on equity than most of its brethren in that index. In addition, its dividend yield was well below that of the average company in the index.

Notwithstanding management's rapid and forceful moves to protect the public and allay escalating fears, investors reacted with a panic of their own, sending the stock into a swift decline. Almost instantly, the stock went from being a Wall Street darling to a Wall Street pariah as investors reacted to the headlines and raced for the exits.

With the perfect vision that hindsight affords, one can say that the crisis created a wonderful opportunity to acquire Johnson & Johnson stock at a bargain price. In a few days, the stock's premium valuation to the S&P 500 Index had eroded substantially. To put it differently, its value relative to that particular benchmark had increased considerably in a short timeframe. And investors who seized the moment, taking advantage of its newly attractive relative value, were well rewarded.

Relative Value Defined

Relative value is an approach to investing in common stocks that seeks to find value in a stock's current price compared to historic norms relative to a general benchmark, usually a stock index. In the Johnson & Johnson case, the stock price was falling while the value of an often-used benchmark, the S&P 500 Index, was rising. As this was occurring, its value relative to the index, by definition, was becoming more attractive. In other words, its relative value was improving. *Relative value is an approach to investing that seeks to invest in companies that are statistically out of favor versus their own trading history relative to a benchmark.* Its appeal is that it focuses the investor's attention on companies that are cheaper today and, accordingly, represent better value than in the past. This approach seeks to reduce risk by emphasizing companies for purchase that are trading below their historic norms.

It is important to define relative value statistically rather than just conceptually. At our firm, for example, we evaluate five criteria to create an overall relative value score for each company in the universe. The five criteria are expressed as ratios and evaluate price to earnings, price to cash flow, price to book value, price to sales, and dividend to price. Each criterion is weighted equally in the analysis and is evaluated over a five-year period.

For example, if over the last five years, Company XYZ's price/earnings (P/E) ratio has ranged from a low of 1.0 times that of the S&P 500 Index to a high of 2.0 times the index, and if it is currently trading at the lower end of its range, say, 1.1 times, then one could argue that XYZ is attractive on a relative valuation basis on this criterion. At our firm, each of the five criteria are evaluated statistically and scored accordingly. To determine an overall relative value score for each company, we combine five scores and assign each company a total score to determine if its relative valuation is attractive enough to warrant further research at the current stock price. (See exhibit on facing page)

Swings in investor psychology can be measured statistically, and profitably, by relative valuation analysis. While it might not always be as striking as the Johnson & Johnson example cited earlier, changes in investor psychology might dramatically affect stock prices. For example, the savings and loan crisis of the late 1980s and the early 1990s poisoned the valuation of many bank stocks to the point of absurdity. Relative valuation extremes were readily seen in the dramatic swings in the technology sector between 1999 and 2002, courtesy of the Internet bubble and its subsequent demise.

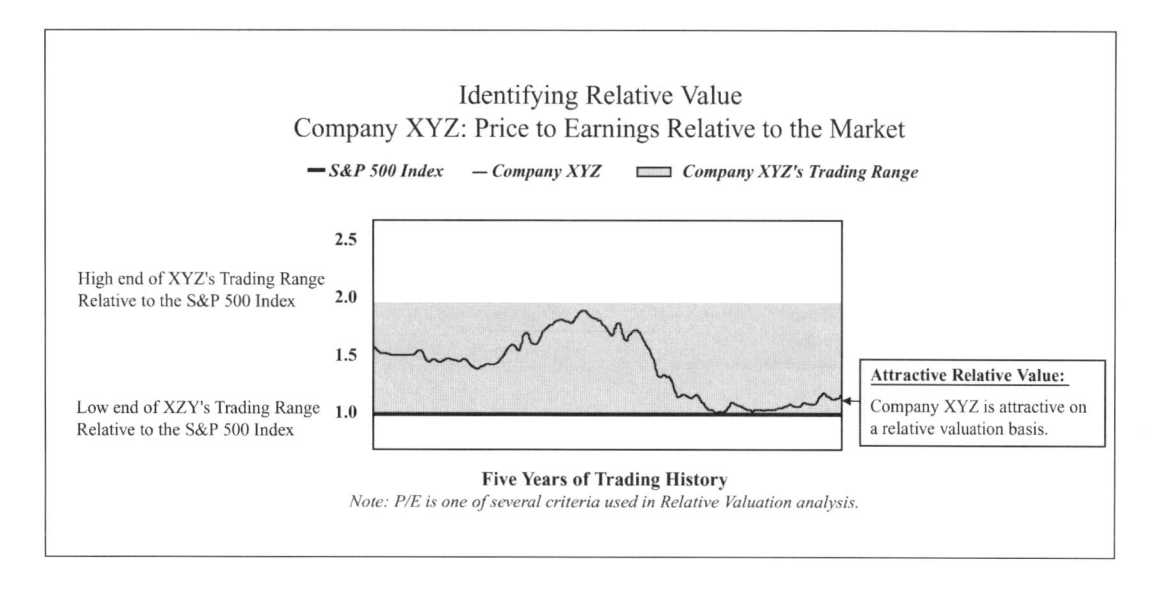

Identifying Relative Value
Company XYZ: Price to Earnings Relative to the Market

Chart showing S&P 500 Index, Company XYZ, and Company XYZ's Trading Range over Five Years of Trading History. High end of XYZ's Trading Range Relative to the S&P 500 Index at 2.0; Low end of XZY's Trading Range Relative to the S&P 500 Index at 1.0. Attractive Relative Value: Company XYZ is attractive on a relative valuation basis.

Note: P/E is one of several criteria used in Relative Valuation analysis.

The pharmaceutical industry was very much in favor through the latter part of the 1980s but fell into severe disrepute in the early 1990s with the gathering force of the HMO industry and efforts to rein in healthcare costs by the newly elected Clinton administration. Each of these psychological imbalances created wonderful opportunities for investors who used relative valuation as a tool to purchase the common stock of high-quality companies at extremely distressed prices.

Absolute Value: Clearing up the Confusion

Relative value is sometimes confused with absolute value investing, and it is important to distinguish between them. Absolute value, sometimes referred to as "deep" value, usually utilizes a single financial variable as a reference point, such as the P/E ratio, to determine if a particular equity offers value as defined by the investment manager.

For example, the manager might define value as any company that has a P/E ratio of less than 12. In this instance, the "buy" universe of stocks would consist of all those companies with a P/E below 12. Following this discipline, the manager may well require the sale of any company in the portfolio once its P/E ratio exceeds a certain amount. Or, perhaps the manager might define value by way of dividend yield or the price/book ratio. In these cases, the manager might find value in any company that has a dividend yield of four percent or greater or, alternately, a price/book ratio below 2.0. Note that in each of these instances, an absolute reference point is used on one, or possibly several, financial statistics to determine absolute value.

This approach often has been contrasted with growth investing wherein the manager might ignore low P/E ratios or high dividend yields in favor of those companies that appear to be offering the most dramatic earnings growth potential, sometimes regardless of price.

Often, depending on how the economic cycle is unfolding, absolute value and growth investing correlate negatively with one another. Think of a childhood seesaw. When one end is up, the other is down. And so it has been with absolute value and growth. For instance, in the latter part of the 1990s, growth investing rewarded its adherents with stupendous returns, while value investing languished in the nether reaches of the playground. Accordingly, with the advent of the new millennium, many investors became impatient with the absolute value discipline and pursued the higher rewards of growth investing, the poster child of which was the Internet frenzy.

Unfortunately, their timing was terrible: just as they made the switch, the seesaw was on the cusp of reversal. Many consultants, aware of the seesaw effect of growth and absolute value, advise their clients to allocate assets across both disciplines in an effort to dampen the volatility and risk levels associated with investing solely in one or the other.

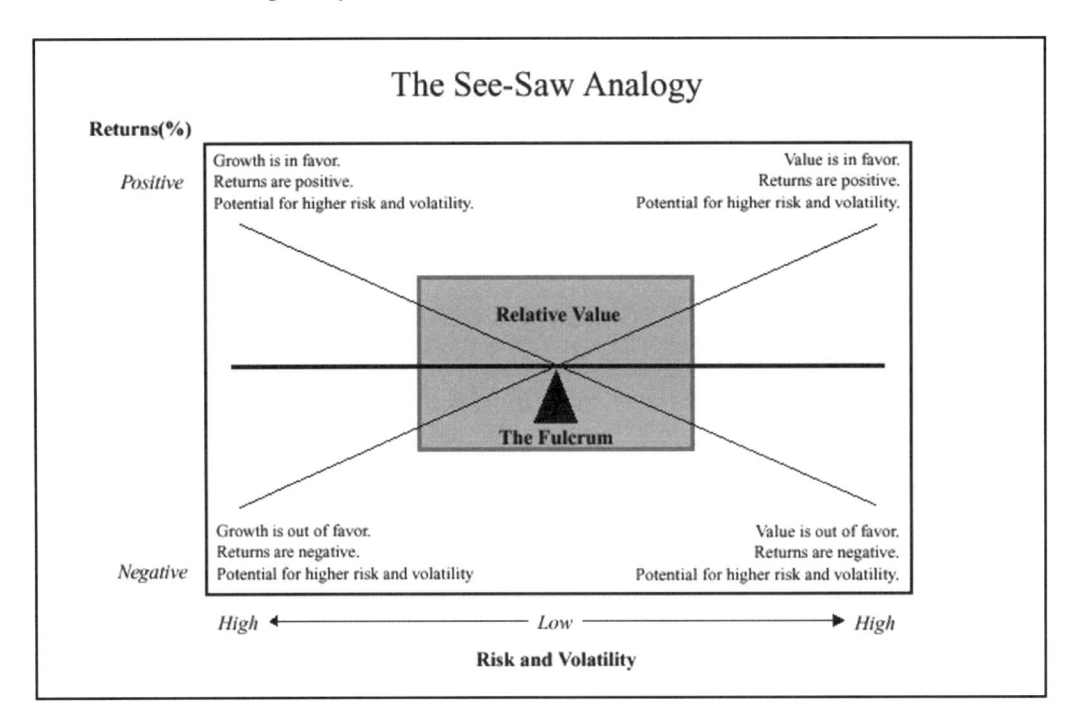

The See-Saw Analogy

Returns (%)

Positive
- Growth is in favor. Returns are positive. Potential for higher risk and volatility.
- Value is in favor. Returns are positive. Potential for higher risk and volatility.

Relative Value

The Fulcrum

Negative
- Growth is out of favor. Returns are negative. Potential for higher risk and volatility.
- Value is out of favor. Returns are negative. Potential for higher risk and volatility.

High ← Low → High

Risk and Volatility

An alternative approach is to utilize the relative value discipline. Returning to the seesaw analogy, relative value often finds itself, from a return standpoint, firmly rooted in the middle of the growth and absolute value extremes, thereby positioning itself as the fulcrum. While the fulcrum is unlikely to match the best returns of either of the "ends" when they are in favor, neither is it likely to suffer the same magnitude of downside when either growth or value is out of favor.

Thus, relative value is an approach that, through ups and downs, can be expected to capture more of the upside and less of the downside of the entire investment cycle, thereby dampening volatility along the way.

Sector Rotation, Core, and GARP

Relative value is an investment discipline that often has been compared with sector rotation, core, and growth-at-a-reasonable-price (GARP) investing. While it may capture some elements of each in its approach, it differs from each in meaningful ways.

The basic premise of sector rotation is that not all sectors of the economy perform well at the same time. At different points in the economic cycle, certain sectors are more likely to be in favor than others. For example, early in a recession, cyclical sectors would be far more vulnerable than non-cyclical sectors. All other things being equal, an investment manager who employed the sector rotator style, and who had correctly predicted the incipient recession, would favor healthcare issues and other non-durables over basic industry and consumer cyclical issues. Then, when economic improvement appeared on the distant horizon, the deft sector rotator would start to tilt the portfolio toward more cyclical sectors. So, the sector rotator starts with the premise that a particular sector is attractive and, accordingly, searches out companies in industries that comprise that sector.

Note that the starting point is the sector choice and the end result is the ownership of companies that fall into that sector. The relative value manager differs from this approach in that the starting point is the search for individual companies that offer attractive relative value. It is certainly possible that many companies in the same industry or economic sector show up with attractive relative value and the relative value manager may elect to concentrate his or her holdings in those industries and sectors. So, at least some of the time, it is possible, though improbable, that the relative value manager and the sector rotator might end up in the same place, even though they started with vastly different premises.

Core investing seeks to invest in large capitalization, stable, blue-chip companies that have strong balance sheets, superior and consistent earnings records, and bright future prospects. Typically, these companies reside in the S&P 500 Index or in the Russell 1000 Index. Companies that are deeply cyclical or have highly leveraged balance sheets need not apply. Of course, a relative value manager who specializes in large capitalization holdings may want to own many of the same companies a core manager owns *if they meet the established relative value criteria.* Once again, the starting point is different. The relative value manager starts from a far broader universe of companies, many of which may not qualify as core. However, to the extent that the relative value manager seeks the highest quality companies, and to the extent that they qualify for inclusion in the relative value portfolio, it is possible that the core and relative value portfolios might have similar holdings, if only temporarily.

As explained earlier, GARP is an acronym that stands for Growth at a Reasonable Price. In a sense, the GARP investor seeks to combine the best premises of value and growth investing. This investor seeks earnings growth, but sets value parameters on what he is willing to pay for that growth. Often, this investor may use the PEG ratio to determine if a stock might qualify for his portfolio. This is simply the P/E ratio divided by the earnings growth rate. To wit, if a company has a P/E ratio of 20 and is growing its earnings at 10 percent a year, its PEG ratio is 2. The GARP manager will set his own rules and parameters on what he is willing to pay and own. For example, a conservative GARP manager might be willing to buy a company with a PEG below 1.0 and sell any company with a PEG above 1.2. In a sense, there are several similarities between a relative value manager and a GARP manager. Both care deeply about what they are willing to pay for a company and have disciplines in place to ensure that they don't overpay. Consequently, if they are shopping in the same universe, it's quite possible that they could end up owning many of the same companies.

However, once again, the starting point is the difference. Recall that the relative value manager compares today's valuation with historic norms relative to a benchmark, typically the S&P 500 Index. In the example above where the GARP manager was happy to buy the stock below a PEG ratio of 1.0, no consideration was given to where the stock historically had traded relative to a benchmark. At the end of the day, the relative value manager may or may not overlay a PEG ratio analysis on top of the relative value analysis, but it is certainly not the starting point. Even if a company looks attractive by this criterion, it won't even make it to the relative value radar screen if it is trading above its historic norms relative to its benchmark.

Relative Value as a Starting Point

Relative value, like any other investment discipline, has limitations. We have found it to be a great *starting* point for our own investment research process. *Those investors who rely on relative value as their sole input will most likely fail.* Companies that show attractive relative valuation are, by definition, inexpensive by historical standards. The great investment challenge is to discern how and why they fell into disfavor and what their prospects are for regaining their former stature. Often a stock falls into disrepute for good reasons. Perhaps a technology change will affect the company's business model forever. In this instance, unless management adapts, the company's prospects may never recover.

Interestingly enough, in the early stages of this deteriorative process, the stock may show up as having attractive relative value. Manufacturers of buggy whips were flourishing in the early days of the automobile, but investors, in their wisdom, recognized that the future of the buggy whip industry was clouded at best. So the stocks may have sold off even while the financial statistics remained strong. And that would set up the hypothetical relative value trap.

In other words, it is very possible that the cheap will get much cheaper. And so we recognize that relative value is a wonderful tool that should not stand alone. Accordingly, we overlay a series of disciplines and fundamental research on top of our analysis to assist us in determining if attractive relative value is a great opportunity or a possible ambush. We start our process by subjecting our investment universe to a relative value screening process, using the five criteria and methodology outlined earlier in this chapter. Companies that survive this screen are then subjected to an *earnings momentum* screen. In this screen, we are looking for upward revisions in consensus earnings estimates from the analysts on Wall Street. The rationale for including this screen is that upward earnings revisions usually mean that something positive is occurring at the companies involved.

And so, the ideal profile for a potential investment is a company that has attractive relative valuation and has earnings momentum in the form of upward consensus earnings revisions from Wall Street analysts. At this point in the process, our work has just begun! We now set about conducting a rigorous fundamental analysis of the company and its prospects, including interviews with senior management. At the end of the day, we want to ensure that the company, even though it has met all of our screening criteria, is absolutely the best current choice for our portfolios. We like to think of relative valuation as a road map: it can point an investor in the right direction, but there may be potholes and detours along the way that require attention if one is to navigate safely to the destination.

Relative Value Case Histories

Equities develop attractive relative value for a host of reasons. Sometimes, as noted in the Johnson & Johnson example, some kind of external event affects a stock's valuation. In other instances, investors, caught up in "groupthink," push valuations to extremes as they get caught up in the fear or greed of the moment. Sometimes, psychology sours on a particular stock, or even an entire industry, notwithstanding that prospects for the future are strong. The big benefit of relative valuation is that it helps the investor to identify, *from a quantitative standpoint*, when valuations are running to extremes relative to historic norms.

In 1994, The Federal Reserve, under the leadership of Alan Greenspan, went on a tear, raising the Federal Funds rate six times from three percent at the outset of the year to 5.5 percent at the end. Generally, investors in financial stocks have a knee-jerk reaction to rising interest rates, and that is to dump them. The year 1994 was no exception. Investors still had the savings and loan crisis of several years earlier very much on their minds and weren't interested in being caught in the trap again should conditions deteriorate. Accordingly, even as the general market remained flat under the onslaught of higher rates, bank stocks gave up continuous ground, thereby raising their relative value scores as the year wore on.

Relative Value

Even as the stock prices were deteriorating and the relative value scores were rising, we noted that earnings estimates were rising with each passing earnings announcement. We surmised that sooner or later the stocks would react positively to such attractive relative valuation scores, especially when accompanied with rising earnings estimates. We had our ideal profile: attractive relative value, coupled with rising consensus earnings estimates! As a result, we started buying the stocks of high-quality banks in the fall of 1994 and were pleased to see them dramatically outperform a rising market in 1995. We never would have started this journey without the benefit of relative value alerting us to the fact that the stocks were so inexpensive.

Relative value can keep an investment manager out of trouble as well as highlight stocks that are excellent purchase candidates. Stocks that trade well above their historic norms on the theory that "it's different this time" or that "a new era" is dawning usually offer a poignant example of excessive risk. And every time that happens relative value is there to point the way.

In 1998, 1999 and the early part of 2000, growth stock investing took on a new meaning with the Internet craze. While it was fashionable to own those stocks and brag at cocktail parties how much money everyone was making, relative value demurred, keeping its adherents out of the fray. Perhaps they couldn't brag at cocktail parties on the way up, but they were spared the hangover on the way down. After the crash, relative value offered a chance to look at the sector with a fresh eye and much less risk than had been extant only a few years earlier.

One company that survived the technology crash of 2000 to 2003 in good financial condition was Cisco Systems. The stock of this company, a worldwide leader in networking for the Internet, got caught up in the technology euphoria of the moment, advancing 16-fold between 1997 and 2000 alone, trading at well over 100 times expected earnings at its peak. Needless to say, no self-respecting relative value manager could even *think* about initiating a position in a company trading at ever-ascending record valuations relative to the market during that heady period.

Then, as the technology bubble started to deflate, the stock started a descent, somewhat mild at first; perhaps investors were reluctant to throw in the towel because, unlike many other companies in the sector, Cisco had earnings and a very strong balance sheet. Nonetheless, as the storm intensified, it became apparent that many of Cisco's customers were in trouble and would not be ordering anywhere near the amount of gear that Cisco had anticipated would be in the order pipeline only months earlier.

And so, with declining earnings, investors started selling the stock in earnest. From its high of $82 in 2000, it started its journey south, moving into the $30 range in 2001 and ignominiously into "single digits" in 2002. Finally, it hit rock bottom, a shadow of its former self, having lost 90 percent of its value along the way. While this was occurring, earnings and sales were deteriorating, but at nowhere near the same rate that was occurring with the stock's valuation metrics relative to the S&P 500 Index. Consequently, its relative value was steadily improving with each downtick in its stock price. In the spring of 2002, trading below $10 a share, Cisco's relative valuation score had never been cheaper.

Then, in August, Cisco announced earnings that were 20 percent above expectations, causing analysts to collectively raise their earnings estimates. Once again, we had our ideal profile of attractive relative valuation coupled with rising consensus earnings estimates. It turned out to be an excellent time to acquire shares of Cisco: As of this writing in December 2003, the stock has dramatically outperformed the market in the interim and the story is still being written.

Conclusion

Relative value is a powerful discipline that, properly implemented, can enhance investment returns while reducing risk and volatility in investment management. It offers the investor important differences from other management styles, yet presents an intriguing palette of characteristics that is embraced by other approaches to investment management.

It is not growth, but can embrace growth stocks such as Johnson & Johnson or a Cisco Systems under the right circumstances. It is not absolute value, but is content playing in the same sandbox, adjacent to the childhood seesaw, if conditions so warrant. Nor, as was pointed out earlier, is it core, GARP, or sector rotation, but may wind up in the same place, at least from time to time, and at least with a portion of the portfolio, as each of them.

Lastly, it is not a "black box" computer-driven discipline that can stand on its own and fend for itself in the competitive world of investment management. It is a model that acknowledges that euphoria and depression, fear and greed, and success and failure drive the psychology of investment decisions every day, year in and year out. It is a model that sometimes screams "Stay away!!" and sometimes whispers "Come on in and take a look." It is a model that consultants and advisors can use for their clients as their sole approach to investment management, or a model that is comfortable in the presence of other investment disciplines. It is conservative. It is comfortable. And it is effective.

❖ ❖ ❖

Disclosure: Rorer Asset Management, LLC, an investment management firm founded in 1978, is based in Pennsylvania and manages accounts for institutions and individuals. The views expressed represent the opinions of Rorer. It should not be assumed that any securities discussed herein are investment recommendations, or were or will prove to be profitable.

23

PASSIVE AND ACTIVE MANAGEMENT
A BALANCED PERSPECTIVE EMERGES

Patricia Sanchez-Marin, Principal
John Tucker, CFA®, Principal
State Street Global Advisors

Discussion surrounding active versus passive management has been copious and, at times, confusing. Historically, strong proponents in both camps have offered different rationales for choosing one style over the other. Traditional arguments in favor of both passive and active management will be examined here, and how and why investors choose one style over the other also will be illustrated. This chapter should also help advisors work with investors to assess which approach best fits their clients' individual needs. Closer examination of the issue could show that the two styles are not mutually exclusive. The best strategy for sophisticated investors may be one that utilizes *both* active and passive management.

What is Passive Management?

First, what is meant by "passive?" Passive management rests on the assumption of market efficiency, a topic upon which the academic community has focused exhaustive theoretical and empirical studies. In fact, Modern Portfolio Theory (MPT) as understood today is based primarily on the pioneering research of two Nobel Prize winners, Eugene Fama and Harry Markowitz.

Efficient Market Hypothesis—Though it emerged as a concept years earlier, the theory of market efficiency was first formalized and supported with empirical evidence by Eugene Fama in 1965, when the Journal of Business published Fama's doctoral thesis titled "The Behavior of Stock Market Prices."

In his thesis, Fama articulated the Efficient Market Hypothesis (EMH).

When individuals or institutions invest in the stock market, they do so with the aim of generating a return on the capital invested. Many investors not only try to generate profitable returns, but to outperform or beat the market. Fama's Efficient Market Hypothesis (EMH), however, suggests that it is impossible to beat the market because at any given time, prices fully reflect all available information on a particular stock and/or market. The nature of the information does not have to be limited to financial news and research alone; indeed, information about political, economic and social events, combined with how investors perceive such information, whether true or rumored, will be reflected in the stock price.

Thus, according to the theory of market efficiency, no investor has an advantage in predicting a return on a stock price since no one has access to information not already available to everyone else. As prices only respond to information available in the market, and because all market participants are privy to the same information, no one will have the ability to "out-profit" anyone else. [1]

Modern Portfolio Theory—Modern Portfolio Theory, formalized by Harry Markowitz in 1952, goes further than the Efficient Market Hypothesis in that it posits a working framework for developing efficient portfolios.

▸ Risk: Two of the most basic and important assumptions about investors and their behavior implied in Markowitz's Portfolio Theory are:

1. Investors are rational and make reasonable decisions over time; thus, they seek to maximize the utility of their investments.

2. Investors make decisions based on an evaluation of each investment's risk and return potential.

Markowitz suggested that rational, risk-averse investors make investment decisions based on a desire to maximize returns for the least amount of risk. Put another way, investors who want high returns must be willing to assume greater risk, and investors who desire a lower level of risk must be willing to accept smaller returns. Given this premise, Markowitz set out to determine how to construct efficient portfolios, i.e., portfolios that would deliver the maximum return for a given level of acceptable risk.

While taking the simple average-weighted return potential of every asset contained within a portfolio will result in the total return potential of a portfolio, Markowitz discovered that taking the weighted average of the risk of each asset (where risk is measured as the standard deviation[2]) contained within the portfolio would not give an accurate measure of total portfolio risk. Instead, Markowitz proposed that rational, risk-averse investors should view each investment *in the context of an overall portfolio* to determine a price that best reflects the return opportunity and potential risk of the total portfolio.

The critical insight of MPT, then, is that the risk of an individual asset is not as important as its contribution to the overall risk of the portfolio. Each asset class carries its own expected rate and variance of return, as well as covariance of returns with other asset classes, i.e., a variability in the rate of return of an entire asset class as compared with another. As a result, the risk of an individual higher risk asset is reduced when combined with less risky assets in a portfolio. The power of diversification is the fundamental lesson of Markowitz's portfolio theory.

▸ Efficient Frontier: Markowitz proposed that if we were to graph the return rates and standard deviations for every single security in the market, as well as for all of the portfolio combinations we can construct by allocating among those securities, we would end up with a region bounded by an upward-sloping curve called the "efficient frontier."

Figure 1

The Efficient Frontier of Diversified Assets

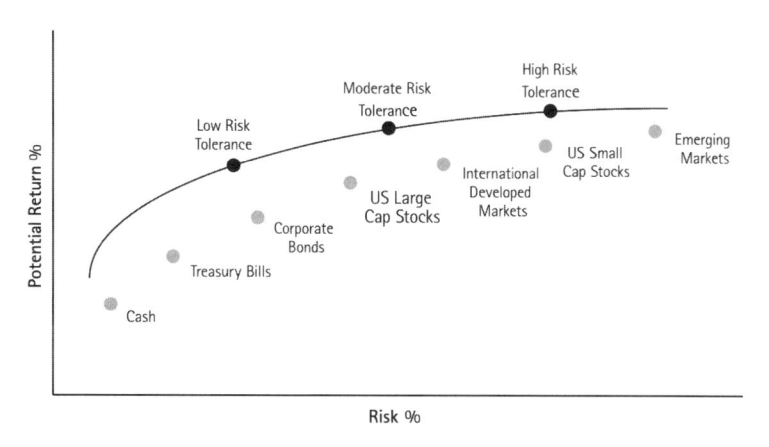

Source: SSgA Advisor Strategies-Advisor Consulting Services Research. For Illustrative Purposes only. Past performance is not indicative of future results. Risk/return will vary for each asset class.

All optimal portfolios that lie along this efficient frontier offer the maximum possible expected return for a given level of risk. Typically, the portfolios that comprise this efficient frontier are more highly diversified portfolios. Again, diversification is paramount.

The Efficient Market Hypothesis and Modern Portfolio Theory together support the notion that the "market portfolio" is an optimal portfolio. Investors, then, may wish to simply own the market. By using a broad market index or a series of specialized indexes investors can build a portfolio that essentially replicates the market. This investment approach is called indexing. Indexing can effectively set passive management principles into action.

▸ Indexing: What is an index? An index tracks a group of investments that are representative of an entire asset class or market, as a way of measuring that asset class' performance. Designed to match market performance, an indexing strategy invests in the same securities, in the same proportions as are held by the market or benchmarked index. There is no aim to outperform or to obtain excess return relative to the benchmark.

Most indexes today are capitalization-weighted as opposed to price-weighted or equal-weighted. That is, each stock impacts the index in proportion to its market value. Today, investors can choose from among literally thousands of index funds and strategies that track all major asset classes, regions and sectors.

While still not as popular among retail investors as active investment strategies, indexing has experienced tremendous growth over the past 25 years. What accounts for such tremendous growth? It may be attributed to wider recognition of the potential benefits such an approach can deliver.

Advantages of Passive Management

Diversified, Risk-Controlled Exposure—Passive portfolios or indexed portfolios are market-driven, not manager-driven. As such, they deliver broad, diversified exposure to the market and can effectively eliminate style drift or capitalization "bets" as requested by the investor or client.

Lower Expenses and Improved Tax Efficiency—Index portfolios are usually less expensive to maintain than active funds. It is conventional wisdom that the cost of managing an index fund should be significantly less than that of managing an active fund. Since passive portfolios do not require managers to expend resources researching the market or selecting stocks, passive management should be less costly than active management. Index funds, too, because they track a market index, usually have lower relative turnover. Fewer transactions results in lower transaction costs. Lower turnover, too, results in lower distribution of capital gains and, thus, lower tax costs. Indexing, then, can be inherently tax-efficient as well.

Competitive Performance—Within the context of the efficient market hypothesis, investing is a zero-sum game since the market is comprised of all investors. In theory then, after adjusting for the impact of costs, the returns of passively managed portfolios should be higher than most active portfolios. William Sharpe illustrates this most succinctly in his 1991 article, "The Arithmetic of Active Management":

"If active and passive management are defined in sensible ways, it must be the case that:

1. Before costs, the return on the average actively managed dollar will equal the return on the average passively managed dollar; and

2. After costs, the return on the average actively managed dollar will be less than the return on the average passively managed dollar.

These assertions hold for any time period. Moreover, they depend only on the laws of addition, subtraction, multiplication and division. Nothing else is required."[3]

In theory, index portfolios should deliver higher risk-adjusted returns (returns adjusted for volatility). Passive management should potentially reduce the risk of manager under-performance over longer time horizons. Much empirical evidence and academic research, in fact, supports the notion that it is nearly impossible to beat a market portfolio over time, after accounting for fees, costs, capital gains and taxes.

Disadvantages of Passive Management

While its advantages appear to be compelling, there may be potential disadvantages to passive management as well.

Market Returns Only—Indexing is not about timing the markets or picking stocks. It is a long-term, buy and hold strategy that seeks to generate market returns only. Indexing does not seek to "beat" a benchmark. Investors in search of—and who believe they can achieve—better-than-market returns will not realize those excess returns utilizing a passive investment approach.

No Ability to Defend Against Down Markets—A second potential disadvantage to a passive approach is its inability to provide defensive measures during market downturns. According to a theory called "Dunn's Law," when an asset class does well, an index fund tracking that class should deliver superior returns. Likewise, when the asset class suffers, the index fund should do worse than its actively managed counterparts.[4] Indexes offer purity. When things go bad, indexes have no reprieve from the downfall; but when markets are up, indexes take full advantage of the benefits. Theoretically, active management enables skilled managers to select specific securities or asset classes during times of market volatility, in an attempt to guard against underperformers and hold top performers.

Now that passive has been defined and some of its advantages and disadvantages have been discussed, let's look now at active management.

What is Active Management?

Unlike passive management, active management rests on the assumption that markets are inefficient. One of the premises upon which this inefficiency is based is the notion that investors are not rational beings as Modern Portfolio Theory suggests. In fact, active proponents offer that inefficiencies develop as a result of the irrationality of investors.

The existence of financial bubbles and historical anomalies suggests such inefficiencies may exist.[5] Active management attempts to exploit those inefficiencies in order to beat the market on a risk-adjusted basis as it's measured by a particular index or passive benchmark. Unlike indexing (i.e., passive investing), which seeks to own all stocks within a particular market, active managers only want to buy the most attractive stocks within a particular market.

Active Tactics

Active proponents point to several techniques, whereby they believe highly skilled managers can find and leverage market inefficiencies. Techniques include: stock selection, manager selection, style rotation, sector rotation and market timing. Brief definitions of each tactic follow below.

Stock Selection—Stock selection is the process of investing in stocks perceived to be undervalued or possessing positive price momentum based on price and volume indicators and based on fundamental or quantitative research used to assess the current and/or future value of a company.

Manager Selection—Manager selection involves selecting managers based on their perceived ability to outperform the market, usually based on past performance of those managers.

Style Rotation—Style rotation is the process of shifting back and forth from one style to another, such as from growth to value, based on the belief or prediction that one style will outperform another in the near future. Growth stocks are generally defined as those companies expected to provide above-average growth in the future. Value stocks are generally defined as stocks that appear to be trading below their true value.

Sector Rotation— Sector rotation is the process of continually rebalancing a portfolio to overweight in strong-performing sectors and underweight in poor-performing sectors.

Market Timing— Market timing is the strategy of shifting a portfolio allocation from one asset class to another based on the belief that the chosen asset class will outperform another in the near future.

Advantages of Active Management

In theory, the primary advantage of active management, and the principle reason more investors may utilize active strategies than passive, is the potential for higher returns.

Potential to Beat the Market—Active proponents argue that pricing inefficiencies can be exploited by highly skilled managers. By taking active "bets" relative to the benchmark, or by assuming more risk, active management offers the potential for investors to realize excess returns relative to market returns.

Protection in Down Markets—In theory, active management potentially provides protection in down markets. Unlike indexed portfolios, which have no discretion to adjust cash reserves to act as a cushion during a market decline, active proponents suggest that an actively managed fund could hold more cash reserves, defensively positioning a portfolio to serve as a buoy in bear markets.

Active management proponents also believe that the more highly skilled active managers can successfully predict market downturns and reposition portfolios accordingly. The assumption they make is that the downside protection active management potentially provides will compensate for any underperformance in up markets.

Disadvantages of Active Management

While its advantages are obvious, the disadvantages of active management are not as immediately transparent.

Higher Costs & Fees—If we return again to the assumptions presented in Sharpe's article on the arithmetic of active management, then we accept that, in order to beat or even to break even with a passive strategy, actively managed portfolios must create enough value-added to offset higher fees and costs associated with this management style.

Much of the cost difference is a result of the higher turnover rate associated with active portfolios. Passive portfolios simply replicate the index and, therefore, only buy or sell securities when the index changes or to meet redemptions. As a result, passive portfolios typically take a buy and hold approach to investing, thereby reducing the number of transactions that take place in the open market.

Risk & Unpredictability— Active management requires that investors have full confidence in their ability to hire the right manager and in that manager's skill and ability to consistently outperform the market over time. Some studies suggest that most managers do not outperform the market and any short-term outperformance has typically been unsustainable. Alternatively, indexed portfolios have historically performed in the top third of all funds in the investment universe.[6] This finding may give investors additional cause to carefully consider utilizing passive management for at least some portion of their investment dollars.

Active Versus Passive: Evaluating Performance

In the active versus passive debate, many academics and investment professionals alike have sought to find empirical evidence that supports the theoretical advantages of passive or active management. Approaches to finding such evidence have generally centered around two questions: (1) How does the median active strategy perform? and (2) Is observed performance due to skill or luck?

When Passive Outperforms Active

Historical evidence suggests that active management may not work, on average—especially within the broader asset classes. Original research conducted in the 1960s by Jensen (1968), Sharpe (1966) and Treynor (1965) found that, on average, active funds underperform their benchmarks on a risk-adjusted basis and that the magnitude of underperformance directly relates to the level of expenses.

In Figure 2, we tracked the performance over 10 years of both active and index funds benchmarked against the S&P 500. As this chart shows, index funds outperformed their active counterparts during seven out of ten years.[8]

Research suggests that the level of underperformance may even be understated in some studies as a result of "survivorship bias." In other words, some studies, when evaluating the historical perfor-

Figure 2

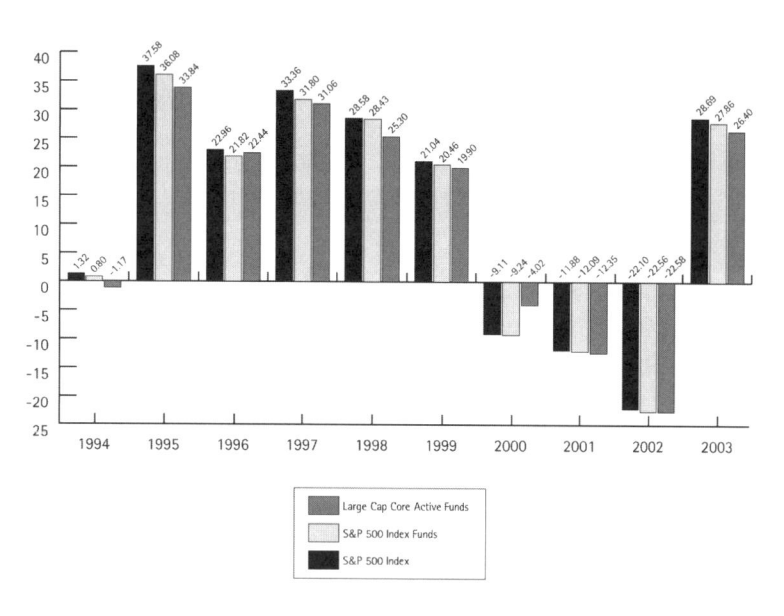

Performance of Index Funds vs. Active Funds

Year	Large Cap Core Active Funds	S&P 500 Index Funds	S&P 500 Index
1994	1.32	0.80	-1.17
1995	37.58	36.08	33.84
1996	22.96	21.82	22.44
1997	33.36	31.80	31.06
1998	28.58	28.43	25.30
1999	21.04	20.46	19.90
2000	-9.11	-9.34	-4.02
2001	-11.88	-12.08	-12.35
2002	-22.10	-22.56	-22.58
2003	28.69	27.85	26.40

Source: Lipper. For index strategies, the Lipper average expense rate of 0.47% was used. For active strategies, the Lipper average expense rate of 1.45% was used.

mance of funds, did not account for those funds that no longer existed due to poor performance. Research conducted from 1970-1990 made adjustments for survivorship bias and risk exposures and concluded that the average active fund fails to add value relative to its passive benchmarks. Some estimates suggest that adjusting for survivorship bias decreases the performance of the average active fund by about 1.5% per year.[9]

Inconsistent Performance of Active Managers—Studies also addressed the second question of to what to attribute performance—skill or luck? In other words, does outperformance persist? After adjusting for factor exposures to control for risk-taking and after adjusting for survivorship bias, studies found that the probability of good performance repeating is consistent with what chance would suggest—approximately 50%. It would seem, then, that luck and risk explain most active manager performance.

Also, a study by Callan Associates Inc. defined rising and declining market cycles from 1974-1997. The study concluded that out of the six declining markets, the median manager outperformed three times and underperformed three times. According to Callan Associates, the median manager would have had to outperform the S&P 500 by an annualized 3.5% during market downturns since 1974 in order to compensate for underperformance during market expansions.[10]

Evidence Contradicts Active Protection in Down Markets—Additional empirical evidence refutes the theory that active management will provide protection in down markets. Institutional money managers have been under increasing pressure to remain fully invested. As a result, though cash positions were at a high point when the bull run of the 1990's began, cash positions were at a low point when the bear market of 2001 arrived.

Despite the research findings described above, actively managed funds and strategies can outperform—and have outperformed—passive strategies at times. Let's look more closely at those examples of active outperformance.

When Active Outperforms Passive

A research study published by Robert Wermers in April 2003, titled "Are Mutual Fund Shareholders Compensated for Active Management 'Bets,'" concluded that active management does provide value but that the value is reflected in only a minority of funds that take relatively large volatility bets. Study results show that funds taking large bets away from the market, or style portfolios, generally perform well during simultaneous time periods.[11]

The study is careful to acknowledge, though, that while results cast a somewhat positive light on some active managers, results also indicated a good deal of risk of underperformance of funds taking higher levels of risk. For example, during the 1998 to 2000 period (a relatively good period for the average fund that took on high levels of risk), substantial numbers of high-risk funds underperformed the S&P 500 index by a wide margin.[12]

Active performance advocates insist that active managers can add the most value in less-efficient, less-liquid areas of the markets, including small stocks and international stocks. Over a 10-year period, from 1993 to December 2003, for example, international stock funds returned an average 4.71% per year, according to Lipper, topping the 4.47% return on Morgan Stanley Capital International Europe, Australasia, and the Far East Index (MSCI EAFE). Ten year returns of small cap stocks averaged 10.04%, again topping the 9.47% return of the Russell 2000 Index. The average return of Emerging Markets stocks over that same 10-year period at 1.42% bested the MSCI Emerging Markets Free Index (MSCI EMF), which delivered an average return of 0.18%.[13] There exists, then, some empirical evidence that active can outperform passive in less-efficient markets over a sustained time horizon.

How can investors, given this plethora of theoretical and empirical research that appears, at times, to be contradictory, make the best decisions as to which approach most appropriately pursues their individual goals and objectives?

Making the Decision: Passive versus Active

The decision to employ active versus passive management should be made by the advisor in the context of an investor's overall investment objectives and ability to tolerate risk. In making the active/passive decision, there are several questions advisors and investors should carefully consider together. Following are some guidelines for investors:

1. What is your tolerance for underperformance?
2. How comfortable are you with taking on active risk?
3. Do you believe markets are efficient or inefficient?
4. Do you believe skill-based managers can add value?
5. How confident are you in your ability to select the top-performing active managers?

The answers to the questions above could help guide investors in making the active/passive decision. Additional indicators investors might use as guidelines in determining which approach best suits their individual needs follow.

Passive and Active Management

Passive Personality Indicators
- Believe markets are efficient
- Unwilling to tolerate high level of active risk or variance in return potential vs. the benchmark
- Believe performance of individual asset classes and styles is unpredictable

Active Personality Indicators
- Believe markets are inefficient and assets are priced above or below fair value
- Believe skilled managers are able to identify mispriced assets in advance
- Able to identify skilled managers in advance
- Willing to assume higher level of risk and variance in return potential

Some investors, when considering the questions and guidelines above, may find that they and their beliefs do not fit neatly into one category or the other—but rather lie somewhere in between. Sophisticated advisors and investors, upon close examination of the rationales for passive and active management may find themselves fluctuating between the two. Does a middle ground exist? Is a compromise between active and passive camps possible?

Passive and Active Management: A Peaceful Co-Existence

Active and passive management approaches are not philosophically incompatible and are increasingly being used in complementary ways to meet the objectives of investors. Let's examine more closely how both investment approaches can be used together to best pursue a sophisticated investor's financial goals.

Risk Budgeting—The concept of risk budgeting helps illustrate why active and passive strategies can co-exist and how an investor might utilize both concurrently. Risk budgeting is essentially the process of identifying, understanding and measuring the component parts of the aggregated risk to which a portfolio is subject. In other words, every investment decision has an associated level of risk. Attributing targets to those various individual investment decisions, bearing in mind the investor's overall tolerance (e.g., budget) for risk, is called risk budgeting.

The efficiency with which a risk budget is spent is defined in terms of a manager's skill in identifying, evaluating and implementing investment choices. Skill is the value-added a manager delivers relative to the benchmark. Taking a ratio of skill to risk (or value-added to tracking error) results in a measure of how efficiently a portfolio is spending its risk budget. This ratio is called the Information Ratio (IR).

The objective of prudent long-term investing is to maximize this Information Ratio, or the excess return per unit of risk taken. Portfolios with higher Information Ratios typically produce more value-added per unit of risk than those portfolios with

Figure 3

$$\text{Information Ratio (Efficiency)} = \frac{\text{Average Excess Return (Value-Added)}}{\text{Standard Deviation of Excess Return (Tracking Error)}}$$

The World of Money Management

lower ratios. However, as investors add more and more risk to a portfolio, they should be wary of expecting commensurate levels of return. There is a diminishing trade-off between risk and reward.

Core-Satellite Strategies—Risk budgeting helps make a strong case for implementing core-satellite solutions that truly incorporate both traditional active and passive management approaches. Information Ratios provide a means for measuring manager skill, or for quantifying a manager's ability to add incremental value relative to incremental risk taken.

Information Ratios, when calculated for various asset classes and styles can provide significant insight as to where it makes sense to use passive versus active managers. The data in Figure 4 (Information Ratios Measure Asset Class Efficiency) indicates that the average investment manager in many market segments is unable to consistently provide incremental return in exchange for incremental risk over the benchmark. The obvious exception to this, in this example, is within the small-cap growth segment. IRs, then, may serve as a good indication of where passive management is most efficient and highlight market segments in which active management is more likely to add risk-adjusted value.[14]

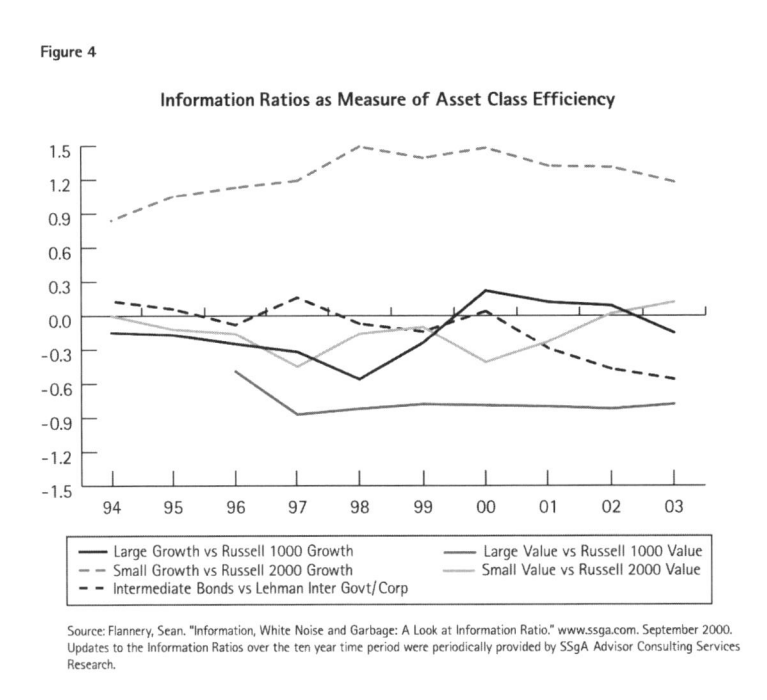

Figure 4

Information Ratios as Measure of Asset Class Efficiency

— Large Growth vs Russell 1000 Growth
— Large Value vs Russell 1000 Value
- - Small Growth vs Russell 2000 Growth
— Small Value vs Russell 2000 Value
- - Intermediate Bonds vs Lehman Inter Govt/Corp

Source: Flannery, Sean. "Information, White Noise and Garbage: A Look at Information Ratio." www.ssga.com. September 2000. Updates to the Information Ratios over the ten year time period were periodically provided by SSgA Advisor Consulting Services Research.

As seen previously in this chapter, evidence suggests that markets may not be perfectly efficient—just that they are efficient enough to make active management, or beating benchmarks, very difficult in the broader market segments. Figure 5 illustrates the percentage of active managers that have outperformed their respective indexes over a 15-year period. Based on these statistics, it appears that large cap value is relatively efficient (only 8.1% of active managers outperformed the Russell 1000 Value Index) and small cap growth is inefficient (100% of active managers outperformed the Russell 2000 Growth Index)—a finding consistent with efficiency levels suggested by the Information Ratios calculated in Figure 4.

Given these results, it makes sense to allocate a greater portion of one's risk budget to those areas where opportunities to add value are good and to go passive where opportunities are relatively poor. That is, employ active managers in asset classes where the manager has a greater chance to outperform and utilize passive for those market segments deemed to be efficient.

Investors may choose to employ an indexed core for more efficient asset classes and pursue alpha—or excess returns relative to the benchmark—via active satellites for less efficient asset classes. By employing this type of strategy, portfolio efficiency is potentially maximized. A simple example will help illustrate this.

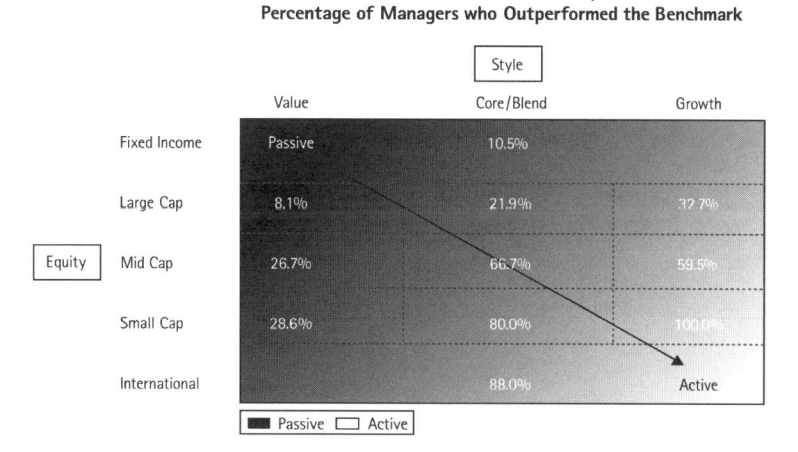

Figure 5

Asset Class Efficiency
Percentage of Managers who Outperformed the Benchmark

		Value	Core/Blend	Growth
	Fixed Income	Passive	10.5%	
	Large Cap	8.1%	21.9%	32.7%
Equity	Mid Cap	26.7%	66.7%	59.5%
	Small Cap	28.6%	80.0%	100.0%
	International		88.0%	Active

*Based on Lipper data for the past 15 years, ending June 30, 2002.
The following indexes were used as benchmarks: Lehman Aggregate Bond Index for Fixed Income, Russell Indexes for the respective domestic equities and the MSCI EAFE Index for international equities.
For illustrative purposes only. Past performance is not indicative of future results.

Source: SSgA Advisor Consulting Services Research.

In Figure 6 (page 196) we have created three portfolios with equivalent asset allocations and analyzed the returns over the same 15-year period. The first portfolio is 100% passive; the second portfolio is 100% active; and the third portfolio—the efficient portfolio—utilizes passive management for bonds, large cap growth and large cap value and then active management for small cap and international equities.

When we take a 100% passive approach for each one of these asset classes, the excess return is 0.0% as we would expect, with little or no tracking error. When we take a 100% active approach, we obtain an excess return of -0.14% and a tracking error of 1.31% relative to the benchmark. The excess return is negative because active managers have not sufficiently outperformed in the inefficient asset classes to offset the underperformance in the efficient asset classes. It is also important to note that the higher degree of turnover in the active funds may generate taxable capital gains and further reduce returns of taxable investors (a topic that will be addressed in the next section of this chapter).

The third portfolio in this example incorporates what was learned previously about the efficiency of asset classes and risk budgeting. By passively managing the large cap allocation and actively managing international and small cap exposure, we can increase the return per unit of risk of the portfolio. As illustrated in Figure 6, the core-satellite portfolio achieves a higher excess return of 0.33% with a lower level of risk as measured by the standard deviation. The tracking error of the core-satellite portfolio decreased, too, relative to the active portfolio. More pointedly, the Information Ratio of the core-satellite portfolio has increased to a positive 0.29. The core-satellite portfolio is spending its risk budget much more efficiently than the active portfolio.[15]

An alternate core-satellite construct to consider could be one that uses a broad market benchmark as a passive core and then pursues active alpha via non-correlated assets or segments, i.e., investments that do not correlate to the broader stock market—such as emerging markets, small cap equities, real estate, private equity, and commodities.

Figure 6

Build an Efficient Portfolio for your Client
Utilize Passive for Efficient Asset Classes and Active for Less Efficient Asset Classes

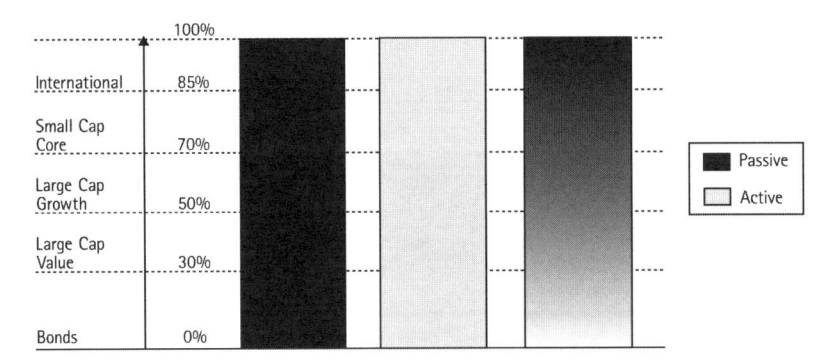

	100% Passive	100% Active	Efficient Portfolio
Total Portfolio			
Return	9.03%	8.89%	9.36%
Risk	10.61%	10.37%	10.36%
Sharpe Ratio	0.35	0.34	0.39
Excess Return	0%	-0.14%	0.33%
Tracking Error	0%	1.31%	1.15%
Information Ratio	N/A	-0.11	0.29

The passive portfolio represents the weighted index returns of the Russell 1000 Value Index, the Russell 1000 Growth Index, the Russell 2000 Index and the MSCI EAFE Index. The active portfolio represents the weighted median manager returns from the Lipper universe for the large cap value, large cap growth, small cap core, and international equity market universes; returns are net of fees. The efficient portfolio represents the weighted median manager returns from the Lipper universe for the active allocation and the weighted index returns for the passive allocation. The passive allocation has been reduced by an estimated 20 bps for equity and 15 bps for fixed income. For illustrative purposes only.
Past performance is not indicative of future results.

Source: SSgA Advisor Consulting Services Research.

Core-Satellite With Active Tax Management

As mentioned in the previous section, investors sometimes fail to consider how quickly taxes can erode portfolio wealth. Active tax management of a core-satellite portfolio potentially offers investors even greater opportunity to create and retain capital.

Too often, investors do not consider the implications of dividend income, capital gains taxes, transaction costs, and management fees on their portfolio returns. Capital gains taxes can be a significant drag on portfolio performance; and investors could discover that portfolios which at first appear to outperform the index on a pre-tax basis may, in fact, significantly lag the market on an after-tax basis.

What is "active tax management"? After implementing a tax-efficient indexed core, investors then utilize aggressive tax-loss harvesting to mitigate the tax consequences of the non-core strategies, e.g., active satellites. After-tax portfolio performance is the key focus of a tax-managed core-satellite strategy.

For example, if an investor's non-core strategy were to generate $200,000 in short-term taxable gains and the client were in the 35% tax bracket, the client's tax liability would be $70,000. The client's core tax-efficient portfolio could potentially realize $200,000 in losses to offset these gains, while matching the pre-tax benchmark returns, thus possibly saving the client $70,000. During years when an investor does not have many gains to offset, the portfolio manager could potentially harvest losses to be carried forward.

How does this process of tax loss harvesting work in practice? If the finance sector were to drop dramatically, the portfolio manager could sell some of the depreciated finance securities to harvest losses. He or she could then replace the sold securities with other finance companies with similar characteristics, thereby ensuring that the portfolio's overall risk characteristics continue to track the index closely. Realized tax losses could then be used to offset realized gains in the core-satellite portfolio or another of the investor's portfolios. Alternatively, the tax losses could be carried forward.

By opportunistically realizing losses throughout the year and by maintaining cost controls, investors could significantly grow after-tax returns, while earning the pre-tax returns of the benchmark.

Finally, for investors who lack the necessary assets or resources to invest in more sophisticated investment strategies such as the core-satellite strategies just described, there exists a relatively simpler and more accessible approach to capturing the benefits of both active and passive management: enhanced indexing.

Enhanced Indexing

Enhanced indexing offers a very cost-effective and a less complex approach, relative to a core-satellite construct, toward combining active and passive management. With an aim to deliver on the benefits of both active and passive management strategies, enhanced indexing attempts to combine the predictability, discipline and low cost of passive management with the typically slightly higher relative returns of active management.

The first step in the implementation of an enhanced indexing strategy is the selection of a benchmark index by which to construct and track the portfolio. This passive portfolio is designed to perform no better and no worse than the market index selected. The portfolio manager then begins to increase portfolio alpha step-by-step by making small, but frequent, changes or building intentional biases into the portfolio, such as underweighting or overweighting specific stocks or industries contained within the benchmark.

These intentional deviations from the index are designed to generate only moderate excess returns relative to the benchmark while controlling for risk. Enhanced indexing strategies typically seek to manage active risk by eliminating unintentional biases or tilts, thereby remaining size and style neutral on an overall portfolio basis.

While borrowing from active management in the sense that enhanced indexing strategies utilize quantitative and fundamental techniques to build small intentional biases, enhanced portfolios still seek to maintain the characteristics of the chosen benchmark; and, like passive strategies, enhanced indexing strategies require low turnover, resulting in lower associated transaction costs. Enhanced indexing strategies seek to optimize the information ratio, thereby providing investors with a very efficient use of their risk budget. That is, the potential for return is high relative to the amount of risk taken. In sum, enhanced strategies seek to capture the risk control and reliability of indexing while still offering the potential for modest relative outperformance.

Conclusion

"Imagine what a harmonious world it could be if every single person, both young and old shared a little of what he is good at doing." — **Quincy Jones**

The World of Money Management

There is a sea of research available to advisors and their clients—both theoretical and empirical—covering active and passive arguments in great depth and tremendous, almost mind-numbing detail. Investors can seek out and digest this avalanche of information at their own risk, but should be wary of any expectation that they will be led to a definitive conclusion as to which approach is best. Compelling arguments can be—and have been—made for both. Amid this ever-widening sea of information and potential misinformation, it is important that advisors provide guidance and direction in helping their clients understand the key distinctions, advantages and disadvantages of both active and passive management.

Discussions in this chapter illustrate that both approaches have their merits and that, perhaps, now is the time for a truce in the perennial active versus passive debate. There is no longer a need to take sides. Advisors have an obligation to protect and promote the financial interests and objectives of their clients and it just may be that the interests of their clients are most favorably served by sophisticated investment solutions that leverage the best of both passive and active management.

❖❖❖

---

1 Source: http://www.investopedia.com
2 Standard deviation is defined as the variability of returns of an asset compared to its average or expected return.
3 Sharpe, William. "The Arithmetic of Active Management." *The Financial Analyst's Journal.* Vol 47, No 1, Jan-Feb 1991, pp7-9.
4 Di Teresa, Peter. "Is Indexing or Active Management Better?". www.morningstar.com. September 27, 2002.
5 Bodie, Zvi, Alex Kane and Alan J. Marcus. Investments. Fifth Ed. New York: McGraw-Hill Higher Education, 2002. 359-374.
6 Source: Lipper. Performance quoted on a yearly basis from 1994 to 2003. The yearly returns were calculated for the S&P 500 and Russell 3000 only. All funds did not report performance every year, so the range for the S&P was a high of 722 funds and a low of 539 funds. For Russell it was a high of 44 funds and a low of 25 funds. Lipper is an industry research firm whose rankings are based on total return performance and do not reflect the effect of sales charges. Each fund is ranked within a universe of funds similar in investment objective. Past performance is no guarantee of future results.
7 Laux, Dr. Paul A. "Traditional Approaches to Investing in Common Stock: A Modern Perspective." Teaching Note 2B Fall 2003 for course BAFI 429: Investment Management. Weatherhead School of Management at Case Western Reserve University. 2003.
8 Source: Lipper. Expenses were calculated for both active and index funds. For the index funds the Lipper average expense rate of 0.47% was used and the average rate of 1.45% was used for active funds. Lipper is an industry research firm whose rankings are based on total return performance and do not reflect the effect of sales charges. Each fund is ranked within a universe of funds similar in investment objective. Past performance is no guarantee of future results.
9 Bernstein, William. The Four Pillars of Investing. New York: The McGraw-Hill Companies, Inc., 2002. 82.
10 Callan Associates.
11 Wermers, Russ. Are Mutual Fund Shareholders Compensated for Active Management 'Bets'? Department of Finance, Robert H. Smith School of Business, University of Maryland at College Park. April 2003.
12 Ibid.
13 Source: Lipper. Average returns were used. Lipper is an industry research firm whose rankings are based on total return performance and do not reflect the effect of sales charges. Each fund is ranked within a universe of funds similar in investment objective. Past performance is no guarantee of future results.
14 Flannery, Sean. "Information, White Noise and Garbage: A Look at Information Ratio." www.ssga.com. September 2000.
15 Fleites, Gus. "Using ETFs to Optimize Risk/Return within an Asset Allocation Framework." www.advisors.ssga.com. January 2003.

The information contained herein does not constitute investment advice and it should not be relied on as such. It should not be considered a solicitation to buy or an offer to sell a security. It does not take into account any investor's particular investment objectives, strategies, tax status or investment horizon. Past performance is not indicative of future results. We encourage you to consult your tax or financial advisor. The views expressed are the views of Patricia Sanchez-Marin and John Tucker only through the period ended March 5, 2004 and are subject to change based on market and other conditions.

24

BEHAVIORAL FINANCE AND VALUE INVESTING

The Brandes Institute Staff
Brandes Investment Partners, LLC

"To enjoy a reasonable chance for continued better than average results, the investor must follow policies which are (1) inherently sound and promising, and (2) are not popular in Wall Street."[1]

— Benjamin Graham

Here's a simple question: *How good a driver are you?* Think of the other drivers you encounter on the road and estimate your driving ability on a scale of one to 10, with 10 being the best. Feel free to use any reasonable set of criteria to evaluate yourself – reaction time, years of experience, driving record, etc. After weighing these factors, what number did you assign yourself?

If you rated yourself a seven or better, you are a typical respondent. If you ranked your driving skill as greater than five, you are in the overwhelming majority. Regardless of your actual driving ability, it is highly unlikely that your self-appraisal was four or less. When researchers pose this question to virtually any group, the average answer is around eight or nine. Think about that for a moment: on a scale of one to 10, the *average* answer is eight or nine. In other words, a majority of participants all believe they are substantially above average — which, of course, is *statistically impossible.*

This example[2] illustrates one of many systematic errors of judgment that impede our daily decision-making. Psychologists have studied these "biases" for decades to better understand human behavior.

So what does this have to do with value investing? Despite theories that the markets are always "efficient" and that investors tend to act "rationally," we (along with other managers) believe that investors, being human, make decisions that include psychological biases, generally without realizing they're doing so. Often, these biases influence a substantial proportion of market participants in the same direction, contributing to the short-term irrationality of stock prices that value investors see as an opportunity.

The 2002 Nobel Prize winners in economics were Daniel Kahneman and Vernon L. Smith, two researchers who integrated psychological factors into their studies of economic and financial markets. The Royal Swedish Academy of Sciences cited Kahneman for applying psychological factors to "human judgment and decision-making under uncertainty." His experiments showed that investors tend to exhibit "shortsightedness in interpreting data that could explain large fluctuations on financial markets."[3] Awarding Nobel prizes to Kahneman and Vernon reflects a growing recognition of behavioral biases and their influence.

Such acknowledgment of psychological factors influencing actions in economic and investment markets echoes the quote from Benjamin Graham that opens this chapter and validates what many value investors have believed for years. Namely, profits may be made in the stock market for patient investors who do two things: conduct thorough, fundamental analysis and have the fortitude to act rationally in an often-irrational environment.

Decades before the term "behavioral finance" was coined, Graham realized that investing in sound businesses was an important component of long-term success – but not the *only* component. He was aware of the market's irrationality and urged investors to exploit its short-term swings in temperament by purchasing out-of-favor stocks when selling at bargain prices, and selling as emotion drives them toward— or beyond— their true, underlying value.

Human nature is far more predictable over time than the day-to-day gyrations of the stock market. By understanding the lessons of behavioral finance, we believe investors can apply a rational approach in a market crowded with irrational participants, and expect much improved results. But (and this is a key point) value investors only can profit from behavioral factors if they set up investment disciplines to make sure they don't fall victim to the very foibles they seek to exploit. This is precisely where professional guidance may have a significant, positive influence. Financial advisors (FAs) may help prevent investors from succumbing to behavioral biases. (Later in this chapter, we'll share tips on how FAs can do this, including working with clients to develop a disciplined approach that stresses a pre-established rational process rather than personal preference or out-of-context judgments.)

But for now, let's look at another flaw that FAs can use as an example to introduce or discuss behavioral finance with clients and prospects – and how understanding such flaws may help better position investors to take advantage of this knowledge.

Extrapolation

While sitting in a traffic jam, maybe you've thought, "It took me 30 minutes to go one mile. At this pace, I'll get home tomorrow afternoon." Or perhaps, while playing golf, you made a birdie putt on the 13th hole and thought, "If I keep this up, I'll shoot a 33 on the back nine!"

These are examples of *extrapolation* – basing a longer-term forecast on an emotional reaction to short-term developments. With respect to performance, market participants often look at negative short-term results and think, "If this continues, I'll lose all my money in three weeks." Or if performance is good, they may say, "At this rate, I'll quadruple my money in six months!" From the tulip bulb craze in Holland during the 17th century to the Internet stock bubble, history is full of examples of the dangerous effects of extrapolation. Much like the example of being stuck in traffic or playing golf, the results are rarely as good, or as bad, as we envision. We often set ourselves up for disappointment or surprises when reality differs from our expectations. It's a quirk of human nature – and one that consistently has surfaced in the investment industry.

Evaluating driving skills, getting stuck in traffic, analyzing golf scores – these examples may be fun stories to share with friends at a party or to help illustrate fundamentals of behavioral finance. But what about objective facts? Is there any broad, statistical evidence that really illustrates that "doing what is not popular on Wall Street" pays off in better, long-term performance?

The Brandes Institute conducted a number of research projects designed to quantify the effects of behavioral biases. Here are highlights from findings of the "Value vs. Glamour" and "Falling Knives" research projects.*

Value vs. Glamour

Amid the Great Depression, Benjamin Graham and David Dodd (a colleague of Graham's at Columbia University) wrote a book that has become the cornerstone for evaluating individual stocks. In *Security Analysis*, published in 1934, Graham and Dodd argued that out-of-favor stocks sometimes sell for prices well below the actual, underlying value of their corresponding business, and that investors cognizant of this phenomenon could capture strong returns. Conversely, the duo theorized prices for widely popular stocks often are buttressed by high expectations, are thus overpriced, and could be vulnerable if these expectations prove too enthusiastic.[4]

Seven decades later, the philosophy espoused by Graham and Dodd is widely known as "value" investing, and the unpopular value stocks they advocated are often associated with companies experiencing hard times, operating in mature industries, or facing similarly adverse circumstances. Alternatively, fast-growing "glamour" firms frequently function in dynamic industries with a relatively high profile. This stark contrast in attributes leads to a natural question: which stocks perform better, value or glamour?

While this is not a simple inquiry, we believe historical analysis can shed light on the relative performance of value stocks and glamour stocks – largely because their divergent traits often manifest in their respective valuation metrics. Specifically, value stocks typically feature low price-to-book (P/B), price-to-earnings (P/E), or price-to-cash flow (P/CF) ratios, while glamour stocks are generally characterized by valuation metrics at the opposite end of the spectrum. As a result, these metrics can be used to split a sample of equities into either the value or the glamour camp – and subsequently track each group's performance over time. As we'll discuss below, this is precisely what we did.

For the purposes of our research, we adopted the "value vs. glamour" methodology employed by three university professors who published a seminal entry in the value vs. glamour canon. In 1994, academics Josef Lakonishok, Andrei Shleifer, and Robert Vishny (collectively, LSV) published "Contrarian Investment, Extrapolation, and Risk," a detailed study of value and glamour stocks in *The Journal of Finance*, a respected academic journal.[5]

---

*Editor's note: The complete research reports are available at www.brandes.com/institute.

Using data from 1968 through 1994, LSV grouped U.S. stocks into value and glamour segments based on price-to-book, price-to-cash flow, and price-to-earnings ratios, as well as sales growth. The academics concluded that, for a broad range of definitions of "value" and "glamour," value stocks consistently outperformed glamour stocks by wide margins. In addition, this outperformance remained robust when the stock samples under review were limited to the larger-capitalization stocks favored by large investors.[6]

We sought to build on LSV's results by extending the time period of the study through the volatile markets of the late 1990s and into 2003, and broadening its scope to include stocks outside the United States.

The Results?

In both the United States and abroad, we found that value stocks we identified:

- Outperformed their glamour counterparts substantially over the long term
- Outperformed glamour stocks consistently

Before we look at the results of our study in more detail, let's quickly review the methodology that we followed to arrive at these conclusions. Following in the footsteps of LSV, we started with all the firms traded on the New York and American Stock Exchanges on April 30, 1968. Then we sorted these stocks into deciles based on price-to-book ratios so that the 10 percent with the highest price-to-book ratios were grouped in decile one. Thus, deciles 1-3 represented glamour stocks while the last deciles (roughly 7-10) represented value stocks.

Once we had grouped the entire universe into deciles, we treated them like portfolios and measured their performance over the five years following their formation. We also formed a whole new set of price-to-book deciles from the sample as of April 30, 1969, then as of April 30, 1970, April 30, 1971, and so on. Then we measured the five-year performance of those deciles (1969 to 1974, 1970 to 1975, 1971 to 1976, etc.). We continued to track performance for deciles formed on every April 30 up through 1989. This last group of deciles gave us returns for the five-year period from 1989 to 1994. Here, in addition to looking at the results, we'll address how we sharpened the focus of the LSV study and extended the period originally covered.

As cited earlier, value stocks, as measured by low price-to-book ratios, outperformed glamour stocks (those with high price-to-book ratios) over the long term. Exhibit 1 illustrates average decile-by-decile returns for the 22 decile sets we created applying the LSV methodology based on the price-to-book metric. To be clear, by "returns," we mean annualized performance over five years. (For more information about this, and other exhibits, please see the *Disclosure* section at the conclusion of this chapter.) As shown, the average annualized five-year return for all 22 sets of decile 1 stocks was 9.3 percent. In other words, on average, the decile 1 stocks LSV identified in each of the years 1968 through 1989 averaged an annualized return of 9.3 percent over five years. (Exhibit #1, top, following page)

Moving from left to right in this Exhibit – from glamour deciles to more value-type deciles – annualized average performance increased substantially. While stocks in decile 1 gained 9.3 percent, the value stocks in decile 10 delivered an average return of 19.8 percent per year over five years.

In Exhibit 2, we show LSV's results along with those generated by the Brandes Institute. The lines don't match exactly, but they are very close. We attribute the minor variation to small differences in our methodology and our sources. For example, LSV used data from the Center for Research in

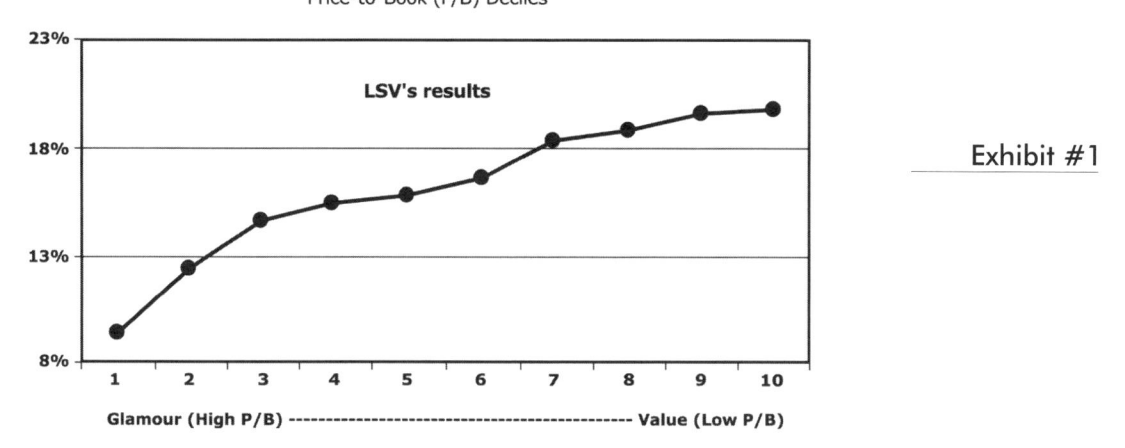

Annualized Average 5-year Returns, 1968-1994
Price-to-Book (P/B) Deciles

Exhibit #1

Security Prices (CRSP) for their performance calculations. In contrast, we used data from Compustat for our performance analysis. Minor differences in these two databases might have contributed to slight disparities between LSV's data and ours. Overall, however, we're confident that these two lines are fairly close to identical—and that our methodology is sufficiently similar to LSV's.

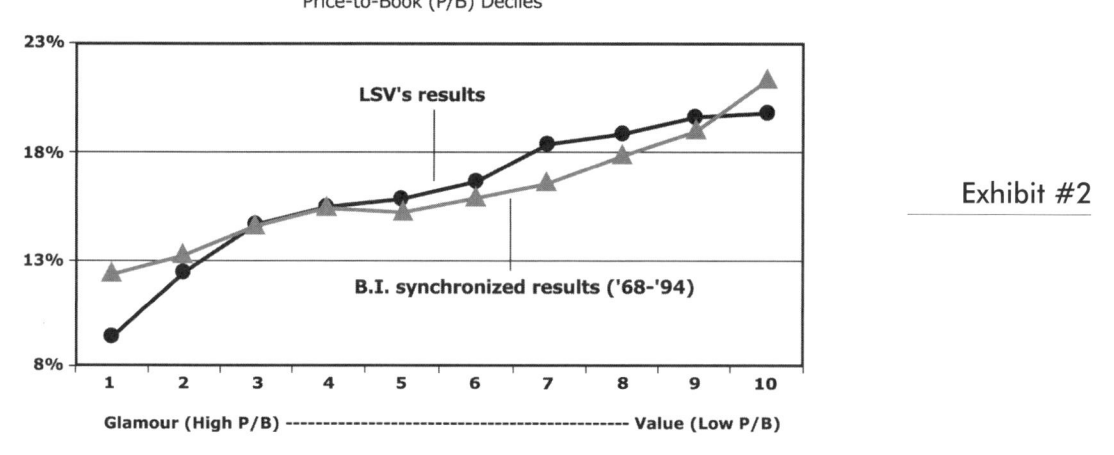

Annualized Average 5-year Returns, 1968-1994
Price-to-Book (P/B) Deciles

Exhibit #2

(It is important to note that this chart only shows results for deciles formed based on the price-to-book criterion. Like LSV, we also achieved very similar results for deciles formed using price-to-cash flow and price-to-earnings ratios. Regardless of the value vs. glamour metric employed, value stocks substantially outperformed glamour stocks between 1968 and 1994.)

Having closely approximated LSV's approach, we wanted to see whether value stocks' outperformance persisted when the study period was extended through 2003. We also wanted to focus on stocks more indicative of a substantial investor's universe. LSV's study contained many micro-cap stocks – those with very small market capitalizations that do not accommodate significant investment. LSV also excluded Nasdaq stocks from their study. Building on LSV's work, we extended their original study in four ways:

• We extended the time period through April 30, 2003 (effectively increasing the number of decile sets we studied from 22 to 31).

- We added Nasdaq firms traded between 1968 and 1998.
- We eliminated the smallest 50 percent of all firms (as measured by market cap) in the sample before forming decile sets each April 30.
- We also extended the universe to value and glamour stocks outside the United States.

Let's look at the results for our extended, or what we called our "focused" study. In Exhibit 3, the black line (punctuated with circles) shows our results for the 1968 to 2003 period before we added Nasdaq firms and extracted firms with small market caps. The gray line (punctuated with triangles) shows the results for our focused sample, after we added Nasdaq stocks and dropped small caps. Despite the addition of Nasdaq companies – a number of which were glamour stocks and among the best performers in the late 1990s – value outperformance remains evident for our focused sample. Returns for decile 1 stocks in our cap-screened sample averaged about 10 percent, while decile 10 stocks averaged just over 17 percent — a margin of 700 basis points. Our findings suggest that this diminished outperformance (it was roughly 1100 basis points in our original sample) is the result of excluding micro-cap stocks. While the margin of outperformance for this sample is smaller, value stock outperformance remains substantial.

Exhibit #3

Annualized Average 5-year Returns, 1968-2003
Price-to-Book (P/B) Deciles

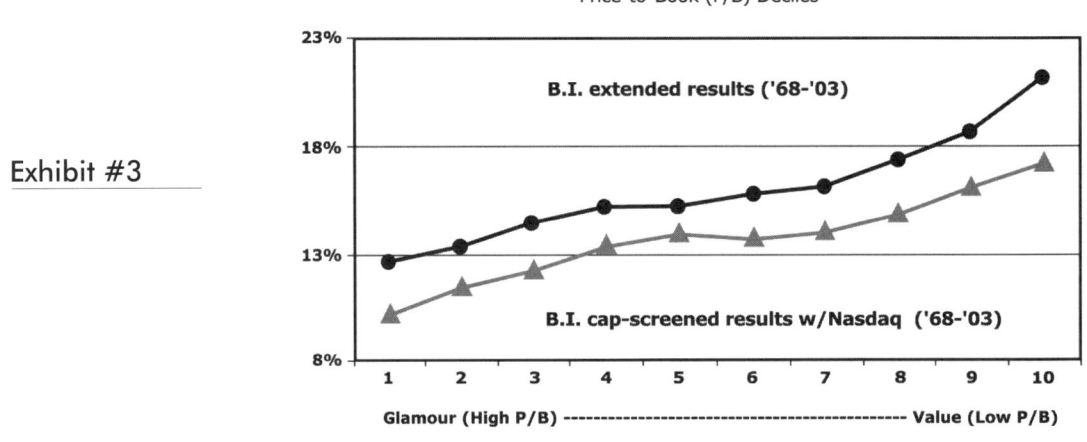

Glamour (High P/B) -- Value (Low P/B)

As cited earlier, value stock outperformance was evident regardless of the valuation metric used. Exhibit 4 on the following page illustrates the average decile-by-decile annualized returns over the entire 1968 to 2003 period measured by price-to-book, price-to-cash flow, and price-to-earnings ratios. Returns for stocks at the glamour end of the spectrum are anchored around 10 percent. Returns for stocks at the value end, in contrast, are up around 15 percent per year, and higher.

Given these results, we wondered: How consistent is value stock outperformance year to year? To answer this question, we examined our findings on a decile set by decile set basis. In other words, we studied the relative performance of value stocks versus glamour stocks for each of the 31 decile sets we examined, from the set formed on April 30, 1968 through the set assembled on April 30, 1998.

For each decile set, we calculate relative performance by subtracting the cumulative five-year returns of stocks in decile 1 (glamour stocks) from the cumulative five-year returns of stocks in decile 10 (value stocks), and then annualizing the result. Effectively, this segments our review of the relationship of value and glamour into 31 rolling five-year periods, starting with the 1968 through 1973 period and ending with the 1998 through 2003 span.

Annualized Average 5-year Returns, 1968-2003
Cap-screened, Nasdaq-inclusive P/B, P/CF, and P/E Deciles

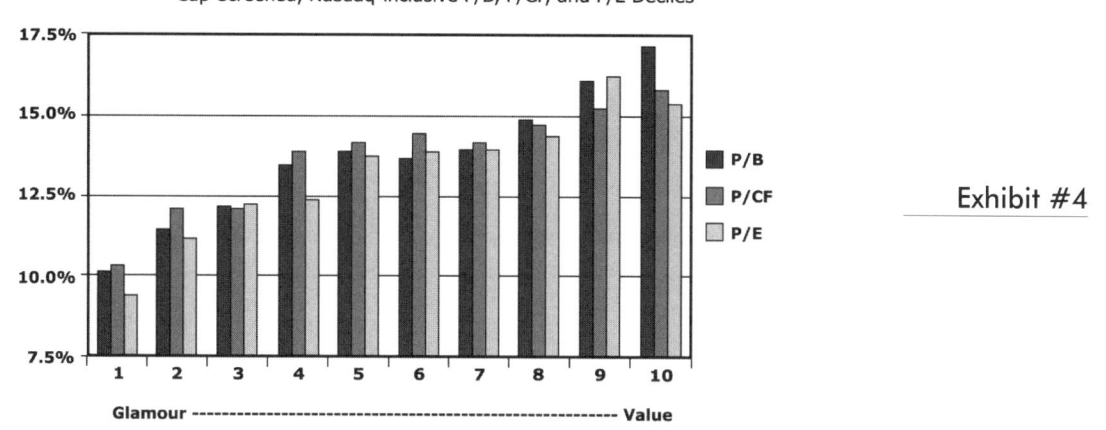

Exhibit #4

In our opinion, this approach suggests the consistency of value stock outperformance between 1968 and 2003. As Exhibit 5 shows, returns for value stocks outdistanced glamour stocks for 28 of the 31 price-to-book decile sets studied. In addition, value's margin versus glamour was an annualized 10 percent or more in seven of these instances. Conversely, glamour stock outperformance of more than 10 percent only occurred once – for the decile set formed in 1995, which happened to capture perfectly the technology-driven glamour stock boom that peaked in early 2000. Even including this anomalous decile set, value stock outperformance averaged an annualized 5.5 percent over the 35-year period. And again, we noted similar results for P/CF and P/E deciles.

Annualized 5-year Relative Performance of Value vs. Glamour
by Price-to-Book (P/B) decile-set

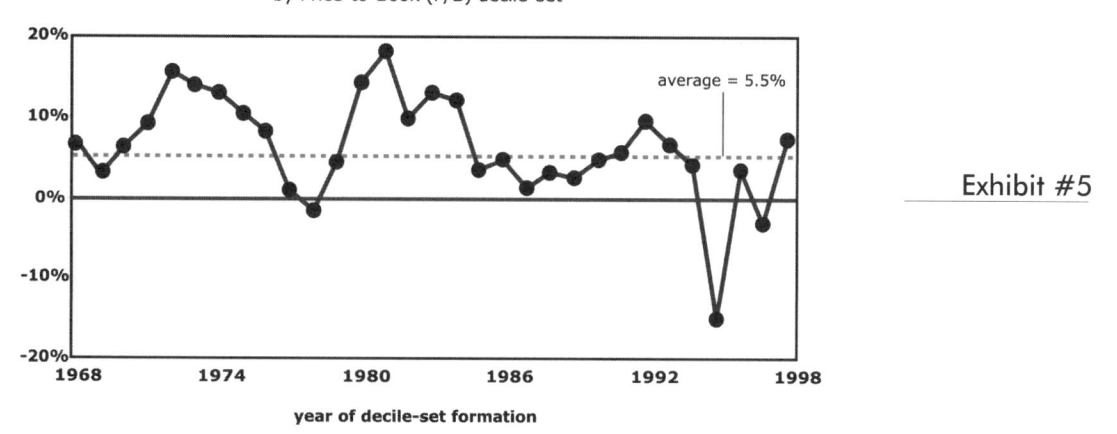

Exhibit #5

Value vs. Glamour: The Value Premium in Non-U.S. Markets

Extending our study to non-U.S. stocks yielded conclusions similar to those in the United States. We applied the same methodology to all common stocks traded in each of the 22 countries that compose the MSCI World Index excluding USA. To sharpen the relevance of our sample, we again excluded micro-cap stocks, taking out the smallest 50 percent of all companies in each country.

After removing each country's micro caps, we divided the remainder of the sample into large-cap and small-cap components. Specifically, we grouped the largest 30 percent of the remaining companies in a large-cap segment and assigned the smallest 70 percent to a small-cap segment. While not exact, we found that this segmentation corresponded reasonably well with other definitions of large- and small-cap stocks in most countries. With this segmentation in place, we examined differences in the relationship between value and glamour at the large- and small-cap levels. The period of our study was 1980 (the inception of the Worldscope database from which we drew our data) to 2003.

To study the relationship between value and glamour in non-U.S. markets in general, we aggregated data from six of the 22 countries in the MSCI World Index excluding USA: the United Kingdom, Japan, France, Germany, Canada, and Australia. In our opinion, these six markets – which contributed more than 70 percent of the Index's market cap as of June 30, 2003 – are representative of developed non-U.S. markets in the North America, Europe, and Asia/Pacific regions. Additionally, Worldscope data for these markets is relatively robust, which contributes to the statistical significance of our findings.

On an aggregate basis, value stocks in these six countries outperformed their glamour counterparts substantially in both the large-cap and small-cap segments. As Exhibit 6 indicates, annualized average five-year U.S. dollar returns for glamour deciles were significantly outdistanced by returns for deciles at the value end of the spectrum. For example, large-cap stocks in decile 1 – those with the highest P/B ratios – posted average returns of 7.0 percent. In contrast, large-cap stocks in decile 10, or those with the lowest P/B ratios, registered average gains of 15.7 percent. These annualized figures are equivalent to cumulative rates of return of 40.5 percent and 106.9 percent, respectively.

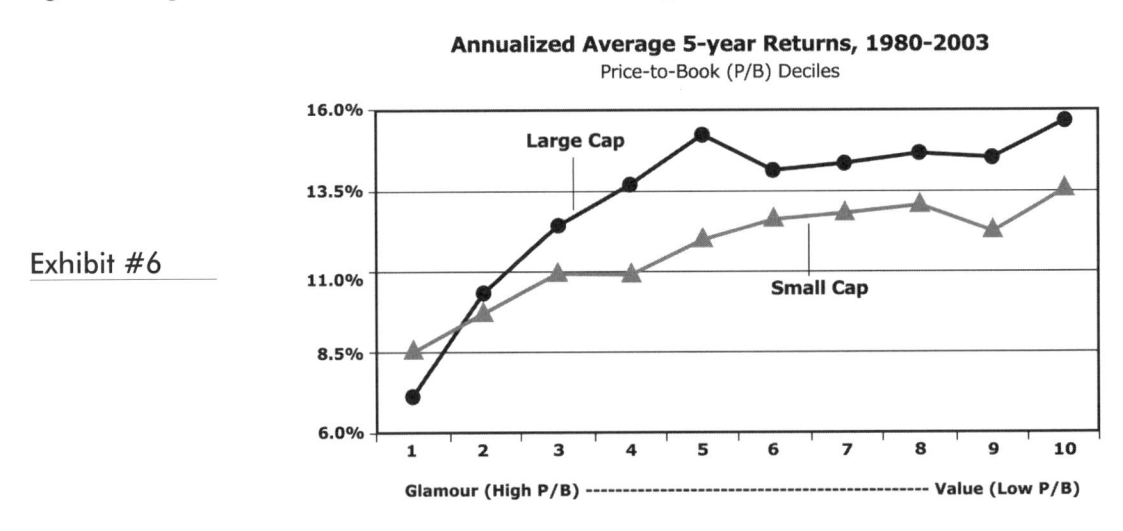

Exhibit #6

Annualized Average 5-year Returns, 1980-2003
Price-to-Book (P/B) Deciles

Glamour (High P/B) -- Value (Low P/B)

With respect to the consistency of value stock outperformance in non-U.S. markets, our results were comparable to our U.S. findings. Applying the same methodology, we effectively segmented value and glamour deciles into 19 rolling five-year periods, starting with the 1980 through 1985 period and ending with the 1998 through 2003 span. As Exhibit 7 on the following page illustrates, value stocks beat glamour stocks in nearly every period, for both the large-cap and small-cap segments of our six-country sample. In addition, value's margin versus glamour was typically substantial: outperformance averaged 9.0 percent for large-cap stocks and 6.2 percent for small-cap stocks. In our opinion, this illustrates the consistency of value stock outperformance over time.

We believe our value versus glamour findings reflect the potential benefits investors can achieve if they are willing to invest in stocks that are not popular. Beyond out-of-favor value stocks, we believe there may be similar benefits for investors who have the courage to purchase "falling knives," stocks that have fallen sharply in price in a relatively short amount of time.

Annualized 5-year Relative Performance of Value vs. Glamour
Non-U.S. Markets

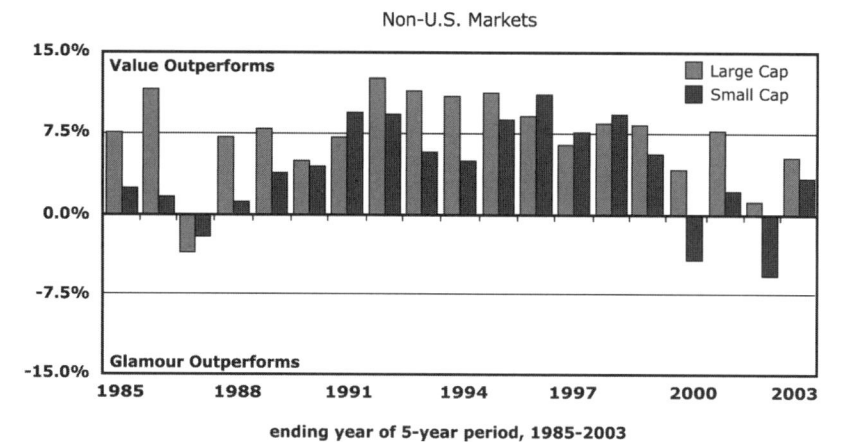

Exhibit #7

Falling Knives

There's an adage on Wall Street: "Never catch a falling knife." This maxim is designed to protect investors from making bad investments by purchasing shares in firms whose stock prices have plummeted and might even appear destined for bankruptcy. But is this true? Are falling knives bad investments?

In this section, we share findings from Brandes Institute research that explores why it may be rational to seek out actively "falling knives" in a portfolio context rather than avoid them entirely. High-profile failures, such as Enron and WorldCom, may galvanize some investors into "zero tolerance" for investing in any stock that has been severely punished in the market. Yet, perhaps because this aversion exists, such situations may offer opportunity for investors who go against the grain to create profit where others see only peril.

Before we review the results of our falling knives research in detail, let's address the methodology. We used performance data provided by Ford Investor Services (now known as Ford Equity Research), an information vendor that manages databases containing price history for a broad universe of equities. We selected data from Ford's U.S. universe, conceived in 1986 with stocks in the S&P 500 Index and the larger-cap members of the ValueLine Index, and then expanded through the 1990s to include constituents of the Russell 1000 and 2000 Indices.[7] For expediency, our research ignored dividends and focused on price-level performance.

Initially, we defined falling knives as stocks that shed 60 percent or more over a 12-month period and had a post-fall market capitalization exceeding $100 million. This definition yielded a group of 1,091 stocks during our study period of December 31, 1986 through March 31, 2002. We also examined groups of falling knives generated by sharper falls and shorter fall periods – and noted that similar results were visible across all groups.*

In essence, our research suggests:

- In the three years following a sharp decline, falling knives did, indeed, experience a higher-than-normal bankruptcy rate.

*Editor's note: To compare results from the various groups the Brandes Institute studied, read the full text of the research report available at www.brandes.com/institute.

- Overall, however, these stocks delivered substantial average gains in absolute terms.
- In addition, falling knives, on average, demonstrated outperformance relative to the S&P 500 Index.

The cumulative bankruptcy rate among the companies we studied was 13.0 percent in the three years after their shares became falling knives. Comparatively, research by LoPucki and Kalin notes that only 0.8 percent of publicly held companies went bankrupt annually between 1983 and 1999 (a period that approximates the time frame for our study).[8] These findings underscore the risk associated with such companies. At the same time, we believe investors tend to focus – almost exclusively – on this risk and ignore the potential for strong returns falling knives may offer.

Despite their high bankruptcy rate, the falling knives we identified delivered substantial gains in absolute terms on an equal-weighted basis. (See Exhibit 8) To gauge the extent to which this solid performance was independent of any broader market effect, we repeated our analysis, focusing on each stock's return versus the corresponding price performance of the S&P 500 Index. For example, if ABC Company became a falling knife at the end of 1992, we compared its subsequent one-, two- and three-year returns against the performance of the S&P 500 Index over the same periods. We aggregated these results.

Average Annualized Performance

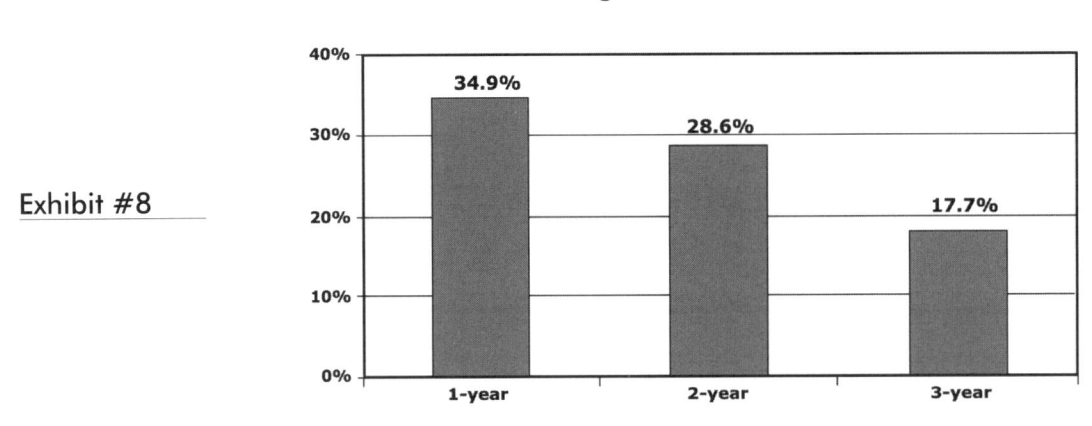

Exhibit #8

Period	Performance
1-year	34.9%
2-year	28.6%
3-year	17.7%

As shown in Exhibit 8, average absolute performance was greatest in the year immediately following the stocks' initial falls, and then regressed toward the market average each year thereafter. Exhibit 9 on the following page, however, illustrates a peak in average outperformance for the two-year period following their initial declines.

Falling Knives in Non-U.S. Markets

When we studied falling knives outside the United States, our research yielded similar conclusions. Drawing on the Worldscope database, we built a universe of all common stocks traded in each of the 22 countries that compose the MSCI World Index excluding USA between July 1980 and July 2003. We limited our sample to stocks with post-fall market capitalizations of $100 million or more; this excluded micro caps, or firms with prohibitively small market capitalizations, and yielded a sample that more accurately represented a truly "investable" universe in our opinion.[9] For every falling knife we identified, we tracked its absolute performance and its outperformance relative to its country's MSCI index over the three years following its fall.[10]

Average Annualized Outperformance

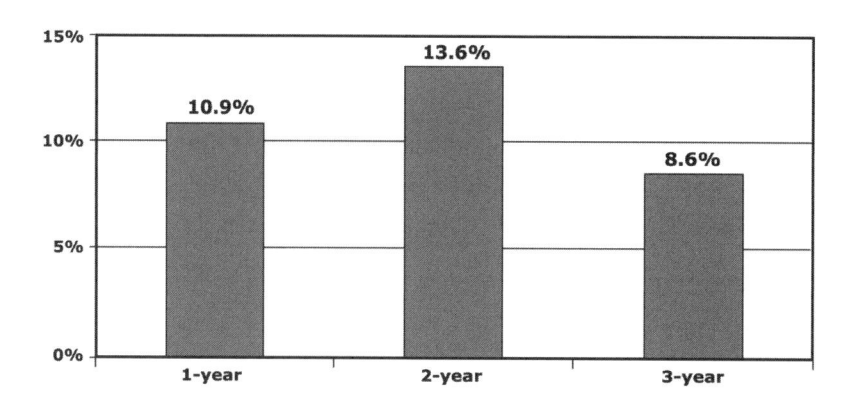

- 1-year: 10.9%
- 2-year: 13.6%
- 3-year: 8.6%

Exhibit #9

Our criteria yielded 1,142 falling knives. As Exhibit 10 indicates, the average non-U.S. falling knife outdistanced its country's MSCI index significantly in the first two years following its initial fall and underperformed its benchmark in year three.[11] On average, the knives we identified gained 19.0 percent in the year after their fall, while the average return for each knife's MSCI country index over the same period was 9.6 percent; in year two, the average falling knife gained 22.2 percent versus an advance of 14.8 percent for its MSCI country index. In year three, knives declined 6.6 percent versus an average loss of 2.7 percent for their benchmarks.

Average Performance, 1980-2003

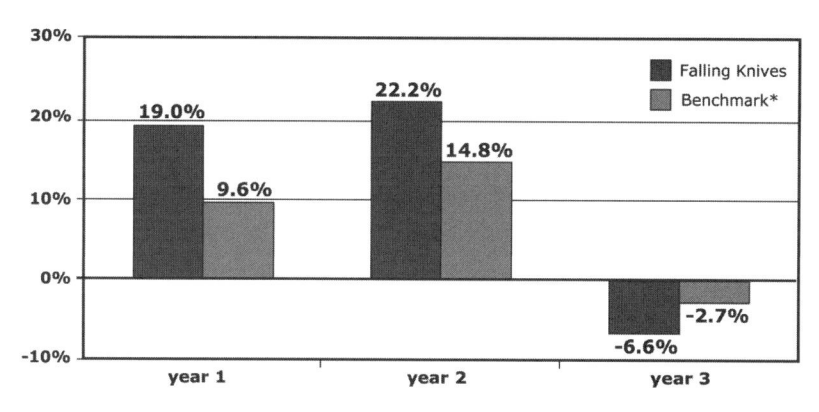

	Falling Knives	Benchmark*
year 1	19.0%	9.6%
year 2	22.2%	14.8%
year 3	-6.6%	-2.7%

Exhibit #10

* We define the benchmark's return as the average return earned by each falling knife's MSCI country index over each of the three years following the knife's initial fall.

Interestingly, the bankruptcy rate for non-U.S. falling knives was sharply lower than the bankruptcy rate we uncovered for their counterparts in the United States. While 13.0 percent of U.S. falling knives went bankrupt, only 22 of the 1,142 non-U.S. falling knives we identified in this study went bankrupt – a bankruptcy rate of 1.9 percent. We believe this disparity stems from differences between bankruptcy conventions in the United States and those in other countries. In the United States, corporate bankruptcy proceedings tend to emphasize the reorganization and rehabilitation of the stricken firm. This differs from nations such as the United Kingdom, for example, where a greater focus on immediate liquidation of assets and reimbursement of creditors could discourage bankruptcy as an option for a company in distress.

Applying What We've Learned

This empirical evidence – the results showing the potential for strong gains among falling knives and value stocks – begs the question: if investing in out-of-favor value stocks and unpopular stocks such as falling knives can help investors achieve better-than-average results, why don't more investors adopt this approach? LSV cited the following reasons:

- Ignorance – in its purest sense. In other words, investors just don't know of the benefits that value stocks can deliver.

- A preference for glamour stocks – based largely on faulty expectations that recent short-term gains in stock price or improving earnings growth will continue for years.

- Short-term thinking.

- Reputation risks – Financial advisors and/or money managers may be worried that clients will have a poor perception of them when they learn of out-of-favor portfolio holdings. These professionals may fear that poor perceptions will lead to them being fired – adversely affecting their firms and/or their personal careers.

Note the trio's comments on the influence of reputation risks and short-term thinking: "Institutions might prefer glamour stocks because they appear to be 'prudent' investments, and hence are easy to justify to sponsors. Institutional money managers . . . often cannot afford to underperform the index or their peers for any nontrivial period of time, for if they do, their sponsors will withdraw the funds. A value strategy that takes three to five years to pay off but may underperform the market in the meantime . . . might simply be too risky for money managers from the viewpoint of career concerns, especially if the strategy itself is more difficult to justify to sponsors."[12]

A Japanese proverb contends, "Beginning is easy. Continuing is hard." Adopting an investment approach that includes purchasing out-of-favor stocks may, at first, seem like a wise choice. But owning unpopular stocks over the long term demands conviction and patience. As Benjamin Graham noted, there are profits to be made in the stock market for patient investors who do two things: conduct thorough, fundamental analysis and have the fortitude to act rationally in an often-irrational environment.

But how can investors avoid the irrational quirks that tend to plague investment decisions? How can they prevent themselves from succumbing to the very behaviors they seek to exploit? How can they develop the fortitude to stick to a value investment approach over the long haul? In the last section of this chapter, we offer some suggestions.

First, we believe it's important for investors to bolster their defenses. As Socrates said, "Know thyself." While the Greek philosopher wasn't talking about global stock markets when he shared this advice around 400 BC, his words are particularly relevant for investors. We believe it's important for FAs to teach their clients certain essentials when investing. Answering the following questions can be a good start for investors:

- What are my investment goals?
- When will I need the money I'm investing?
- What is my tolerance for volatility?

One way investors can get an *objective* point of view to these questions, of course, is by working with a professional financial advisor. By having a frank discussion with clients, FAs may be able to detect areas of weakness in an approach, unrealistic expectations, or misperceptions that could lead to trouble.

> **A four-step process, to counter self-defeating behavioral tendencies.**

1. Assess risk tolerance and define investment goals and time horizon.

2. Create a written plan designed to achieve goals.

3. In implementing the plan, develop an asset allocation strategy and strict process for rebalancing and security and/or money manager selection and termination.

4. Regularly monitor all aspects of the process versus stated goals and make appropriate adjustments.

Helping clients set objectives can avoid the tendency to constantly compare short-term returns for their portfolios against an index – or a certain brother-in-law who likes to brag about how much money he's making in stocks. It might make clients feel better to have owned the best-performing stock each quarter, but it is far more important to evaluate periodically how their overall portfolio is doing compared to the specific goals they have set.

In addition to assessing risk tolerance and gauging time horizons, there are other factors to consider when creating objectives, including: return requirements, income and liquidity needs, tax considerations, and legal and regulatory concerns.

FAs can explain to prospects and to clients that having a written game plan for buying or selling a stock greatly reduces the potential for making emotional decisions and can be an excellent defense against the kinds of psychological pitfalls addressed earlier. A written action plan also can help bring greater consistency. As for reviewing progress toward goals, we suggest establishing how often this should be done. FAs and their clients may want to examine portfolios every six months or once a year. We suggest putting a lot of time into *developing* the plan and far less time into *tinkering* with it. Unless long-term goals or objectives change, clients probably will make few adjustments to the plan once it's established.

In Conclusion

Long-term value investors recognize that financial success doesn't happen overnight. There will be periods when stocks aren't performing well. That is when patience becomes especially important to success. During down markets, FAs should remember to remind clients that the fundamental principles of purchasing undervalued businesses and doing what is not popular on Wall Street outlined in this chapter retain merit.

But knowing and understanding those principles won't be enough unless FAs (and their clients) practice patience and self-discipline. How critical are patience and discipline for the successful investor? We turn again to Benjamin Graham, who makes the argument for restraint in *The Intelligent Investor*:

"For indeed, the investor's chief problem — and even his worst enemy — is likely to be himself…We have seen much more money made and *kept* by 'ordinary people' who were temperamentally well suited for the investment process than by those who lacked this quality, even though they had an extensive knowledge of finance, accounting, and stock-market lore." [13]

While the rest of the world rushes to buy great concepts or the latest high flyer, the successful value investor must hang tough and stick to basics. In our opinion, maintaining a disciplined approach, trusting individual convictions (versus those of the crowd), and patience will contribute to a rewarding pursuit when investing in undervalued businesses around the world.

❖❖❖

---

1 Graham, Benjamin. "The Intelligent Investor: A Book of Practical Counsel." Fourth Revised Edition. New York: Harper & Row. 1973 (page 13)

2 Kahneman, Daniel, "The Psychology of the Non-Professional Investor," article presented at Harvard seminar on Behavioral Finance, November 1998.

3 Huuhtanen, Matti. "Two Americans win Nobel Price for Economics." *The Seattle Times*. October 9, 2002. (pulled from the Internet on Dec. 2, 2002) at seattletimesl.nwsource.com/html/businesstechnology/ 134551407_webnobe109.html.

4 Graham, Benjamin and David L. Dodd. "Security Analysis." McGraw-Hill, New York, 1934. See chapters 1 and 17.

5 At the time of publication, Lakonishok taught at the University of Illinois, Shleifer at Harvard University, and Vishny at the University of Chicago. Also in 1994, the trio founded LSV Asset Management, a quantitative value equity manager that uses proprietary models to manage money for institutional investors. In October 2003, the firm's website (www.lsvasset.com) listed its assets under management at over $9.0 billion.

6 LSV's conclusions are summarized on pages 1543-1544 of their report.

7 As of 12/31/86, Ford's U.S. universe included approximately 2000 stocks. At the close of our study on 3/31/02, stocks in the universe numbered over 4500. For more info on Ford, visit www.fordinv.com.

8 LoPucki, Lynn M. and Kalin, Sara D. "The Failure of Public Company Bankruptcies in Delaware and New York: Empirical Evidence of a 'Race to the Bottom.'" *Vanderbilt Law Review*. Vol. 54. Number 2. March 2001, pages 231-282.

9 Companies are not completely removed from the database after their first appearance in our sample; instead, each falling knife rejoins the database 12 months after its fall. As a result, a knife can reappear in our study if it experiences a subsequent 60 percent fall in a separate 12-month period and still maintains a post-fall market capitalization above our $100 million minimum.

10 We calculate outperformance by subtracting the return of each falling knife's country index from the knife's absolute return. All performance is in U.S. dollars.

11 We define the benchmark's return as the average return earned by each falling knife's MSCI country index over each of the three years following the knife's initial fall.

12 Lakonishok, Josef, Shleifer, Andrei, and Vishny, Robert W. "Contrarian Investment, Extrapolation, and Risk." *The Journal of Finance*. Vol. XLIX, No. 5. Dec. 1994.

13 Graham, Benjamin. "The Intelligent Investor: A Book of Practical Counsel." Fourth Revised Edition. New York: Harper & Row. 1973. (page xv)

Disclosure: The information provided in this material should not be considered a recommendation to purchase or sell any particular security outside of a managed account. It should not be assumed that any security transactions, holdings, or sector discussed were or will be profitable, or that the investment recommendations or decisions we make in the future will be profitable or will equal the investment performance discussed herein. Investing outside of the United States is subject to certain risks such as currency fluctuation and social and political changes; such risks may result in greater share price volatility. Please note that all indices are unmanaged and are not available for direct investment.

With respect to all exhibits in this chapter, past performance is no guarantee of future results. No transaction costs or taxes were included. Your actual results will vary.

For "Value vs. Glamour" exhibits (Exhibits 1-7), performance results reflect total returns. Typically, stocks of small companies tend to experience more volatility than mid- and large-sized companies. While LSV's paper connects "value" stocks with recognized value investing proponents such as Benjamin Graham and David Dreman, it does not explicitly associate "glamour" stocks with growth investing, the value strategy's traditional foil. Accordingly, we note that, for the purposes of our study, "glamour" is not necessarily synonymous with "growth."

Like many researchers studying value vs. glamour, LSV actually used reciprocals of the P/B, P/CF, and P/E metrics to distinguish between value stocks and glamour stocks. We note that this approach yields identical results, and we focus on P/B, P/CF, and P/E for simplicity. Our source for P/B, P/CF, and P/E data, as well as performance information, was the Compustat database, which we accessed using FactSet. For the purposes of our study, price-to-book was defined as market value of equity on April 30 divided by book value of equity as of the most recent fiscal year-end. For performance measurement, decile weights were rebalanced annually. As a result, deciles began each year with equal weights for all stocks.

For "Falling Knife" exhibits (Exhibits 8-10), performance results reflect price-only returns.

The foregoing reflects the thoughts and opinions of the Brandes Institute, a division of Brandes Investment Partners. Brandes Investment Partners is a registered trademark in the United States.

PART IV

Eye On The Investment Portfolio

25

IDENTIFYING INVESTMENT MANAGER SKILL

Ronald J. Surz, CIMA
President, PPCA Inc.

Do investment managers have skill? Can these managers be identified? Are my consultants personally invested with these managers?

These important questions asked by clients could not be answered with confidence just a few short years ago. The motto of professional investment performance evaluators has long been, "Evaluate skill, not luck."

For years everybody attempted to make this distinction by using Modern Portfolio Theory (MPT), but this didn't work, primarily because the focus of MPT is solely on broad market effects. However, about five years ago, researchers discovered the significance of investment style in identifying skill.*

Researchers learned that skill could be properly identified only by lifting the thick clouds of style that routinely distort one's perspective, in addition to accounting for the broad market effects dictated by MPT. It was more complicated than MPT would suggest, but not that much more. Put simply, good growth equity managers tend to continue to be good growth equity managers, and ditto for value, but if you're only looking at broad market effects you'll never see this persistence. In the past, the problem with identifying skill had been that it was routinely confused with *style.* Witness the numerous firings of value managers that occurred as the growth stock bubble of the late 1990s inflated. Accordingly, the motto for 21st century evaluators is gradually becom-

*Editor's Note: A list of some of these studies is provided in the Appendix to this chapter.)

ing, "Evaluate skill, not style." The term "gradually" is used because the evolution beyond MPT has been slow, and some may not agree with concepts in this chapter.

The following is written from the perspective of the professional evaluator. Professional evaluators have an advantage over the academic researchers who have discovered style-adjusted persistence in *performance* because these evaluators understand the other three Ps: People, Process, and Philosophy. Accordingly, they can use style-adjusted alpha as a first cut in their search for skill. This determination of positive risk and style-adjusted value added is called *performance evaluation*. Professional evaluators can then determine the reasons for the alpha and verify that these reasons substantiate the other three Ps. The examination of the reasons for performance is called *attribution analysis*. The reasons revealed by attribution analysis are stock selection and sector allocation. Importantly, to make sound decisions, evaluators look for persistence over time in these sources of added value. Furthermore, they confirm that the value added is coming from a source consistent with the management process. If the management process is predominantly top-down, one would expect alpha to derive primarily from sector allocation. Similarly, a bottom-up manager should excel in stock selection. This total performance evaluation and attribution picture is shown in Exhibit 1.

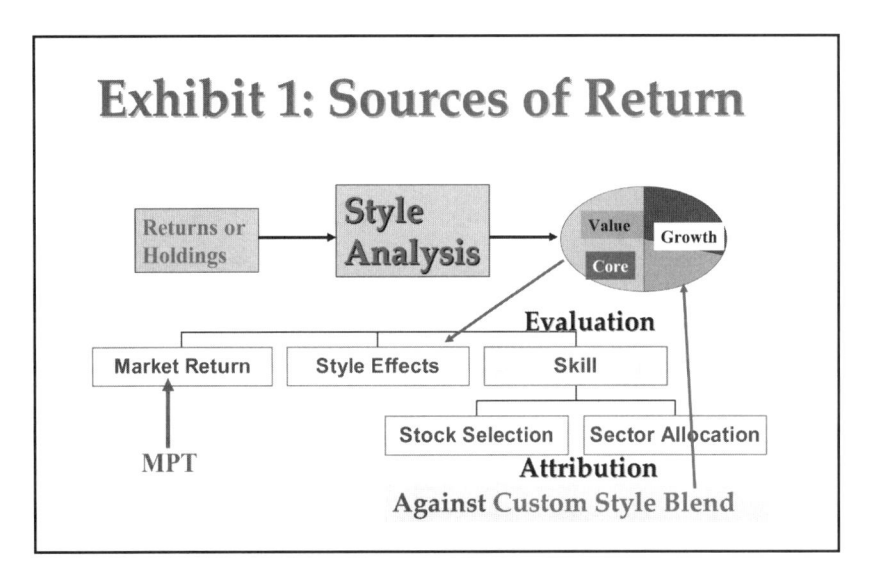

Exhibit 1: Sources of Return

Note that while alpha, or skill, can be estimated using either holdings or returns, holdings are required to complete the picture with the components of skill, or attribution analysis. Note, also, that it is important that style be taken into account in both performance evaluation and performance attribution. Performance evaluation will be discussed first, followed by performance attribution.

As a practical matter, the search for skill ought to begin at the macro level with managers whose performance is good. Then due diligence can proceed with an understanding of the people, process and philosophy that produced the good performance. And then last, but not least, performance attribution confirms that the sources of this good performance are consistent with the people, process and philosophy. Throughout this process, keep in mind that the resultant decisions are all about the future, even though we use the past as a guide.

Performance Evaluation

The answer to the question, "Is performance good or bad?" rests on yet another question: "Relative to what?" The investment industry has two answers to this second question: passive alternatives and peer groups. Most evaluators use both benchmarks. Passive alternatives are indexes, or combinations of indexes, that could have been purchased for a low fee in lieu of the active manager actually selected. Peer groups are collections of other managers that could have been hired instead of the active manager actually selected. Both of these benchmarks have problems, but there are solutions to them.

Peer groups

The investment industry has been using peer groups for so long that no one thinks to question them, except for the occasional discussion about survivor bias, which seems to be the only bias that people know and understand. Survivor bias raises the hurdle by including only those portfolios that have remained in business for the entire evaluation period, which is generally five years or more.* In actuality, peer groups suffer from a collection of biases, only one of which is survivor bias, and each peer group has its unique set of idiosyncratic distortions. As a result, the exact same performance number will rank differently against different peer groups, even when all of the peer groups are for the same management mandate, such as large cap growth.

Benchmarks

Even if a bias-free peer group existed, it still would not qualify as a valid investment performance benchmark as defined by the criteria established by Richards & Tierney, a Chicago-based investment consulting firm specializing in custom benchmarks, and supported by the Association for Investment Management and Research (AIMR). These criteria are summarized below:

Criteria for Good Benchmarks

1. Unambiguous: Names and weights of securities are clearly stated.

2. Investable: Investors have the option to forego active management in lieu of a passive alternative.

3. Measurable: The benchmark's return can be calculated on a reasonably regular basis.

4. Appropriate: The benchmark accurately represents the manager's approach.

5. Reflective of current investment opinions: The manager has current knowledge of the securities constituting the benchmark.

6. Specified in advance: The composition of the benchmark is agreed to and constructed prior to the start of all evaluation periods.

Traditional peer groups meet none of these criteria, except possibly No. 3.

Performance evaluation is all about making a judgment as to whether performance is good or bad. This judgment ought to be made relative to a passive alternative. *It doesn't matter how other managers in a particular peer group have fared,* since they, too, should each be evaluated against their respective passive alternatives. Put another way, "If you don't like your ranking in one peer group, choose another peer group." *What matters is the degree of success or failure experienced relative to*

---

* The analogy that's frequently used to describe survivorship bias is the marathon with 1000 runners and 100 finishers. Is the 100th finisher dead last, or in the top decile? He's in the top decile.

a chosen benchmark. This can only be captured through a relatively new technique that creates all of the portfolios that could have been held by the manager, selecting from stocks in a benchmark that meet the criteria on the preceding page. This new approach combines the better characteristics of peer groups with those of passive alternatives, while eliminating the problems of each. A manager's ranking in this scientific universe is an indication of the degree of his success or failure.

Passive Alternatives (Indexes)

Scientific universes bridge the gap between peer groups and passive alternatives. Passive alternatives have two problems: defining them, and waiting. The industry's experience in manager performance evaluation has led it to conclude that most managers use a blend of styles. This conclusion has been reached with the help of a relatively new technology called returns-based style analysis (RBSA). RBSA solves for the blend of style indexes that has behaved most like the manager, and identifies this blend as the manager's effective style mix. Note the similarity of this approach to that of a "normal portfolio." Normal portfolios are custom benchmarks designed to capture the essence of an individual manager's process and philosophy. Sometimes called "information-neutral portfolios," these designer benchmarks were intended to reflect the portfolio to which the manager would retreat if one day he had no insights or ideas to implement. Almost everyone agreed at first that normals were a great idea, but it turned out that only a few consulting firms could construct them properly. Due to the cost and effort involved, normal portfolios never really caught on. By contrast to normal portfolios, which are composites of individual securities that are extremely difficult to construct, effective mix portfolios are blends of styles that are easy to create. The old idea of designer benchmarks is back, and this time it is actually doable.

The collection of style indexes used in RBSA is called a "style palette." It's important that this palette be the best possible so the analysis is reliable. It's like finding the best color master for creating custom-blended paint. RBSA uses return history and optimization techniques to determine the blend of styles that most closely emulates the behavior of the investment portfolio. As with any statistical process, data problems in RBSA may go undetected, leading to faulty inferences. One such problem is "multicollinearity," which occurs when the style indexes used in the regression overlap in membership. Multicollinearity invalidates the regression and usually produces spurious results. While most users of RBSA focus on optimal fit, it is important to note that good style palettes should also possess certain characteristics, as described below. The first two characteristics have been put forth as requirements by the developer and creator of RBSA. The last two characteristics are ours, and represent our opinion of good characteristics.

Characteristics of Good Style Palettes

- Mutually exclusive: No stock is categorized into more than one style. Accordingly, multicollinearity is minimized.

- Exhaustive: All stocks are classified. Some index vendors throw out data, e.g., stocks with negative earnings or small companies. Finding a good fit is impossible if any of the portfolio's stocks have been eliminated.

- Inclusion of core: This continues to be a novel idea. It's a way to deal with stocks in that gray area between value and growth. Most index providers deal with this problem by either throwing out these stocks, violating the exhaustive rule, or by classifying them into mul-

Identifying Investment Manager Skill

Characteristics of Good Style Palettes

tiple styles, violating the mutually exclusive rule. Interestingly, core doesn't always perform between value and growth. Sometimes it is better than both, and sometimes it is worse.

- Quarterly rebalancing: Things change rapidly. Calling a cheap high-tech stock "growth" because it had a high price/earnings ratio a year ago doesn't make sense. Of course, more frequent rebalancing makes an index harder to track because its composition is changing.

Be aware that the popular style palettes meet none of these criteria. Popularity is not synonymous with quality when it comes to RBSA.

Regardless of the style palette, the resultant style blend meets the criteria for a good benchmark, and, importantly, represents a portfolio that the investor could have purchased for a low fee instead of hiring an active investment manager, so the problem of defining the benchmark has a contemporary solution. The next problem is somewhat more difficult to solve. It takes many decades to develop statistical confidence in the manager's ability to beat his benchmark. For example, if a manager's return is 12 percent per year, and the custom style mix has returned 10 percent, one will have low confidence that this two percent annual spread is skill if it occurred over a five-year period, and might still have insufficient confidence over a 55-year period. This is because it takes a long time to develop confidence in the parameters that define the underlying statistical process.

This waiting time problem can be solved by operating in the cross section, rather than across time. By forming all of the portfolios that could have been formed from the passive style blend, statistical significance can be determined in a very short period of time. It's classic statistics: "I'm testing the hypothesis that the manager has succeeded, so I let the monkeys form portfolios at random. If my manager's performance is in the top 10 percent of this random distribution, I accept the hypothesis with 90 percent confidence, and I do so even if the measurement period is as short as a few months or weeks."

Put another way, if a manager delivers a 50 percent return in a month, and his custom index is flat, there's a good chance that this is a significantly good return, and one shouldn't have to wait decades to come to this obvious conclusion. Cross-sectional performance evaluation produces the statistical backdrop necessary to make this determination, while traditional cross-temporal regression approaches (aka "alpha") do not.

Performance, therefore, is best evaluated against a scientific universe formed from all of the portfolios that the manager could have held, selecting stocks from his custom style blend. The next question is, "Why is performance good or bad?"

Performance Attribution

Like performance evaluation, there has been an evolution in performance attribution. The performance measurement industry is fairly young, having started in the 1970s. Much of the attribution analysis that had been used until recently was developed in the 1980s, when we were only beginning to understand that there was more to life than MPT. We knew back then that characteristics like capitalization, price/earnings ratio, and dividend yield mattered, but hadn't figured out how to best integrate these factors into attribution analysis. Consequently, we wrote "slicers and dicers" that segmented the portfolio and the benchmark by whatever characteristic we liked. To see how the segment of one's portfolio with high P/Es fared against the comparable segment of stocks in the S&P 500, one would just draw the P/E line wherever one wanted, and voila!

The problems with these old approaches are standardization and benchmark inflexibility. If you draw the P/E line at 15 and I draw it at 20, we'll each get different insights. Also, as described above, those who wanted to use a custom style blend as the benchmark couldn't do so with the 1980s technology because it didn't provide the ability to customize the benchmark as a blend of indexes. So, with the old technology we could peel the apple like an orange or slice the orange like an apple, but the end result was a rotten fruit salad.

By contrast, contemporary technologies encourage the use of custom style-blended benchmarks, and standardize style definitions so there is comparability across managers. In this way a manager's stock selection and sector allocation skills are not confused with his style. Exhibits 2 and 3 summarize this evolution.

In the search for skill, one must look for persistence in the reason(s) for good performance, and for confirmation of the People, Process, and Philosophy. Exhibit 4 (facing page) shows a manager who has consistently added value through stock selection, although the amount of value added has slowed somewhat in the recent past. This particular manager is a bottom-up stock picker, and the attribution analysis confirms his skill in this endeavor. Sector allocation has also added some value, which is consistent with bottom-up stock picking. Only Trading Activity has had a modest negative effect on performance. Trading Activity measures the intra-period effects on performance of transactions executed during the period. If this manager were looking for ways to improve performance a place to start would be the trading desk.

These relatively new tools give the professional evaluator the insights needed to determine whether good performance is likely to continue into the future. The discussion thus far applies to all types of tradi-

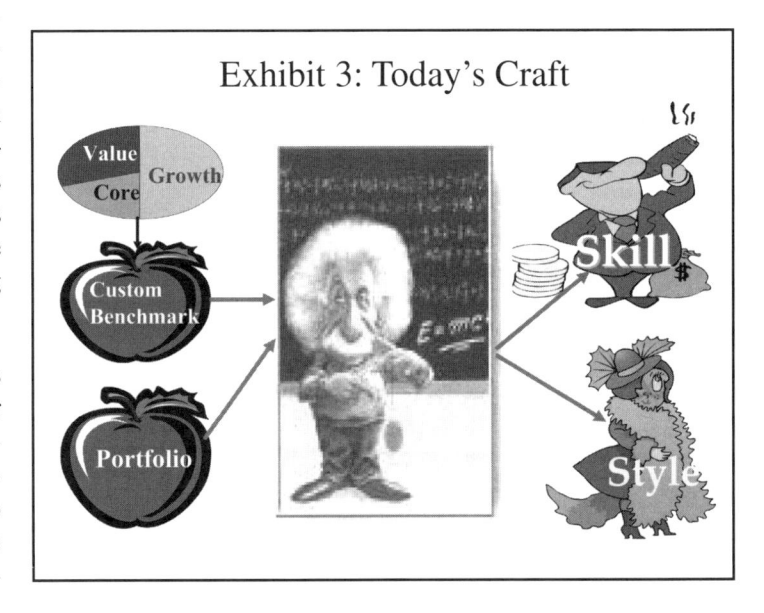

Exhibit 2: 1980's Slicer & Dicer

Exhibit 3: Today's Craft

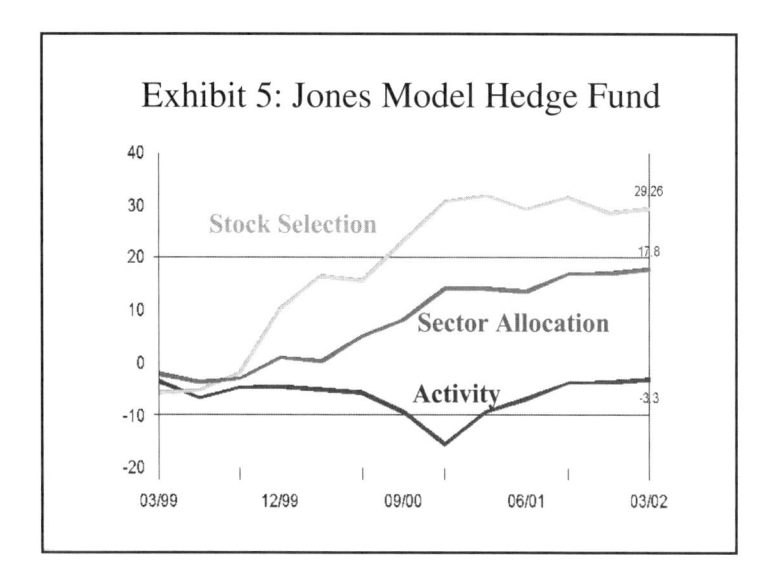

Identifying Investment Manager Skill

Exhibit 5: Jones Model Hedge Fund

(Chart showing Stock Selection reaching 29.26, Sector Allocation at 17.8, Activity at -3.3, from 03/99 to 03/02)

Exhibit 5: Jones Model Hedge Fund

(Illustration of a scale balancing Short and Long, with Leverage above and Direction below)

tional portfolios – U.S. stocks, foreign stocks, bonds, etc. With some extensions, it can also be applied to hedge funds.

Hedge Funds

The growing popularity of hedge funds has engendered a tendency to confuse form with substance. The hedge fund form is excellent for skillful managers, since they can implement efficiently on most of their insights. As a result, some equate hedge funds with skill, even calling them "skill-based strategies." This skill part is not necessarily true, so the substance may, in reality, be missing from some hedge funds. Because of the fees involved and the degree of latitude afforded to the hedge fund manager, it is even more important that skill is present in hedge funds than in traditional investing. This determination must consider all of the moving parts in a hedge fund, as depicted in Exhibit 5.

In this context, style and attribution analyses begin by looking independently at the short portfolio and the long portfolio, just as if they were each long-only portfolios. Attribution analysis then blends the two portfolios, adding in the effects of directional bets, which are amounts long or short away from the target long and short exposures for the fund. The final level of attribution is leverage. Here the effects of the targeted leverage can be measured, as well as any deviations from this target. As in traditional analyses, the end game is persistence in one or more of these sources of value added, and persistence that confirms the skill of the people, process and philosophy of the manager.

Conclusion

The search for investment manager talent puts a lot of emphasis on recent past performance. Unfortunately, in evaluating past performance, style is routinely confused with skill. The retirement industry is particularly notable for making this mistake as a group. Perhaps it's because the test of fiduciary prudence rests partially with what other fiduciaries have done.

After general market effects, the most important determinant of performance is style, followed by a distant third residual that we use to find manager skill. Detecting skill is tough for this reason. Although it's easy to confuse style with skill, it's hard to make good decisions once this mistake has been made.

❖ ❖ ❖

References : Studies Finding Evidence of Persistent Style-Adjusted Excess Return
Coggin, Daniel T. and Charles A. Trzcinka,, "A Panel Study of U.S. Equity Pension Fund Manager Style Performance," *Journal of Investing*, vol. 9 (Summer 2000), pp 6-12
Gruber, Martin J. "Another Puzzle: The Growth in Actively Managed Mutual Funds," *Journal of Finance,* vol. 51, no. 3, 1996, pp 783-810
Ibbotson, Roger and Amita Patel. "Do Winners Repeat With Style," Ibbotson Associates research paper, November 2001.
Kahn, Ronald N. and Andrew Rudd. "The Persistence of Equity Style Performance: Evidence from Mutual Fund Data." The Handbook of Equity Style Management, 2nd ed., (New Hope, Pa: Frank J. Fabozzi Associates, 1997)
Stewart, Scott D. "Is Consistency of Performance a Good Measure of Manager Skill?" *Journal of Portfolio Management*, vol. 24, no. 3, 1998, pp 22-32.

26

THE SIGNIFICANCE OF STYLE DRIFT

Steven Maslow, CFP®
Managing Director
GroupRed, LLC

"A foolish consistency is the hobgoblin of the mediocre mind."

–Ralph Waldo Emerson

The fall of the stock market and the rise in popularity of the television series, "Survivor" coincided at the turn of the 21st century. Why, you may question, would we link a frivolous television series with something as serious as the capital formation process? Because the driving force behind their valuations is the same: audience participation.

The comparison is the sort that Wall Street professionals like to dismiss as anecdotal—as correlation, not causation, the way a previous generation used to joke about average skirt lengths and the Dow Jones Industrial Average (DJIA). But in the late 1990s, common stock ownership became so widespread that Wall Street itself entered the popular culture, creating an unprecedented level of "audience participation"[1] and sending valuations to historic highs.[2] Equity ownership reached a high of 48.2 percent of U.S. households in 1999, and 49.5 percent in 2002; in 1983 the figure was 19 percent. The average number of individuals owning equities per household rose to 1.6 in 1999, a record to this day. The record high for the DJIA was reached on Jan 14, 2000: 11,722.98 During the 1990s, while Survivor became the most widely watched show in U.S. households, the DJIA climbed from approximately 3700 to its aforementioned peak, an unprecedented rate of growth and not, owing to the dearth of small companies in the index, largely attributable to Internet-related valuations.

The capital markets and the TV show have more than a superficial resemblance: One player—the investor—is pitted against the stock market—a powerful opponent indeed. Playing to win against such an opponent is likely to be a sure recipe for losing. By making the most of a bad bargain—by resorting to long-forgotten atavistic, if not primal, behaviors—the investor at least maximizes the probability of survival.

Style Drift - The "Survivor" Pitfall

For investors, the behavior in question is diversification. By making the most of a bad bargain—by diversifying instead of striving to make a killing—the investor at least maximizes the probability of survival. For financial advisors then, diversifying client assets is mission-critical and fundamental. Style drift undermines diversification, and places financial advisors in a position where they inadvertently diversify client assets not wisely, but too well. Minimizing style drift, conversely, permits the kind of diversification that aligns market returns with market risks, if not survival. Advisors, in other words, cannot control returns, but they can manage risks: diversification is their principal tool; style drift, their nemesis.

Professor Harry Markowitz, winner of the Nobel Prize in Economics for his pioneering work on the mathematics of stock market "survivors," was single-minded only, perhaps, in his insistence that risks could be managed, not eliminated, through diversification of assets. Perhaps his best-known concept is the "Efficient Frontier" through which Markowitz established the highly counter-intuitive process by which assets are included or excluded from a portfolio based on the way they behave in concert; not just individually. Markowitz, in other words, established that performance and risk are inseparable metrics where portfolios are concerned.

Markowitz's work is the intellectual foundation underlying the current hyper-trend upon which investors hitch their assets together and turn the reins over to a professional in order to achieve a level of diversification and management they could not manage themselves. The impetus to diversify drives the explosive growth in the categories of mutual funds, hedge funds and funds of funds. And what salt is to the seasoning of food, diversification is to portfolio management. The finest ingredients would provide subpar, if not indigestible, cuisine were they under- or over-seasoned; and so, too, would a portfolio, were it under- or over-diversified. It *is* in the mix.

Moreover, the financial equivalent of hybrid vigor (the genetic concept in which the blending of certain parent traits produces offspring with characteristics superior to those of either ancestor) is the properly diversified portfolio.

Hence the great threat to investors' (and, soon after, their advisors') survival is improper diversification. When a money manager accepts an investor's money into Portfolio or Fund A, and contractually agrees to invest it in specified ways, the investor's exposure to various risks, both inside and outside Portfolio or Fund A, can be measured and mitigated through diversification. When the same manager exposes the investor to risks outside their agreement, the road to hell is well-paved: not only is the portfolio or fund out of balance, but the investor is exposed to risks that undermine the diversification among his or her other assets as well.

Style Drift in Action

In ordinary commerce, when professionals accept fees and represent they will perform a service according to rules and then break them, at the very least it is called a breach of contract. Are damages caused by mere *exposure* to harm, and if so how much? This is a question for attorneys. When a money manager does the same, it is called "style drift." Is a manager drifting and, thereby, destroying the balance in the clients' portfolios? This is a question, if not *the* question, for financial advisors.

Our definition of "style drift" is what happens when a manager makes changes from a specific style, asset class or index that is described as the investment purpose of a portfolio or fund.

Imagine that an advisor had placed client funds with a fixed income arbitrage manager and he or she "drifts" by investing the clients' funds into speculative growth stocks. This is a substantial problem if the advisor carefully determined the individual client's risk capacity and matched it to a defined risk exposure, which is what, after all, financial advisors are essentially advising about. In our example, the only certainty is that potential returns, volatility and risk are going to change. Sound familiar? This is a pattern of behavior that led to the demise of Long Term Capital Management and the loss of billions of dollars of investor money.

Financial advisors face an extraordinary dilemma when they inform clients that a manager is drifting, very often because the manager is chasing higher returns from a different asset, and the client responds by saying, "I don't care." The visceral excitement generated by this breakdown of investment discipline captivates investors when it works, and exerts an equal and opposite vehemence when it does not. Unless the advisor is comfortable playing the role of the client's pharmacist to the manager's doctor, the advisor must be prepared to either counterbalance the client's portfolio to account for the manager's style drift, or fire the client. Furthermore, it is legally ambiguous whether the advisor can be held accountable were the client to override the advisor's recommendation to maintain proper diversification.

Unbalanced portfolios do not survive the capital markets over time because the odds are overwhelming. To those who say "Diversification is a hedge against wealth" we say, "You are oversimplifying. It is over-diversification that is a hedge against wealth." Nevertheless, no financial advisor we know of has been brought before the regulators for attempting to over-diversify a client's portfolio, though several have for under-diversifying. Avoiding style drift requires a manager to possess both an extraordinary depth of knowledge about individual assets and an encyclopedic breadth of familiarity with the markets in which they trade. Avoiding style drift requires discipline. And between discipline and a risk-appropriate return lies style drift.

The Style Drift Persona

Style-drifters are, in fact, more common than conventionally thought because they are only too human. They get bored with sticking to their routine; they wish to avoid pain when their investment style is out of favor, and they especially want to seek the pleasure of generating high returns "*uber alles*," an experience which, as Sigmund Freud said, can only enter our consciousness via a contrast to—and not from a maintenance of—our routine activities.

Some financial advisors have been "enabling" style-drifters. Many tend to ogle five-year average returns without measuring the risk undertaken to achieve them. How often do they monitor the degree of variation within those five-year periods and, less often still, compare those variations with the index returns for the asset or style under investment consideration? The Internet has placed unprecedented amounts of such information at the advisor's disposal; yet rarely, except for alternative investments, are such metrics considered, such as the Sharpe Ratio and its variants (metrics that measure return in the context of risk).

Sticking to one's investment style requires temperance, a virtue witnessed in our time by the actions of money managers like Buffet, Soros and Niederhoffer or conveyed during performances of Shakespeare's *Henry IV*. The great money managers are distinguished not so much by novelty nor intelligence nor connections, but by their ability to live paradoxically: they operate both consistently (but not foolishly so) and flexibly (but within bounds)–an iron-clad adherence to a flexible set of rules from which they do not drift. Bernard Baruch, world renowned financier and advisor to presidents in the early 1900s, bought all his straw hats in winter as reliably as Warren Buffet buys stocks with intrinsic values less than their current prices. Which hats and which stocks defined the boundaries of their "style."

The stock-in-trade of all great money managers is the ability to recognize a subtle, regular recurring pattern from one characterized by high drama and brief duration. Because great managers drift least, their investment patterns are highly predictable. Advisors can reliably diversify their clients' assets among them. Hence, their enormous "audience participation" and consequent portfolio valuations. However, an advisor's concern with style drift does not end with selecting Berkshire Hathaway and a set of gold coins for every client.

The Best Defense

Unlike tigers, securities can change their stripes. When Warren Buffet, the avatar of value investing, began purchasing Coca-Cola common stock in the late 1980s, the security wore "growth stripes" as measured by the difference between the then-current prices and the Graham & Dodd intrinsic value. By the mid-1990s, the prices of Coca-Cola's common stock began to show "growth stripes" as both the price and the rate at which it grew doubled. Financial advisors who were fortunate enough to have exposure to Coca-Cola common during this time would have had to adjust their clients' portfolios, perhaps by paring back less successful growth investments and counter-balancing the portfolio with alternative investments. Surely this is not "style drift" but is yet another way in which financial advisors can explain the importance of monitoring and balancing the activities even of luminary investors, in order to create additional returns in—and ensure the survival of—their clients' portfolios. To avoid the "foolish consistency" that characterizes mediocre minds, we must learn to tolerate and prepare for ambiguity; e.g., the limits a manager may reach in placing "big bets."

A prime example of giving adequate notice to advisors is the Fidelity Magellan Fund prospectus. Fidelity makes a point of disclosing to investors the extent to which the manager's investment style may diverge from various indices and the principal factors likely to influence fund returns. Fidelity is clearly signaling that its managers may choose to over or under weight securities within the Fund's portfolio—but the limits of these arrangements are disclosed. In fact, many investors select managers precisely because they are skilled at over or under weighting securities in a given asset class in order to capitalize on market inefficiencies. CNN/Money interviewed Bob Stansky, the manager of Fidelity's giant Magellan Fund on April 15, 2002 and asked him quite bluntly, "How do you beat the S&P 500?" He responded, "You beat it by over weighting some groups, under weighting others, and by owning stocks that aren't in the S&P 500. Sometimes I think if people knew how risky I was acting in the portfolio they'd be really surprised. Just go back a bit—I made AOL very big; I made Yahoo very big. I'm not afraid to make any bet."

Our point is clearly illustrated by the anecdote above: style drift is toxic because it cloaks the investor's true risk, creating an over weighting or under weighting of exposure to a kind of asset. Stansky's investment vehicle—the Fidelity Magellan Fund—makes clear in its prospectus that the manager may choose to place up to a certain percentage of the fund's assets in single stocks ("big bets"), and, therefore, advisors may diversify their clients' other holdings to allow for Stansky's investment style. In other words, to be a successful "survivor" financial advisors may wish to counsel their clients to compensate for the possibility of exposure to "big bets" with other types of investments. If a manager is drifting, advisors can neither plan nor act, and their performance becomes more a matter of chance than skill.

The prevalence of style drift is so great that it causes a serendipitous opportunity to add greater value to client portfolios. By now it should not be surprising that this is accomplished not so much by asset selection as by asset diversification, mentioned earlier. That is, advisors add the most value by designing portfolios whose asset prices not all move in concert. It is, therefore, incumbent upon the advisor to be able to articulate conceptually— and in dollar terms— the dangers of style drifting and the benefits of diversifying well. Ask yourself, in dollar terms, "Which will have the greatest perceived and actual impact on my clients' portfolios over time? (1) Choosing common stock value manager A over common stock value manager B (the differences in returns are often measured in single basis points), or (2) diversifying my clients' assets such that an unwelcome event affecting value manager A is counterbalanced by holdings with manager C, who makes direct real estate investments?" Advances in technology permit financial advisors an unprecedented degree of precision to measure risk, and, with that information comes the power to diversify properly and add real returns to client portfolios without depending on "make or break" bets.

Style Drift and Risk Management

Risk means different things to different people. Webster's defines it as the "possibility of loss" and most of us would agree risk in securities investment is the degree of likelihood of an unfavorable outcome. A 65-year-old retiree may have a different attitude toward this possibility than someone midway on the journey through life, but risk has a fundamental and quantifiable meaning to all investors. On Wall Street this concept has been measured operationally as the variability of anticipated returns, and is measured mathematically with a concept called standard deviation. At the heart of this metric is the notion that the past is prologue to the future, and, sooner or later, an investment's returns will conform to an historical, recognizable and predictable pattern.[3] Recognizing those patterns is another way of saying advisors must compare the standard deviation of a particular investment with those of other investments in order to determine how many dollars may be allocated to each.

As the time value of money is used to compare cash flow streams of different investments, the standard deviation allows an advisor to compare the riskiness of different assets. While it is outside the scope of this chapter to delve into the precision of standard deviation as an investment metric, it is defined as the square root of the average squared deviation of each *possible* return from the *expected* return. In common-sense terms, if a biotechnology company has an expected return of 20 percent and a standard deviation of 40, we may reasonably anticipate that the actual investment returns will fall between –20 percent and +60 percent two-thirds of the time, that is 20 percent anticipated return, + or –40 percent standard deviation. Surely this calculation of standard deviation for a single security does not provide much certainty; it is more a description of the climate than the weather. But the importance of standard deviation is clear when investments are compared as they are in a portfolio.

Since the attractiveness of a security with respect to its return and risk cannot be predicted in isolation, more than one asset should always be held. *Not selection, not timing,[4] but diversification is the principal determinant of "survival."* For example, say that an investment in a local firm that owns restaurants has the same expected 20 percent return as the biotechnology company illustrated above, but with a standard deviation of 10. Now we would consider the biotech investment excessively risky. In the technical jargon of modern portfolio theory, the restaurant company is said to dominate the biotechnology one. In plain English, the restaurant company has the same anticipated return as the biotech, but is less risky.

What if we compare the investment in the restaurant company with one in a voice-over-IP Internet telephone company, an investment in which the anticipated rate of return is 50 percent, but in which the standard deviation is 75? In this example, when one investment has both a higher expected rate of return and greater risk, our investment decision will be determined by the financial advisor's assessment of an investor's risk tolerance. A 65-year-old retiree will have a different attitude toward risk than a 40-year-old in mid-career. The choice of one investment over the other is an expression of taste and preference about risk and return. Because portfolio managers cannot possibly take into account the tastes and preferences of each investor when making decisions, it is the role of financial advisors to define the limits of exposure to assets for their clients. That is, to help investors diversify in order to survive the overwhelming odds against them in the marketplace.

A Classic Example

In November of 1985, Pennzoil was awarded the then-unimaginable sum of $10.5 billion by the courts against Texaco for misconduct in "tortuously" outbidding Pennzoil in Texaco's acquisition of Getty Oil Company. Based on this single event, Pennzoil's stock almost doubled, from $46 to $90 per share, in a matter of days. (Texaco declined from $38 to $25.)

Now the date is March 25, 1989 and imagine the client owns Exxon stock. When the advisor awakes that morning and notices the leading article in *The Wall Street Journal* is headlined, "Alaskan Oil Spill Largest Ever," the advisor might infer this is not good news for their clients' holdings. Following this event, the stock of Exxon declined for several months.

What happened to Pennzoil and Exxon were events unique to these two companies, and the stock market reacted accordingly. The prices of the stocks changed in light of new information. While one might have wished they owned Pennzoil in 1985, or didn't own Exxon in 1989, everyone likes to avoid uncertainty, which is to say everyone is, to some degree, risk-averse. Most would want to reduce the risk associated with the investment portfolio without having to lower the expected rates of return. Diversification accomplishes this task effectively by dividing and conquering the variability of returns.

Risk can be isolated, measured and reduced (but not eliminated) because some of the volatility in returns of any asset is unique to that asset. And that uniqueness can be countered by the uniqueness of another asset. We cannot expect to eliminate all risk from our portfolios, because of the correlation factor. But we can divide risk into (1) firm-specific risk (e.g., the performance of the stocks of Pennzoil in '85 and Exxon in '89) and (2) market-related risk (the performance of the S&P 500 in '85 and '89). A better term for firm-specific risk would be "diversifiable" risk because it can be diversified away.

A Different Kind of Risk

Market risk cannot be diversified away when securities are the assets under discussion, though the recent surge in popularity of funds of funds, in which investment managers are assembled like securities into a portfolio, and other alternative investments, seek to accomplish precisely this task. Nevertheless, the principle remains the same: the markets do not provide us with extra rewards for assuming risks that could be avoided by simply diversifying. Therefore the *only* relevant risk is non-diversifiable risk.

The Significance of Style Drift

A manager who drifts will destroy the balance among the assets in client portfolios, especially those assets not under control of the manager. Hence, style drift increases exposure to diversifiable risk, for which the market does not compensate and reduces exposure to non-diversifiable risk, the relevant risk. And advisors who choose consistent managers reduce diversifiable risk and earn increased returns for their clients and a good night's sleep for themselves. Ironically, ultimately this requires advisors to accept that a manager's "bad" returns in a given year were "good" because they evidence the manager's consistency. In the wider context of total portfolio risk, the client's investments' survival may depend on it.

Two types of risk in a stock market portfolio are illustrated in the footnote.[5] Total risk declines until there are approximately 20 securities, and then the decline becomes very slight. The remaining risk, typically about 40 percent of the total, is the portfolio's market risk. At this point, the hypothetical portfolio is highly correlated with all securities in the marketplace.[6]

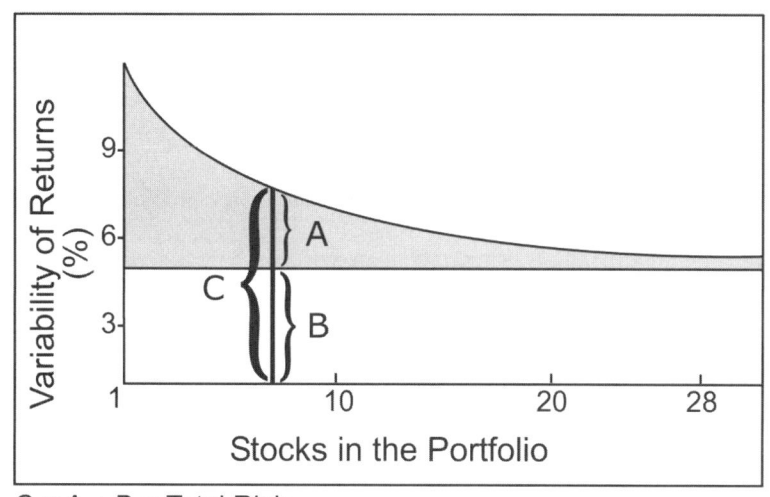

C = A + B = Total Risk
A = Diversifiable Risk
B = Non-diversifiable Risk (Result of general market influences)

The danger implicit in style drift can now be understood in all its dimensions. It over weights asset-specific risks, essentially putting too many of an investor's eggs in too few baskets. And, because it is undisclosed, investors may not become aware of this until too late.

A recent study by the Association for Investment Management and Research (AIMR) found that approximately 40 percent of actively managed funds are classified inaccurately, based on the stated goals versus actual investments. In other words, fund managers, except for those of index funds, are drifting along. These style drifts often entail shifts in positions, which drive up trading costs, generate higher taxes, alter risk, and lower returns.

Moreover, it is not merely investment professionals who need to be vigilant about style drift. Many financial establishments and even state bodies, including the Chinese and Italian central banks, found this out on September 23, 1998, when the president of the Federal Reserve Bank of New York found it appropriate to call on the cream of the crop of the international financial establishment to prevent the bankruptcy of Long Term Capital Management (LTCM). In view of the extraordinary persons and sums involved—$4.8 billion in capital, $200 billion portfolio and securities (derivatives) with a notional value of $1.25 trillion with two Nobel prize winning experts in the "science" of risk, Myron Scholes and Robert Merton, as principal shareholders—it is astonishing that the managers' style drift led them to mistakenly place too large a bet on the convergence of interest rates.

It was thought the liquidation of LTCM might disrupt the U. S. economy, hence the intervention of the Federal Reserve into a private hedge fund. The two great lessons learned from this debacle are:

1. ***Nesson Dorma ("No one may sleep")***: there is no such thing as "cruise control" where investments are concerned and advisors are paid, in large measure, to monitor the activities of their managers and maintain diversification of client portfolios

2. ***Over time, it is better to sleep well than eat well*** because client survival is a function of the advisor's ability to diversify them properly, against which style drift is a stealth killer.

The Role of the Advisor

Once an advisor has monitored and determined, through that monitoring, that the manager has drifted, he or she must decide what actions to take. If this chapter has a "takeaway" for advisors it is that monitoring for style drift (as part of, or separate from, portfolio attribution) is one of the advisor's most important responsibilities. What the advisor *should* do can significantly vary from what the advisor *does* do, so let us separate the theory from the reality.

The Theory

The first step, taken in the interests of fairness of objectivity, is to allow the manager to respond to the advisor's finding. The advisor should contact the manager, lay out the findings, and let the manager respond. The manager might have an explanation (temporary aberration, market condition, capital structure arbitrage, offsetting position) the advisor finds acceptable, thus eliminating the problem.

Assuming the advisor believes even after discussions with the manager that there is style drift, the next step is to attempt to have the manager correct the problem. If in a separate account, the advisor may instruct the manager to take whatever steps are necessary to bring the portfolio back into compliance with the original intent.

If the manager will not correct the situation, the next step is quite clear and simple: the advisor should fire the manager (remember, this is the theory part) and select another one who fits the style. In the theoretical world, this completes the issue. The advisor has performed his or her role and the client is receiving what he or she has sought.

The Reality

Let us take the most difficult variation on the theme first: the advisor determines that the manager has drifted in style, but the performance is still positive (versus the underlying perception that style drift invariably leads to losses). A diligent advisor is faced with recommending to the client the termination of a manager who is producing positive performance. This is clearly not an easy thing to do. It is, however, the correct thing.

The client is not receiving what he or she expected when the manager was hired. The investment may not be fitting into the overall asset allocation the advisor constructed. It is not consistent with the investment policy.

Here's the variation that is most troublesome:

1. Advisor finds style drift and recommends termination.
2. Manager is profitable.
3. *Client* does not want to terminate the manager (does not care, likes the profits, likes the manager, etc).

The Significance of Style Drift

This is called the *reality* section because things can get *extremely* difficult. The advisor is now left deciding whether or not he and she should terminate *the client.* Some advisors may seek a midground by having the client sign a statement acknowledging awareness of the drift so that subsequent events do not allow for criticism of the advisor who is, essentially, *surrendering control over the account while being paid to control it.*

All advisors know how difficult it is to attract and retain clients and, thus, confronting the possibility of terminating a client is by no means an easy decision. What is easy to determine is that it goes to the integrity of the advisor and the performance of his function. To state it differently— it is where principle overcomes principal.

Although proper diversification can seem a simplistic answer to the style drift problem, it addresses all the potential consequences of style drift when implemented properly. Some clients may resist (in a sense the extent to which they believe they are invulnerable to adversity "drifts" when it requires counterbalancing positive returns from an asset. Advisors may have to notice their clients in writing that they are, in fact, "drifting" from the advisor's counsel, and, if the wake-up call goes unheeded, advisors may have to terminate the relationship or trust that clients will accept responsibility for adverse developments.

Advisors and clients, both, can be "survivors," but only if they collaboratively apply proper diversification and its risk management benefits. This is their only defense against the "survivors" nemesis, style drift.

❖ ❖ ❖

---

[1] Sources: *The Wall Street Journal*, ICI/SIA equity ownership surveys and Survey of Consumer Finances, Board of Governors of the Federal Reserve System.

[2] IBID

[3] Bear in mind that most investment performance measures are computed using historic data but are justified on the basis of predicted returns. Implicitly or explicitly, it is assumed that historic results have some predictive ability.

[4] It is interesting to note that Gary P. Brinson, Brian D. Singer and Gilbert L. Beebower, in their "Determinants of Portfolio Performance "*Financial Analysts Journal* (May-June 1991) found that timing investments explained a meager 1.8 percent of the variation in pension fund returns. That is, none of the investors of these pension funds were any better than their peers at timing market movements when making investments.

[5] x-axis: number of stocks in portfolio; y-axis: variability in returns (standard deviation)

[6] A large number of studies have noted that portfolios consisting of approximately 20 randomly selected common stocks have virtually no firm-specific(diversifiable) risk. See Robert C. Klemkosky and John D. Martin, "The Effect of Market Risk on Portfolio Diversification," Op. Cit. (March 1975, pp. 147-154).

PART V

WEALTH MANAGEMENT SOLUTIONS

27

SEPARATELY MANAGED ACCOUNTS

Don Gartlan, Director
Russell Managed Portfolios
Russell Investment Group

The history of separately managed accounts is rich and filled with colorful stories about the men and women who pioneered the concept of fee-based consulting, managed accounts, and the value of advice. Many such legends are chronicled in industry books about the roots of this business. But today, the growing popularity of managed accounts is largely the result of hard-working and talented consultants and advisors who continue to serve clients—both retail and institutions—using a proven investment consulting process. The technology supporting the use of SMAs by advisors also has improved greatly in recent years, making the vehicle easier to use.[1]

To better understand managed accounts' beginnings, let's flip the calendar to the 1960s when our country was in a state of political unrest and economic change. Wall Street witnessed irrevocable changes in its markets and its players that altered the financial services industry. Several landmark pieces of legislation affected pension funds. The most significant was the Employee Retirement Income Security Act (ERISA) of 1974, which forever changed the landscape of managed assets.

Performance measurement was virtually unheard of at the time, and there were no benchmarks or similar vehicles to compare investment results. After a few major mutual fund performance studies were undertaken by such firms as Russell Investment Group, SEI (AG Becker) and RogersCasey, institutional consulting was born.

The World of Money Management

In addition to legislative changes, a series of events occurred in the financial services industry (including the end of fixed commissions, the 1970's bear market and portfolio managers leaving banks) which further accelerated the trend toward skilled financial advisors capturing larger assets—the middle market, $50 to $150 million—an under-serviced market that could truly benefit from the type of management that, until then, only Fortune 500-type companies enjoyed.

Initially, the managed "product" included the three-step process of developing client investment objectives, evaluating and choosing suitable managers, and monitoring their ongoing performance. This gave smaller investors comparable institutional-caliber oversight which many early consultants believed was an important service for that market. In the 1970s, the first wrap fee program was launched by EF Hutton and offered to the public on an all-inclusive fee basis. Then, six months from the industry's "May Day," Hutton rolled out a product that discounted commissions to zero. Other firms such as Merrill Lynch, Dean Witter and Kidder Peabody joined the fray in the mid-1980s.

Today, it's generally accepted that the term, "wrap fee" does not adequately reflect the true definition or comprehensiveness of separately managed accounts. Rather, the term focuses on the fee aspect only, and not the significant value of the investment process and the consulting effort of the advisor. Increasingly, the industry is using the terms SMAs, managed accounts, fee-based business and managed money to describe this area of investment strategy. The focus is on the process, and not the actual product or fee.

In the early days, it was difficult to determine whether the industry was driving technology, or technology was driving the industry, but by 1980, technology systems had become more sophisticated, and as account minimums began to decrease substantially, the number of accounts for money managers to handle blossomed. Eventually fees came more in line with minimums and gave advisors the ability to attract more assets.

This added to the proliferation of new product and catapulted the industry into the 1990s, a period where gathering significant market share was the name of the game–all events that would mold the industry into what it is today.

SMAs More Popular Than Ever

Today, wealth transfer demographics along with the aforementioned technology, are largely responsible for the potentially explosive numbers the industry will continue to experience over the next decade. According to Financial Research Corporation, the number of individuals with more than $1 million in investable assets is projected to grow at 16 percent annually for the next three years.[2] This segment of the population will control $30 trillion by the end of 2004 as reported by Web Finance in their World Wealth Report.[3]

This segment is growing five times faster than the general population. According to the US Census Bureau, one in 14 households is a millionaire household, and this number has quadrupled in the past 10 years. Currently there are 14 million millionaire households in the United States, and wealth transfers between generations are projected to be $12 trillion over the next 20 years.

As a result of this phenomenal growth in wealth, the assets held in separately managed accounts industry-wide totaled $456.29 billion at the end of 2003's third quarter. Assets held by year-end 2002 totaled $391 billion. These numbers are based on a survey conducted by the Money Management Institute of managed account sponsor firms.[4]

Separately Managed Accounts

Assets Under Management in Separately Managed Accounts Programs

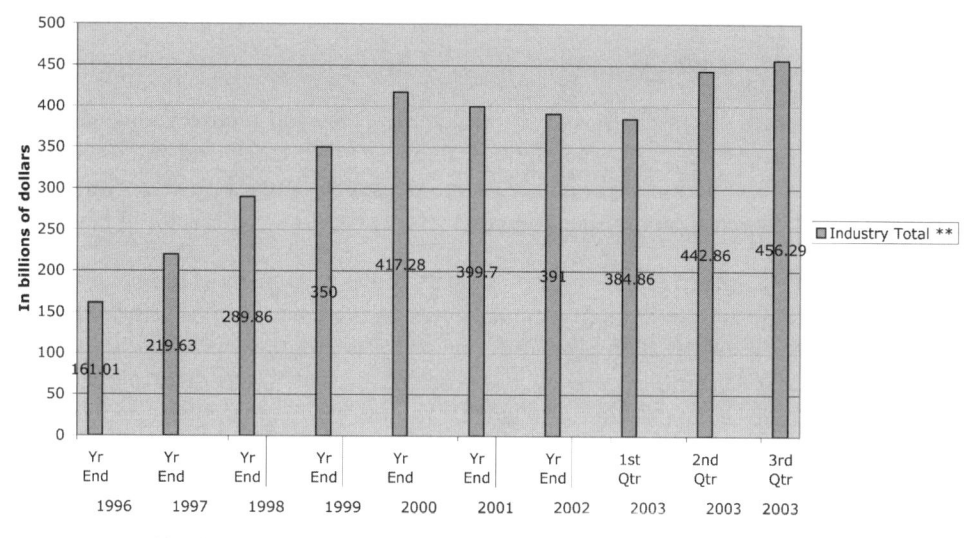

Period	Industry Total** (in billions of dollars)
Yr End 1996	161.01
Yr End 1997	219.63
Yr End 1998	289.86
Yr End 1999	350
Yr End 2000	417.28
Yr End 2001	399.7
Yr End 2002	391
1st Qtr 2003	384.86
2nd Qtr 2003	442.86
3rd Qtr 2003	456.29

** Estimate based on observations of other proprietary databases and projections from MMI sources

Estimates vary, but the most reliable industry sources suggest that today fewer than 20 percent of financial advisors use separate accounts on a regular basis. Even in the wirehouses, which hold more than 70 percent of all separate-account assets, estimates are that as few as five percent of the advisors drive more than 80 percent of the business. This leaves much room for further growth. [5]

Separate accounts have even shown strength during difficult times in the market when other investment products showed signs of weakness. They have grown so dramatically in recent years for several reasons. In part, some popularity is due to the increasing popularity of fee-based advice. The industry also has benefited from the entry of many new, well-financed players who have helped spread the word about separate accounts and lent credibility to the product.

Because of their popularity among advisors, and the marketing momentum they have gained, the controversial debate about whether SMAs are a product or whether they are a process rages on.

SMAs became relatively mainstream in the 1980s and early 1990s as an investment venue through which investors could gain more control over the effects of their portfolio results. They enabled them also to effectively manage those results, with the help of their advisors, to achieve their financial goals and objectives.

SMAs, therefore, are best viewed as products that can be used in the basic investment planning process. The process might consist of several steps. Advisors first profile a client, gathering information on investment goals and risk tolerance. Second, they analyze their clients' existing portfolios to determine whether they are correctly invested or whether they are saving enough money to retire at a desired age. The third step is for the advisor to allocate a client's portfolio in a way that accords with findings relating to the profile and the analysis. Fourth, the advisor implements the allocation findings. The final step is to report back to the client so that the results can be reviewed.

The World of Money Management

An advisor might decide at the implementation stage of the process to suggest that a client be invested in an SMA product. Viewed in this way, the SMA is a component of the process of basic investment planning.

Benefits of Working With SMAs

By now, most advisors are familiar with the differences between mutual funds and separate accounts, and many successfully articulate those differences to prospects and clients. Although both vehicles offer access to professional managers who follow a particular investment strategy or objective, and provide the opportunity for portfolio diversification, that's where the similarities end.

Whereas certain benefits of mutual funds—such as access to more asset classes, next-day liquidity, and lower minimums—are attractive to many clients, the features of SMAs far outweigh those differences, especially for the high net worth investor. For example, portfolio customization, no embedded gains, tax control, transparency, and other features of SMAs draw a higher-level, loyal, clientele. The fee-based compensation structure also allows the client to believe advisors truly have their best interests at heart.

(For a complete comparison of mutual funds versus separate accounts, see chart on facing page)

One of the greatest benefits to advisors and consultants is the leveraging of income by allowing market returns to bump up their income. Since the SMA annual fee is based on the value of a client's portfolio every quarter, the good performance of the selected manager(s) boosts an advisor's income, thereby creating a long-term annuity stream.

Here's a typical example: If an advisor receives two new SMA accounts a month at $500,000 each, for a total of $12 million in assets under management that first year, $90,000 in fees will have been generated if calculated on 75 basis points.

Advisors should realize, however, that they need to earn the fees. They need to provide services along with selecting the SMA product for their clients. Such services including preparing comprehensive profiles of their clients, guiding them with advice, and providing analysis.

Another significant advantage to working with separate accounts is the amount of time advisors can leverage. By removing themselves from the day-to-day process of personally managing money, more time is available to service clients and capture more assets. Of course, the potential for conflict of interest also is eliminated for those advisors who do transaction-based business, because they now sit on the 'same side of the table' with clients.

There also is more time to develop quality service and maintain deeper relationships with clients. And, most likely, an added benefit of building substantial relationships will be more referrals. Advisors have increased opportunities to work with larger clients, i.e., ultra high net worth, foundations, endowments, and small to mid-sized institutions. With this business model, advisors also can attract larger assets which require fewer clients to build a bigger business—again saving time for relationship building.

Currently, there is no mandatory separate account reporting system, so comparing and evaluating SMAs and their managers is no easy task. However, two familiar industry services, Morningstar and CheckFree (with Mobius data) are attempting to rate separately managed account performance by providing such information as 10-year performance history, portfolio composition, performance, sector weightings compared to various benchmarks, and a broad analysis of the account's holdings.

Separately Managed Accounts

GENERAL FEATURES	MUTUAL FUNDS	MANAGED ACCOUNTS
Access to professional money managers	Yes	Yes
Diversified portfolio	Yes	Yes
Ability to customize portfolio	No	Yes, investors can restrict specific securities from their portfolios
Manager independence from the "herd instinct"	No, if clients want to redeem shares, fund managers must sell to raise the cash to do so	Yes, money managers can buy when the "herd" is selling and vice versa, customizing the decision to the client's objectives
Unlimited withdrawals/redemptions	No, most funds have restrictions	Yes
Typical account minimum	$1,000	$100,000
Liquidity	Typically, next day	Three-day settlement of trades
Access to asset classes	Numerous	Somewhat more limited than funds
Performance Reporting Features		
Performance reporting	Typically semi-annual, some more frequent	Customized performance rating
Customized performance reporting	No, investors must calculate their own performance which is problematic, particularly for investors who dollar cost average	Yes, automatically sent to investors every quarter, includes performance of individual portfolios and of aggregate of multiple portfolios
Tax-Related Features		
Separately held securities	No, investor owns one security, the fund, which in turn, owns a diversified portfolio	Yes, investor owns securities in an account managed by their money managers
Unrealized gains	Yes, average US mutual fund has a 20% embedded, unrealized capital gain[1]	No, cost basis of each security in the portfolio is established at the time of purchase
Customized to control taxes	No, most funds are managed for pre-tax returns, and investors pay a proportionate share of taxes on capital gains	Yes, investors can instruct money managers to take gains or losses as available, to manage their tax liability
Tax-efficient handling of low-cost basis stocks	No, stocks cannot be held in an investor's mutual fund account, so there is no opportunity to manage low-cost basis stocks	Yes, the handling of low cost basis stocks can be customized to the client's situation, liquidating in concert with offsetting losses, etc.
Gain/loss distribution	Virtually all gains must be distributed, losses cannot be distributed	Realized gains and losses are reported in the year recorded
Cost-Related Features		
Expenses, excluding brokerage costs (Note: advisor fees may not be included as it may vary)	1.42%[1,3]	1.00%
Expenses, including brokerage costs (Note: these are estimate and do not include advisor fee which may vary)	1.56% average[2,3]	1.25%
Volume fee discounts	No, all investors pay the same expense ratio	Yes, larger investors enjoy fee discounts
Other costs	12b-1, sales loads, redemption fees, etc.	None

Chart reprinted with permission of SMA Forum, Lockwood, and MMI. 1) Morningstar Principia Plus for Windows, Feb. 2002, 2) Brokerage costs estimated at 0.13% for the 10 largerst funds, 3) Costs do not include Advisor fee, which will vary

Information on the manager's organization, structure, investment philosophy and style, statistical data and other useful material is available. Helpful tools that they are, though, the advisors and consultants still need to address the customization and tax issues that are a major part of the SMA attraction. These industry research tools are intended to help advisors compare managers only; the value-added work is in the decision-making process by the individual advisor.

Benefits of SMAs to the Client

The unique benefits of separately managed accounts to new and experienced investors drive their popularity. Portfolio customization and tax considerations are two of the most important benefits of separately managed accounts. Customization is generally thought of as tailoring the treatment of specific investment results to address the needs of an investor's individual tax, retirement, or risk management considerations.

SMAs allow for a full range of customization needs, and innovative technological developments over recent years have made customization cost-efficient, timely and expedient for investors. Mutual funds do not provide the level of customization capabilities necessary, in particular, for most high net worth individuals. Some of those customization needs are: to create liquidity, to hedge investment positions, to diversify a concentrated position, and/or to transfer wealth.

Monitoring and controlling tax liability from trading activities are main benefits of an SMA. The client can instruct the manager to harvest offsetting losses or gains. Tax losses also can be "saved" and used to offset gains realized in future years. Advisors and consultants working with high net worth individuals already know that one of their primary concerns is tax liability. High tax liabilities are easier to control by using an SMA. They don't want their assets to be subject to the trading activities of other investors, as they are in pooled accounts, such as mutual funds.

Another chief advantage is that investors also can choose to prohibit the purchase of specific securities or industry sectors in an SMA. And since all securities held in an SMA are owned directly by the investor, he or she can see exactly what securities are in the portfolio at any time.

When compared with other alternatives, managed accounts offer additional value to investors. Much of this value lies in the knowledge and experience of the advisors and consultants who work closely with investors to ensure that their long-term goals are achieved. Managed account programs include a number of services that might otherwise be cost-prohibitive, including the five hallmark features of a written policy statement – determination of risk tolerance, asset allocation, selection of money managers, monitoring of performance and rebalancing of portfolios–professional portfolio management, and performance measurement reports.

Clients also appreciate that there are no hidden charges, and fees are clearly disclosed and, typically, charged on a quarterly basis. Fees also may be tax-deductible.

All of the above benefit information is suitable for an advisor to use while explaining the viability of separately managed accounts. The importance of teaching clients the underlying reasons for choosing these vehicles is paramount.

These questions, which can be asked of a prospective client and which relate to product as well as process, will help determine exactly who is a typical SMA investor:

- Do you have more than $250,000 in investable assets? (relates to product)

- Did you incur a large tax bill from your investments in the last tax year? (product or process)
- Do you know the total fees and commissions you now pay as a percentage of your assets? (product)
- Do you receive advice that helps match your investments to your goals and risk tolerance? (product or process)
- Are there certain securities you can't or don't want to own? (product)
- Do you have a long-term financial goal that requires a specific investment strategy? (process)
- Are you interested in exploring investment strategies beyond mutual funds? (product)

Advantages and Disadvantages of SMAs

As with any investment solution, no one vehicle is perfect for everyone. Pros and cons can be found in all products and it's up to the individual advisor or consultant to evaluate each on its own merits and how best suited the solution is for each client.

The numbers are proving that high net worth individuals are seeking separately managed accounts for many of the reasons stated earlier in this chapter. Industry research suggests that affluent individuals are tired of receiving retail treatment. A major advantage of offering a truly institutional-quality and institutionally priced investment vehicle allows clients the professional management they require. Add to that a quality consulting process and these advantages dwarf even the best alternative product offerings in comparison.

Undoubtedly, SMAs provide clients with numerous advantages such as: Working within a comprehensive investment process continuously; appropriate asset allocation for their specific needs; manager search, selection and monitoring, flexibility to accommodate client preferences; and informative and useful quarterly reporting processes.

Clearly, the advantages all relate to the advisor's ability to serve clients better.

Advisors recommending SMAs also can solve what behavioral finance scholars refer to as "value expressive" issues, and what lay people usually refer to simply as issues of preference. Many advisors still focus on the purely rational investment science side of the business and ignore issues of client preference. They are aware that their clients will spend thousands of dollars to buy a Rolex when a Timex keeps time just as well, but they somehow think that these preferences are unimportant in an investment context. As separate accounts become more mainstream, clients will begin to ask about them and may even develop preferences for them. It will not be a good answer for advisors to say they use only mutual funds if clients want their money managed by an institutional manager through the separate account vehicle.

Dispersion in account performance sometimes can be a drawback of SMAs. Dispersion occurs when clients have similar portfolios and yet find that they have widely differing results. Some dispersion is acceptable. Other dispersion can be viewed as a disadvantage of separate accounts and can be difficult to explain to clients.

Acceptable dispersion occurs when the accounts are opened at different times, obviously thereby encountering different market conditions at the time of investment. Different performance as a result of the size of the account is also acceptable dispersion as a larger account may need to be invested differently from a smaller account.

Client-driven changes also can result in acceptable dispersion. One person, for example, may add more money to an account at a later stage. Others may want their accounts to be rebalanced regularly.

Unacceptable dispersion occurs when two accounts opened at the same time with the same amount of money are invested using the same product and yet they show widely differing results. No individual dispersion should be seen in today's wrap accounts being managed for a model account.

Disadvantages include fewer choices than in mutual funds, less experienced junior portfolio managers handling the accounts and non-timely investment strategy implementation. Sometimes, too, historical composite performance records can be difficult to interpret.

In addition, compromising the consulting process by focusing on a certain style in the allocation portion of the process—rather than being driven by the client's risk tolerance and long-term objectives as stated in the investment policy statement—will have a profound impact on the client's plan.

Advisors need to remember that an SMA will not be appropriate for every client or for every situation, but it's still a tool to have in the arsenal when the right situation arises. For those who work with high net worth investors, the "right" situations will arise frequently. What advisors should not do is recommend separate accounts either because they are the new, hot product or because a portfolio of individual securities carries prestige.

Depending on the type of client and/or account, portfolio transparency can be viewed as an impediment. Because clients see all transactions and daily holdings, they may focus on the short-term gyrations rather than the long-term planning aspects. Real-time delivery of information to the client, which may be more confusing than helpful in some cases, may cause potential problems for the advisor. Transparency may encourage individual investors to focus on security selections of professional money managers rather than the overall portfolio strategy.

A challenge may be the level of advisor education needed to teach the client about the SMA itself. While this area of training is growing, many clients and investors still have not heard of SMAs or don't fully understand them. Up-front and ongoing education is essential to the long-term SMA relationship.

As advisors gain experience, they get better and better with the product. In fact, many of those who have used separate accounts for a while are every bit as adept at using them with their individual clients as pension consultants are in working with institutional clients. The key is experience and education.

In addition, understanding the investment consulting process, and the fee-based business is one thing—but do advisors and consultants truly understand what qualities comprise a good money management firm? What is the actual process for evaluating and selecting these managers and then combining them for style diversification? (See chapter 11 and 12) While many firms do an excellent job of manager due diligence, Wall Street could be well advised to improve training and education to advisors in these areas.

Perspective on Tax Strategies

Advisors and consultants emphasize measuring after-tax portfolio performance, but it's important to consider hiring managers that have an appreciation for, and experience in, managing taxable portfolios. Many managers "grew up" on the institutional side of the business and, thus, have been managing without regard for taxes.

Separately Managed Accounts

For example, some managers might hit their stock price target, and their process will be to sell that stock. Other managers who've grown up in a more taxable environment will consider a group of accounts, and recognize that by continuing to hold the particular stock for another 30 days, for instance, it becomes a long-term gain vs. a short-term gain.

The concept of tax efficiency may have first arrived as a bull market phenomenon that evaporated in the previous three years with the market decline. But many believe tax efficiency today is a significant part of the investment process and advisors and consultants are searching for managers with a solid investment process that includes tax strategies.

An advantage of SMAs is that they enable clients to have some degree of control over when taxes are paid. Sometimes a client can benefit from moving money around at different times to make it more tax-advantageous. But the "tax tail should never wag the investment dog."

Another advantage can occur if the client has some sort of taxable event, such as the sale of a business, or an investment property or, perhaps, realizes the gain in another part of a portfolio. The gains can be offset with the harvesting of tax losses.

Fees Associated With Separate Accounts

It has been said many times, "Fees are only an issue in the absence of value." This is a concept that many successful advisors and consultants explain to their clients when—and if—a need to defend fees becomes necessary. Fees, in general, cover all services an advisor offers, and they are more cost-effective in the long run. They are competitively priced relative to many other investment vehicles. Mutual funds, for example, cost an average of 2.4 percent (not including advisor fee, which may vary) Most advisors charge less than this, and their fees are completely up front, budgetable, and tax-deductible.

According to Financial Research Corporation (FRC), the average size of a managed account is $260,000 and the average fee range is 1.9 – 2.0 percent In understanding separate accounts, it is important to know how they are priced and what services the fee covers. This allows valid comparisons between separate accounts and other investment vehicles. One of the benefits of separate-account pricing is that the fees are easy to understand.

Typically, the separate account fee has four components. They are:

- The manager's fee—anywhere from 30-100 basis points, depending on the size of the assets and asset class
- A fee for the sponsor of the separate account program (typically 25 to 60 basis points, which includes services such as housing the securities, trade execution and clearing or settlement functions)
- All custody and trading charges (see above)
- A fee for the advisor—ranging from 40 to 100 basis points. This part of the fee varies significantly, depending on the amount of consulting services provided.[6]

Often a single fee covers all of the services provided to the client. When all fees are "wrapped" together this is called "bundled pricing." Occasionally the various components of the fee may be broken out so that the client sees the manager's fee, the sponsor's fee, custody and trading charges and the advisor's fee separately. This is called "unbundled pricing."

Another difference in separate account fees emanates from the source of an advisor's separate account platform. For example, an advisor in the employ of a large wirehouse will have an all-inclusive fee that combines the manager's fee, the custodial and sponsor fees, and the advisory fee paid to him or her. The client may see an all-inclusive fee ranging from approximately 1.5 percent to 2.25, broken down aslisted on page 239. The wirehouse advisor is accustomed to different methods of compensation based on the investment instrument used. Mutual funds have sales loads; separate accounts have fees; hedge funds have sales charges plus, in many cases, a share of the profits for the manager.

The independent advisor, on the other hand, tends to work on a fee basis for all of the products used. Each product will have a management fee which will vary, but since independent advisors use no-load funds and other investment instruments that are structured differently than at the wirehouses, they offer an entire planning program that is structured on a fee basis. One of the easiest ways to distinguish the wirehouse advisors' fee structure from the independent advisors' fee structure is to go back to the wrapped and unbundled concepts. One could say that wirehouse advisors wrap all the components of the fee presented to the client in the all-inclusive format. An independent advisor, however, takes the various components such as the investment product used, the custody and clearing fees, the manager fees, and the advisory fee and breaks them all down so that the client can see what part of the fee is going for what part of the service.

Wirehouses have a different dimension to their culture than independent advisors: that of being compensated in different ways according to the investment product used. A wirehouse may have a sales agreement with a mutual fund company, for example. That is why many wirehouse advisors do not sell no-load funds. They have no method of being compensated for using them. An independent advisor receives no sales load from a mutual fund. He or she simply passes on the fund expenses to the client, adding advisory and other fees on top.

In most cases, the fees associated with separate accounts are expressed in terms of basis points. Fees are usually reduced as account sizes increase and reach established "breakpoints." [7]

Some clients might argue that managed account fees are too high and that they can receive an equal benefit from mutual fund investing for a lower cost. However, it's important for a client to understand that mutual funds also net out fees before their Net Asset Value (NAV) is calculated, keeping them unaware of the exact amount being deducted from the account. Also, SMA fees are negotiable and are reduced for large accounts, and this is not so for mutual funds. SMA fees are not necessarily higher, but they are more visible.

The Future of SMAs

According to Russ Alan Prince, president of the marketing research and consulting firm Prince & Associates, investors in the not-so-distant future will have the option to select an entire portfolio, including SMAs, mutual funds, individual securities, and other investments, which will all be available under a fee-based separate account pricing structure. Hedge funds and insurance companies are examples of financial service providers that are already exploring how to transform their products from a commission-based structure to a managed account or fee-based structure.

The advantage of a Unified Managed Account (UMA) is simplicity. By having all the accounts in one, it allows for a comprehensive view of a client's portfolio. The new generations of accounts are called Multiple Discipline Accounts (MDA™), Multiple Style Accounts (MSA), Multiple Style Products (MSP), and other similar acronyms. Not only do these accounts combine different managers into one account, but they allow for an overlay portfolio manager (OPM). This manager coordinates the accounts and so is able to check on loss-managed accounts or aspects that may be overlooked, such as buys in one account and sales in another, which may result in wash sales. The key is coordination of the accounts.

As more and more advisors venture into the world of separate accounts there will be an increased need for guidance to ensure the high standards that, by and large, exist today continue to be maintained. Helping to drive this effort are ongoing advances in technology, coupled with continually evolving portfolio management and assessment tools. Organizations such as the Association for Investment Management and Research, Investment Management Consultants Association, Money Management Institute, the Center for Fiduciary Studies, and a host of other individual and institutional researchers significantly contribute to the effort.

Separate accounts have huge potential to lead the investment industry forward or to stop it dead in its tracks. High, ethical standards are the key.

The trends supporting separate account growth will continue, and there is every reason to believe they will become a tool used by an ever-increasing number of advisors, thereby adding a higher level of service to all segments of the investing public.

❖ ❖ ❖

---

1 "Legacy: The History of Separately Managed Accounts," Sydney LeBlanc, Money Management Institute, 2003; The Evolution of Separately Managed Accounts, Sydney LeBlanc, Effron; Money Management Institute.
2 Financial Research Corporation, Boston, MA, www.frcnet.com
3 WebFinance-Wealth Report 2003
4 Money Management Institute, 2002
5 "Do Separately Managed Accounts Make Cents for Your Clients?" Scott MacKillop, Trivium Consulting.
6 Money Management Institute, "Benefits of Separately Managed Accounts" www.moneyinstitute.com
7 *Financial Advisor Magazine*, Sept '02, "Pros and Cons of SMAs, Advisor Roundtable;" Scott MacKillop, Trivium Consulting.
Additional references: The Spectrem Group; "Separate Accounts: An Essential Tool for Every Advisor," SMA Forum; Financial Research Corporation.

28

SEPARATE ACCOUNTS
CLIENT-FOCUSED INVESTMENT SOLUTIONS

Scott MacKillop
Co-founder, President and Principal
Trivium Consulting, LLC

Let's start with an understanding of the characteristics that make separate accounts such a useful tool for financial advisors and their clients. First, let's define the term. A separate account is:

- a portfolio of individual securities
- held in a brokerage or custodial account
- managed by a private money manager
- solely for the benefit of the account's owner

The assets in the separate account are not pooled with the assets of other investors as they are in a mutual fund. Instead, securities in the account are owned directly by the client. Traditionally, an SMA is managed by a single investment manager. This is true of most separate accounts.

Within the past few years a new type of separate account has emerged. Commonly referred to as a "multi-style portfolio" (MSP*), it combines a variety of managers in a single account, each managing a different style or asset class. The allocations to each style or asset class are well-defined, and the portfolios are automatically rebalanced to those allocations on a periodic basis. Typically an "overlay portfolio manager" (OPM) coordinates the trading activity of the managers in the MSP and handles certain administrative activity within the account.

Client application

*Also known as MDA and MSA

Benefits of Separate Accounts

Separate accounts are well-suited to the needs of affluent investors and are an excellent complement to other investment vehicles that advisors already use to service their clients. By using separate accounts, advisors can expand the range of solutions they provide and create investment solutions more closely tailored to client needs.

Professional Management: The first and most obvious benefit of separate accounts is that they give investors access to professional investment management. Many of the world's best money managers offer their services to investors through separate accounts.

In most cases, separate account managers must pass rigorous due-diligence requirements before they are offered to investors. Managers are screened on a quantitative basis to make sure they have a solid track record of consistent performance and experience managing money in different market environments. They also are screened on a qualitative basis to make sure they have a well-disciplined philosophy of investing and a motivated team that applies that philosophy consistently through time. In the separate account world, consistency and predictability are highly valued. The due diligence process gives investors confidence that their managers have demonstrated a high level of experience, consistency and accomplishment.

By using separate account managers, an advisor can build portfolios overseen by managers who invest only in their respective areas of expertise. So portfolios are built using specialists in each style and asset class. And often, investors can access these specialist managers for significantly lower minimums than they could if they opened up an account directly with the manager.

Separate account managers know that advisors use their services to build portfolios for their clients using carefully constructed combinations of styles and asset classes. They also know that advisors and their clients can see the transactions they make in the accounts they manage. Accordingly, they tend to adhere closely to their style mandates.

They also tend to maintain less cash in accounts they manage since separate accounts are not subject to the same level of asset inflows and outflows that mutual funds experience. Therefore, separate account managers are often more fully invested than mutual fund managers.

Tax Management: One of the primary attractions of separate accounts are the advantages they can provide to taxable investors. For example, separate account investors can avoid the embedded capital gains problem that can exist with mutual funds. A mutual fund investor may end up paying taxes on gains that were generated in the fund before he or she became an investor. This never happens to a separate account investor because the investor owns the securities in the account directly and takes his or her own basis in the securities when they are purchased for the account.

Separate account investors also have the ability to harvest losses in their accounts. This means that investors can intentionally realize losses in order to shelter gains realized elsewhere. Alternatively, an investor may choose to realize gains that can be sheltered by losses the investor incurred elsewhere.

Another benefit to taxable separate account investors is the availability of tax-efficient managers. These managers manage portfolios with a true sensitivity to the needs of the taxable investor. They try to minimize the amount of taxable gain they generate and make an effort to ensure that any gains they do generate are taxable at lower rates.

Customization: Direct ownership of securities also permits a level of personalization not available through other professionally managed investment vehicles. Separate account investors can tell their managers not to buy certain securities for their portfolios. Investors also can restrict the purchase of certain types of securities, such as tobacco stocks or securities in the technology sector.

An investor also may be able to transfer an existing stock position into a new separate account. In some cases, the manager may actually incorporate some or all of the existing position into the portfolio. In other cases, the manager may work with the investor to sell off the position over time to smooth out the tax impact.

Managers differ in their willingness to customize portfolios for investors. If customization is important to the client, then it is important to determine a manager's level of willingness to customize a portfolio before investing with that manager.

Control: Because separate account investors have direct ownership of the securities in their portfolio, they have more control over the holdings and activity within their accounts. For example, if certain events cause a large number of mutual fund investors to redeem shares of their fund, all shareholders are affected. The fund's manager must sell securities to meet shareholder redemptions, whether he believes it is a good time to sell or not. A separate account manager maintains complete control over when to sell securities in the account.

Transparency: In addition, separate account investors always know what securities are held in their accounts. This is because they receive information about purchases and sales for their account when these transactions take place. Mutual fund shareholders do not have the same access to information about the securities in their funds because that information typically is disclosed on an infrequent basis.

Separate Accounts and the Investment Consulting Process

Although separate accounts are an investment product just like mutual funds, they usually are offered through the "investment consulting process." The process starts with an assessment by the advisor of the client's needs, goals and objectives. Then the advisor develops a diversified investment strategy for the client based on that assessment. This strategy is set forth in a statement of investment policy that describes the client's asset allocation approach, other aspects of how the client's portfolio will be managed and how long-term progress will be measured.

The advisor then works with the client to select managers to implement the strategy. The advisor monitors progress toward the client's goals, reports on that progress on an ongoing basis and works with the client to make needed adjustments along the way.

The characteristics of this process are ideally suited to the needs of the affluent investor. First, the process is client-focused, not product-focused. This satisfies the client's desire to be at the center of the advisory relationship and to base all investment solutions on their personal goals. It makes the client's particular situation of paramount importance and reduces emphasis on performance-oriented stories that frequently leave the client feeling disappointed as markets go through their inevitable cycles.

Success is measured more in terms of the overall portfolio's progress toward the client's goals than on the performance of specific investments. This benefits the advisor, too, because it heightens client satisfaction and makes the advisor less dependent on uncontrollable factors such as the fortunes of particular companies, which investment style happens to be in favor at a particular time, or the direction of the market.

By offering separate account managers through the investment consulting process the client gets the benefit of objective, expert investment management and the advisor assumes a supervisory role, watching over all managers with the client's best interests in mind. This eliminates a common problem that exists when the advisor is actually managing the client's assets. It is difficult for an advisor to be objective about personal performance. However, when the advisor assumes a supervisory role, if action needs to be taken to replace a manager, the advisor can discuss the issue with the client and then take action without jeopardizing the client relationship.

The consulting process has other benefits that are, perhaps, even more important. The consulting process instills discipline into investing and provides a framework for measuring success and taking action. For this reason, anxiety associated with market volatility and client mistakes based on emotion and fear are reduced. Thus, clients are in a better position to weather the storms that all long-term investors eventually encounter.

In addition, the consulting process establishes the foundation for excellent client relationships by incorporating meaningful and frequent communications into the process. This communication flows from the advisor's role in monitoring and reporting on the client's portfolio. An integral part of the consulting process is periodic meetings between the client and the advisor. And, ideally, these interactions are supplemented with frequent communications regarding significant developments affecting the client's portfolio. Separate account managers often support this process by providing advisors with a stream of research and commentary to keep the advisor fully informed.

Building Portfolios with Separate Accounts

The level of diversification that can be achieved using separate accounts allows advisors to address an investor's concerns about reducing risk, limiting volatility and avoiding unpleasant surprises. Separate accounts are available in a wide range of asset classes, including domestic and international equities, fixed income and real estate. This allows advisors to design portfolios with a wide variety of risk and return levels.

Diversification also can be achieved by combining separate accounts with other types of investments. For example, an advisor may build a portfolio for a client using separate accounts, hedge funds and mutual funds. This type of flexibility allows advisors a wide range of alternatives in accommodating specific client needs.

As the technology that supports separate accounts improves, it will become increasingly simple to combine separate accounts with other types of investments. The technology that supports multiple-style portfolios already allows for the combination of multiple separate account managers in a single account. As new technologies are perfected, financial advisors will be able to use the investment consulting process to develop investment strategies and implement them on a truly "product-neutral" basis.

The obstacles that make it difficult to efficiently build multi-product portfolios today will begin to disappear. Advisors will no longer think in terms of building separate account portfolios or mutual fund portfolios for clients. Today's product-focused orientation will fade away and be replaced by attention to developing client-focused investment strategies and implementing them with the best combination of investment products for the client's situation. And separate accounts will be an important part of the solution for many clients, particularly taxable investors and investors with customization needs.

❖❖❖

Editor's note: This article is an extremely valuable pass-along tool for advisors or consultants to give to their clients. For reprints, go to http://www.fisherleblanc.com. Important: Before distributing to investors, please have materials approved by compliance and/or management.

29

MULTIPLE STYLE ACCOUNTS

Mark E. McMeans, CFA®, CPA
President and Chief Operating Officer
AIM Private Asset Management, Inc.

It sounds like alphabet soup: MDAs, DSPs, MSPs, DMAs, and MAPs. These initials can be confusing to investors and, at times, to the most knowledgeable advisors and consultants. But no matter what the label, the generically-termed Multiple Style Account (MSA) is quickly becoming the investment "vehicle dujour" on separately managed account menus.

Among the fastest growing segments of the managed account industry, Boston-based research firm, Financial Research Corp. (FRC) predicts that MSA assets under management will grow to $46 billion (conservative estimate) in 2004, accounting for 17percent of total managed account assets, up from the $26 billion in assets at year-end 2003. FRC predicts that by 2007 assets will grow to approximately $175 billion (aggressive estimate). (See Chart #1- page 252)

Introduced in 1997, more than 40 financial institutions either have announced their intent, or have introduced an MSA-type product, according to FRC. Several unique and appealing features help to explain the growing popularity of MSA's. But what are they exactly, and what are the major benefits to advisors and their clients?

Basically, an MSA is a portfolio that incorporates several different invest-

Projected MDA* Asset Growth -- Three Scenarios

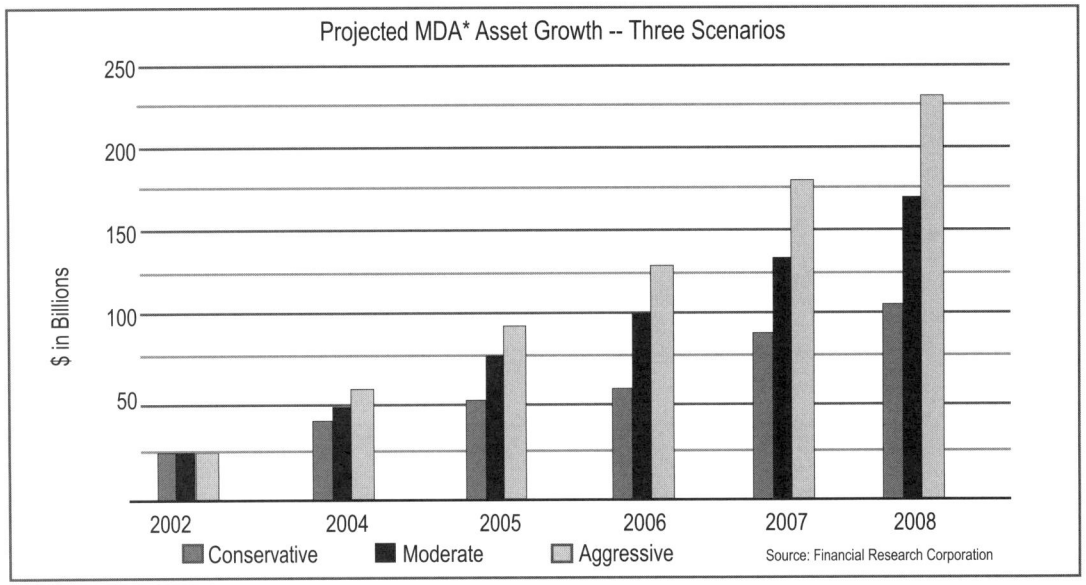

Conservative = MDPs will capture 10% of SMA industry-wide net sales
Moderate = MDPs will capture 20% of SMA industry-wide net sales
Aggressive = MDPs will capture 50% of SMA industry-wide net sales
Assumption = 8% market appreciation of existing assets

*Also known as Multiple Style Account (MSA)

Source: Financial Research Corporation

ment style managers into one account. Clients receive one statement, one performance report, and access to the Overlay Portfolio Manager (OPM) who oversees asset allocation, rebalancing, and monitoring of the portfolio.

MSA Benefits

In a word, diversification is the greatest benefit of the MSA. The fact that it can be obtained in a one-stop-shop is icing on the cake. While providing the critical ingredient of diversification, MSAs allow investors this diversification at generally lower minimums —some as low as $50,000 for one management style (or sleeve) — than those of the traditional separately managed account (SMA). Although the minimum for an MSA account tends to be higher than the traditional SMA, ranging from about $150,000 to $250,000 or more, the investor gets the benefit of spreading that investment out over several investment management styles reducing the minimum "entrance investment" for each "sleeve" significantly.

MSAs offer high net worth investors and, increasingly, ultra high net worth investors a wide selection of investment products and solutions covering different investment management styles within the SMA environment. It includes all the key benefits of the typical separate account, featuring direct stock ownership, customization, tax advantages, portfolio re-balancing, professional management, and consolidated reporting. The streamlined client reports are a perfect example of efficiency and an enhanced client experience.

Because minimums are higher for the typical stand-alone separately managed account, some clients may be taking on more risk than they should. The Money Management Institute (MMI) reports that a large percentage of SMA clients are using only one manager with one style, and may, consequently, be overexposed to risk. An MSA normally will help to mitigate some of that risk.

An attractive solution especially for the smaller high net worth investor, MSAs allow for strategic asset allocation, more flexibility in how their assets are managed and, quite possibly, a reduction in risk.

One of the main advantages for both investors and their financial advisors is the automatic rebalancing that takes place in a MSA that might otherwise be left to adhoc portfolio revisions. To keep an asset allocation strategy on course, it is imperative to rebalance on a regular basis. Not only must the portfolio be geared toward individual goals and risk tolerance, but portfolios also need periodic fine-tuning to keep them in line with stated objectives. Assets do not grow uniformly, and, over time, a well-structured portfolio can shift away from its desired asset mix. The value of certain assets may grow faster than others, resulting in a shift in allocation levels. By rebalancing the portfolio, the goal is to liquidate assets whose prices have risen. Proceeds from sales are then redeployed to buy lower-priced securities. A buy low/sell high strategy returns the portfolio to its target allocation. Most MSAs offer automatic rebalancing. If market conditions cause the portfolio to be overweight in one type of investment, the portfolio is automatically re-adjusted by the overlay portfolio manager (see next section for more discussion on the OPM) to the target allocations.

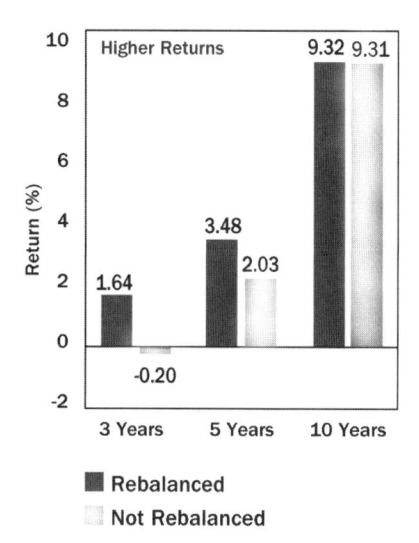

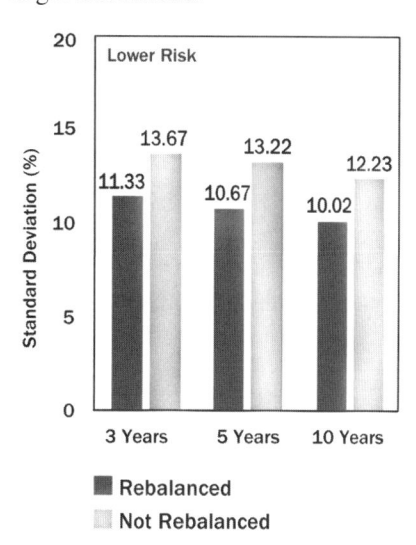

Advisors are correctly encouraging their clients to think more like institutional investors so they can take advantage of the benefits of using high-caliber institutional money managers. Although many original MSAs were targeted at the clients who were just beyond program minimums, anecdotal industry evidence suggests the average account size is somewhat higher than expected.

This points to another industry finding—the more experienced, higher-level advisor is now introducing this investment solution to their affluent prospects and clients, thereby capturing larger assets for MSAs. *Many advisors report using the MSA as a core account strategy*, placing "serious money"— upwards of $1 million or more— into the MSA and utilizing other investments vehicles around it.

This trend suggests that the multiple style account appeals to a wide audience, and is recommended both by advisors newly entering the separate account business, and skilled veteran consultants with large practices. Regardless of the size of the account, each client should have the benefit of a basic working knowledge of an MSA. An advisor can explain the concept and the components simply, like this: "Essentially MSAs are portfolios incorporating various management styles into one account. The portfolio might offer a Large Cap Equity mix of 40 percent value, 40 percent growth, and 20 percent international, with a separate professional manager or team overseeing each style or "sleeve" of the portfolio. Typically an investor can choose from different asset allocation models built around varying levels of risk. MSA accounts offer a more streamlined approach, including receipt of one account opening form, one statement, one performance report and periodic rebalancing."

The benefits to advisors also are advantageous, and offer numerous ways to build a high-level practice with long-term clients.

Main Benefits of MSAs to the Advisor

There are numerous positive benefits for the advisor working with MSAs. First, these accounts have a user-friendly interface that cuts down on the administrative burden for them. There is much less paperwork, so it is less cumbersome to open new accounts. For example, let's focus on a client who wants to invest $1 million utilizing separately managed accounts. Typically, the advisor might hire four different managers at $250,000 each which would include four different manager searches, four different sets of account opening forms, resulting in the client receiving five statements— one from each manager and one for the overall account. Additionally, if the advisor has a supervisory structure, the branch manager needs to sign off on four different account applications.

With the MSA, the paperwork for the advisor is streamlined and bundled into one set of materials—one new account form, one manager profile, one client statement, and so on. The customer experience is superior, and is a major leap for the advisor with a client-centered practice.

Additionally, instead of dealing with multiple managers, the advisor relies on an overlay portfolio manager who acts as a liaison with the money managers. The OPM oversees asset allocation, rebalances the portfolio, and monitors each manager's holdings. The overlay function can be performed by the sponsor, an outsourced third party, or the asset manager.

With the market's increased volatility in the last few years, advisors and their clients are well-incented to get back to the basics of investing: assessing risk, asset allocation, long- term discipline, and utilizing a comprehensive wealth management process. The MSA builds on the importance of these investment principles in the tradition of the SMA.

During the volatile markets, though, some investors and advisors have, in some instances, "short-circuited" the consulting process at the asset allocation and risk assessment level. However, now, instead of picking the hot manager or hot fund, clients are learning more about diversification and re-balancing and their importance to the overall portfolio.

According to Financial Research Corp, only 23 percent of affluent investors rebalance their portfolios—this is compared to about 91 percent of institutional investors who do so. This only furthers the case for having a systematic approach through the MSA concept.

Why Rebalance?	• Rebalancing is an integral part of an investment policy. • The process fosters a buy low/sell high approach. • A clear policy avoids the risks of adhoc portfolio revisions. • Rebalancing helps to maximize the value-added benefits of diversification.

Without a disciplined system (like in an MSA) it is easy to "run with the winners," and neglect to bring the asset allocation back in line with what was the client's overall objective, or target allocation. Human nature has proved that individuals will buy what has worked best in the previous 12-24 months, and that contributes to the volatility in the marketplace. The MSAs utilized within a well-structured plan focus the client on the long-term goals rather than individual manager performance.

MSAs also offer an easy way for less experienced advisors to move into consultative relationships. This is a good solution for professionals in transition who want to customize portfolios without devoting themselves entirely to the consulting process, thereby having additional time to build their businesses.

MSA Generations

The industry defines the various types of MSA programs in terms of its "generation." There are several generation levels that reflect either the simplicity or complexity of MSA progression, and the relationship the investment managers have to the sponsoring organization. Here is a brief overview of definitions:

First generation— Client portfolios and asset management are provided from a single investment organization that is affiliated with the sponsor broker/dealer firm that controls the styles and trading of the MSA account.

Second generation—The program sponsor partners with a single unaffiliated asset management firm that is responsible for trading the account and providing all of the strategies within the MSA product.

Third generation— The program sponsor selects several unaffiliated managers for their MSA program; each manager provides a portfolio for their individual investment style. An overlay manager at the sponsoring broker/dealer firm level must be utilized in this model. In some instances, the sponsor firm may also hire a third-party firm to oversee the overlay process (ex: Manulife).

Fourth generation— An extension of each prior generation, a program sponsor's financial advisor has the ability to set dynamic strategy allocation to match the risk profile for each client.

Fifth generation— Predicted to be the next evolution in MSAs by Cerulli Associates, and coined in the industry as a Unified Managed Account (UMA), this model pulls together an MSA as a core account, individual separate account manager investment styles, alternative investment products such as hedge funds and ETFs, and mutual funds. At its heart are client–centered services that include client profiling, asset allocation, performance and client reporting. This type of account demonstrates steady movement toward comprehensive asset gathering and sophisticated wealth management services often found today in family offices through higher-end wealth management firms and trust companies.

In the first generation MSA (with only affiliated investment managers running portfolios) and the second generation MSA (managed by unaffiliated investment managers), one investment firm is chosen to run the entire MSA strategy. The portion of the account allocated to each style, and the managers included in the account, are predetermined by the firm sponsoring the MSA. So, in effect, MSAs are prepackaged, multi-style, multi-manager portfolios (drawn from a single asset management firm, affiliated or unaffiliated) maintained within a single brokerage account.

Citigroup pioneered the first generation of MSAs within the Smith Barney system. The Citigroup MDA™ (Multiple Discipline Account) is an affiliated model. The sleeves are all managed by Citigroup. Merrill Lynch's CDP, on the other hand, has affiliated managers (second generation) offered in one bundle. For example, they have sister companies AIM and INVESCO together, as well as MLIM, Alliance, and CDC IXIS. In this model, the advisor is investing with one parent or holding company that encompasses multiple investment organizations. The individual sub-portfolio sleeves of the MSA are discreet investment portfolios with individual portfolio managers assigned to each sleeve who are responsible only for managing their particular portion of the overall portfolio. Then investment styles and risk category allocations are predetermined and an advisor cannot make individual sleeve manager substitutions.

In the third generation, the Wachovia Diversified Managed Allocation (DMA) serves as a good example. All managers are unaffiliated with the sponsor program and Wachovia acts as the overlay manager. As in the other generations, the research groups at the sponsor programs determine the manager selection and the appropriate allocations for each risk profile. However, in this model the advisor can choose a predetermined manager allocation or custom select the individual sleeve managers from a menu of managers. Additionally, this model gives the advisor the flexibility to substitute individual sleeve managers as they see fit.

Special Features of MSAs: Overlay Portfolio Manager (OPM)

The success of the MSA hinges on the role of the overlay portfolio manager and without one the concept can't deliver. Depending on the type of MSA, this function may reside at the investment manager level or at the sponsor firm level. Generally, the individual portfolio managers do not have access to the holdings of the other portfolios, so the OPM serves an important role. Typically, the OPM does most of the "heavy lifting" for the MSA. Primary responsibilities include: reviewing and executing aggregate trades for all the portfolio managers, watching overlap, rebalancing, and helping to reduce the investor's tax bill (i.e., combating potential "wash sale" issues where one manager may be buying a particular security that another manager is selling within a particular MSA).

MSA Fees: The Breakdown

Like stand-alone separately managed accounts, MSA fees are flexible and negotiable. Fees greatly depend on the construct of the offering. On a wholesale basis, if a complete package of portfolio managers, accounting, and related services is provided, fees can range (industry-wide) from approximately 80 bps to 135 bps. These fees include the manager's fee (35-50 bps), the custody/trading expenses (25-35 bps) and the sponsor's fee (20-50 bps).

Overlay portfolio manager fees can range overall from around 20 bps to 40 bps. These are the fees the OPM charges the advisor or the sponsor firm. If an OPM is involved, generally their fee would not significantly change the cost of the product, if at all. Investment manager fees tend to be a little lower if an OPM is involved because of the reduced burden, so the addition of an OPM's fee is often offset in whole, or in part, by a reduction in the asset manager's fee.

In most cases, the advisor's fee, another 100 bps (at the high end) is added, which is, typically, a negotiated amount based on asset size and overall relationship size. Like a stand-alone SMA, an advisor has this advantage of flexible pricing. For example, they may place a higher fee on a smaller account that may take more time to service, and pass along a discount to a larger account that may require less time or that might require a competitive advantage for the advisor.

Overall, according to industry sources, there has not been a noticeable fee premium over the stand-alone SMA to the end client for MSAs.

Typically, no sales commissions are generated from placing clients in an MSA, so there is no perceived conflict of interest and the advisor is able to "sit on the same side of the table" with the client. This way, advisors better position themselves as wealth managers or consultants.

Potential Challenges with MSAs

One of the challenges advisors may encounter in MSAs is what to do about a poorly performing manager within an account. Another is how to handle the account if the performance does not meet the goals of the client's investment policy statement (IPS). As mentioned above, since MSAs exist in several generations, or models of affiliated and unaffiliated managers, not all sleeve managers can be replaced; in some cases, the entire portfolio must be replaced, possibly triggering unwanted taxable events.

But, even though a style sleeve may underperform, an advisor needs to consider that the market may be favoring a certain style at the time, of course. The structure of the MSA as a diversified concept, in and of itself, is designed to compensate for market cycles. Even though a manager may be out of favor, the other sleeves are pulling the weight during that time period to meet the expectations of the chosen risk category.

Unless there is something significant occurring within an individual manager's team, the MSA is doing what it should be doing—buffering risk and maximizing return over time. The point is that the MSA is a diversification vehicle and, chances are, the portfolio will not have superior performance in every sleeve, in every time period, in every market.

Another challenge—or ongoing debate—in the advisor/consultant community is that the MSA takes the advisor/consultant out of the loop from the consulting process since some of the steps (i.e., rebalancing, overseeing managers etc.) in the consulting process are built into the account. We would contend that the advisor must still perform the critical task of investment risk profiling for their client and monitor that on an ongoing basis. And, after choosing the appropriate MSA, the inherent conveniences of the product serve as an opportunity for the financial advisor to focus on the other aspects of their client's financial well-being (i.e., estate planning, retirement planning, charitable giving, succession planning, and so on). Focusing on these aspects of a client's financial picture may often lead to additional asset gathering opportunities. In a sense, MSAs take some of the guesswork out of the equation, but, by no means undervalues the financial advisor.

Some advisors may encounter the problem of having to justify their fees to clients. But if their business models and core business beliefs integrate the very hands-on client financial goal analysis and risk assessment, due diligence of manager search, selection, and monitoring, as well as rebalancing and ongoing client reporting, there is no question the fees are well-deserved. Especially in times of high market volatility when it has been proven that investors need a professional advisor most. If clients expect high-level service and real value in return for the fees they pay, and receive it, there is no need for a fee defense. Fees are only an issue in the absence of value.

Another current concern is that the assets are concentrated in the hands of a rather small group of managers who have the infrastructure and retail marketing acumen to compete in this space. It may, then, prove difficult for advisors to differentiate themselves from an investment solution standpoint when their competitors are touting the same list of asset managers.

Looking Ahead

TowerGroup Research predicts that MSAs will continue to be a growing component of managed account sales. The promise of customization at the investor level and coordination across multiple styles means operational challenges will grow as well. Critical to success with multiple style accounts is the availability of portfolio management technology adapted to meet individual demands of advisors and their clients.

Overlay portfolio management will play a critical role (and will likely increase) in the management of MSAs, and outsourcing will allow for better coordination across styles in a conflict-free way. Considering not only the operational and structural complexities of assembling the various portfolios, but also the "coming together" of unaffiliated managers in one account, the OPM concept works well for all manager parties. Strategies remain confidential within each portfolio as the third party arrangement oversees each manager's activities. This will allow for the next generation of MSAs to improve the ability of unaffiliated managers to coordinate with one another – providing for greater tax management, optimization of tradeoffs among risk and return, and buy/sell coordination for the investor's total portfolio.

As technology continues to improve, the industry will embrace the single client account that encompasses MSAs along with exchange-traded funds (ETFs), hedge fund strategies, single securities, mutual funds and more. The universal-type account that acts as a "wrapper" for all types of investments for clients of all shapes and sizes—including the ultra affluent—would fill this need. More than a new generation of MSA however, the universal account (or unified account) may be thought of as an asset-gathering tool. The universal or unified account will help make the advisor's practice even more client-centric, and will provide a framework that will offer a higher level of tax sensitivity, customization, and flexibility to the portfolio.

A movement is underway by the Money Management Institute (MMI) to help develop standards that eventually will ease the burden of connectivity among managers, sponsors, custodians, and overlay portfolio managers. According to the TowerGroup, the lack of data standards, as well as getting the various players to adopt the standards will be an equally, if not more difficult, task. But, with industry leaders working toward common structural and operational goals, ultimately, the client is better served.

The future is very bright for MSAs as more assets, further development, improvements, and choices, and more education of the product flows in. As a subset of the separate account, the MSA is in its infancy, so it has a lot of room in which to grow as witnessed by the steady pace of new MSA programs being launched by product sponsors.

Summary

MSAs reinforce the investment process. The importance of a quality consulting process dwarfs even the best product offerings. Research shows that investors, especially the affluent, are tired of receiving the traditional retail treatment. An advisor or consultant who can offer a truly institutional-quality and institutionally priced multi-manager, multi-asset class product, has a valuable tool in their arsenal. There are many talented managers and third-party providers available to advisors, and that list will continue to grow.

Financial Research Corporation reports that advisors currently are earmarking almost $500,000 on average to MSAs, almost twice the assets in the average SMA. For those who truly appreciate the process, and have their client's best financial and personal interests in mind, the multiple style account is a very real way to add tangible value and build a client-centric practice.

❖ ❖ ❖

References: Cerulli Associates; Financial Research Corporation (FRC), Kevin Keefe, "Rise of the MDP in the SMA Market"; Multiple Discipline Products Bring Separately Managed Accounts to Main Street" and "ABCs of MSPs", CheckFree Investment Services, Charles Smith, SMA Forum, Sept 2003; *Financial Advisor Magazine,* "The Pros and Cons of Separately Managed Accounts," 2002; "Legacy: The History of Separately Managed Accounts," Sydney LeBlanc, Money Management Institute, 2003; The Tower Group, Inc. TowerGroup Research, "Portfolio Management Systems for Multidiscipline Accounts."

30

THE MYSTERIOUS UMA

Leonard A. Reinhart, President
James J. Seuffert, Chief Operating Officer
Lockwood
A BNY Securities Group Co.

There's a lot of talk about unified managed accounts (UMAs) these days. Industry participants talk about who *has* the UMA and who doesn't. Some talk about the UMA as a new type of separate account. Others define it as an offshoot of the fourth generation multiple style account or MSA. Like the MSA, the UMA is personified through different initials at different firms. At Smith Barney, it's called an Integrated Investment Services (IIS) account. At Lincoln Financial it's LineSolutions (LS).[1]

Thus, as with a plethora of other industry buzzwords, the unified managed account has taken on a life of its own. Its implications and explanations can vary widely, depending on who is delivering the requested information at the time. The advisor population at large is barely beginning to use and fully understand the separately managed account concept; MSAs and UMAs are even farther down the education chain. And although the excitement and potential of the UMA are genuine and appropriate, its actual realization is only just beginning. Buzzwords can be cool to use—especially in the early stages of a new development—but they also can shroud the benefits of such a valuable new solution set through misunderstandings and misuse. So, in an effort to unveil the mystery once and for all, a clear definition of the UMA along with common misconceptions, challenges, and future possibilities follow.

The UMA Defined

The unified managed account is a multi-product solution set for the client. Unlike its often compared, mis-associated sister, the multiple style account, the UMA is not a product in and of itself. Rather, it is a conduit through which a comprehensive solution is effected for the client by gathering a custom designed collection of products under a single umbrella.

Where the MSA allows a new product to be made by combining several different asset managers within a single account, the UMA serves as an umbrella which includes a variety of *baskets,* which house various types of investment products. The umbrella then allows an overall treatment of those products through a single venue, most notably realized by the UMA statement.

Therefore, the UMA is a blending of different investment products and with integrated benefits to the client. The particular version of a UMA offering depends on the capabilities of the firm. At its simplest level, firms are taking separate accounts and mixing them with mutual funds to form a UMA solution for the client. The sponsor and the advisor get paid the same fee regardless of the investment product used. That is a simplistic, but accurate, definition of a UMA. The problem lies in the multitude of names given the solution set, the varying levels of development of UMA platforms, whether at a large firm or through a third-party vendor, and the quick-study type of advisor education that surrounds most new investment products. Such factors easily breed misconceptions, inaccurate perceptions of what a UMA is, and what it can do for advisors as well as their clients.

The Ideal Picture

What *should* a UMA look like? The ideal picture of a UMA would allow advisors to be totally independent within the sponsor's scope of research. Sponsors would provide research on different investment products but would own none of them. The palette would be broadened and would allow the higher level advisor to be more flexible by being able to use a broader spectrum of research. Other advisors would have access to the same breadth of research, but the sponsor would provide more guidance in advising clients. It would be the sponsor's or RIA's responsibility to determine the level of decision-making and advice-giving under which an advisor could work.

Once decisions are made about asset allocation and which managers or funds, annuities, ETFs or other investments should be used, each product would compete to get into the sponsor's programs within the research confines of that sponsor, which is similar to the way asset managers compete now. Product manufacturers would compete to get into sponsor programs, but there would be no incentive for the sponsor to pass on to entice the advisor to use one product over another.

The advisor would get paid a standard fee based on total assets regardless of the products used for any particular client. The sponsor would get paid a standard fee based on total assets regardless of which products are recommended and used. The products within the UMA would be completely no-load. The combination of the fee charged by the product and the sponsor and advisory fees comprise the overall UMA fee to the client. Different products might have different fees. The sponsor's job would be to provide the due diligence and research on that product so that the advisor could concentrate on doing the right job for the client and find the right combination of products to help the client reach his or her objectives.

This scenario would completely free the advisor to change focus back on to the client and not on compensation, incentives, or back office solutions. Although each product would have to be no-load to the client, each product could, however, have a different fee structure as long as neither the sponsor nor the advisor were compensated out of that fee structure. That's the ideal way to do it. If there are two money managers with two different fees, then deciding between the two becomes part of the overall decision process. The client asks, "Do I want the more expensive one, and is the more expensive one worth it?" The advisor can be totally objective, because there is no extra compensation for him or her from the more expensive one, but if that's the product the client chooses, that's the one he or she chooses. It's all just a part of the decision tree.

The avoidance of ownership of the managers allows advisors to hire and fire them based on doing the right thing for the client with no worries about how hiring one manager over another will affect that advisor's relationship with the firm or with any particular manager. Another advantage of this ideal set-up is that advisors would then be able to have a dialogue with a high net worth investor with $1.5 million in liquid net worth ready to be invested. It would go something like this: "We're going to use an MSA as the core of your portfolio and use the various styles to control risk. We're also going to create a tax sensitivity overlay by using another outside manager so that tax optimization can be accomplished all the way down to the tax lot level." So now, the high net worth individual has a hub, and they can then add ETFs, mutual funds, alternative investments, real estate, whatever is available to fit within the structure of the UMA at that point in time.

Ideally, that fit would accommodate any product that is available anywhere for the client to use in his or her portfolio. A market value could be put on the art collection, the real estate holdings, private equity investments, the jewelry collection and all those values could be rolled up along with the financial investments into the back end of the UMA. As well, any new product that's created would, in the process of its creation, be designed for use either outside of the UMA umbrella or structured so that it could readily be included if the client so desired.

That would be the ideal scenario, but for several reasons, that ideal does not exist today. The UMA concept is so new that everyone is running with it and firms are claiming they *have* it as soon as they have any type of platform that will accommodate more than just a separate account or MSA. The fact is that nobody *has* it. It doesn't exist and cannot exist fully with today's technology—especially at the wirehouses. Most of the firms involved at this early stage of UMA development simply are using "one process to develop portfolio recommendations that include separate accounts and mutual funds."[2] Depending on the firm's UMA platform capability, other investment products such as ETFs, hedge funds, and municipal bonds can be included as additional baskets within the umbrella.

Misconceptions

The primary misconception about UMAs is that they are another investment product. They are not. Neither are they another type of separate account. Nor are they an extension of an MSA. In fact, they are not products at all. Again, they are umbrella-like venues through which clients can see their entire portfolios, receive tax optimization over the entire portfolio nestled within that umbrella, and see one comprehensive statement that encompasses allocation, performance reporting, activity, attribution, and all the rest.

The UMA does not provide an overlay manager. In an MSA, an overlay portfolio manager (OPM) is given discretion to choose the most appropriate group of managers based on the client's IPS. A first or second generation MSA simply involves more than one asset manager, pre-selected, within a separate account structure. Third and fourth generation MSAs provide more variety, with fourth generation MSAs offering the OPM. The OPM can offer several advantages. The two primary advantages are tax management over the combined separate accounts and monitoring of overlapped positions.

Overlay portfolio management is not required in a UMA. Rather, the UMA offers an overview of all of the investment products selected for the portfolio, the tax implications resulting from the selection of those products, and the comparative performance and effectiveness of the overall portfolio asset allocation—in an ideal UMA picture, of course. Realistically at this writing, these overview advantages do exist and are limited only by the technological capability of the sponsoring firm or third-party platform which, in turn, limits the variety of product baskets that are included. But the advisor is the one who provides the overall advice. The primary advantage the UMA affords today's advisors is the ability to focus their concentration exactly where it should be—on the client—rather than on back-office operations.

Most firms that say they have the UMA are referring to the fact that they aggregate everything on the back end. It's all at one custodian and they get a feed from a retail account that rolls up into a performance report and, voila, it's a UMA. Well, it's really not. A true UMA starts with taking the client through the consultative process: it rolls from there into a complete solution using any security, mutual fund, separate account, hedge fund, or whatever the client may choose. That just doesn't exist now—the technology at most firms does not make that a scalable option.

Hurdles to Overcome

One of the largest hurdles stemming the growth of the separate account industry today is the amount of attention to back-office operations required for advisors who use separate accounts. As these operations become more standardized, a function that the UMA innately provides, advisors can turn their focus on client relationships and business development. The UMA, in fact, is never going to be *done*. The firms that *have* it now have it all worked out on the back end, which involves the aggregation of all the things mentioned earlier such as asset allocation, performance, attribution, and tax all rolled up into one report. Again, no firm has the ideal UMA front to back.

Here's an example. A financial institution may want to incorporate securities, SMAs ETFs, mutual funds, and RICs (registered investment companies or hedge funds of funds) all within a single questionnaire. Therefore, there would be only one questionnaire, one account set-up, one contract, all the way through to a single statement. Therefore, different silos or buckets are created for each product. The risk/return spectrum, the efficient frontier, asset allocation, and tax optimization are all cut up in slices so that an ETF falls into one bucket, a mutual fund into another, a separate account or an MSA into another—and they're value, growth, whatever—and they are all dropped into their respective risk silo.

This process enables the single questionnaire which subsequently enables the client to decide: a) if they want the advisor to make all the decisions for them based on their IPS, or b) if they want to make all the decisions themselves, and if they make an incorrect choice according to their IPS, the advisor would tell them. At this point, such a scenario doesn't exist, which is why no firm really *has* the UMA. But this scenario typifies the ideal UMA functionality and has the ability to expand to include any and all investment products.

Within the most advanced UMA capabilities offered today, sophisticated advisors and clients want to see a minimum of three options available in each asset allocation style and to be involved in the selection process. In a small enough account, the taxable money might be placed in an MSA with an overlay portfolio manager, the IRA might be put into mutual funds, and the trust might be set up an entirely different way. To reduce risk, they might buy bonds or they might decide to make riskier plays using ETFs. For example, a client might want to make a play in healthcare or technology using an ETF that can be either held or traded as opposed to trying to pick the right healthcare or technology stocks himself or herself or hire an asset manager for the purpose.

The primary hurdles currently limiting the potential of the UMA are pricing methods, data aggregation and reporting, technological synchronicity, and client education. With the larger wirehouses, the old legacy systems add to these hurdles because these firms have been so focused on front-end components such as portfolio construction and proposal generation that the data aggregation and reporting (middle and back-end functions) are constantly falling through the cracks. As a result, firms are in a constant state of playing catch-up and keep-up. These are root problems in the big firms' approach to technology. These problems will have to be resolved or the same technology boons that have helped the separate account industry develop to this point could become the very nemesis that causes its demise.[3]

Another hurdle is in getting advisors to actually use the UMA platform. At this point in time, only a small percentage of the advisory population even uses separate accounts, much less MSAs and certainly less UMAs. A large part of this involves the required change in the way in which advisors are compensated—the old fees versus commissions. Advisors will have to start looking on a longer term basis for their compensation and realizing that the fee structure will serve them better over the long haul than the immediate gratification that commission-based compensation provides. The UMA facilitates putting the client first and fosters a better way for advisors to build their businesses.

Yet another hurdle involves what always happens with the latest *new thing*. Firms hurry to have it first and, in their haste, create confusion. Each firm develops its own name for the new thing. It is only partially defined and understood, and then the 'first-to-market' syndrome causes the new thing to be sold without full knowledge and understanding of its purpose and proper use and or gets represented as something it may not be.

Obviously, first-to-market syndrome is not in and of itself a bad thing. It does create an awareness of the *new thing* and it fosters the spread of initial availability to the extent that it is viable. So it is a mixed phenomenon that invariably requires stepping back, educating firms and their advisors, and creating parameters for optimal implementation. The beauty of the UMA is that, as a solution rather than a product, its very use fosters those parameters and supports the sea change occurring toward compensation for advice rather than product.

The Broad Jump

The "advisor-use" hurdle is based in getting advisors to embrace fee-based compensation and that hurdle is deeply embedded within the product-oriented culture at advisory firms. But factually, there are so many investment products today that they have become commoditized. The only way for firms and advisors to distinguish themselves will be through the UMA. ETFs, index funds, mutual funds, hedge funds of funds—they're all products competing for shelf space with other products. Merrill Lynch, Smith Barney, Charles Schwab all have 90 percent product commonality. The UMA allows the personality of the firm and of each advisor to come through. If the UMA is done correctly, each firm will be different, which is the very attribute to which people will be attracted.

Another hurdle for the large firms to overcome lies in aligning what have traditionally been competitive forces within the firm. At the wirehouses, the competition may not necessarily be another firm such as Merrill Lynch; the competition is most likely the mutual fund department, the annuity department, tax shelters, or real estate. The internal workings of the wirehouses will have to be adjusted to a 'product-neutral and full disclosure' status. Competition within the firm on a product basis will have to be completely eliminated.

That brings the focus down to the following questions. The products housed with a UMA can likely be bought at any firm, but how does a client get to those products? What's the most efficient, user-friendly venue through which to construct the client's investment strategy? Which research departments are really good? Whose asset allocation is better? Of course, there also will be firms whose UMAs will consist only of their proprietary product, but that, too, becomes another choice for the client. And as everything within the UMA gets rolled up into a single custodian, it all will become cheaper and more efficient.

But the road to that place is farther off for some firms than for others. Larger, older firms have the product mentality and the legacy systems to overcome; newer firms can more quickly adopt a UMA structure because they can start pretty much from scratch. Third-party vendors catering to independent advisors and RIAs also can adopt this structure more easily because they do not have traditional advisory personnel in their employ.

But getting advisors to see and understand all of this is a hurdle unto itself. The higher-end advisors and consultants *get it.* They already do what is described above, but they also pay a couple of hundred thousand dollars a year for the systems needed to do what was just described. Many of these advisors are independents or RIAs and may say they have been doing UMAs for years – that the UMA is really just a wirehouse side of the business kind of thing. Although they technically are correct, the independent advisors are caught in the same trap as wirehouse advisors—they have to spend most of their time on back-end operations in order to produce the unified statement that the client sees.

They also have to fill out a different questionnaire for each manager or product they use, which can become cumbersome for the client. Without a UMA, the independent advisor has to fill out multiple sets of paperwork and any other documentation needed for the products or managers used. But through a UMA, a single questionnaire can be formulated based on the focus of that advisor's practice. If the advisor is a CPA and has a tax focus, the documentation can drill down to the needed tax information by security or product.

So, the UMA creates efficiencies and cost-effectiveness for independent advisors and RIAs as well. The advantage for independent advisors is that they don't have the product-based culture of the wirehouses to overcome. Will the wirehouses be able to fully adopt UMAs? That remains to be seen and depends on how well the firms embrace the concept and how willing they are to change their culture.

Managing Expectations

There are only five questions that drive everything in investment consulting—time, risk, income, downside, and growth. Which objective does the client fall into? If the answer to that question is moderate growth, then that client can accept this range of possibilities; if it's more aggressive, then that range of possibilities can be accepted; if more conservative, this other range can be accepted. The UMA functions as the key to the determination of those answers. The UMA unlocks the shackles of product-based compensation so that the advisor can better serve the client and also better manage the client's expectations.

The primary hurdle on the client side is educating clients on the true meaning of diversification. Clients traditionally have felt that proper diversification means having their investment accounts scattered over a variety of firms—regardless of what those accounts may contain. Therefore, their idea of diversification is based not on their investment and suitability criteria, but on diversification of location. So the client fills out the questionnaires at the various firms with the same investment objectives and risk parameters and ends up with virtually cloned accounts at a variety of investment firms.

Advisors have a duty to educate clients on the true meaning of diversification and the real advantages it can offer them, as well as the dangers their perceived diversification can inadvertently hold for them. The UMA, if done correctly, can serve as a tool for facilitating this education.

Is the UMA the latest *new thing*? That depends on when the mystery behind it is unveiled and how well firms can maneuver the broad culture jump from 'product-based to product-neutral.' Only then will the ideal UMA have a chance to be realized, and only then can it fulfill the potential it holds for firms and advisors who implement it.

❖❖❖

---

1 "Unified We Stand," by Sydney LeBlanc, *Financial Advisor* magazine, December 2003.
2 "The Next Big Thing," by Len Reinhart, *Financial Planning Magazine,* December 2003. http://www.financial-planning.com/pubs/fp/20031201012.html.
3 "The Next Big Thing," by Len Reinhart, *Financial Planning Magazine,* December 2003. http://www.financial-planning.com/pubs/fp/20031201012.html.

31

SERVING THE ULTRA HIGH NET WORTH MARKET

Anthony H. Browne, CEO and Co-CIO
Roxbury Capital Management, LLC

Does having great wealth signify great success? Although it would seem so to most of us, the ideology of success has been challenged by great minds since Plato. The hotly debated notion that anyone could become wealthy—hence successful—through hard work was widely promoted by author Horatio Alger in his more than 100 "dime novels" published in the late 1800s.

Most of Alger's novels told stories about poor boys rising from rags to riches through hard work, courage, faith, and perseverance; not through skill, or by saving money. During the Gilded Age in America (1870-1900), his books instigated much furor among scholars and ideologues. Alger suggested that, in part, his hero's success was due to help from a mentor. Most of his other characters were taken under the wing of an older individual who guided them and helped them on their journey toward wealth.

Today's affluent individuals are looking for "financial mentors" to help them preserve their wealth. As in Alger's novels, working hard to make the money is a key element, however, working hard to *keep the money,* is perhaps an even more important factor in the road to financial success. So, one answer to the question "does wealth signify success?" is "yes," *if* the individual employs a disciplined process of capital preservation and growth, and adheres to a prudent wealth management plan.

Whether their wealth was obtained through fortunate circumstances or hard work, about one-third of the newly rich surveyed in the latest U.S. Trust Study of the Affluent (2002) cited as "worrisome" the fact that they don't put enough time into developing a financial plan or managing their assets.[1]

This chapter will explore these and other financial challenges of high net worth and ultra high net worth individuals, as well as how advisors and consultants can meet such challenges through investment consulting and wealth management strategies.

High Net Worth Defined

According to the U.S. Census Bureau, at the end of 2000, 105 million households in the United States, collectively, controlled liquid assets of $12.9 trillion. The top 0.1 percent of households (those with over $10 million) controlled 16.3 percent of liquid assets ($2.1 trillion excluding the impact of retirement funds).

What do these statistics mean to the financial advisor or consultant of today?

Unfortunately, this top market ($10 million +) has only 268,000 members and, therefore, has limited potential for advisors due to the small number of households in this category. Generally, large brokerage firms identify the mass affluent markets as households with between $100,000 and $1 million in investable assets, leaving households with under $10 million in investable assets underserved.

According to the Merrill Lynch Cap Gemini/Ernst & Young "2003 World Wealth Report," the wealth of the high net worth category is expected to increase at an average annual rate of seven percent over the next five years, totaling approximately $38 trillion by the end of 2007. This projection takes into account the slow growth in wealth over 2001 and 2002 caused by the three-year bear market. Even in 2002, the number of global individuals with more than $1 million in financial assets grew by 200,000. A very abundant market indeed, but one that requires a new approach toward active professional participants and financial managers

Industry experts estimate that only one-third of wealthy individuals' assets are professionally managed, and bank trust departments hold half of that total. This means a majority of these individuals are either managing their wealth themselves, have put their financial plans 'on hold,' or are being advised by someone not thoroughly qualified in the area of asset or wealth management. These potential assets are virtually untouched, according to an often-quoted industry report by researcher Sanford C. Bernstein & Co, and the individuals who hold them will need a consultant or wealth manager more than ever as the transfer of assets reaches staggering levels over the next decade.

Who are the Wealthy and What Do They Need?

For advisors aiming to counsel the affluent, getting inside the mind of a millionaire is the ultimate goal, but getting to know each and every prospective client is a daunting task. A former marketing professor, author Thomas J. Stanley, did just that. In his best-selling book, "The Millionaire Mind," Stanley surveyed 1,300 millionaires and discovered that the average millionaires often were told they were not smart enough to succeed, and so chose careers that matched their abilities. A few of their commonalities included creativity, practicality, goal setting, calculated risk taking, and very hard work.

According to Stanley's study, the average multi-millionaire is a 54-year-old man who has been married to the same woman for 28 years and has three children. Nearly half are business owners or senior corporate executives. When asked, almost none of them credit their success to being smart.

They say the keys to success are honesty and discipline, getting along with people, having a supportive spouse and, of course, working hard.

That said, advisors must understand what these attributes mean to these principled affluents in order to establish or strengthen relationships with them. The old and tired approach of trying to reach the ultra high net worth individual by providing them with some type of product solution is backwards. These individuals want and need an extension of themselves, someone they can trust overseeing their assets. They want an advisor with the same or similar belief system, a good understanding of their station in life, knowing what their financial needs are now, and what they may be in the future.

Successful wealth managers work with the ultra high net worth first from the vantage point of being a family counselor and then an asset counselor— in other words, they understand the dynamics of the affluent family first, then follow with an understanding of their spending habits and, finally, a comprehensive examination of their assets and recommendation of investment vehicles through an overall financial plan.

Life planning and an understanding of their life goals are among the keys to reaching this influential group of investors. In his book, "Advanced Planning for the Ultra-Affluent," researcher Russ Alan Prince says that in addition to brokerage and investment management, there is a third component to successfully working with the wealthy: advanced planning. Says Prince, "Financial advisors are most familiar with brokerage and investment; less so with advanced planning, which covers wealth enhancement, wealth transfer, asset protection, and charitable giving. And it's the advanced planning that makes wealth management both increasingly attractive to affluent clients and viable for financial advisors."

The wealthy want best-in-class advice and ongoing counsel, and are willing to pay for a superior level of service. They are expecting a better platform of products, a team of experts to serve all levels of wealth management concerns, and a disciplined investment consulting process. A greater focus on intimacy and problem-solving will lead to a deeper client connection, which can, in turn, lead to a stronger relationship, greater profitability per client and more referrals.[2]

How To Deliver the Solutions—The Case for Wealth Management

Understandably, the various components of offering investment and wealth management services to the affluent client require a broad understanding of each component and how it fits among an alliance of specialists who can implement and oversee the strategies. The wealth management business model centralizes the affluent client's financial affairs. The advisor is the overseer of the entire program of financial services and is responsible for finding and selecting the specialists who will provide advice, products, and services outside of the advisor's area of expertise. This model includes such elements as tax management strategies, personalized and tax-efficient estate planning, risk management strategies, charitable giving, business succession counsel, life and business insurance, loans, banking, accounting and administrative issues, investment management, and more.

In addition to the various specialties required by team members, many advisors also use their own investment management consulting process. Working with independent money managers, the comprehensive steps of the consulting discipline include developing the investment policy statement (IPS); asset allocation and rebalancing; manager search and monitoring; manager and portfolio evaluation; and performance reporting. But the newly affluent are requiring more than just lip service attention to the basic tenets of the consulting process. Advisors wishing to attract this underserved wealth segment will have to refine their business models to include deeper relationship-building skills. The 2003 Cap Gemini report cites the migration of the demands of the ultra-affluent down to lower wealth segments. Their needs are growing more and more complex, therefore, their demands are also becoming increasingly complex.[3]

According to the report, these are the primary concerns of wealth segments.

- Wealth preservation and risk management
- Estate planning
- Tax planning
- Retirement planning
- Stock purchases

Such concerns involve much more than plugging the answers to a questionnaire into a computer program to generate an investment proposal, asset allocation, and investment policy. It involves integration of the consulting process and the resulting investment plan with the work of outsourced professionals so that the attention is given to these concerns in light of the wealthy individual's entire financial picture, not just his or her investment portion of that picture. It should be noted that the individual's entire financial picture also includes liabilities as well as assets. Both should be managed prudently in order to achieve the investment goals of the affluent. The advisor has the enviable advantage of being able to position himself or herself "point person" for this team of advisors on the client's behalf in addressing each of these concerns. This, in turn, builds significantly more trust with affluent clients.[4]

Russ Alan Prince's investigation into this type of business model consisted of more than 40 surveys during the last decade of affluent investors and their advisors. It involved more than 18,000 respondents and proved the attractiveness of the model. The findings showed "wealth management is not only regularly more profitable than the more traditional approach toward financial guidance of one advisor for each product and service, it's also the model that affluent clients tend to prefer."

Spending and Inflation: An Overlooked Element of the Wealth Equation

Advisors desiring to work with this prestigious group of individuals and families can make inroads to them by differentiating themselves in meaningful ways. For example, instead of approaching wealthy investors with traditional methods of marketing such as recommending unique investment strategies, a more commonsense dialogue would, instead, focus on the important subject of spending or liability activities. To illustrate, an advisor clearly could demonstrate that while an individual may receive an appealing annual investment return of 10 percent, if they have a 20 percent increase in their spending every year they will experience a depreciating accrual of assets—whether it is through the family foundation, trusts, or other vehicles. Simply, if less money is spent, less growth is needed to achieve the wealth target.

Discussions with the affluent individual and/or family about capital expenditures and discretionary spending is an essential first step in establishing a successful plan. A true wealth advisor positions himself or herself as a counselor on spending habits as well on investments. However, it is important to keep in mind that training—or gently reminding— an individual who overspends to be more careful is a difficult task and some may be unwilling to heed the advice.

One successful wealth manager who utilizes the concept of total relationship solutions uses an approach preferred by most high net worth prospects and clients. Here is how the model unfolds:

- The first element of the plan is to protect the clients assets against unforeseen events. This is accomplished through a comprehensive review of the insurance needs and the placement of any additional policies to cover – automobile, home, business, liability, life, etc. The purpose is to eliminate any stress associated with the potential loss of material assets.

- Determining and allocating assets to ensure financial liquidity is the second step of the financial process. Depending upon his or her own financial situation, of course, a client may require five or more years of expenditures in cash outside of the market, for example. The discussion then turns to inflation, unexpected expenses or long range spending for eldercare or education for children.

- The final step in this planning process focuses on growth of assets. The growth element follows with a comprehensive investment discussion and subsequent plan. Most advisors discuss growth *before* discussing spending, which, of course, is backwards.

In addition to direct spending habits, other factors having an effect on the outcome of a wealth management plan include an individual's *personal* inflation number. The client's personal inflation figure may be significantly different than what traditionally is used in an asset allocation model.

Since inflation can rob wealth creation, this is an important topic an advisor should discuss with a client. It is easy to put a number of five to six percent on inflation, but how different is that than saying, "I think in the year of 2008, you're going to have a 10 percent return on your portfolio." The reality—and the challenge—is that no one knows for sure. Most advisors will assume a figure. However, assuming a 10 percent inflation rate and a 10 percent return, the client's wealth will not grow nearly as much if the plan assumed two percent inflation and 10 percent return. Which answer is correct? Both assumptions of inflation can be correct, it depends on the spending pattern of each specific client. It is critical to communicate with each client the need to control their own personal inflation and the direct connection it will have on achieving their personal goals in accumulating or protecting wealth.

The ultimate point is that considerable up-front time, effort, and energy is involved in properly building a solution for the high net worth client; significantly more than in "selling" on performance. And as a business for the advisor, the profit margin initially may be lower with this model. Think of it as basic micro-economics: even though the margin may go down, the advisor will provide such a better solution for clients that the gross margin dollar potential will be much higher.

Wealth Transfer Strategies

According to a *More than Money* journal interview in 2003 with Paul G. Schervish of the Social Welfare Institute,[5] upwards of $41 trillion will be transferred between generations over the next 55 years through inheritance, philanthropy, and taxes. The 1999 study conducted by Schervish and John J. Haven has been validated despite the economic and market downturn of 2000 – 2003. Most investors do not realize the potential impact taxes will have on their inheritances, much less the impact such exponential wealth may have on their lives.

The transfer process has already begun. One result has been an increasing interest in philanthropy. Families with wealth are not only setting up foundations to promulgate the family legacy, but also for use as a training ground for young heirs in wealth management. But philanthropy should be approached very cautiously. Individuals inheriting or receiving "sudden money" tend to be overly generous in the beginning. They immediately begin creating charitable remainder trusts, charitable lead trusts, and grants to their schools without fully exploring the implications such trusts may have on their long-term investment planning. Counseling these wealthy individuals to be extremely careful about long-term philanthropic commitments that they may not be able to keep is a vital service to them.

In his book, "Wealthy and Wise," Claude Rosenberg, Jr. suggests that as a result of the growing realization of the personal rewards philanthropic giving can offer, individuals and families need to become enlightened about the advantages of philanthropy. They need education about which charitable opportunities are legitimate and, further, which will best match the interests of the benefactor.

This is a vital and growing area where advisors and consultants can be of service to clients. Advisors either can become knowledgeable about philanthropic matters themselves, or they can outsource philanthropy experts for their clients who need such expertise. Philanthropy, as noted earlier, is directly involved with estate planning and tax planning. Astute advisors and consultants will seek to be a resource for information and expertise in these areas and will integrate their investment advice with these growing areas of wealth management.

Making Inroads to the Super-Wealthy

Many advisors have discovered that much of an affluent family's money is tied up in long-term trusts and other accounts created a generation ago with private banks and trust companies. To a great extent, the plans are written so that the trustee cannot be replaced. However, traditional trust investment management today is being supplanted by the desire of clients to hire outside professional money managers. The hiring of these outside managers offers advisors and consultants an opening to the trust/client relationship.

Advisors can begin to build trust with a focus on relationships and position their practices as those that care more about their clients than do the trust companies that traditionally serve the old-money set. The new wealth management practices help individuals sort through their issues with family and wealth.

Also, advisors can look outside their current client base to target local foundations that may need professional investment advice. An advisor or consultant might offer a service to trustees such as reviewing the foundation's investment policy statement (IPS) to ensure it is in line with their investment goals, fiduciary guidelines, and standards. Reviewing the foundation's IPS can also serve as an introduction to other generations of the family involved in the family legacy, paving the way for advisors and consultants to build multi-generational relationships with their clients and access to larger assets.

One popular resource, Guidestar, a national database of charitable organizations, allows advisors to research the finances of foundations in their geographic area and beyond. Organizations such as The Council on Family Foundations (www.cof.org) and The American Foundation (www.americanfoundation.org) can be invaluable resources for advisors and consultants wishing to learn more about the process of establishing foundations and the needs their interested clients may have as a result.

Family Foundations

As noted earlier, the family foundation can serve as the perfect training ground for young heirs who will someday inherit the family fortune. Family offices have decades of experience helping families establish, run, and preserve their legacies through such foundations. Controlling generations, the baby boomers currently, are beginning to question leaving vast sums of money to their heirs. Many are bequeathing their fortunes to foundations, forcing heirs to make their own fortunes rather than rely on their inheritances.

Establishing a family foundation is best done with the advice of an estate and tax attorney so that the proper structure will be implemented. Foundations must meet certain requirements to establish and maintain their non-profit status, their funds must be prudently managed, and grants for funds must be carefully considered. It doesn't take much imagination on the part of advisors and consultants to see opportunities for service to philanthropic clients. Organizations such as the Institute for Private Investors (IPI) and Family Office Exchange (FOX) are excellent places for advisors to find out more about serving high net worth clients in these areas.[5]

For less affluent families, donor-advised funds may be a workable alternative. Investors make irrevocable contributions to such funds, then are granted influence over how the funds are used. Donors get the advantage of making the contribution and determining which grant proposals are accepted without having to go through the rigors of setting up a family foundation. Donor-advised funds, therefore, offer many of the advantages of promoting a philanthropic interest for those with less than sufficient funds to establish a separate philanthropic entity.

The Family Office

A family office is an entity dedicated to serving the personal, financial, and social needs of an individual family and, ideally its future generations. When a wealthy family reaches a critical level of wealth, usually around $100 million, and needs a separate, dedicated team of professionals to help manage all aspects of their wealth and some aspects of family members' lives, they form a family office. That critical level of wealth depends upon the extent of the services needed by the family, and how much they can expect to grow their wealth in order to justify the costs and any overhead. The basic services provided by family offices include: integrated asset management, confidentiality, intergenerational wealth transfer, management of international financial and non-financial assets, and, in many instances, philanthropy.[6]

Family offices represent a growing market for the financial advisor or consultant who understands the unique needs of wealthy families. To run a successful family office, a firm grasp of the services needed by ultra high net worth clients is required. Ultra high net worth individuals face complex planning issues, including generational tax and estate planning, all-inclusive consolidated reporting of asset classes, charitable gift-giving, concierge services and lifestyle management, and, most important, education of family members in all areas of wealth preservation and management.

In theory, working with five families each representing $30 million in assets would be a preferable business model, versus servicing 150 high net worth investors with assets of $1 million. But, practically speaking, starting a family office requires taking on new and/or unfamiliar challenges of providing the multi-faceted, complex set of services that most ultra high net worth clients and family offices require. This set of services includes much more than just asset management. Personal desires must be catered to; family dynamics must be considered in wealth management and growth, as well as business succession, partnership accounting, and other issues. However, by acquainting oneself with the needs of the ultra wealthy (defined as $25 million in assets and above) and developing relationships with other professionals who may provide expertise in the needed areas, advisors and consultants can position themselves as important liaisons for these families.

Developing such relationships is not an overnight process. Transitioning to a family office model requires understanding operational and administrative issues, which services to offer, and how to provide them. There are several business models from which to choose, depending on the type of clients and how much an advisor is willing to collaborate with other professionals.[7]

According to the Family Office Exchange, an educational organization for family offices and affiliated professionals, there are six levels of wealth management services for family. Here are their dimensions: family continuity, strategic philanthropy, risk management, investment diversification, integrated planning, and lifestyle enhancements.[8]

These six dimensions clearly indicate that the family office focus is not always on traditional money management. It also shows that it takes a number of strategic partners to deliver these myriad services as well as considerable capital to pay for the team, the support staff, office space, and the technology necessary to run a successful family office. However, outsourcing is a viable option for many of these services and relationships with outsiders who excel in tax and compliance work, charitable and estate planning, back-office reporting, and concierge services.

Investment Strategies and Vehicles for the High Net Worth Investor

Ultra high net worth investors have invested in private investment partnerships since at least the 1950s. Warren Buffett's, Buffett Partnership Ltd., was formed in the mid-1950s and by the time Buffett liquidated his partnership in 1969, many others already had been formed. Buffett ignited interest in private partnerships with his 1984 "Super Investors of Graham and Doddsville" presentation at Columbia University that was widely reported in the financial press.

The go-go years of the 1960s saw the advent of the phrase "hedge funds." Leading hedge fund managers of the 1960s were A.W. Jones and his disciple Carlyle Jones. During the 1960s, the SEC became concerned about the market impact of hedge funds, which were exempt from SEC regulation, and launched a major study of the funds. The benign conclusions of the study paved the way for people like George Soros and Michael Steinhart to legitimize these investment vehicles by achieving outstanding investment results for nearly three decades into the 1990s.

By the late 1990s, hedge funds had proliferated and, like other investment strategies, became more and more specialized. Large brokerage firms like Goldman Sachs and speculators like Ivan Boesky, for example, initially ran arbitrage funds. These funds also became more specialized and included convertible bond arbitrage, fixed income arbitrage, currency, and commodity arbitrage.

Family Offices and Institutions Get Involved

Family offices like the Rockefeller's and the Whitney's are active in venture capital and real estate. Rockefeller Center is a 1930s example. By the 1970s, these and other sophisticated family offices embraced "alternative investment strategies."

The bear market of 2000-2002 devastated most traditional "long only" stock portfolios and stimulated broad interest in alternative investments, such as hedge funds with non-stock market related returns.

The popularity of alternative investments is a result of excellent risk-adjusted returns, which attract investors and high fees and, in turn, attracts premier investment talent. Alternative investment returns, particularly during the period of 2000-2002, were significantly better than traditional separate account strategies. The result has been a stampede into hedge fund strategies by family offices, pensions, and endowments.

Absolute, consistent, and market neutral returns, typically about 10 percent or more, equal or exceed long-term returns of the major stock indexes, but with less volatility. Bond returns will not likely match the returns of the past 25 years (about 10 percent) with bond rates currently below 6 percent. In this world, it is easy to understand the popularity of hedge funds.

Fund of Fund Services

Investors are faced with many challenges in choosing alternative investments. When available, the data on investment strategies and techniques of thousands of hedge funds are difficult at best to understand. Fund of fund consultants have provided a valuable resource to institutional and ultra high net worth investors by analyzing fund strategies and policing the funds to stick by their disciplines.

Risk can be great in funds that employ substantial leverage, such as Long Term Capital Management, whose bankruptcy nearly caused a national financial panic in 1998. The potential to lose 100 percent of one's investment is certainly present in the alternative investment world, and there are many examples to prove it.

Summary

The primary focus of this chapter has been the multiple avenues through which advisors and consultants are gaining viable access to service options sought by high net worth and ultra high net worth individuals. More importantly, this chapter highlights the changing attitudes and needs demanded by today's affluent investor. Advisors and consultants serving as financial mentors to this group must become aware of these changes in order to remain competitive in the years to come.

❖ ❖ ❖

---

1 US Trust Survey of the Affluent, 2002
2 Wealth Management: The New Business Model for Financial Advisors by Russ Alan Prince, 2004
3 Merrill Lynch/Cap Gemini Ernst & Young *World Wealth Report* 2003, p. 12 .
4 IBID
5 "Wealth Transfer in an Age of Affluence," by Pamela Gerloff, *More than Money Journal,* Spring 2003. http://www.morethanmoney.org/articles/mtm32_schervish.pdf
6 Institute for Private Investors – www.memberlink.net; Family Office Exchange – www.familyoffice.com
7 Cerulli Associates, "Family Offices," p217
8 "The New Family Office: Innovative Strategies for Consulting to the Affluent," by Lisa Gray, Euromoney Books/Institutional Investor, p. 111, March 2004
9 Family Office Exchange

This material is provided for informational and educational purposes only. The statements contained herein are the opinions of Roxbury Capital Management, LLC and are subject to change without notice.
This report contains no investment recommendations and should not be construed as specific tax, legal, financial planning, or investment advice. Clients should consult their professional advisors before making any tax or investment decisions. Investing entails risk including the loss of principal and there is no assurance that an investment will provide positive performance over any period of time. It is important to review investment objectives, risk tolerance, tax objectives, and liquidity needs before choosing an investment style or manager. Information was obtained from third party sources, which we believe to be reliable but not guaranteed. Past performance is no guarantee of future results.

32

ABSOLUTE RETURN OPPORTUNITIES AND RISK MITIGATION WITH HEDGE FUNDS

William Turchyn, Partner
Mariner Investment Group

Hedge fund managers are mysterious people. They are industry renegades, striking out on their own to escape the shackles of big organizations and regulation. They are demanding and brilliant with few "people skills." They eat, sleep, and breathe their craft.

True or False?

Well, the above is partially true. The personalities of these exceptional men and women are often described as driven and focused, and the consistency of the investment returns that they have produced for their partners and clients is remarkable. Many of the most successful of these managers have been able to achieve this with significantly lower risk than have traditional investment managers.

But exactly what is a hedge fund and why are they attracting so much attention from investors?

Hedge Funds Defined

"Hedge funds engage in a variety of investment activities. They cater to sophisticated investors and are not subject to the regulations that apply to mutual funds geared toward the general public. Fund managers are compensated on the basis of performance rather than as a fixed percentage of assets.

'Performance funds' would be a more accurate description."

—-George Soros, "Open Society: Reforming Global Capitalism" 2000

Simply put, a hedge fund is an investment pool (usually a limited partnership or limited liability company). The hedge fund manager has investment discretion to manage assets in the fund, and the hedge fund structure provides the flexibility to accommodate a variety of hedging strategies. Hedge fund managers seek to generate portfolio performance regardless of the direction of the capital markets, and unlike traditional asset managers, many managers try to create value primarily through limited exposure to the traditional capital markets.

Return opportunities come from identifying a dislocation in the value of one or more securities, and then quickly acting upon this conviction. Managers take advantage of these dislocations with an expanded universe of securities from which to trade; and a wider array of investment strategies that are not as constrained as most traditional strategies. For example, hedge fund strategies may take corresponding long and short positions in equities, fixed income securities, commodities, options, and other derivative securities, whereas, a traditional manager is usually long these types of securities. Consequently, hedge funds possess unique risk and return characteristics that are very different from those of traditional asset management strategies.

This means that when analyzing potential managers and strategies there is more information to process and different measures are used in manager selection and portfolio construction. The hedge fund structure can also combine a diverse set of strategies since investment objectives vary widely among hedge fund managers. Some hedge fund strategies, such as market-neutral, attempt to avoid systematic exposure to the capital markets and are true diversifiers. Other hedge fund strategies, such as equity long/short, are more sensitive to the same market factors as traditional capital market strategies[1], since these strategies usually have net long exposure to the equity markets.

A factor lending to the relative anonymity of hedge funds, heretofore, is that hedge funds have had relatively little oversight by regulatory bodies, allowing hedge fund managers to be extremely discreet in the investment positions they take. Although most hedge funds report performance on a regular basis (monthly), they rarely disclose their positions. This privacy and lack of transparency provides the manager and investors several advantages, the most obvious of which is the ability to effect control over trading positions without open competition from other mangers and traders who may seek to trade against them, creating the potential for losses in the portfolio and ultimately harming the performance of the fund. This issue has been particularly troublesome for institutions that, as fiduciaries, need to know where they are exposed to risk and how such risk relates to their overall portfolio. This gap is seemingly being bridged through risk reporting software that gives fiduciaries and institutions the risk oversight they need without revealing each security position.

Misconceptions about Hedge Funds

Most people correctly identify hedge funds with the ability to have both long and short security positions in one portfolio. The ability to use a variety of financial instruments such as options and derivatives has led many investors to believe that hedge funds offer the opportunity for outsized performance that can yield 25-30 percent annual returns. This is a myth. Those who truly understand hedge funds and their strategies, specifically the institutions, are not buying them with the hope of making these outsized returns (of course, this does not imply that there are no managers trying to hit "home runs" every year). But the largest, most successful hedge fund firms are the ones *not* delivering the very large returns, but rather, more modest absolute returns with high *consistency* and lower volatility. High risk-adjusted returns is the objective and, over time, can be in the range of 10-14 percent. For example, a return of 10 percent with annualized standard deviation of 2 to 3 is performance that institutions find very attractive.

Both the investor and advisor are attracted to the absolute return that hedge fund managers attempt to produce. The attraction for hedge fund managers is the potential to earn a fee based on their performance. Because of these two factors, new capital is flowing into hedge funds (and especially those strategies that can produce consistent absolute performance). According to the Putnam Lovell study, "Institutional or Institutionalized—Are Hedge Funds Crazy?", hedge fund assets are expected to reach the $2 trillion mark by 2010.[2] As of this writing, hedge fund assets have just surpassed $800 billion according to HedgeWorld.[3]

Because their primary objective is to produce a positive return regardless of market direction, hedge funds are increasingly sought after by investors of all levels of wealth. In practice, hedge funds may not actually produce an independently positive (or absolute) return, but that is, indeed, their goal and to find those funds with the best potential that are open to accepting new capital is not easy.

Depending on the strategy a hedge fund manager employs, the fund may still have a high correlation to the traditional equity and debt markets. Similarly, low or no correlation does not guarantee a positive return; instead, the return simply may be less negative. For example, many long/short equity managers can have a 60 percent or greater net long exposure to the equity markets due to the generally accepted positive bias of those markets. Generally, the higher the percentage of long equity exposure, the more the funds' returns will be correlated to stock market returns. When market downturns occur, funds with higher net long exposure will usually experience greater losses in the downturn. Even if hedge fund managers adjust their funds' exposure, they still may produce a negative return during a down market. For instance, the CSFB/Tremont Long/Short Equity Index generated a negative return of 1.6 percent in 2002. But that was much better than the 22.2 percent loss experienced by the S&P 500 that year. Individual funds with greater net long exposure may have fared much worse, but this average return significantly outperformed the S&P return.

Another big misconception regarding hedge funds is hedge fund's use of leverage. Leverage is one of the most misunderstood hedge fund practices, largely as a result of spectacular failures by over-leveraged funds. But the actual use of leverage by most hedge fund managers is quite limited and (when used properly) enhances returns. Despite the publicity well-known funds may receive each time one blows up or closes down, there are many more funds, in fact, that send back gains and do not take new money. According to the Managed Accounts Reports, Inc. (MAR/Hedge) data, the majority of funds using leverage do so at a ratio of less than 2 to 1. If placed visually on a bell curve, managers who have outperformed significantly would be at one end, managers who produced some level of positive returns consistently over time (the majority) would be in middle, and notorious firms such as Long Term Capital Management (LTCM) who used leverage and illiquid securities (by virtue of their size) to the extreme would be at the other end of the curve.

The large body of available hedge fund performance data indicates that a high ratio of hedge fund managers make money each month, effectively managing risks and dispelling the misconceptions fostered by publicized hedge fund debacles and failures. Obviously, this information does not mean that these managers will never have a losing month, but it does indicate that the best hedge fund managers are effectively managing these risks and that the down months they have experienced have been minimal in size and number.

Hedge Fund of Funds

Most seasoned hedge fund managers traditionally have not accepted investments into their funds of less than $1million and, in many cases, $5-10 million. Of course, many institutional clients may not have much difficulty dealing with this account minimum, but for individual clients—except for the most affluent— it would be an impossibility. In order to reduce the minimum investment requirements and increase the ability to diversify, a structure called *fund of funds* has evolved and is becoming increasingly popular. A fund of funds is structured with a variety of underlying hedge fund manager portfolios that are overseen by a fund of funds manager. This structure provides value to investors in that the fund of funds manager conducts extensive due diligence and monitoring, portfolio construction, and risk management of underlying funds and strategies. Fund of funds managers provide investors the expertise of a professional manager who constructs a diversified portfolio of hedge funds and reduces the risk of investing in one manager. They also offer the ability to access hedge fund managers that investors otherwise might not be able to afford due to high minimums or "closed" status.

There are fund of fund managers who allow investors to participate for $250,000 or less. In this respect, a fund of funds can actually accept even smaller investment minimums as long as the total fund is large enough to bear the expenses of operation and still provide acceptable performance. Because funds with these low minimums require large numbers of investors, they are sometimes SEC-registered. Whether these vehicles are registered or unregistered, investors must meet specific suitability standards relating to their investable assets, income and sophistication.

Hedge Fund Strategies

Although the specific application of basic hedge fund strategies is discretionary to each hedge fund manager, a fundamental understanding of these strategies is imperative for financial advisors and their clients. Below is a list and brief explanation of the most common strategies employed by hedge fund managers.[4]

- Directional

    Equity Non-Hedge funds do not use hedging consistently and are commonly called "stock pickers." Their investments are based on market conditions, both favorable and unfavorable.

    Equity Hedge funds have a core holding of long equities that are consistently hedged with short positions or index options. Leverage is commonly used and hedging most often involves [some ratio of] dollars in long and short positions. Conservative managers limit their net equity exposure from zero to 100 percent; more aggressive managers exceed 100 percent exposure and may use leverage to invest a limited amount of assets in other types of securities.

    Macro strategies involve taking leveraged, directional exposure on price movements of equity markets, interest rates, foreign exchange markets, and physical commodities. The strategy most often involves a top down global approach and has the freedom to invest in any instrument and any market that appear over or under valued. These movements occur as the result of economic shifts, world events, and global supply and demand factors. Managers may use derivatives to exaggerate the exploitation of the price movements.

    Emerging Markets investments involve the debt of developing or "emerging" countries in nations experiencing governmental upheaval or change. Hedge funds employing emerging market strategies are obviously global and may shift their holdings between a variety of debt from emerging countries or those experiencing financial distress. Many of these funds are predominantly long, although funds may go long on one country's bonds and short another's.

Short Selling involves the sale of a security not owned by the seller in anticipation of a decline in the price of that security. Profit is made by borrowing securities, selling them short, then repurchasing the securities at a lower price than the short sale price. Unlimited loss is possible if the security price rises or "goes against" the position. Therefore, short sellers must pledge cash or other securities equal to the value of the borrowed securities to mitigate this risk. As the price of the shorted security moves, investors may be required to make additional deposits.

- Event-Driven

Event-Driven strategies exploit non-market driven events in a companies' development or business cycle. Corporate events drive the strategy and may include mergers, buyouts, spin-offs, recapitalizations, and share repurchases. Long and short securities as well as preferred stocks, options, and debt instruments may be used.

Distressed Securities represent companies that have experienced situations that have negatively affected their value. Such companies may have high bank debt, other corporate debt, trade claims, or depressed common stock, preferred stock, and warrant prices and may be experiencing bankruptcies, reorganizations, or other corporate restructurings. Strategies include investments in the bank or corporate debt while shorting the underlying stock.

Merger (Risk) Arbitrage, sometimes called ***Risk Arbitrage***, involves event-driven strategies around leveraged buy-outs, mergers, and hostile takeovers. Usually, the acquiring company's stock is sold short and the stock of the target company is purchased. Equity options are sometimes used to reduce risk exposure and hedging is accomplished by purchasing index puts or put option spreads.

- Relative Value

Equity Market Neutral seeks profits by taking advantage of equity market price inefficiencies and combining long and short positions in an attempt to neutralize market fluctuations and the risk associated with it. Strategies may include long equities and short index futures or long positions in strong companies' stocks and short positions in weak companies' stocks.

Relative Value Arbitrage strategies try to exploit discrepancies in pricing relative to specific investment instruments, namely equities, bonds, options, and futures. Inefficient security prices that are misvalued relative to the underlying security or the overall market or sector are exploited using dividend arbitrage, pairs trading, options arbitrage, and yield curve trading.

Convertible Arbitrage usually involves hedging long convertible bond positions with short positions in the underlying stock. Managers generally employ leverage ranging from 1:1 to 6:1 with the equity hedge ratio ranging from 30 to 100 percent. The strategy inherently provides the return generated by the interest income from the bonds. Some managers employ additional profit strategies such as trading short positions on the underlying stock and hedging interest rates, whose movements significantly affect the value of the bonds. Low-grade bonds are typically used, but the hedge provided by shorting the underlying stock mitigates the risk normally assumed by investing in such bonds.

Fixed Income: Arbitrage is a market neutral strategy that attempts to add profit by exploiting inefficiencies in value between fixed income securities and hedging against interest rate risk. The focus is on reducing exposure to changes in the yield curve and capitalizing on dislocations in the relationship of different Fixed Income securities. Municipal bonds, corporate bonds, and global fixed income securities are the most commonly used instruments.

Fixed Income: High-Yield Credit managers invest in non-investment grade corporate debt. The fund manager focuses on the assessment of the issuer's credit risk and may use extendible/reset securities, increasing rate notes, pay-in-kind securities, step-up coupon securities or split-coupon securities.

Fixed Income: Mortgage-Backed invest primarily in AAA-rated bonds such as government agency bonds, government-sponsored enterprise securities, private label fixed or adjustable rate mortgage pass- throughs, CMOs, REMICs, and stripped SMBSs. Hedges involve protection against prepayment risk and may use leverage, futures, options, and short sales.

Benchmarks for Hedge Funds

Hedge fund indices are evolving into investment instruments, much like major market indices. They allow investors to participate in hedge fund-like returns and achieve diversification without having to invest directly in a single strategy hedge fund or fund of funds. But hedge fund indices are much different than major market indices and are not always the best tools by which to achieve "benchmark" performance. Because hedge fund managers seek to deliver an absolute return, they inherently deliver a wide range of returns—even two managers using the same hedge fund strategy may produce returns that are quite far apart. If an analyst took such returns and plotted them on a graph around a hedge fund index, the returns would be all over the chart resulting in a high level of dispersion.

In contrast, a chart illustrating traditional investment managers' returns would show those returns in a tight pattern around the performance of the benchmark they are trying to beat. There's a very simple reason for the disparity between the two charts; traditional managers compare their returns to their peers and to the index that most closely represents the holdings in their portfolios. They are judged on their relative performance. Hedge fund managers focus on an absolute return—a return that is, for the most part, not related to a market or to their peers.

The entities that have made significant headway in forming reliable investible indices are CSFB/Tremont (www.hedgeindex.com), Hedge Fund Research, Inc. (www.hedgefundresearch.com), and, the S&P Hedge Fund Index (www.standardandpoors.com). Although indices can give an investor exposure to the hedge fund asset class, an actively managed fund of funds with superior good selection has the potential to significantly outperform the index because the dispersion between the best and worst managers is large when compared to dispersion of managers in traditional asset classes.

Regulation

There is a major evolution under way in many of the larger, more substantial, and better- known hedge fund firms: they are beginning to look like traditional asset management firms. They are taking on the responsibilities of registration as registered investment advisors (RIAs)— in part for ERISA compliance, and their desire to offer registered products such as funds of hedge funds, that are usually offered in the form of SEC registered investment vehicles.

There is formalized governance in the hedge fund world, primarily in the form of investment committees, management committees, and advisory boards. The most successful funds have a well-developed infrastructure similar to traditional asset management firms. They have legal and compliance staffs, accounting staffs, investor relations departments, and significant operations and administrative support. A number of functions used to be outsourced, but the institutionalization of hedge funds has reversed this trend.

The SEC held a roundtable discussion in May 2003 that focused on whether greater disclosure and increased regulation of the industry is needed. It should be noted here that registration is not the same as regulation; a fund can fall under certain regulatory requirements even if it is not registered. Prime examples of such regulations include the anti-fraud, anti-money laundering, and anti-terrorism provisions that govern all hedge funds regardless of registration. Another example is the requirement for hedge fund managers to be subject to the laws governing securities and investment advisors in their state of operation. Both of these examples cite regulations hedge funds must follow without being registered, *emphasizing the fact that hedge funds, contrary to popular myths, are not unregulated investments.* Registered funds of funds— or registered investment companies (RICs) — are subject to the regulations of the acts under which they are registered in addition to the regulatory parameters cited above.

Until the May 14, 2003 SEC roundtable discussion, private hedge funds avoided registration under the Investment Company Act of 1940, the Investment Advisors Act of 1940, and the Securities Exchange Act of 1934, all of which register and regulate mutual funds and their advisers. Private hedge funds avoid registration because they can lay claim to one of two significant exemptions to the SEC's definition of an investment company. Under Section 3(c)1 of the Investment Company Act, a fund is allowed to have up to 100 accredited investors without triggering registration requirements. The other significant exemption is listed under Section 3(c)7 of the Act. This section permits a fund to have an unlimited amount of investors provided each investor is a qualified purchaser. A qualified purchaser is either an individual with a net worth of at least $5 million or an institution with investable assets of at least $25 million. The reporting company provisions of the Securities Act effectively limits the number of investors in a qualified purchaser fund to 499. Other regulatory exemptions to registration can be found by visiting the Securities and Exchange Commission website at: http://www.sec.gov/about/laws.shtml.

None of these exemptions, however, mean that hedge funds are, or have been, totally unregulated. Private hedge funds that use commodities and futures must register with the Commodity Futures Trading Commission (CFTC). Hedge funds also are subject to recordkeeping and reporting requirements, including the Patriot Act, set forth by the U.S. Department of the Treasury. Hedge funds also must be cognizant of each state's regulations, which may differ from the federal regulations outlined above. The amount of regulation hedge funds should be subject to will continue to be debated and advisors and consultants should be aware of actions by the SEC and other regulatory agencies.

Manager Selection, Due Diligence and Risk Management

A thorough discussion of the process of manager selection and due diligence incorporates an extensive list of guidelines that increases in depth with each step. However, for purposes of this chapter and in the interest of available space, the discussion will be limited to the highlights of a comprehensive and rigorous due diligence process.

Fund of fund managers, investment consultants, family and wealth management firms, along with third party platform providers all have developed proprietary approaches to manager selection and due diligence. Most will use a set of "screens" to identify a core group of potential managers. This pool of managers usually will number in the hundreds, and will be broadly diversified by strategy and market sector. The sources of these managers often are proprietary as well, and are the result of referrals from existing managers as well as a deep network in the investment management and proprietary trading community. Many of the most successful hedge fund managers began their careers trading proprietary capital for large securities firms. Similarly, many of the most sophisticated hedge fund strategies can trace their origins to Wall Street proprietary trading desks.

The qualitative tools used at the initial stage of due diligence are somewhat standardized and among others, include: an analysis of maximum drawdown, standard deviation and use of leverage. The next level of due diligence usually includes a deeper look into historical performance, fee structures, risk/return characteristics and pricing policies, among other factors. It also includes an in-depth examination of the fund's organizational documents. These include offering memoranda, subscription agreements, presentations, audited and unaudited financial statements as well as a review of the manager's employment history.

A deep understanding of the manager's investment process, risk management parameters, trading support systems, compliance standards, and the overall stability of the organization is critical. In line with this, a number of firms have the ability to conduct a detailed analysis of a prospective manager's security positions as well as current and historical trades. Whether it is performed early or late in the process, the firms that have an ability to do this usually will come away with a much deeper understanding of the manager's disposition for risk and investment philosophy, and often leads to better decision-making in selecting managers. Not all managers, of course, will offer this level of transparency at this stage (or ever, for that matter) and it requires a high degree of trust and understanding between the two parties.

An onsite visit is mandatory and can offer valuable clues about the firm's staff, accounting and risk controls, as well as the manager's integrity and experience. It can also be the source of references to be followed up after the visit.

Searches are then usually performed using a number of the following databases, Lexus Nexis, SEC enforcement actions, NASD enforcement actions, news reports, Edgar (SEC) position reports, ADV review (if applicable), and NFA enforcement actions.

A key distinguishing characteristic of hedge fund managers is that a large percentage have a substantial portion of their net worth invested in their funds. It is not uncommon to see 60 percent or more of a manager's liquid net worth invested in his or her fund. This is especially prevalent among smaller-sized managers. In addition to the obvious benefit of alignment of interests between investors and managers, a manager who has a significant amount of his or her own capital in the fund usually will not allow the fund to grow too large. The best managers will not allow the size of the fund to affect their ability to manage the fund efficiently. If necessary, they will close the fund to new investors.

After the completion of these in-depth processes, the asset allocation team or investment management consultant evaluates the effect of the proposed investment on the existing portfolio. The appropriate managers are then chosen.

Ongoing Monitoring and Risk Management

The manager selection and due diligence process provides the basis for an expectation of how a manager is expected to perform and the steps they will undertake to contain risk in the portfolio. These expectations are based on the information provided by the manager as it relates to the many factors described above. Over time, however, markets change as do portfolios and the individuals who manage them. The ongoing due diligence and risk management process involves staying in frequent communication with the manager. It also requires a complete understanding of the quantifiable aspects of the fund's portfolio.

These data points are too numerous to mention here but include asset growth, employee turnover, appropriate use of leverage, portfolio pricing, and a change in investment strategy. To be effective, this ongoing due diligence usually will involve some degree of portfolio transparency and position information. This information is usually gathered monthly or bi-monthly through a formal questionnaire and electronic data transmission. As mentioned earlier, many consultants and fund of fund firms are using risk-reporting services to gain portfolio level information. This is especially important for fiduciaries and their consultants who, armed with this information, can view the portfolio under a number of "what if" scenarios. These scenarios stress the portfolio under various stock market, interest rate, and shock events. By considering the impact of these various scenarios, investors can better forecast overall performance of the portfolio and make changes accordingly.

The largest and most sophisticated university endowments, foundations, and very wealthy individuals have been investing in hedge funds for some time, as mentioned earlier. One of the beneficial byproducts of the increasing capital flows into hedge funds from institutions is that institutional investors and their consultants have high quality standards for process, compliance and due diligence. Looking ahead, this should benefit all levels of investors and provide a better educational framework for investors to evaluate prospective hedge fund managers.

The Place of Hedge Funds in Today's Portfolios

It is clear that some amount of hedge fund or fund of funds allocation should be added to a traditional 60 percent equity/40 percent fixed income portfolio based on the un-correlated and potential risk reducing nature of this asset class. For individual investors who do not have the deep pockets of institutional investors, the best venue for hedge fund investing is through funds of funds. Financial advisors do not have time or, generally, the skills to perform the level of due diligence conducted by funds of funds managers. Funds of funds can also offer investors access to the best managers, which is the result of their thorough due diligence and evaluation.

Hedge fund clients—especially those with smaller net worths—must be educated regarding the risks and expected returns of hedge funds. They also need to understand how an investment in hedge funds will impact their entire portfolio. The types of hedge fund strategies selected must also be suitable for clients relative to their risk tolerance and objectives for investing in the funds. Aside from these basic considerations, the ability of hedge funds to help qualified investors manage risk and obtain non-correlated investment returns are other aspects of hedge fund investing about which financial advisors must educate investors. Methods of risk management and measurement used by the fund of funds manager, the appropriateness of the investment instruments used by the underlying managers, the draw-down history of the underlying managers, the sensitivity of the portfolio to potential shock "events," and what that may mean to investors' overall portfolio performance are additional areas advisors would be well-advised to cover.

In working with hedge fund or fund of funds managers, financial advisors will want to keep in mind the personality traits of many of the best hedge fund managers:

- They usually do not like to talk to people very much as they think it's a waste of their time to educate unsophisticated investors
- They have limited patience
- The best are brilliant at what they do
- They know more about their companies and the financial instruments they invest in than almost anyone else

- They live their passion for their work and they eat, breathe, and sleep it every day
- They stick to what they know

It is crucial that an advisor rely on individuals they trust to keep them abreast of any important changes occurring within a hedge fund portfolio and its business. The due diligence and manager research departments, as well as the fund of funds organizations and institutional consulting firms, are in the best position to report on significant developments within a specific hedge fund or about a manager that may potentially impact the advisor's clients. These are the best sources to help advisors keep up to date on the latest news and events surrounding the managers and the fund.

As with other investments, advisors should inform their clients of the dangers of chasing performance. A hedge fund producing 20 to 100 percent returns one year may deliver a 20 to 100 percent loss the next. Consistency of returns is a wiser focus. This consistency helps investors mitigate the overall risk in their portfolios and provides overall portfolio stability through lower volatility and non-correlated investment performance.

Conclusion

Hedge funds are sophisticated investment vehicles about which financial advisors and their qualified clients must be well-educated. Advisors who wish to provide hedge fund exposure to appropriate clients must ensure a high level of due diligence either through conducting that due diligence personally or through due diligence performed by consulting firms or fund of funds managers. Funds of funds are the most advantageous and practical forms of hedge fund investing for less-affluent individual investors. Generally, they are more cost-efficient, accept lower investment minimums, and offer added diversification.

The growing interest in absolute return strategies is one that will have broad ramifications for investment managers, advisors, and their clients. As more investors make these strategies permanent additions to their portfolios, new definitions of "good performance" will emerge.

❖ ❖ ❖

---

1 "Investing in Hedge Funds Strategies for the New Marketplace," by Joseph G. Nicholas, Chairman, Hedge Fund Research, LLC, 1999, Bloomberg Press

2 "Institutional or Institutionalized☐Are Hedge Funds Crazy? " by Neal M. Epstein, CFA, Neil O. Brown, CFA, Darlene DeRemer at NewRiver, Inc. and Joseph R. Hershberger and Donald H. Putnam at Putnam Lovell NBF, p. 1, December 2002.

3 *HedgeWorld,* February 10, 2004

4 "Hedge Funds: Issues for Public Policy Makers," Managed Funds Association (MFA), Appendix I: Strategy Definitions, reprinted with permission from Hedge Fund Research's web site, http://www.mfainfo.org/subsechedgefrm3.htm April 1999. http://www.mfainfo.org/subsechedgefrm3.htm

Recommended Reading: "Pioneering Portfolio Management," by David F. Swensen; "Where Genius Failed: The Rise and Fall of Long Term Capital Management," by Roger Lowenstein; "Market Wizards: Interviews with Top Traders," by Jack D. Schwager; "The New Market Wizards: Conversations with America's Top Traders," by Jack D. Schwager; "Hedge Funds," by Jesse Lederman and Robert A. Klein; and "Absolute Returns, The Risks and Opportunities of Hedge Fund Investing," by Alexander Ineichen

Editor's note: Financial advisors can find more information on hedge funds and funds of funds through their firms' alternative investment departments or by reviewing the additional resources available at http://www.fisherleblanc.com.

PART VI

The Future

33

TECHNOLOGY TODAY

Fisher LeBlanc Group

Technological innovation is vital to the growth of the separate account industry. It enables new products such as the Multiple Style Portfolio (MSP), and new solutions such as the Unified Managed Account (UMA). But, what is technology's function in today's separate account industry, what role will it play going forward, and how do sponsor firms, their advisors, and independent advisors and RIAs choose and implement the technology that will help them best in growing their businesses?

Let us explore these and other issues advisors and consultants face today. First, most would agree that it is easy for advisors to get lost in the world of technology. The excitement of innovations that sport more bells and whistles, create more efficiencies, and make implementation of the consulting process easier, can unwittingly absorb and displace the attention that should be directed toward clients. These innovations run the gamut from improving the stodgy back-office functions to offering sleek new methods of investment policy formation, asset allocation, and performance measurement and attribution. But before advisors can fully appreciate the reason for—and impetus behind—this diversion, they must first take a close look at the actual products, features, and capabilities to gain a better understanding of how they can help.

The Innovations

The quest for high-quality advice from today's clients is the power behind a strong tidal wave of solutions, and most technological developments are geared toward providing what advisors and their clients need, instead of toward grabbing the gusto of frenzied new product development. Clients looking for quality advice appreciate advisors who have quality tools supporting that advice. Clients see very little of what actually goes on in the advisors', sponsors', and asset managers' behind-the-scenes worlds, but the fulfillment of their quest is stark—their advisors either have the expertise and supporting tools or they don't. Consequently, sponsor firms, their independent counterparts, and money managers are all scrambling to meet the challenge.

One of technology's most valuable aspects is the efficiencies it provides. For example, an advisor may feel he or she easily can perform the tax lot harvesting and rebalancing calculations needed to manage risk in a client's portfolio. But, in fact, those calculations involve a large number of securities and, therefore, involve a complex mathematical process—a process beyond the scope of the human mind. Technology's role is to perform those types of tasks for the advisor so that the advisor's core value as a relationship manager is in the forefront.

Other technology efficiencies are readily apparent through new investment products and other service solutions. Some service solutions are invisible to the client and translate into efficiencies identifiable only to the advisor. All the client sees is clean, efficient, timely service. The solutions involved in these behind-the-scenes efficiencies include portfolio construction, monitoring of asset managers, performance measurement and attribution, performance reporting, rebalancing, tax management, and customization.

Today, some of the above services are included in the multiple style portfolio (MSP), one of the latest technology innovations. CheckFree Investment Services (CIS), a provider of automated services for investment management, trading, portfolio performance, and reporting requirements, notes that MSPs are now accommodating assets upwards from the original $100,000 to $250,000 foreseen by early participants. Advisors are recommending them as viable solutions for high net worth clients. The fourth generation MSPs offer the added benefit of an overlay portfolio manager (OPM) to coordinate tax management, performance monitoring, rebalancing, and other services that can be provided more efficiently by incorporating several managers under one account umbrella. (See Chapter 29 for more information on Multiple Style Portfolios.) PlaceMark Investments, Inc. specializes in providing this type of overlay management and frees the advisor to focus on serving the client rather than on administrative and account management functions. Included in this type of technology service are tax management, performance evaluation and reporting, and centralized discretion across account components. Tax management can be switched on or off, depending on the client's needs and the tax status of the portfolio.

The UMA, discussed indepth in Chapter 30, is a solution set of which the MSP will be a critical component. The ability to diversify clients' assets through the use of an MSP along with other types of investment vehicles will vastly streamline paperwork, account set-up, reporting, statement generation, monitoring and any other function associated with the consulting process. The one thing a UMA cannot do, however, is provide the quality advice for which clients are clamoring. As a support tool for that advice, the UMA will be a powerful solution.

Technology's Proper Place

Many would agree that the financial services industry needs to focus more on solving specific industry problems. FinanceWare, a provider of web-based probability analysis tools, for example, focuses on refining the definition of need regarding technology tools. An advisor who only has 100 deeply developed client relationships will probably know those relationships intimately, eliminating most of the need for a contact management system. Other advisors who have not yet transitioned their businesses to fee-based may have 2,000 customers, none of whom they know very well at all. For them, a contact management system is imperative.

Family Office Metrics, LLC, works on the same principal. As a completely impartial technology consulting firm, it objectively searches for the appropriate technology providers to fill the needs of its broker-dealer and advisor clients. Focusing primarily on providing family-office-level services, the firm also knows the business practices that can create the bridge between the normal financial services technology offerings and the translation of those offerings into high-quality services tailored to the high net worth markets.

Setting up the proper technology platform of services requires vision. Technology must provide what is needed now, plus make way for future needs and service enhancements. A three- to five-year time horizon is needed to anticipate those needs and to help transform the bulky, legacy, ad hoc systems so prevalent today into the streamlined, scalable web-based systems of tomorrow. The process of designing solutions that solve the problems of today while leaving room for the needed solutions and capabilities of tomorrow creates efficiencies regardless of the existing technology state. Firms tend to latch on to the new technology and spend high dollars without creating a developmental plan for implementation to serve the increasingly complex and changing needs of the marketplace. Such planning inherently streamlines the technology adoption process and enhances decision-making regarding outsourced services from vendors.

Challenges

The large wirehouse firms are fighting the biggest technology battles because of their pieced-together legacy systems and their lack of sensitivity to books and records firewalls. Outsourced technology tools related to clients' holdings must be carefully mapped to the existing system so that the clients' privacy is protected, yet the systems have the access they need to add the efficiencies they are designed to provide.

Another problem is lack of standardization. Each component process of the overall consulting process must become commoditized. The application paperwork at one firm should mirror the application paperwork at any other. The basic proposal generation, asset allocation tools, and manager search capabilities should be standardized at all firms. Complete open architecture should be available, with a focus on the firm's differentiating capabilities such as research and advice. Each firm can then create value added through its research and the quality of its advice. The entire focus of competition will be able to change with the ongoing development of technology. The marketplace is driving such change—with advisors and clients at the center of it. The days of the industry driving advisor and client offerings are dwindling.

All of this adds up to the primary problem of slow adoption. Industry experts predict full transition to web-based applications will take years because of the legacy systems in place and because of the added complexity resulting from the sheer numbers of separate accounts in the marketplace. Stodgy systems combined with large volume and lack of standardized processes form the foundation for the technology problems in the industry today.

But firms are aggressively searching for answers, and although this chapter highlights some of the innovations in the technology marketplace today, increased visibility of these firms and their innovations will increase adoption rates. The Money Management Institute serves as a central venue through which to keep up with technology developments as well as new products and services solutions for separate accounts. Although some of these innovations may not seem to have a direct bearing on advisors' ability to do business, that view is a mistaken one. The trickle-down effect of these innovations, wherever they are located in the consulting process continuum, directly or indirectly affects the efficiency and quality of service advisors and their firms can offer clients. They free the advisor to do what advisors should be doing—providing quality advice and guidance.

Other hindrances lie in the age-old problem of "what can and cannot be done." But change is an ongoing phenomenon. At one point, for example, banks were trying to build a standard system so that customers could bank online, get the banks' software and dial into their systems to see their transactions. Then Quicken entered the scene and all the banks' plans fell by the wayside. Quicken was much simpler to use. The same thing is occurring with separate account industry technology today. The technologies that are easier to use will win out and create capabilities previously chalked up to "it can't be done."

Rather than writing more software packages, the focus must shift to creating solutions to solve the problems the industry faces today. This has tremendous implications, but the leadership of wirehouses and independent broker-dealers will have to recognize the need for the shift before it will be expedited. The nature of competition has changed, and those who latch onto this changing nature rather than being slow to adapt will benefit the most. To cite a corporate example, many ascribe Apple Computer's dip in market share during its early years as the refusal to recognize the changing face of competition. Apple wanted to keep its software and processes exclusive so that people would have to buy all Apple products. But Microsoft realized that by licensing (sharing) its software, it could set a standard throughout the industry, regardless of the actual hardware used. The same principal applies to technology in the separate account industry today. The competitive landscape has changed. Every participant has the basic capabilities. The real differentiation will lie in the quality of the research and the quality of advice.

Platforms and Tools to Help the Advisor: A Sampling

The response of industry technology firms to the needs of today's clients and their advisors is overwhelming and exciting. Initially, these innovations generally have been produced from the viewpoint of providing a better mousetrap, but at this stage of development, increased quality of service and distribution efficiency is becoming the decided focus.

From a technology standpoint, the various components of the separate account process have been offered at the large firms either through their proprietary systems, or individually, through early adopters of the process (individual advisors and consultants who took it upon themselves to build their own systems in addition to what their firms provided). Independent advisors faced certain challenges since they did not have the resources of a large firm's basic system as an advantage. In years past, this situation made it very difficult for independent advisors to provide separate accounts; thus they tended to adopt the wrapped mutual fund as their fee-based business anchor.

Today, the advent of third-party platforms enables independent advisors access to the same basic separate account services as their large firm counterparts. The third-party providers serve as the program sponsor, with the independent advisor plugging into a program designed by the third-party sponsor. Prices and available services vary and many new platforms, as well as the new offerings of some of the more established providers, offer integrated services that allow advisors to access various components of the process, such as proposal generation, asset allocation, manager search and selection, and ongoing monitoring from one access screen, many of which are already web based.

The move to web-based technology will make each component of the process, including behind-the-scenes back office functions and asset manager tools, more efficient and easier to access. This will, in turn, greatly enhance client service, enabling the advisor to add more value for the client. With this in mind, a closer look at a few of the most important value-added tools being developed for advisors, both at large firms and through third party platforms, follows.

General Platform Services

Development of separate account offerings for independent advisors is finally catching up to that of the big houses. The Internet has played—and will continue to play—an even larger role in that development going forward. The Internet enables integration of proposal generation all the way through to the new account, a feat easier to accomplish through the Web since it uses information from the big firm's legacy systems—a problem third-party providers can manage more easily since they built their systems from a "new company" advantage.

The workflow discussion that follows applies to both large firms trying to streamline their processes and to independent advisors seeking to loosen the grip of back office functionality on time that is needed to better serve clients.

Web-based platforms use databases (housed in large, legacy systems at big firms and at database outsourcers for third parties) to help sell separate accounts. Workflow software is being developed to accept new account data from the back office or from a proposal system and to automatically post it into a management system, so that the entire process supports the SMA sale for the advisor.

With such workflow applications, advisors can gather the information needed to profile the client and input the information once. When the account is funded, the information doesn't have to be keyed in a second time, thus eliminating duplication and triplication. The information also is fed to the money managers who have been hired—all with one information entry. The complete version of this process is not yet available (at the time of this writing), but the above description is a peek into what is to come for advisors on both sides of the sponsor fence.

Manager Search/Performance Measurement and Attribution

In the due diligence process performed while searching for managers to implement the asset allocation, both the tenets of Modern Portfolio Theory (MPT) and the Efficient Market Hypothesis (EMH) (traditional ideas and solutions that do not necessarily allow for value added to the client) are heavily relied upon. Although such tenets are true, research is turning up new ideas and solutions that can enhance the appropriateness of their real-life ability to fit the needs of today's advisory and its clients. The trio of people, process, and philosophy must be added to the application of MPT and EMH. The numbers component of the process primarily should be used for evaluating the prospective manager's performance and the comfort level associated with future performance attribution to that manager.

Performance attribution is often provided by the managers themselves, but objective attribution can be provided only by an outside assessment. Most performance measurement used today is based on a manager's conglomerate returns, typically over a three-year period. The ability to discern actual manager skill from style, however, is more accurately measured with holdings-based analysis rather than with returns-based analysis. In holdings-based analysis, the individual positions of the manager's portfolio are classified into their corresponding management style such as growth, value, large, and small. The positions are then compared to the appropriate benchmark rather than to a peer group.

Ideally, the benchmark will be a customized benchmark that will more closely resemble the manager's portfolio. This allows a clearer attribution of style performance as opposed to manager skill.

Holdings-based analysis using customized benchmarks, according to PPCA, creator of the StokTrib attribution tool and the portofolio opportunity distribution (PODs) is preferred over returns-based analysis. StokTrib attributes performance, based on stock selection and investment style. Customized benchmarks are the only reasonable comparisons against which to measure performance based on these factors. Why use these factors? Because they more accurately reflect the real-life performance of the portfolio and more clearly delineate the factors underlying the performance.

For example, if the investment style is small cap and the capitalization for measurement purposes is restricted to companies above $10 billion using the S&P as a benchmark, the comparisons of that small cap portfolio to S&P companies above $10 billion market cap make no sense. The companies below $10 billion are not even on the radar screen, therefore, performance measured against such a benchmark leaves much room for error.

The POD system takes the best parts of peer group and benchmark performance measurement, and eliminates the weak parts. It starts with the benchmark notion and turns the customized benchmark into a peer group by taking all the securities in the benchmark and forming all the possible portfolios that could be formed from it. This newly created peer group allows the identification of the desirable and less desirable portfolios. The ranking of a particular portfolio within that peer group can provide the confidence needed for reliable measurement in a very short period of time as opposed to the 40 to 50 years needed to institute credibility for traditional benchmarks.

Platforms and Decisioning Tools

Platforms—The fiduciary aspects of the consulting process are more familiar to the institutional side of the separate account business than the retail, although the same basic principles apply to both. Fiduciary Analytics, the technology arm of the Center for Fiduciary Studies was created to match the technological capabilities of software with the fiduciary responsibilities set forth in the consulting process. The software tools include a proposal generation, IPS template, asset allocation tool, manager search and selection, and performance monitoring—all of which are designed to meet the criteria of the Fiduciary Checklist, a core component of the program. The checklist serves as a guide for addressing the minimum fiduciary issues involved in investment decisions.

Decisioning Tools—Some advisors believe searching for better manager customization for client portfolios is akin to searching for the Holy Grail. One example of a technology firm attempting to do just this is Klein Decisions. During the search process, the software goes through a multiple screening process, much like current vendors do, but with one important difference: Klein's system never eliminates the managers who fail the screening process, it just reorders them within the list of screening candidates. With other systems, those managers are discarded and the advisor never has the opportunity to go back and reexamine them. Case in point: an advisor wants a manager with a beta less than 1. A manager showing a beta of 1 might actually have a beta of 1.01, so this manager fails the screening process. That may be the manager best suited for the client's needs, but the advisor is never allowed to go back and make that decision. With Klein's program, it is possible. The software can be embedded in large firm systems, third party platforms, or in business-to-business applications such as from one section of a bank to another.

Klein takes the decision-making process capability a large step further. Its product offers the advisor the opportunity to incorporate the advice component directly into the implementation phase of the consulting process, allowing higher-quality service to be delivered. The screening questions have to be customized and other data must be input so that the advisor can tailor his or her practice to clients' needs, highlighting their expertise and value added.

Yet another method of making portfolio allocation decisions is offered by RowPyn Investment Partners, LLC. RowPyn has developed a method of using 38 algorithmic formulas as a foundation and overlaying 28 variable regression models to effectively drive the process. The regression model allows the shortening of the lag method to an optimum time frame, so that the model effectively moves dollars from underperforming investment styles and toward outperforming styles. For domestic equities, the method has been useful in limiting downside losses during turbulent markets and enhancing portfolio returns during more favorable markets. RowPyn's proprietary process then draws on Rowe Decision Analytics software to implement the investment policy.

A Look into the Future

As newer platforms develop and offer greater capability and efficiency, sponsor firms and their advisors, as well as independent advisors and RIAs, will be able to compete on the quality of their advice and on fulfilling the needs of their clients. Standardization of processes will allow complete automation, commoditizing most of the physical services involved in the consulting process. For example, asset allocation will be facilitated by programs that can determine the best exposure based on the client's risk and the market and economic environment. That same software will be able to facilitate performance monitoring from the standpoint of rebalancing needs. The implementation of the investment policy will be facilitated by tools that provide more accurate due diligence information so that manager selection can be more accurately based on the client's individual objectives and parameters. Portfolio manufacturing will be streamlined so that any manager's model portfolio can be well monitored across any number of client accounts. Performance reporting and attribution will be more accurate, offering more effective alerts to trouble signs and making it easier, quicker, and less painful to adjust portfolios as market conditions and style definitions change. Manager skill will become more readily identifiable, making active/passive decisions easier and more appropriate.

Finally, the automation of all of these processes will not only facilitate the customized service of the mass affluent, but will also enable firms and high-level advisors to attract and properly serve higher net worth clients, allowing more time and ability to provide the softer services to which those clients have become accustomed, while streamlining the problem areas they currently experience in the daily management of their larger wealth clients.

Of course, any system has its limitations and always will, but the combination of choices on a web-based platform will allow those limitations to be overcome through added flexibility, true open architecture, and scalable offerings. Technology already has reached the point where the time required to produce a 70- to 80-page reporting package has been reduced to the short time it takes to image the document into a PDF file. Such reports used to take two minutes per report. With the imaging process, according to ADVISORport, it now takes a couple of seconds. Data in these packages has to be verified and reverified.

Advisors today find themselves slaves to their own portfolio accounting systems as a result of trying to verify accuracy of reports. ADVISORport's platform helps to leverage advisors' time, which is their most precious commodity. The platform attempts to combine all the capability the advisor needs to accomplish each task in the consulting process in a more efficient manner.

ADVISORport is simply one example of such a platform. Bank of New York/Lockwood, Brinker

Capital, and many others also offer platforms that offer independent advisors and RIAs the capabilities of larger firms, only with greater efficiency because they are less encumbered by the legacy systems and processes. However, it is the large firms that have the deep pockets to drive technology adoption. But it is the nature of technology to level the playing field. In years to come, it will be interesting to see how the various areas of the separate account industry affect service to clients and, therefore, the market share of participants.

There are myriad technology firms that offer a plethora of technology solutions to the separate account industry of today—and of tomorrow. The excitement lies in seeing the developments occurring, and discovering how they can help streamline the delivery of existing services as well as future ones. The key is continuity, standardization, and web-enabled. The combination of these three components will open the floodgates of growth for the separate account industry and any number of investment products and solutions that are made available through it.

It has been said that leaders use their own insight and foresight to prey on the complacency of ignorers and followers. The separate account leaders of tomorrow will differentiate themselves with their advice and the quality of their service. Technology is the tool and "right-focused" consulting is the bedrock that will enable them to provide such leadership.

❖ ❖ ❖

Editor's note: Due to the proliferation of third-party technology platforms, web-enabled programs, software and hardware providers, only a few representative firms were mentioned in this chapter. A more complete list of other firms is provided on http://www.fisherleblanc.com.

References: Many thanks to the following industry experts for helping us with this chapter:
Ron Surz, PPCA; David Loeper, Financeware; Jon Carroll, Family Office Metrics LLC;
Bill McVay, Zephyr/Style Advisor; Jamie Waller, CheckFree; Bob Rowe, RowPyn Investment Partners LLC; Bob Padgette, Klein Decisions; Lee Chertavian, Placemark; Greg Horn, ADVISORport; Bill Poulin, LifeHarbor; and, Don Trone, Center for Fiduciary Studies/Fiduciary Analytics.

34

THE FINANCIAL ADVISOR OF THE FUTURE

Stephen C. Winks, Publisher
Portfolio Construction Technologies
Publisher, *Senior Consultant*

The ultimate arbiter of how an industry evolves is the consumer. It's no mystery within the financial services industry that investors want value to be added. So, today, with the advent of new technology tools and information, the financial advisor is demanding from the industry a higher level of accountability and the support necessary to add value and to fulfill their fiduciary responsibility.

Now, thanks to advances in technology, investors know whether value is being added. Enterprising advisors are making it clear whether fiduciary responsibility is being fulfilled. Thus, financial advisors of the future must leverage themselves with the processes and technologies necessary to address and manage a broad range of investment and administrative values required by regulatory mandate.

This level of investment and administrative counsel is the "continuous, comprehensive" counsel envisioned in the regulatory parameters within which all advisors must work. With access to real-time information and analytical tools, all it takes to become an advisor of the future is the access and/or development of the processes, technology and support infrastructure necessary to add value.

This evolution of the role of the financial advisor represents a profound shift within the financial services industry. Look at it this way: Human beings are capable of thinking only in three dimensions. If one tries to think in the fifth or 10th dimension, it is not humanly possible to fathom 25 or 100 possible interrelated outcomes. Now consider a financial advisor's role. Suppose an advisor wants to help 500 clients with one objective— say, retirement. To address and manage the values of risk, return, tax efficiency, liquidity, cost structure and time as required by regulatory mandate (UPIA, ERISA, IMIFA, UMPERS) and to use the 10,000 investment options at their disposal, each having at least 100 description points, an advisor would have to manage a three-billion dimensional equation with nine quintillion possible interrelated investment outcomes.

This illustrates how mind-boggling today's financial product and service menus have become. No one can understand this equation in its entirety, much less articulate it. Clearly, a process is needed to manage this information in terms meaningful to each client. Financial advisors who cannot reason beyond the three dimensional can add very little, if any, value for a client. So, for the thousands of financial advisors who want to add value, fulfill their fiduciary responsibility, and attain the highest level of professional achievement, their success will be increasingly tied to their access to enabling processes, technology, and support infrastructure. Historically, this has been available within the commission brokerage community.

Success will be determined by process and technology. All advisors are indebted to the work of pioneering investment management consultants in the high net worth and institutional markets where fiduciary responsibility is viewed more seriously. These advisors, by necessity, have designed a six-financial-services investment process (asset/liability study, investment policy, strategic asset allocation, manager search and selection, performance monitor and tactical asset allocation), which consistently allows them to address and manage a broad range of investment and administrative values.

Research by the Center for Fiduciary Studies, citing case law, statutes and regulatory opinion letters, confirms the six financial services investment process.[1] This process may sound like a foreign language to some, and many advisors may work for firms that have not prepared them for such a discussion. That's because most financial advisors, whether they are commission brokers, financial planners, insurance agents or bankers, are compensated by firms for selling products, not necessarily for adding value. Though it would be nice to add value, many supporting firms do not find it essential. This is why a discussion of process and technology is so important to elevating a financial advisor's role and counsel.

Many advisor support organizations do not acknowledge fiduciary responsibility or its associated liability. They maintain that advisors do not render advice; they are just making the client aware of investment alternatives. Investors must serve as their own counsel, exercising their own judgment. Hence the caveat: "Buyer beware." Yet, if no advice is implied, provided or supported, how is it possible for the advisor to add value?

This is perhaps the most perplexing conundrum a financial advisor faces today. They are compelled by clients and professional integrity to add value and fulfill fiduciary responsibility but, again, the institutional support and processes/technology necessary to add value are not in place. Even with the tools and processes, there is the question of whether a firm would allow them to be used because of the implied fiduciary liability. There is the legitimate fear that a different skill set is required of both the firm and the advisor to address and manage a broad range of investment and administrative values as required by regulatory mandate.

There also is the very real fear that many advisors want to add value, but don't know how. So, many firms opt to limit their role to product access, trade execution and facilities management.

The Financial Advisor of the Future

Therefore, most advisors must take it upon themselves to add value and take on fiduciary responsibility. This is why only a small number of advisors advise a disproportionately large portion of investable assets at the high end of the high net worth and institutional markets, which contain more than 90 percent of investable assets. There is a significant difference between commission sales and running an advisory services enterprise that offers counsel for an on-going fee. This is how an advisor can add more value, advise more assets, work with fewer clients and make more money.

Nothing discussed here is rocket science. In fact, addressing and managing values like risk, return, tax efficiency, liquidity, cost structure and time can be understood by the typical investor, which is why the opportunity is so great. Financial tools and information accessible through the Internet have made account performance increasingly clear to investors, who understand that value isn't added through a series of disjointed, unrelated transactions called commission brokerage. Still, technology works in an advisor's favor. Only when an investment recommendation is viewed in the context of all a client's holdings can the advisor know if their recommendation actually improved overall portfolio return, reduced risk or enhanced the tax efficiency, liquidity or cost structure of the total holdings.

Investors are beginning to realize there is no accountability in investment recommendations for commission sales once the product is sold, the trade has cleared and the commission is earned. It is not the investment product itself that adds value; it bears repeating— it is the process or what one does with the investment product that adds value. *The advisor becomes the value added, not the investment product.*

Here, in more detail, are the investment processes, the technology and the support advisors need within their practices to add value and fulfill fiduciary responsibility.

The Process

A highly disciplined investment process comprised of six financial services enables advisors to address and manage a broad range of investment and administrative values as required either by regulatory mandate (UPIA, ERISA, UMIFA, UMPERS, proposed Uniform Trust Code) or client directive. Each service adds value in its own right; and when they are aggregated in sequence into an investment process, it constitutes an extraordinary level of professional investment and administrative counsel.

The Six Financial Services
1. Asset/Liability Study
2. Investment Policy
3. Strategic Asset Allocation
4. Manager Search and Selection
5. Performance Monitor
6. Tactical Asset Allocation

Each service is described in detail below:

1. *Asset/Liability Study*—Most investors are unclear about how their assets (and liabilities) work in unison in an investment portfolio. They can't explain the return they have achieved on all their holdings as an investment portfolio. They can't explain if they have taken 150 percent of the market's risk for 50 percent of its return. They don't know if their assets are structured in an income and estate-tax efficient manner. They have no idea about the cost structure of their investment portfolio.

They don't know that mutual funds are three times more expensive than managed accounts or that ETFs and folios are just 40 percent of the cost of managed accounts. They don't understand the trade-off between tax efficiency, liquidity, cost structure and performance. They don't know when they have contradictory investment positions.

Essentially, nine out of 10 investment portfolios are a mess. Investment counsel has been confined to a series of disjointed, unrelated stand-alone transactions, and a large number of the investor's many financial advisors do not assume responsibility for the investor's on-going financial well-being. Investors want someone to be accountable; and an advisor fulfills that need through the asset/liability study. This is an immediate value-added service.

The asset/liability study evaluates all of a prospective client's assets within an investment portfolio. Think of it as the "before" photograph that is used as a reference point to measure the value an advisor adds with their on-going investment and administrative counsel. This diagnostic assessment provides an advisor with 20 to 30 specific recommendations on how to significantly improve a prospect's financial well-being. Often an investor's portfolio shows great need for improvement, and the asset/liability study allows advisors to demonstrate the depth and breadth of their investment and administrative counsel in a dynamic and understandable fashion.

Rather than selling investment products, an advisor addresses and manages a broad range of investment and administrative values essential to achieving an investor's goals and objectives. For this on-going service, the investor is more than happy to pay an advisory fee. They like the fact that the advisor is accountable, focused on their objectives and have acknowledged fiduciary responsibility. The advisor no longer has an economic incentive to make an investment recommendation based on a commission.

2. ***Investment Policy***—Investment policy is a management document that defines the roles of the investor, money managers, custodian, administrator, recordkeeper and the investment management consultant (or advisor). The investor is defined in specific terms (risk/return, goals/objectives, tax sensitivity, special instructions, etc.) that serve as parameters around which a portfolio will be constructed and managed. The policy sets forth the conditions in which a money manager will be engaged and terminated. It quantifies, through diagnostic testing, key values such as risk and tax sensitivity, and translates the client's stated goals and objectives into an agreed-upon and well-reasoned investment strategy.

Investment policy is the heart and soul of professional investment and administrative counsel. Investment policy is the discipline that keeps the client focused on a long-term strategy, and not chasing after alluring, but highly elusive, short-term returns. The policy serves as the corporate conscience of all parties engaged in helping the client and is essential to making sure everyone fulfills their fiduciary responsibility.

3. ***Strategic Asset Allocation***—Technically, strategic asset allocation is a subset of investment policy, but it is a key element of the investment process because 93.6 percent of the value an advisor adds is by determining the appropriate configuration of asset class in which to invest.[2] (When there is a reference to a four-step investment process, strategic asset allocation is typically part of the investment policy, and tactical asset allocation is not acknowledged separately.)

Nobel Prize-winning investment theory states: If a client/client's portfolio can be determined in terms of risk, return, tax efficiency, liquidity, cost efficiency and time, and if the investments can be defined in terms of risk, return, tax efficiency, liquidity, cost structure and time, then a mechanism in which an advisor can construct a portfolio is in place that, with reasonable probability, will approximate the desired result over a long time-frame. When a financial advisor can formulate, evaluate, and monitor such an investment strategy, clients will marvel at how their objectives were reached.

Strategic asset allocation is based on the long-term performance characteristics of asset classes, ranging from five to 60 years, depending on the model used. The longer this time period, the more reliable the model. Using historical returns as a proxy for future performance, one can exercise judgment as to what configuration of asset classes would achieve the desired result given a specific level of risk. Of course, there are periods of time when current market conditions contradict historical precedent. For example, equities generally outperform fixed income, but there may be times when the opposite occurs. In such periods, one would tactically allocate assets, rather than automatically allocate according to historical precedent. (This is tactical asset allocation, which will be discussed later.)

Without question, the single most important decision an investor will make is where to allocate capital assets among asset classes. A variety of research and tools can assist in asset allocation.

4. *Manager Search and Selection*—Most clients believe all the value that is added occurs in manager search and selection, but the truth is that most of the value previously was added when the investment strategy was determined and assets were allocated. Once it is determined how much of the portfolio should be in large-cap value, small-cap growth, international, fixed income, etc., manager search and selection becomes a straightforward task of objectively evaluating proven, accomplished managers against a specific investment mandate. An advisor determines which large-cap value manager(s) best represent the large-cap value investment mandate set forth in investment policy. Of course, the advisor also has to adjust for style bias, skill-versus-luck issues, etc. In the end, the job goes to the manager with the most financial strength, consistency and skill, and who provides the highest return, lowest risk, and lowest cost structure.

One of the most critical aspects of manager search and selection is determining the form of ownership in which assets will be held. For example, the use of trusts, family foundations and other contractual means are used to move the ownership of assets outside of one's estate, thereby averting income and/or estate taxation. These tax-efficiency considerations should be articulated in the investment policy to help determine what percentage of the client's assets should be held and managed within a different entity, such as a trust. The impact of managing the income and estate tax-efficiency considerations on portfolio returns ranks second only to the impact of strategic asset allocation.

5. *Performance Monitor*—Additional value added by an advisor's professional investment and administrative counsel is "continuous and comprehensive" monitoring of all the client's holdings. An advisor is accountable for addressing and managing the full range of investment and administrative values as directed by the client and quantified in the asset/liability study and investment policy. The discipline of the six-financial-services investment process is manifested in the performance monitor.

As Charles Ellis, a leading authority on investment policy, states in his highly regarded book, "Winning the Loser's Game," *"In investment management, the real opportunity to achieve superior results is not in scrambling to outperform the market but in establishing and adhering to appropriate investment policies over the long-term that position the portfolio to benefit from riding the main long-term forces at work in the market."*[3] The emphasis in monitoring performance is not to chase short-term performance from quarter to quarter, but to focus on affirming and adjusting long-term investment policy and strategy so they remain consistent with the client's goals and objectives.

Quarterly, an advisor will (1) confirm the client's economic circumstances, goals and objectives, risk and tax sensitivities; (2) gauge the client's reactions to actual market conditions, and accordingly affirm or adjust investment policy and strategy; (3) explain what is happening in the capital markets and how that impacts the client's portfolio; (4) review the performance of each investment manager against their investment mandate; and (5) adjust the client's portfolio appropriately.

Annually, an advisor will review all vendor relationships that impact custody, clearing and reporting, and disclose all forms of compensation derived from the client's account, as required by law. This level of counsel has unique nuances for each market segment, whether an advisor is dealing with the high net worth market or defined contribution plans. The depth and breadth of on-going counsel elevates an advisor's role far above those engaged in commission sales.

6. *Tactical Asset Allocation* — Although strategic asset allocation is helpful in explaining the performance of capital markets and in helping the advisor develop an investment strategy, it requires tactical adjustment. This is because there are times when current market conditions contradict the historical precedence upon which strategic asset allocation is based. For example, over the long term, equities always outperform fixed income; but there are times in a declining interest-rate environment when fixed income actually outperforms equities. This was the case for several years in 1980s and 1990s, during the strongest bull market on record. At such times, the wisest counsel was to *not* follow historical precedent. By overweighting fixed income, one actually reduced risk and enhanced performance. This is tactical asset allocation.

Today, as many advisors move to real-time attribution analysis, portfolio opportunity distributions (PODs), Omega access, and post-Modern Portfolio Theory, they no longer have to wait a week or two after each quarter for peer group performance rankings in order to evaluate manager performance and provide counsel to their clients. With less lag time, advisors can make corrective adjustments more quickly and the promise of continuous, comprehensive counsel (required by regulatory mandate) is achieved.

Technology

Today, technology provides the means to manage an incredible amount of data on both the client and the investment alternatives that drive the overall investment strategy. Until recent breakthroughs in process and technology, high-level counsel historically has been out most financial advisors' reach. Thanks to the Web and advances in Web-based portfolio management technologies, it is now economically viable for financial advisors to create within their own practices the division of labor, the process and the enabling technology to add value and fulfill their fiduciary responsibility. The process can be brought in-house via technology and support staff.

By way of example, let's follow an advisor (or partnership of advisors) who has $50 million under advisement (200 clients at $250,000 each). The advisor can redirect the $350,000 (70 basis points x $50 million) that is now being paid for working in a wrap-fee program, to hire a chief administrative officer and portfolio manager and buy the enabling technology to create a pre-emptive value proposition to any wrap-fee program offered by a major financial services firm. [4]

For the first time, financial advisors have a technological edge over their supporting organizations. Because advisors are closer to the client than the distant systems-and-technology personnel within the firm – who have little or no practical understanding of fiduciary responsibility or of addressing and managing a broad range of investment and administrative values – the advisors can act more quickly and decisively than their firms.

The Financial Advisor of the Future

A Personal Discussion on Budgeting

If you choose, here are the specific steps you can take to oversee and manage clients' accounts in a cost-effective, efficient and highly professional manner. Assuming a budget of $350,000 (deploying what is now paying to work within a wrap-fee program) to build a support infrastructure (people, process, technology) within a practice. Here are the elements for consideration:

Infrastructure—The first step in bringing a technology and support infrastructure in-house is to determine a division of labor. Client acquisition/service (the advisor's strength) must be separated from portfolio construction/management and administration/operations. More time will be gained for client acquisition and service, but also will find others who may be far better suited to portfolio construction/management and administration/operations. The chemistry and complementary skill sets of this group are important. Client acquisition/service requires different skills than those required in administration/operations or portfolio construction/management. Both the administration and the portfolio management positions are partnership-level positions. If your colleagues assume ownership of the positions, they become an integral part of your value proposition.

If you decide to expand your financial services practice, there are several important qualities and qualifications to consider in your prospective partners. For the portfolio construction/management (PCM) position, consider hiring a bright young MBA from a good school who is eager to learn and wants to work toward becoming a partner. Cost: $55,000 to $75,000. You will spend $5,000 putting your PCM through (1) the online CIMA program offered by IMCA, (2) the online accredited investment fiduciary (AIFA) program offered by the Center of Fiduciary Studies and (3) enrollment in the Chartered Financial Analyst curriculum. If you haven't gone through the CIMA and AIFA programs yourself, you should consider it.

CIMA gives you the language of high-level counsel and educates you in how to evaluate money managers and how to engage in more sophisticated forms of portfolio construction. AIFA gives you an authoritative understanding of fiduciary responsibility and provides the knowledge required to perform a fiduciary liability audit, which is particularly important at the higher end of the market. You should budget $10,000 per year for professional development within your practice.

Your chief administrative/operations (CAO) person will turn a complex array of technology functions into a seamless system that allows you and your firm to do extraordinary things. The CAO function is a partnership-level position. Cost: $65,000 per year. Thus, the cost of starting and training your practice's support infrastructure is $150,000 per year, leaving $200,000 of your $350,000 budget for enabling technology.

Account Aggregation Technology—As stated earlier in the chapter, it is impossible to add value unless you can evaluate an investment recommendation in the context of all a clients' holdings, both assets and liabilities. Only then can you determine if a recommendation improved overall portfolio returns, reduced risk or enhanced the tax efficiency, liquidity and cost. The aggregation, verification, reconciliation, and management of investment information provided by multiple custodians into a common format was cost-prohibitive until recently. Thankfully, several account aggregation firms have emerged to help greatly reduce the labor and cost of aggregating account information. These firms offer incorporated analytics to establish the risk and return characteristics of aggregated data.

By making a few analytical adjustments of your system to measure tax efficiency, liquidity and cost structure, an electronic asset/liability-study capability can be achieved. This extraordinary time-saving technological breakthrough will cost approximately $65,000 the first year and $45,000 in year two for the first 220 accounts, and then $140 per account thereafter. This leaves $135,000 remaining in your budget.

Investment Policy—Creating an investment policy statement is the heart and soul of high-level counsel. It requires extensive knowledge of the client, fiduciary responsibility and investments, and takes hundreds of man-hours. Online investment policy capabilities that address the high net worth and institutional-market segments are available.[5] These templates are designed to be customized for each client, reducing the time required to create an institutional quality statement of investment policy to just a few hours. Importantly, legal opinions can be generated to state that each investment policy statement and its associated portfolio are in compliance with the regulatory parameters set forth in UPIA, ERISA, UMIFA and UMPERS. Investment policy capability should cost $1,500 per year, leaving $133,500 in the budget.

Strategic Asset Allocation/Monte Carlo Simulation—Strategic asset allocation is available at little or no cost from multiple sources. You and your team/firm may have an interest in going beyond strategic asset allocation and using a tool such as Monte Carlo Simulation (MCS), which helps explain the random nature of the capital markets and can zero in on risk by defining it in a more understandable manner than the more conventional institutional can. Cost for such an asset-allocation tool: $3,500. Your budget is now $130,000.

Manager Search and Selection—Manager search and selection lends itself to outsourcing because of the expense of analytical tools, access to managers and the ongoing nature of due diligence in a dynamic investment environment. A second set of eyes dedicated to managing the research and evaluation of managers is well worth the cost. By outsourcing manager research, the PCM can focus on portfolio construction, and the management and monitoring of investment strategies.

To fulfill fiduciary responsibilities, you are required to engage non-related "prudent experts" to manage clients' assets. This requires expertise in evaluating managed accounts, mutual funds, ETFs, folios, hedge funds, managed futures, etc. Depending upon the strength of your PCM, you may want to engage outside counsel on specific portfolio recommendations until collective judgment is up to speed. Even if it is, having a highly skilled second opinion is prudent. Several organizations for manager search and selection are available to help with this task. [6]

Cost: $9,500 for managed account and mutual fund research to $13,500 for specific portfolio recommendations. If you are active in the institutional market, research and consulting relationships with large institutional consulting firms (focusing on the $100+ million market) can be helpful, but will require a retainer fee of $100,000 per year. After spending $13,500 for this service, you have $116,500 in the budget.

Performance Monitor/Reporting—In this age of the Internet and real-time information, no financial services firm can provide all its financial advisors with performance reports on all their clients' holdings, including those custodied outside of their firm. Yet, without this information, it is impossible to add value. The solution? The Excel spreadsheet is the industry's top performance reporting tool used by advisors to develop their own required composite-performance monitors. Technology greatly has reduced the labor intensity and cost of aggregating account information in a usable form, especially for accounts custodied outside of an advisor's firm. (Note: account aggregation technology already was subtracted from the initial $350,000 budget.)

Real-time reporting, accounting, and trade-and-order routing technologies essentially run an advisor's core portfolio-management engine. Several popular systems for sub-accounting and reporting, and for trade-and-order routing are available to advisors building their practices. [7] These web based, AIMR-compliant systems automatically can report on any configuration of assets, automatically rebalance portfolios and offer extensive training and support; they also are very expensive. By linking Advent, (an industry standard, for example) and account aggregation technology, you can gain access to all clients' account information in a stand-alone system. To replicate the functionality, accuracy and support of this technology and the level of counsel it facilies would be cost-prohibitive. Advent costs about $75,000 for the first year, and $25,000 annually thereafter. This leaves you with $41,500.

One of the most exciting aspects of real-time information and web based technology is that data can be taken far beyond one-dimensional performance reporting and used to more dynamically manage client portfolios. Services offering real-time monitoring, analytics and attribution technologies are highly effective in managing portfolio detail for a very large number of accounts.[8] Rather than waiting each quarter to evaluate the key performance values (risk, return, tax efficiency, liquidity, cost structure, etc.) as outlined in the client's investment policy, it is possible to electronically establish and manage these values as constraints within each client's portfolio. Upstream linking these particular services, in effect, ties these electronic gating values to a real-time performance monitor. Any transaction that knocks a portfolio out of compliance with the desired values will be electronically suppressed, and the PCM can manage by exception. Real-time analytics (using links) [9] can allow your PCM to provide an extremely high level of continuous, comprehensive counsel as required by regulatory mandate. You will know at all times how each portfolio, each manager and each holding is performing. With $12,000 budgeted for the real-time monitoring, analytics, and attribution technologies, plus $10,000 for the links, $19,500 remains in your budget.

With access to real-time information, you no longer has to wait 30 to 45 days after each quarter to receive peer-group-performance comparisons (used to evaluate money managers). Comparisons using PODs and PIPODs methodology [10] allow for a more immediate assessment of manager performance adjusted for style bias, resulting in a faster and clearer view of manager performance. The PIPODs technology costs about $1,100. You now have $18,400.

Tactical Asset Allocation—As stated earlier, there is fear within the financial services industry that financial advisors are not capable of adding value through portfolio construction. This is why some firms will not acknowledge that advisors are rendering advice or assuming fiduciary responsibility. This is mitigated, however, by having a CFA-candidate PCM monitoring all client portfolios in real-time, by your engaging an institutional authority to assist in making or confirming portfolio construction recommendations, and by purchasing proven, established tactical investment methodologies (research) that will guide the PCM in making tactical adjustments. Many investment methodologies are available with documented results that significantly outperform their benchmarks.[11] Typically, these investment methodologies either take the form of real-time buy-and-sell instructions (research) or tactical signals that require interpretation and individual execution. These investment methodologies cost about $15,000 to $20,000 a year, fully expending your budget.

Bullrun Financial, for example, has four investment methodology overlays that can help you and your PCM understand what sectors are coming in and out of favor and why. In the budgeting scenario, when the cost of Advent drops from $75,000 for the first year to $25,000 for the second year, and the cost of account aggregation drops from $65,000 to $45,000, it will be time to budget for one or more of these investment methodologies to reaffirm portfolio construction decisions.

There are other tools a PCM may find valuable, such as real-time, style-adjusted attribution analysis, and post-Modern Portfolio Theory methodologies [12] that can significantly enhance performance and elevate counsel. In year two and thereafter, there will be financial latitude within the budget to secure those capabilities.

Summary

This budgeting scenario proves that any financial advisor (or partnership of financial advisors) who advises $50 million in assets or who has 200 clients with $250,000 in investable assets, can personally create a pre-emptive value proposition (if they decide to choose an alternative environment) to any competing financial services firm. If clients are engaging their counsel for a fee, there is no need for securities licensing and they can become RIAs using the services of a Schwab, Fidelity, or Ameritrade, for example. If an advisor would like to retain their securities licenses, they can become correspondents to major firms retaining access to support services, but achieving 100 percent payout by virtue of having their own firm.

An advisor does not have to be an investment guru; he or she simply needs a PCM with access to investment gurus. An advisor does not have to be a technology expert; just employ a chief administrative officer who makes non-integrated technology function as a seamless system that empowers an extremely high level of counsel.

Advisors must facilitate a division of labor that allows them to do what they do best – acquire and service client relationships in a manner that no institutional competitor can. Advisors have a choice to re-deploy the 70 basis points they are paying their firms to participate in wrap fee programs, and build their own process, technology and infrastructure within their practice. This is the way to attain the highest level of professional achievement, provide a higher level of counsel, add more value, advise more assets and win more clients than ever. The number of investors looking for added value far outnumbers the advisors capable of adding value. That is why this is the marketing opportunity of a lifetime.[13]

Rewards are high for advisors who act quickly. There are only 15 million U.S. households with more than $100,000 of liquid investable assets, which is the most economically viable market segment for a fee-based advisor to address to engage their counsel. Once the early adopters start providing continuous, comprehensive counsel, the pool of available clients will decrease, making it difficult for those advisors who follow to succeed. As with institutional markets, the high net worth market will become a zero-sum game. To win a client, an advisor must take the client away from another advisor.

The only way to "win" is to have a better value proposition and a better service culture. At last, advisors know how to control their own destinies.

❖❖❖

---

[1] "The Center for Fiduciary Studies Proposes Practice Standards, SEC and DOL Very Receptive," *Senior Consultant*, December/ January 2001, http:// www.SrConsultant.com/Articles/2000-12-FiduciaryStudies.pdf.

[2] Brinson, Hood, Beebower examined the quarterly investment returns of 91 large pension plans over a 10-year period (1974-1983), concluding that investment policy explained an average 93.6 % of the variation in total plan returns. An update to the study in 1991, using data from 1977 to 1987, similarly found that 91.5% of returns could be explained by policy decisions.

[3] Charles Ellis, "Investment Policy," McGraw-Hill, September, 1992

[4] "How Are Top Advisors Growing Their Business in a Difficult Market," *Senior Consultant*, April 2003, http://

www.SrConsultant.com/Articles/ 2003-04-Top-Advisors-Grow.pdf.

5 Rowe Decision Analytics, http://www.MyInvestmentPolicy.com

6 Prima Capital is emerging as the leading organization for manager search and selection, and is used by the largest global accounting firms. [author endorsement]

7 Advent's Moxie (trade-and-order routing) and Axys (sub-accounting and reporting). [author endorsement]

8 Bullrun Financial, Inc. www.bullrunfinancial.com

9 Qantal and Upstream links; www.bullrunfinancial.com

10 PIPODs technology offered by PPCA.www.ppca-inc.com; See *Senior Consultant*'s Toolbox http://www.srconsultant.com/Toolbox/toolbox.html#PIPODs.

11 Dynaporte, www.dynaporte.com. Quantitative Advantage, www.qadvantage.biz. RowPyn Investment Partners, LLC, www.rowpyn.com.

12 StokTrib, a real-time, style-adjusted attribution analysis. www.ppca-inc.com; DynaPorte, a post-Modern Portfolio Theory methodology. www.dynaporte.com.

13 "Speaking the Unspeakable: The Marketing Opportunity of Our Lifetime," *Senior Consultant*, October 2003, http://www. SrConsultant.com/Articles/2003-10-Speaking-the-Unspeakable.

ND Management

EDUCATIONAL ORGANIZATIONS AND ASSOCIATIONS

Education. It is the backbone of the investment management consulting profession. Education took consulting from an idea to a marketing opportunity in the 70s, and from a practice in the 80s to the growing profession it is today. Increasingly, separate account managers, mutual fund companies, private coaches and trainers, wirehouses, and other broker-dealers are all providing their own brand of fee-based or managed account training and education to advisors. E-learning or e-training is also popular because professionals can learn at their own pace, and online universities are beginning to offer specialized courses and continuing education credits. Industry trade organizations will continue to offer high level designations and professional education through conferences and study courses.

With increased competition for niche markets, advisors and consultants can stand above the crowd through professional advancement. Industry organizations that provide courses for continuing education and professional designations are vital to their practices. In addition to the knowledge gained by earning the title, professional trade organizations assist consultants and advisors with sales and marketing issues, regulation, compliance issues, networking and support from others in the field. Here are a few industry organizations worthy of investigation:

- *Association for Investment Management and Research (AIMR)*
PO Box 3668 (560 Ray C. Hunt Drive)
Charlottesville, VA 22903
Tel: 800-247-8132
http://www.aimr.com
Thomas A. Bowman, president and chief executive
Members: Individual financial analysts and financial consultants

- *The American College*
270 S. Bryn Mawr Avenue
Bryn Mawr, PA 19010
Tel: 888-263-7265
http://www.amercoll.edu

- *College for Financial Planning*
6161 So. Syracuse Way
Greenwood Village, CO 80111
Tel: 800-237-9990
http://www.fp.edu
Michael Cates, CFP®

- *Family Office Exchange LLC (FOX)*
100 S. Wacker Drive
Suite 900
Chicago, IL 60606
Tel: 312-327-1200
http://www.familyoffice.com
Sara Hamilton, Founder and CEO

- *Financial Planning Association (FPA)*
5775 Glenridge Drive
Suite B-300
Atlanta, GA 30328
Tel: 800-322-4237
Denver office:
4100 E. Mississippi Ave , Suite 400
Denver, CO 80246
http://www.fpanet.org
Janet G. McCallen, executive director
Members: Individual financial services professionals

- *Financial Women's Association (FWA)*
215 Park Avenue South
Suite 1713
New York, NY 10003
Tel: 212-533-2141
http://www.fwa.org
Nancy Sellar, Executive Director
Members: Individual financial professionals, men and women

- *Foundation for Fiduciary Studies*
Center for Fiduciary Studies
2004 E. Carson Street
Pittsburgh, PA 15203
Tel: 412-390-5080
http://www.cfstudies.com
Donald Trone, cofounder

- *Institute for Private Investors (IPI)*
74 Trinity Place
New York, NY 10006
Tel: 212) 693-1300
http://www.memberlink.net
Charlotte Beyer, Founder and CEO

- *Investment Management Consultants Association (IMCA)*
9101 E. Kenyon Ave. Suite 3000
Denver, CO 80237
Tel: 303-770-3377
Website: http://www.imca.org
Evelyn L. Brust, executive director
Members: Consultants, financial advisors, financial planners, wealth managers.

- *The Money Management Institute (MMI)*
1101 17th St. N.W., Suite 703
Washington, DC 20036
Tel: 202-347-3858
Website:http://www.moneyinstitute.com
Christopher L. Davis, executive director
Members: Money managers, sponsor firms, and broker-dealers

- *The National Association of Personal Financial Advisors (NAPFA)*
3250 N. Arlington Heights Road, Suite 109
Arlington Heights, IL 60004
Tel: 800-366-2732
http://www.napfa.org
Ellen Turf, chief executive
Members: Individual fee-only financial advisors

- *National Association of Philanthropic Planners (NAPP)*
754 111th Ave., N.
Naples, FL 34108
Tel: 800-342-6215
http://www.napp.net
Johnne D. Syverson, president
Members: Individual financial and estate planners

- *Investment Company Institute (ICI)*
1401 H Street, N.W.
Washington, DC 20005
Tel: 202-326-5800
http://www.ici.org
Matthew P. Fink, president

- *Managed Funds Association (MFA)*
2025 M Street, N.W., Suite 800
Washington, DC 20036
Tel: 202-367-1140
http://www.mfainfo.org
John G. Gaine, president
Members: Individual alternative investment professionals

- *National Association of Insurance and Financial Advisors (NAIFA)*
2901 Telestar Court
PO Box 12012
Falls Church, VA 22042
Tel: 703-770-8100
http://www.naifa.org
David F. Woods, chief executive
Members: Individual life, health, and financial advisors

- *National Association of Investment Professionals (NAIP)*
Financial Services Policy Institute (FSPI)
12664 Emmer Place, Suite 201
St. Paul, MN 55124
Tel: 952-322-6247
http://www.naip.com
Thomas O'Keefe, president
Members: Individual brokers, financial advisors, financial planners.

AUTHOR BIOGRAPHIES

A

Anthony, Dianne Pagano, CFA®
Principal and Director of Fixed Income
Rorer Asset Management, LLC

Dianne P. Anthony, CFA, is the director of fixed income at Rorer Asset Management, LLC, where she is responsible for the firm's fixed income policy, strategy, and investment process. She also is responsible for interpreting and monitoring economic statistics and market trends. Before joining Rorer, she served as senior fixed income portfolio manager at Meridian Investment Company from 1989 to 1995, and as municipal bond liaison with Legg Mason from 1986 to 1989.

Ms. Anthony is a member of the Financial Analysts of Philadelphia, the Municipal Bond Club of Philadelphia, and a board member of the Bond Club of Philadelphia. She earned her BA, Summa Cum Laude, from Immaculata College.

Arnold, Jennifer
Partner, Director of Communications
Capital Market Consultants, LLC

With more than 10 years of experience in the financial services industry, Jennifer Arnold is partner and director of communications for Capital Market Consultants (CMC), LLC. There she is responsible for the strategic marketing, brand development and communication needs of both CMC and its clients. Prior to joining CMC, Ms. Arnold was the marketing manager for the Investment Consulting Services business unit at Robert W. Baird & Co. in Milwaukee, Wisconsin, from 1998 to 2002.

At Baird, Ms. Arnold was instrumental in positioning and packaging marketing initiatives and played a key role from inception to implementation of strategic guidance and training for financial advisors, rebuilding the managed portfolio image, and retooling the asset management enterprise to achieve greater educational efficiencies. She spent more than four years in Baird's corporate finance division managing desktop publishing and administrative staff, overseeing all corporate acquisition and IPO materials, and overseeing process improvement and technical upgrades.

Prior to joining Baird, Jennifer had 15 years of experience providing marketing research, public relations, strategic planning, corporate communications and cooperative marketing services for General Electric Medical Systems, Miller Brewing Company and Carson Pirie Scott.

Ms. Arnold holds a MA degree in Industrial Relations and a BA degree in Communications and Sociology from the University of Wisconsin- Milwaukee.

B

Bott, Daniel R, Sr. CIMC
Managing Director – Investment Officer
Bott & Associates Investment Consulting Group of Wachovia Securities
Co-founder, Investment Management Consultants Association (IMCA)
Founder, Institute for Certified Investment Management Consultants (ICIMC/IMCA)

Daniel R. Bott, Sr. is the managing director and investment officer of Bott & Associates, a professional investment consulting group within Wachovia Securities. Formerly senior vice president and consulting group director for the Consulting Group Division at Smith Barney, Inc., he consistently was awarded their highest recognition—membership in the Senior Alchemist Society.

Mr. Bott's career began in 1975 at Kidder Peabody. Ten years later, his vision helped convince management at Dean Witter to enter the separately managed account business, where he was responsible for the start-up of what is now one of the largest managed money programs on Wall Street. Recognized as an industry leader, speaker and author, Mr. Bott is one of the first individuals to be listed in the "Who's Who of Investment Management Consulting" of the Senior Consultant Society, and was one of the first advisors in the United States to be recognized as a Certified Investment Management Consultant (CIMC) by the Institute for Certified Investment Management Consultants (ICIMC), now IMCA.

Over the past decade, Mr. Bott has been featured in numerous industry publications, including having been chosen

The World of Money Management

B

as one of the "Top 10 Broker/Consultants" in the United States by *On Wall Street* magazine. He authored the first textbook written on the use of separate accounts entitled, "Wrap Account Investment Advisor," published by Dow Jones Irwin. His latest book, "The Managed Money Process" which is co-authored by Catherine L. Theisen, will be available Fall, 2004.

Brandes Institute, The
Division of Brandes Investment Partners®

The Brandes Institute, a division of Brandes Investment Partners® (BIP), investigates potential opportunities arising from the influence of behavioral and structural factors on global investing. From ideas contributed by BIP colleagues or members of the academic and broader investment communities, a 10-member Advisory Board selects projects and provides guidance toward their completion. The Brandes Institute staff conducts research, often partnering with professionals and academics in the investing and finance fields.

Brandes Institute staff members are:

- Barry Gillman, CFA, Director (middle, top row)
- Robert Schmidt, Manager (right, top row)
- Machel Allen, Project Research Analyst (left, top row)
- Shane Finneran, Financial Writer (left, bottom row)
- David Hecht, Associate Financial Writer (right, bottom row)
- Beth Richardson, Administrative Assistant (middle, bottom row)

Browne, Anthony H.
CEO and Co-CIO
Roxbury Capital Management, LLC

Anthony (Tony) H. Browne, Roxbury's chief executive officer and co-chief investment officer, oversees all aspects of Roxbury's investment and portfolio management process. In addition, he currently is co-portfolio manager of the Large Cap Growth portfolio.

With more than 30 years of experience in the investment management field, Mr. Browne began his investment career with Tweedy Browne & Company, his father's New York-based investment firm. Warren Buffett once named Tweedy Browne as one of the "superinvestors" of the Graham and Dodd value style. Prior to founding Roxbury, Mr. Browne was president and chief investment officer of CMB Investment Counselors, a Los Angeles firm with $3 billion under management. He holds a BA in Economics from Harvard College and an MBA in Finance from Harvard Graduate School of Business.

C

Campanale, Frank
IMCA Advisory Board Member
Member, MMI Board of Governors
Former President and CEO of Smith Barney Consulting Group

During his tenure as president and CEO of Smith Barney's Consulting Group, Frank Campanale was responsible for market research, investment manager research and evaluation, asset allocation advisory, and new product development, sales marketing, training, and technical support.

Starting his career as a financial consultant with Merrill Lynch, Mr. Campanale joined E. F. Hutton (Smith Barney's predecessor) in 1975, because he believed in the consultative approach exemplified by their Consulting Group. He first acted as the Consulting Group's branch advisor, was promoted to district director in 1980, regional director in 1982, divisional director in 1984, national director in 1987 and president and CEO in 1996. Mr. Campanale also was instrumental in the Nikko Salomon Smith Barney joint venture (now Nikko Citigroup).

On the board of several European mutual funds, Mr. Campanale also serves on the advisory board of IMCA (Investment Management Consultants Association), as well as the Board of Governors for The Money Management Institute (MMI). He speaks frequently at national pension and investor conferences and is interviewed by numerous publications including *Fortune, USA Today, The Associated Press, Investment News, Financial Times of London* and

AUTHOR BIOGRAPHIES

The Christian Science Monitor. Mr. Campanale also appears on CNBC's Power Lunch, CNNFN, and in *On Wall Street* magazine's "Broker After Hours" webcasts.

Davis, Christopher L.
Executive Director
Money Management Institute (MMI)

Christopher L. Davis is the executive director of the Money Management Institute (MMI), a national organization representing the managed accounts industry and numerous firms that deliver money management services to individual and institutional investors. Mr. Davis manages the operations of the rapidly growing association and represents the industry on a wide range of legislative, regulatory and investment issues. Before joining MMI, he was with the Washington, DC law firm of Surrey & Morse. Earlier, he held several positions at the White House during the administration of President Carter, including special assistant to the president for Congressional Liaison. Mr. Davis is a 1971 graduate of the University of North Carolina at Chapel Hill where he was elected to Phi Beta Kappa, and was a 1975 graduate of the State University of New York at Buffalo School of Law.

Deakyne, Bill, CFA®
Vice President, Director of Marketing
Franklin Templeton Private Client Group

Bill Deakyne, CFA, is a vice president and director of marketing for Franklin Templeton Private Client Group and has been associated with Franklin Templeton Investments since 1998.

Previously, Mr. Deakyne was a financial analyst with Paul Kagan Associates in Carmel, California. He is a Chartered Financial Analyst (CFA) charterholder and holds NASD Series 24 and 7 licenses. A member of the Security Analysts of San Francisco (SAFS), Mr. Deakyne also is a member of the Association of Investment Management and Research (AIMR), and the Association of Investment Management Sales Executives (AIMSE).

He received a BS degree in commerce with a concentration in finance from the University of Virginia. Mr. Deakyne also received an MBA in International Management from the American Graduate School of International Management (Thunderbird).

Duff, Richard
Managing Director, Head of Private Client Distribution
Co-head, Private Client Group
BlackRock

As managing director and head of BlackRock's Private Client Distribution, Richard Duff also is co-head of BlackRock's Private Client Group. In both capacities, he is responsible for enhancing and expanding wholesale distribution strategies and relationships, and for managing the firm's internal and external wholesalers.

Mr. Duff has been involved in the financial services industry since 1994 in roles including equity portfolio manager, institutional, retail, and high net worth sales, and sales management. Prior to joining BlackRock, he was managing director of Forward Management where he was responsible for managing the sales team for their funds and manager affiliates, including Hoover Capital Management and Uniplan Real Estate Advisors. Prior to that, Mr. Duff was senior vice president and national sales manager for Nicholas Applegate Capital Management. Mr. Duff received a BA degree from the University of California, Berkeley and a JD degree from the University of San Francisco.

Fleites, Gus, CFA®
Senior Principal, State Street Global Advisors

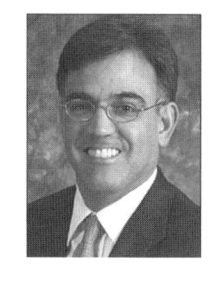

Gus Fleites is a senior principal of State Street Global Advisors and managing director of Advisor Strategies. He is responsible for the distribution of SSgA investment strategies into third-party channels, and the development and implementation of exchange-traded funds, registered investment funds, and managed account strategies. Mr. Fleites is a member of SSgA's Investment Committee; president of SSgA Funds Management, Inc.; and director of SSgA Ireland, Limited and the SSgA Cash Management Funds, PLC (Ireland).

After joining the firm in 1987, Mr. Fleites headed the firm's asset allocation team and is credited with the successful development and implementation of SSgA's asset allocation strategy. He established SSgA's Australian office in 1991 where, as managing director, he was responsible for portfolio management services, client support, and the development of new client relationships. Prior to moving to Australia, Mr. Fleites was a portfolio manager in SSgA's Active International Equity group where he managed several commingled and separately managed active equity funds.

The recipient of a BA degree in Finance and Multinational Management from the Wharton School of the University of Pennsylvania, and an MBA degree in Finance from Babson College, he also is a Chartered Financial Analyst.

Gartlan, Don
Director, Russell Managed Portfolios
Russell Investment Group

As the director of Russell Managed Portfolios, Don Gartlan is accountable for the success of Russell's high net worth managed accounts product. Prior to joining Russell, Mr. Gartlan served as vice president and manager of A.G. Edwards & Sons Investment Management Consulting division from 1996 until November 2001. From 1991 to 1995, he was vice president and manager of the Asset Management Group for Rauscher Pierce Refsnes, Inc., Dallas, Texas. Mr. Gartlan served as a director of the Institute for Certified Investment Management Consultants (ICIMC), now merged with IMCA, a member of the Investment Management Consultants Association (IMCA), and a member of the Corporate Advisory Board of the Graduate School of Business at Texas A&M University.

ING Investment Management
(See corporate profile - page 335)

Iwanski, Richard G., CFA®
Partner – Institutional Client Services
Capital Market Consultants, LLC

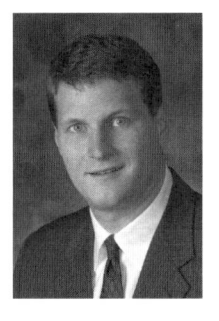

Richard G. Iwanski, CFA®, who has more than 10 years of financial industry experience, joined Capital Market Consultants, LLC, in January 2004 as a partner, servicing institutional and practice management clients, and managing investment manager due diligence. From 1999 to 2004, Mr. Iwanski was vice president and senior portfolio analyst at Robert W. Baird & Co. His primary responsibilities included analysis and research of third-party investment managers in the firm's advisory programs, providing guidance to Baird financial advisors on asset allocation, manager selection and client profiling, and developing the sales platform.

From 1994 to 1999, Mr. Iwanski was employed with Stein Roe & Farnham. His responsibilities included working with the chief economist to produce the economic forecast, analyzing economic data, writing reviews for analysts and portfolio managers, as well as portfolio attribution analysis.

Mr. Iwanski earned his Chartered Financial Analyst (CFA) designation in 2000. He is a member of the Investment Management Consultants Association (IMCA) and the Milwaukee Investment Analysts Society. Mr. Iwanski attended the University of Wisconsin, earning a BA degree in Economics in 1992.

Capital Market Consultants, LLC, is a leading business consulting and investment advisory firm specializing in the development of custom, Open Architecture Investment Management (OAIM) solutions for small to mid-sized financial service firms.

Kahn, David C.
Managing Director and Co-Portfolio Manager-Large Cap Growth
Roxbury Capital Management, LLC

David C. Kahn is a managing director and co-portfolio manager for Roxbury's Large Cap Growth portfolio where his responsibilities include stock selection, sector allocation, portfolio construction, and benchmark analysis. Prior to joining Roxbury in 1994, he was a vice president with the Investment Management Consulting Groups at Oppenheimer and Smith Barney.

AUTHOR BIOGRAPHIES

Mr. Kahn has 18 years of experience in the investment management field, including seven years with a New York-based proxy solicitor and merger strategist, where he developed and ran a division providing defense strategy and investor relations consulting to Fortune 1000 companies. He received his BA in Economics from Bucknell University and his MBA in Finance from New York University.

MacKillop, Scott
Co-founder, President and Principal
Trivium Consulting, LLC

Scott MacKillop is the co-founder, president and principal of Trivium Consulting, LLC. Trivium works with financial institutions, investment advisors and money management firms to develop or improve their managed account or investment consulting capabilities. Trivium's services include strategic planning; competitive analysis; product development; manager search and due diligence; creation of marketing, sales and training programs; technology assessment and development; design of back office systems and processes, and hands-on implementation assistance in all areas of program development and operations.

From 1998 to 2000, Mr. MacKillop served as president of PMC International, Inc. the first firm to provide separately managed account services to independent advisors. He also served as a member of PMC's Investment Committee. Before joining PMC, Mr. MacKillop served as president of ADAM Investment Services, Inc., in 1997. He also served as vice president to ADAM's affiliate, LCG Associates, Inc. He began his career practicing law in Washington, D.C., specializing in corporate, securities and venture capital matters.

Mr. MacKillop has authored articles on topics including managed accounts, investment consulting and behavioral finance. His articles have appeared in the *Journal of Financial Planning, Investment Advisor, Financial Advisor, Financial Planning, Financial Strategies* and *The Wrap Fee Advisor*. He often speaks to financial services groups and is frequently quoted by industry publications. Mr. MacKillop received a BA degree from Stanford University and a JD degree from George Washington University Law School. He currently holds a Series 65 securities license.

Madison Core Equity Team
Madison Equity Group

- Rich Eisinger, Portfolio Manager (standing, left)

    Rich Eisinger is a senior member of the Madison equity management team, with primary responsibility for the mid-cap portfolios. Prior to joining the firm, Mr. Eisinger worked in the equity research department at Piper Capital Management in Minneapolis, and as an investment manager for Spectrum Advisors. He holds a law degree from the University of Louisville and an MBA in finance from Cornell University's Johnson School of Management.

- Matt Hayner, Equity Analyst (seated, left)

    Matt Hayner is an equity analyst covering stocks in the Industrial and Health Care Sectors at Madison Investment Advisors. Prior to joining Madison in 2002, he worked with the Valspar Corporation as a financial analyst in the information systems group. He graduated with honors from Eastern Illinois University in 1995 with a BS in Chemistry, and from the University of St. Thomas in 2001 with an MBA in Finance.

- Jay Sekelsky, CPA, CFA®, Lead Equity Manager (standing, right)

    Jay Sekelsky serves as the lead equity manager for Madison's stock funds, and has since April of 1995. Previously, he served as co-manager on the equity funds. In 1990, Sekelsky joined Madison Investment Advisors, the managers of the Mosaic funds, as an Assistant Portfolio Manager. Sekelsky joined Madison Investment Advisors from Wellington Management Company, where he worked as an investment officer. He holds BBA and MBA degrees from the University of Wisconsin and also has earned both the CPA and CFA designation.

- David Halford, CPA, CFA®, Portfolio Manager (seated, right)

    David Halford is a member of Madison's equity management team, specializing in technology and telecommunications stocks. Prior to joining Madison, he was an equity portfolio manager for the Wisconsin Alumni Research Foundation and before that, with Firstar Investment Research and Management. Mr. Halford is a CPA and is a CFA charterholder.

Maslow, Steven, CFP®
Managing Director
GroupRed, LLC

Steven Maslow is managing director at GroupRed, LLC, a New York-based firm. Steven Maslow's career began at Bear Stearns in New York City, spanning the years 1985 to 1999. During his tenure, he worked in the investment banking, risk arbitrage, real estate and asset management divisions. In every area, he interpreted, explained and documented the firm's "mandates," the firm's senior managed-underwritings and new product offerings. He also prepared prospectuses, marketing materials, and presentations to "make the case" for financial products across many of the firm's disciplines in coordination with the origination, distribution, and legal divisions of Bear Stearns.

Throughout that time period, Mr. Maslow also retained his "customers' man" status and maintained his brokerage licenses and a base of clients. In 1999 he made a career change, deciding to pursue his life-long love of cooking at the French Culinary Institute from which he graduated in 2003. In addition to his responsibilities at GroupRed, he currently is a line chef at Brasserie 8 in New York City. Mr. Maslow, although a veteran CFP, engages a financial specialist to manage his own accounts because he believes strongly that "perspective is worth about half your returns."

McCall, Patrick J., CFA®
Executive Vice President, Portfolio Manager
Templeton Private Client Group

Patrick J. McCall, CFA, is an executive vice president and portfolio manager for Templeton Private Client Group (TPCG). He is a member of the TPCG portfolio committee and serves as team leader. Mr. McCall has been involved in the securities industry since 1983 and joined Templeton in 1995.

Prior to joining Franklin Templeton Investments, he was a fund manager/equity analyst for the Duke Endowment (1993 to 1995), portfolio manager for NationsBank (1988 to 1993), co-director equity research/senior analyst for NationsBank (1986 to 1987), and equity research analyst for Trusco Capital Management/Trust Company of Georgia (1983 to 1986). He is a Chartered Financial Analyst (CFA) charterholder and holds Series 7, 24, 63, and 65 NASD licenses. Mr. McCall is a member of the South Florida and International Society of Financial Analysts, as well as a member of the Association for Investment Management and Research (AIMR). Mr. McCall received his BS degree in Finance from Indiana University.

McMeans, Mark E., CFA®, CPA
Managing Director, Investment Department, President and COO
AIM Private Asset Management Inc.

Mark McMeans, a managing director of AIM's Investment Department, is president and chief operating officer of AIM Private Asset Management, Inc. (APAM). He assumed his current position in 2000 and oversees APAM's portfolio management, client service, and marketing efforts. Mr. McMeans began his career at AIM Investments in 1992 as project manager and supervisor of the client service and internal sales desks within AIM's Institutional Marketing Department. He led numerous projects, including the internalization of AIM's first transfer agent, AIM Institutional Fund Services, Inc., and AIM's first online trade entry and servicing system, AIMLINK™.

In 1996, he was named senior vice president of AIM's Fund Management Company and was subsequently charged with creating and developing the firm's electronic commerce strategy. In November 1996, AIM launched its corporate website, naming Mr. McMeans vice president of AIM Advisors, Inc. and its first director of electronic commerce. Mr. McMeans was awarded the position of senior equity officer of AIM Capital Management, Inc. in 1997 and became responsible for the day-to-day operations of the AIM equity portfolio management team. Prior to joining the AIM team, he held positions at JP Morgan Chase and KPMG Peat Marwick, LLP.

He currently is a member of the Houston Society of Financial Analysts, the Investment Management Consultants Association (IMCA), and the Money Management Institute's (MMI) Media Relations Committee, which works to promote the separately managed account industry. He also has earned the Chartered Financial Analyst (CFA) and Certified Public Accountant (CPA) professional designations and currently serves on the Oversight Board of the M.A. Wright student-managed funds at Rice University's Jones Graduate School of Management. Mr. McMeans earned his bachelor's degree in business administration from the University of Texas at Austin and his MBA from Rice University.

Mendelson, Barry K., CIMA
Managing Partner
Capital Market Consultants, LLC

Barry K. Mendelson, CIMA, managing partner at Capital Market Consultants (CMC), LLC, has, for the last 15 years, dedicated his time exclusively to Open Architecture Investment Management (OAIM). During this period he was instrumental in helping several firms launch entire OAIM programs and businesses, developed new OAIM products, and has taught advisors how to employ these in the development of client relationships. He speaks frequently at industry events on subjects ranging from investment analysis, client profiling, money manager style analysis, investment consulting, practice management and numerous other topics. His career in the financial services industry spans more than 20 years.

He earned his Certified Investment Management Analysts designation (CIMA) from the Investment Management Consultants Association (IMCA) in 1989, and now serves on its Professional Ethics Committee. He graduated from the University of Pennsylvania's Wharton Business School in 1990. He also is a member of the International Coaching Federation. Mr. Mendelson earned a BS degree from Palmer College in Davenport, Iowa in 1976.

Capital Market Consultants,LLC., is a leading business consulting and investment advisory firm specializing in the development of custom, Open Architecture Investment Management (OAIM) solutions for small to mid-sized financial service firms.

Nersesian, John, CFP®, CIMA, CIS
Managing Director, Wealth Management Services
Nuveen Investments

John Nersesian is managing director of Wealth Management Services at Nuveen Investments where his group provides wealth management and practice development education and consulting support to successful advisors. An experienced financial advisor to corporate executives, affluent families, and non-profit organizations, Mr. Nersesian was a first vice president of Merrill Lynch Private Client Group prior to joining Nuveen in 2000. While at Merrill Lynch he also was a leader of advanced training for financial consultants, providing training in comprehensive wealth management strategies and business development practices.

Mr. Nersesian is recognized within the financial services industry as an expert in investment consulting and financial planning issues and is a frequent contributor to *The Wall Street Journal*, *Bloomberg* and *CNN*. He has earned the Certified Financial Planner (CFP), Certified Investment Management Analyst (CIMA), and Certified Investment Specialist (CIS) designations. He received a BS in Business and Economics from Lehigh University.

O'Keefe Thomas S.
Founder, Financial Services Policy Institute (FSPI)
Founder and President, National Association of Investment Professionals

Thomas S. O'Keefe is the founder and president of the National Association of Investment Professionals (NAIP). He is editor of the organization's quarterly newsletter, *The Advocate*, and NAIP's *Securities Industry Digest*, a compilation of papers written on employment and arbitration in the financial services industry.

Mr. O'Keefe also is founder of the Financial Services Policy Institute (FSPI) a foundation and "think-tank" that provides research on financial regulatory issues affecting investors, and educational material for investors on issues related to this field of study. Both NAIP and FSPI provide research and analysis in areas of securities, employment and arbitration law. NAIP also lobbies Congress on issues that affect registered representatives in the securities industry.

The World of Money Management

Having entered the securities industry in 1986 as a trainee for Shearson (now Smith Barney), Mr. O'Keefe worked for several other well-known brokerage firms, as well as being an independent contractor with Raymond James Financial Services. He holds his Series 7, 65, and 24 licenses and also has worked as a principal in the securities industry. O'Keefe is an Accredited Asset Management Specialist (AAMS), earning that designation through the College of Financial Planning in Denver.

For several years, Mr. O'Keefe's monthly columns appeared in *Registered Representative* magazine where he wrote about NAIPs lobbying efforts in the U.S. Congress, its responses to the regulatory initiatives of the SEC, on NASD regulation regarding employment law, and the NASD arbitration system. He also has been quoted in *On Wall Street* magazine, and *Investment News* on matters related to employment law and market regulation, and has appeared on CNN and CNBC.

Potter, Frances, CFP®
Vice President
Wealth Management Services Group
Nuveen Investments, Inc.

With extensive experience as an investment professional working with investors and advisors at Nuveen Investments and Kidder, Peabody & Co. Incorporated, Frances L. Potter currently is Vice President in the Wealth Management Services Group of Nuveen Investments, Inc. Ms. Potter is a graduate of Transylvania University in Lexington, Kentucky and is a Certified Financial Planner™ certificant. She also has completed the Wealth Management Certificate program offered by the Investment Management Consultants Association (IMCA).

Leonard A. Reinhart, President
Lockwood
A Service of Pershing®
A BNY Securities Group Co.
Solutions from The Bank of New York

Len Reinhart is recognized as one of the founders of the individually managed account industry. He started his career in 1978 at E.F. Hutton, and was directly responsible for developing programs that introduced institutional-level professional investment management services to the individual investor marketplace. Under his leadership, the organization dominated its market, ultimately gathering more than $70 billion in assets under management and serving over 200,000 clients.

Mr. Lockwood founded the Lockwood family of companies in 1995. Lockwood Financial Services, Inc. provided an investment consulting platform to independent broker/consultants, investment advisors and financial planners. Lockwood Advisors, Inc. offered proprietary research on institutional money managers, asset allocation and style allocation recommendations and integrated portfolio design services. Through Lockwood, advisors access a broad array of investment services and products to create customized investment programs for high net worth individual and institutional clients.

Mr. Lockwood also was part of the team that developed and launched Electronic Managed Account Technologies (EMAT), in October 2000. EMAT's managed account technologies provided individually managed account opening and maintenance services on an open-architecture, web-based platform to money managers and program sponsors.

In 2002, Lockwood and EMAT were combined into a single firm, which was acquired by The Bank of New York, which later acquired Pershing, LLC. In 2003, Lockwood and Pershing joined forces to create the most advanced, comprehensive managed money platform in the industry, blending Lockwood's leadership in managed money research and product development with Pershing's operational expertise.

Mr. Lockwood serves on the Board of Governors of the Money Management Institute (MMI) and on the Advisory Board of Directors of the Investment Management Consultants Association (IMCA). He frequently is quoted on the industry by *The Wall Street Journal, Forbes* and other major financial publications. He has been a regular contributor to *Registered Representative* magazine, and currently writes a monthly column for *Financial Planning* magazine. He has appeared on financial programs broadcast over the CNN and CNBC networks.

Rorer, Edward C.
Chairman and CIO
Rorer Asset Management, LLC

Edward C. "Ted" Rorer is the founder, chairman and chief investment officer of Rorer Asset Management, LLC. Having developed Rorer's disciplined approach to investment management, he is responsible for the firm's overall investment process.

Before establishing Rorer Asset Management, he served as executive vice president at Professional Capital Management from 1976 to 1978, and as vice president at Blyth Eastman Dillon from 1971 to 1976. Mr. Rorer earned his BA from Trinity College in 1965, and an MBA from the University of Pennsylvania in 1970.

Sanchez-Marin, Patricia
Principal
State Street Global Advisors

Patricia Sanchez-Marin is a principal of State Street Global Advisors with the Advisor Strategies Group. She is the director of Advisor Consulting Services, a group responsible for delivering value added research, educational tools and practice management services to financial advisors. Prior to her current position, Ms. Sanchez-Marin was part of SSgA's Exchange Traded Funds/Offshore Funds group where her responsibilities included quantitative support focused on indexing and portfolio management, client service, and product development. Before joining SSgA in 2000, she worked for Osram Sylvania within its Benefits Group.

Ms. Sanchez-Marin holds NASD Series 7 and 63 licenses through State Street Capital Markets LLC. In addition, she is a Level II candidate of the CFA® program. She is a summa cum laude graduate of Salem State College with a BS degree in Finance, and currently is pursuing her MS degree in Finance from the Carroll School of Management at Boston College.

Seuffert, James J.
Chief Operating Officer
Lockwood , A Service of Pershing®
A BNY Securities Group Co.
Solutions from The Bank of New York

Mr. Seuffert is recognized as one of the primary contributors to the development of the fee-based consulting industry. He started his career in 1980 at EF Hutton's Consulting Services Division. During his 15-year tenure there, he helped inaugurate many innovative programs that made professional investment management consulting accessible to individual, as well as institutional investors.

In 1995, Mr. Seuffert and his long-time colleague, Leonard A. Reinhart, founded the Lockwood family of companies. Lockwood Financial Services, Inc., the broker/dealer, was the first investment advisory firm specifically designed to provide a turnkey investment consulting platform to independent broker/consultants, investment advisors and financial planners. Through Lockwood, these advisors access the asset management services of a large universe of highly regarded institutional money managers, choosing the appropriate investment style alternatives to create customized investment programs for their clients.

In 2002, Lockwood was acquired by The Bank of New York, which later acquired Pershing, LLC. In 2003, Lockwood and Pershing joined forces to create the most advanced, comprehensive managed money platform in the industry, blending Lockwood's leadership in managed money research and product development with Pershing's operational expertise.

In his current position, Mr. Seuffert is directly responsible for all operations procedures and protocols within Lockwood. He also carries leadership responsibility for the development of the firm's information management systems and proprietary investment advisory software, including the web-enabled technology that provides independent financial advisors with front-end sales, marketing and proposal-generation capabilities, account-opening oversight and ongoing account monitoring and performance reporting.

A graduate of Mount St. Mary's College in Emmitsburg, Maryland, Mr. Seuffert has a BS degree in Business and Finance. He lives with his family in Wilmington, Delaware.

Sinsimer, Lawrence M., J.D.
Senior Vice President
Managing Director
Managed Accounts
Eaton Vance Distributors, Inc.

Lawrence "Larry" M. Sinsimer, J.D., has more than 32 years experience in the financial services industry, and joined Eaton Vance in November of 2000 to lead its managed accounts efforts. For 15 of those years, he was a partner and/or principal in three investment management firms managing in excess of $7 billion dollars, and was a participant on their investment committees.

Before joining Eaton Vance, Mr. Sinsimer worked for six years at Paine Webber, where he was senior vice president and national marketing director for Investment Counseling Services. Prior to joining Paine Webber, he served as senior vice president and national sales manager with Roger Engemann and Associates. From 1987 to1991, Mr. Sinsimer was a senior vice president and director of Regent Investor Services. He began working in the broker/consultant marketplace with Smilen and Safian in 1982.

Mr. Sinsimer is a past member of the Board of Governors of the Money Management Institute (MMI), a member of Investment Management Consultants Association (IMCA). He holds a BBA in Insurance and Finance, and earned a law degree from New York Law School.

Sislen, Alan
President
Managed Account Perspectives, LLC (MAP)

Alan Sislen founded Managed Account Perspectives, LLC (MAP) in 2001, a consulting firm focused exclusively on the separately managed account industry. MAP works with program sponsors and money managers considering entering the separately managed account business, as well as participants who would like to achieve even greater success in this rapidly growing segment of the managed money marketplace. He spent more than 31 years at Merrill Lynch as a financial consultant, branch manager, and national sales manager and, from 1991 to 2001 he was first vice president and senior director of Merrill Lynch's Investment Consulting Group. In that position, Mr. Sislen was the senior executive directly responsible for the fee-based advisory services (ML Consults®, Mutual Fund Advisor(SM), and MFA-Selects(SM), Strategic Portfolio Advisor(SM), and Personal Investment Advisor(SM), as well as Merrill Lynch's institutional level consulting services. Under his leadership and management, ML Consults grew from $4 billion to more than $60 billion in assets and to more than 250,000 accounts, and was one of the most successful separate account programs in the industry. Mr. Sislen's management team was responsible for all aspects of these services, including product design, manager due diligence, sales and marketing, portfolio management, compliance, systems, and trading.

He served on the Professional Advisory Council of the Investment Management Consultant's Association (IMCA) and on the Board of Governors of the Money Management Institute (MMI), from which he received the prestigious Managed Account Pioneer award. He frequently is interviewed and quoted in financial publications such as *The Wall Street Journal, Business Week, Forbes, Fortune* and *FundFire*. Mr. Sislen graduated from Syracuse University with a BS in Finance and holds an MBA from George Washington University.

AUTHOR BIOGRAPHIES

Storms, Clifford B. Jr., CFA®
Executive VP and Director of Research
Rorer Asset Management, LLC

Clifford B. Storms, Jr. CFA, is the director of research at Rorer Asset Management, LLC, where he is responsible for the firm's fundamental, technical, and quantitative research. He is directly involved in setting the firm's investment policy and strategy.

Before joining Rorer, Mr. Storms served as associate director of research and portfolio manager at First Pennsylvania Bank from 1987 to 1990 and as an analyst with Value Line from 1982 to 1984. He is a member of the Financial Analysts of Philadelphia. Mr. Storms earned his BA degree from Dickinson College in 1981, and an MBA from the University of North Carolina at Chapel Hill in 1986.

Surz, Ronald, CIMA
President, PPCA, Inc.
Principal, RCG Capital Advisors, LLC

Ronald Surz has held senior positions in the investment consulting and financial services industry since 1972 and is currently President of PPCA Inc., a firm that provides complex investment monitoring, performance attribution and related analytic tools to the investment consulting industry. He is also a principal of Risk Controlled Growth (RCG) Capital Advisors LLC, manager of funds-of-funds of hedge funds employing a diversified multi-strategy/multi-advisor approach to achieving absolute returns.

Between 1972 and 1986, Mr. Surz served as a senior vice president and head of investment policy consulting at AG Becker/SEI, one of the investment industry's largest and most prestigious consulting firms. In 1986, Mr. Surz was a co-founder and principal of Becker/Burke, a Chicago-based investment consulting firm that provided strategic planning, portfolio and manager evaluation, and performance monitoring services to institutional retirement trusts, foundations and endowments, nationwide. In 1992, he joined Glenwood Financial Group, a fund-of-funds of hedge funds, where he developed institutional relationships and reviewed prospective managers. In 1996, Mr. Surz joined Roxbury Capital Management where he was the Managing Director of Institutional Business Development. Before entering the investment industry, Mr. Surz spent four years as a consulting engineer with Northrop Corporation, where he developed electronic countermeasures to jam heat-seeking missiles

Mr. Surz's original research has been published in numerous professional journals including the *Journal of Investing*, *The Journal of Portfolio Management*, *The Financial Analysts Journal*, *The Journal of Performance Measurement*, *Pensions & Investments*, *Senior Consultant*, *IMCA Monitor*, *Pension Fund Investment Management*, *Portfolio & Investment Management*, and the *Handbook of Equity Style Management*. He also is active with the Investment Management Consultants Association (IMCA) and has served as a member of its Board of Directors since 1998. He also has served IMCA as Chairman of its Standards of Practice Board, editor of the IMCA Monitor, and currently is co-chairman of its Committee on Alternative Investment Strategies. He also is a member of the After-Tax Performance Reporting Standards Sub-committee for the Association of Investment Management and Research (AIMR) and AIMR's Investment Performance Council.

Mr. Surz graduated grada cum laude in 1967 from the University of Illinois, Chicago, with a BS in Applied Mathematics, and in 1969 he earned an MS in Applied Mathematics from the University of Illinois, Chicago. Mr. Surz received an MBA in Finance from the University of Chicago, Graduate School of Business, in 1974.

Todd, Richard M., CIMC
Principal
Innovest Portfolio Solutions, LLC

Richard M. Todd, CIMC, is a co-founder and manager of Innovest Portfolio Solutions, LLC. He has more than 18 years of experience in investment consulting and currently provides extensive consulting services to institutions and individuals. His clients include public funds, corporate plans, Taft-Hartley funds, and wealthy families. In addition to client consulting, Rich is responsible for political and economic analysis and business development.

Prior to establishing Innovest, Mr. Todd was first vice-president of Investment Management Consulting Group of Dain Bosworth and managing director of RPRime Services, the consulting department at Rauscher Pierce Refsnes. Mr. Todd's responsibilities included consulting to the firm's top clients, coordination with other departments and professionals, and department management.

In 1999, Mr. Todd was honored as one of the financial services industry's "best and brightest" for his pioneering work in advancing the practice of investment management consulting. This distinction places Mr. Todd in the top percentile of more than 150,000 financial professionals in the United States and Canada. He is one of only 92 consultants elected into the inaugural class of the Society of Senior Consultants. His election into the Society places him among the elite group of investment management consultants who advise $850 billion in assets or 8% of the $10 trillion in financial assets in the United States. Mr. Todd was nominated and elected by a national advisory board comprised of his peers. The nomination process and criteria for election to the Society were exacting and included standards for exemplary regulatory and compliance history, a focus on investment management consulting, significant experience and assets under advisement. Most importantly, Mr. Todd's business had to represent the highest form of integrity and achievement within the financial services industry.

He is a frequent author on fiduciary and investment-related matters. His works and thoughts have been published in *Financial Advisor Magazine, Private Asset Management, Defined Contribution News, The Investment Councilor, On Wall Street, Colorado Lawyer, Pension World, Journal of Compensation and Benefits, Colorado Society of CPAs News Account, Registered Rep, Quarterly Forum, Pension & Investments, The Denver Post, Accounting Today, Senior Consultant, Plan Sponsor* and *The Denver Business Journal*. Additionally, Mr. Todd has been a guest lecturer at the University of Denver Graduate Tax Program, National Jewish Estate Planning Conference, the Callan IMC National Conference, the Colorado Public Pension Conference, the Western Pension & Benefits Conference, and the Mountain States Employers Council, among others.

Mr. Todd is a member of the National Planned Giving Advisory Council for the National Jewish Center for Immunology and Respiratory Medicine, was on the Greenway Foundation Steering Committee, is on the Citywide Banks Advisory Board and is currently the President of Legatus of Colorado, an organization fostering business ethics.

He has earned the designation of Certified Investment Management Consultant (CIMC) from the Investment Management Consultants Association (IMCA). Mr. Todd previously served on the board of directors for the Institution for Certified Investment Management Consultants (now IMCA), and is active with the Western Pension and Benefits Conference. He holds a BA degree from Western State College.

Trone, Don, AIFA™
President, Founder
Foundation for Fiduciary Studies

Don Trone is president and founder of the Foundation for Fiduciary Studies. The Foundation's mission is to develop and advance fiduciary standards of care for trustees, investment committees and advisors. In addition, Mr. Trone is one of the co-founders and co-directors of the Center for Fiduciary Studies, which operates in association with the University of Pittsburgh's Katz Graduate School of Business. The Center is the first full-time training facility devoted to the subject of portfolio management and investment fiduciary standards of care.

Mr. Trone is the CEO of www.investmgt.com, an Internet company that develops web-based tools to support the decision making process of investment fiduciaries. Investmgt.com evolved from the investment consulting firm, Investment Management Council (IMC), which Mr. Trone founded in 1991. The IMC provided investment consulting services to fiduciaries and trustees, and from 1992 to 1998 operated as a division of Callan Associates, one of the largest investment consulting firms in the country. Clients of the former IMC included four of the Big 6 CPA firms (when there were six), one of the 10 largest U.S. banks, and over 120 other local and regional investment advisory firms.

Mr. Trone was appointed by the U.S. Secretary of Labor in 2003 to represent the investment counseling industry on the ERISA Advisory Counsel. As the co-author of two industry bestsellers, "Procedural Prudence" and "The Management of Investment Decisions" (McGraw-Hill Publishing), he also led the development of the recently released handbook, "Prudent Investment Practices." Mr. Trone's works are now used in numerous professional certification programs including the Chartered Financial Analyst (CFA®) and Certified Financial Planner (CFP®) courses. He also is a sought-after speaker on the subject of investment fiduciary responsibility and speaks at national conferences for accountants, attorneys, financial planners, and investment consultants. He is often quoted by the financial press, and has appeared on CNN.

Mr. Trone graduated as president of his class from the United States Coast Guard Academy, and with honors from the U.S. Naval Flight Training Program in Pensacola, Florida. He served on active duty for 10 years as a long-range search and rescue helicopter pilot and is credited with flying over 100 rescue and 50 drug enforcement missions. In 1997 he was the recipient of the Coast Guard Academy Alumni Medal of Achievement for his distinguished military and business career. Mr. Trone received his Master's degree in Financial Services from the American College.

Tucker, John, CFA®
Principal
State Street Global Advisors

John Tucker, CFA, is a principal of State Street Global Advisors and unit head of the portfolio management team responsible for the firm's exchange-traded funds. He manages a number of the firm's domestic and international portfolios. In addition, Mr. Tucker is responsible for new product research and development.

Previously, Mr. Tucker was head of the Structured Products group in SSgA's London office. Prior to joining the investment management group, he was the operations manager for SSgA's International Structured Products group, where he was responsible for the operations staff and functions. He has been working in the investment management field since 1988.

Mr. Tucker received a BA degree in Economics from Trinity College and a MS degree in Finance from Boston College. He also earned the Chartered Financial Analyst (CFA®) designation and is a member of the Boston Security Analysts Society.

Turchyn, William
Partner
Mariner Investment Group

William Turchyn is a partner at Mariner Investment Group in New York City, a hedge fund investment firm that manages more than $3 billion for institutions and wealthy families. Prior to joining Mariner, Mr. Turchyn was chairman of ING Furman Selz Capital Management and a member of the Management Committee of ING Aeltus, which managed more than $50 billion for institutions and private clients. He was also responsible for the firm's hedge fund businesses, which consisted of 10 internal groups managing more than $2 billion.

Before joining ING Furman Selz, Mr. Turchyn was associated with Shearson Lehman Hutton/American Express where he was executive vice president and head of Private Equity Organization, Asset Management and Real Estate Investment activities. Mr. Turchyn has served as chairman of the Direct Investment Committee of the Securities Industry Association, Chairman of the Investment Partnership Association and a member of the Direct Investment Committee of the NASD.

Mr. Turchyn is vice chairman of the Investment Committee for St. Peter's College Endowment. He has been a director of a number of public and private companies and is co-chairman of the Executive Committee and a member of the Board of Directors of the Money Management Institute (MMI).

Walker, Lewis J., CFP®, CIMC, CRC
Former President, ICIMC
President, Walker Capital Management Corp.

Lewis J. Walker, CFP, CIMC, CRC, is president of Walker Capital Management Corporation and Walker Capital Advisory Services, Inc., financial planning and investment advisory firms. Lewis holds the Certified Investment Management Consultant (CIMC) designation and has served as national president of the Institute for Certified Investment Management Consultants (now IMCA). He also holds the Certified Retirement Counselor (CRC) designation granted by the Institute for Retirement Education (InFre) and has been a Certified Financial Planner (CFP) since 1975.

Mr. Walker is recognized as a pioneer in financial planning, and as past president of the Institute of Certified Financial Planners (ICFP), he was the first recipient of HONORS, an award bestowed by the Georgia Chapter of the Financial Planning Association (FPA). HONORS recognizes Georgians who have made a significant contribution to the development of the financial planning profession

Known as The Investment Coach™, Lewis is a nationally recognized speaker and writer. He writes a monthly column, "Economic Literacy" for *On Wall Street* magazine and is a regular columnist for the *Journal of Financial Planning*. Lewis was cited by *WORTH* magazine in their 10th anniversary issue (July/August, 2002) as one of the Top 250 Financial Advisors in the United States. Mr. Walker earned his BSFS (Bachelor of Science in Foreign Service) degree from Georgetown University, School of Foreign Service, Washington DC, and an MBA in Marketing from Northwestern University, Chicago, IL.

Washburn, Drew E., CIMC, CIMA, CFP®
VP, Regional Marketing Director
The Roosevelt Investment Group

Drew E. Washburn, CIMC, CIMA, CFP is a 25-year veteran in the investment consulting industry. As a former course trainer for the Institute for Investment Management Consultants (now IMCA), and a registered Certified Investment Management Consultant (CIMC), he has extensive knowledge in the educational arenas. Mr. Washburn has been instrumental in successfully building strategic alliances in the broker-dealer, registered investment advisory, financial planning, and banking industries. He also was involved in every aspect of separate account management, holding such positions as equity analyst, head equity trader and portfolio manager.

On the business development side of the money management business, Mr. Washburn previously was VP and regional marketing director for Wells Fargo Private Client Services; senior VP and director of marketing and client service for SCI Capital Management; and senior VP and regional director of marketing for AEGON USA.

An active member of the Investment Management Consultants Association (IMCA) and the Financial Planning Association. (FPA), Mr. Washburn has published booklets and educational materials on Investment Consulting and Fiduciary Responsibility and is the author of numerous articles on these topics.

Waymire, Jack C., CFP®
President
Paladin Investor Resources

Jack Waymire's career in the financial services industry spans 27 years. For 20 of these years, he was the president of a Registered Investment Advisor, a broker/dealer, and a technology company. Prior to these responsibilities, he was a vice president with a global asset consulting firm and a U.S. money management firm. He also spent nine years in the technology industry working for two Fortune 500 companies in various management capacities. Mr. Waymire is currently the president of Paladin Investor Resources, LLC, which has two operating companies: PaladinInvestors.com and Paladin Research Associates.

Mr. Waymire has worked with numerous personal financial advisors, individual investors, and institutional investors. In the 1980s he built what was then one of the largest money management, distribution companies in the industry. In the 1990s, he built a diversified financial services company with several hundred independent advisors. In the late 1990s and early 2000s, Mr. Waymire helped develop an industry-leading fee-based financial service delivery system on the Internet that is used by some of the largest financial institutions in the world.

He is the author of "Who's Watching Your Money? The 17 Paladin Principles for Selecting a Financial Advisor." He also provides content for, *PaladinPrinciples.com*, a website that offers investment and retirement education services and helps investors find, evaluate, select, and monitor competent, trustworthy advisors. Mr. Waymire is also active with Paladin Research Associates, which provides a broad range of consulting services to financial institution in need of integrated wealth management platforms.

Mr. Waymire earned a Certified Financial Planner (CFP) designation and has held Series 24, 65, 63, and 7 licenses. Mr. Waymire received a BA degree in Economics from California State University, Sacramento, and an MBA from Pepperdine University.

AUTHOR BIOGRAPHIES

Winks, Stephen C.
Chairman
Portfolio Construction Technologies
Publisher
Senior Consultant (e-letter)

As chairman of PCT, a company that pioneered the first Internet-based, comprehensive investment process technology tied to a virtual real-time balance sheet and income statement, and publisher of *Senior Consultant,* Stephen C. Winks also is co-founder of The Society of Senior Consultants. *Senior Consultant,* a publication with circulation that includes top-tier senior consultants who advise 25% of all U.S. assets. Mr. Winks is recognized as a leading proponent of the "high-level, comprehensive advice business model" that is shifting the way financial services firms conduct business.

Additional positions Mr. Winks has held include: national product manager with Prudential Securities Consulting Services, where he managed both the retail and institutional investment management consulting initiatives, more than doubling assets under advisement, making it the fastest growing; consultant, Private Capital Markets Group, PaineWebber; senior vice president, National Accounts, Johnstown Capital; president of FSC Advisory, Financial Services Corporation, where he worked with John Bell Keeble, the Father of Financial Planning, and managed the largest nationwide financial planning initiative in the United States. Mr. Winks also served as senior vice president for Financial Services Group, Wheat First Securities, where he built and managed most of the firm's major product areas.

Mr. Winks speaks regularly at industry conferences and regional meetings. He holds a BS degree in Economics from the University of Richmond and is a graduate of the Securities Industry Institute at the Wharton School-University of Pennsylvania.

MONEY MANAGEMENT FIRM PROFILES

AIM Private Asset Management
11 Greenway Plaza, Ste. 100; Houston, TX 77046
Tel: 800.349.0953
Website: http://www.aiminvestment.com

AIM Private Asset Management[SM], a subsidiary of A I M Capital Management, Inc. and part of AIM Investments[SM], offers privately managed investment services to individuals and institutions with considerable assets and fiduciaries responsible for the management of significant wealth. We build individual portfolios by employing time-tested investment strategies that are designed to offset the uncertainties of the market and to produce superior long-term results.

AIM Investments[SM] has managed our clients' money through all kinds of markets. With years of strategic planning and disciplined growth, AIM is one of the nation's top money managers. And as part of the $345 billion (as of Sept. 30, 2003) AMVESCAP Group—one of the world's largest independent investment managers—AIM has become a global presence. AIM is dedicated to building solutions for our clients with exceptional products and services.

Team Management

Investment decisions are made by teams of managers who collectively contribute ideas and help ensure management continuity. Our investment managers are supported by more than 500 investment professionals and local analysts in all major markets. We seek independent thought, both from our own analysts and investment managers, and from trusted Wall Street sources. This team system helps ensure a consistent and continuous management style that has stood the test of time.

Investment Research

Rigorous accounting analysis is at the forefront of our investment research efforts. We employ both internal and external accounting experts and proprietary tools to screen our portfolios for high-risk situations and to look for investment opportunities. By going beyond the reported bottom-line numbers, we strive to understand where a company's growth is coming from and how sustainable it may be. Our discipline takes us through an in-depth examination of financial statements and industry conditions, combined with an evaluation of management's style and strategy. In addition to strong financial fundamentals and attractively priced securities, our investment managers look for companies with experienced and credible management teams. Sometimes this means not accepting the consensus view of a particular company.

Quantitative Expertise

AIM's team of quantitative analysts plays a large role in portfolio construction and performance monitoring. Our state-of-the-art proprietary tools include the means to optimize a portfolio's construction, which includes managing and monitoring risk, analyzing performance and conducting hypothetical trading scenarios to see how they would affect the overall portfolio. These tools offer our investment teams a more acute awareness of how their portfolios stack up against their benchmarks and their peers.

Attribution tools allow us to monitor relative sector and industry weightings, individual security weightings and correlations across different holdings.

AIM's Complementary Investment Strategies

At AIM, we believe different investors deserve different solutions. That's why we manage equity portfolios that follow complementary investment strategies to help investors build a diverse portfolio—growth, value and a blend of growth and value (blend/core). These strategies have been tested over the years through all kinds of markets by our teams of professionals.

AIM's Privately Managed Portfolios

Intrinsic Value: This portfolio is a classic "Graham and Dodd" value portfolio and the team considers three factors before making an investment: (1) calculation of intrinsic value, (2) determination of quality of the business, and (3) current stock price. The management team is looking for quality companies with attractive long-term outlooks that are temporarily selling at a discount to the calculated intrinsic value. Additionally, the management team is looking to buy good companies at great prices that have at least a 50 percent appreciation potential based on a two to three year holding period.

Mid Cap Core: This portfolio seeks long-term capital growth by investing in medium-sized U.S. companies at attractive valuation levels and may serve as a reliable asset-allocation tool. This portfolio employs AIM's Growth at a Reasonable Price (GARP) discipline to find stocks that are undervalued relative to their future growth prospects. The portfolio seeks early but tangible evidence of a catalyst that may cause earnings or cash flow to increase, earning potentially higher valuation multiples. Further, the management team is looking for companies that offer 50 percent upside potential over an 18-month period.

International ADR Growth: The portfolio pursues long-term growth of capital by translating AIM's earnings-driven approach for domestic stock selection to overseas markets. This is a large-cap international portfolio that seeks companies with strong earnings growth, has limited emerging-markets exposure and offers diversification for investors with mostly U.S. holdings.

Large Cap Growth: The portfolio uses a bottom-up approach for picking stocks, and seeks long-term capital growth by investing in companies in the top 50 percent of the Russell 1000 Growth Index. The portfolio invests, using an earnings momentum discipline, to identify companies believed to have the potential for above average growth in revenues and earnings. The investment process utilizes both quantitative and qualitative measures. Several factors influence the buy decision, such as: quality of earnings, sustainability of growth, quality of management, and the company's products and competitive landscape.

All Cap Growth: The portfolio uses a bottom-up, earnings-focused approach to stock selection based on our belief that earnings are the best indicator of a company's financial strength. By striking a balance between stocks experiencing earnings growth and those displaying consistency in earnings, we expect the portfolio to participate in a growth market, while providing more moderate performance during market downturns. We analyze companies based on a number of factors, including earnings and revenue growth, analysts' estimate revisions, earnings stability and sustainability, dividend growth and perceived quality of management. We also use proprietary models for both earnings-momentum and core growth stocks that help us assess attractiveness of a portfolio holding relative to other stocks in the universe.

Small/ Mid Cap Growth: This portfolio utilizes AIM's classic earnings-momentum investment strategy and seeks to provide aggressive capital growth by investing in small and mid-sized companies that management believes will have earnings growth well in excess of the general economy. Additionally, the management team looks for companies with new or innovative products, services or processes that are poised to exceed expectations.

MONEY MANAGEMENT FIRM PROFILES

BlackRock®, Inc.
Contact: W. Michael Hogan, Director
40 East 52nd Street; New York, NY 10022
Tel: 212.754.5300 / 888.825.2257
http://www.blackrock.com

BlackRock is a premier provider of global investment management and risk management products. We offer fixed income, liquidity, equity, alternative investment, and risk management products to clients worldwide. As of June 20, 2003, BlackRock's assets under management totaled $286 billion across various investment strategies. BlackRock is also a significant provider of risk management and advisory services that combine our capital markets expertise with our proprietarily-developed risk management systems and technology. As of June 30, 2003, BlackRock provided risk management services to portfolios with aggregate assets of $2.3 trillion.

Since its inception in 1988, BlackRock has grown from a boutique investment management firm to an established investment manager and a premier provider of risk management services. As a result of BlackRock's initial public offering of common stock in 1999, BlackRock employees and the public own approximately 31 percent of the firm.

The PNC Financial Services Group retains a 69 percent stake. BlackRock is committed to broadening equity ownership by employees and has instituted several programs, including deferred compensation, options grants, a 401(k) company match, and an employee stock purchase plan.

Headquartered in New York City, BlackRock maintains offices in Boston, Edinburgh, Hong Kong, San Francisco, Tokyo and Wilmington.

An Inside View

BlackRock's day-to-day operations are independently managed by its Management Committee, whose members include all founding partners and represent all operating areas of the firm. We enjoy a high level of stability among our senior professionals and continue to attract additional talented professionals to our team.

BlackRock has always focused on a cross-disciplinary team approach in which clients benefit from the pooled expertise of the firm's resources: our investment and risk management professionals and our proprietarily-developed analytical tools, in addition to excellent performance. BlackRock is committed to delivering a high level of client service that is tailored to the needs of each client. BlackRock's global client base includes corporate, public and Taft-Hartley plan sponsors, insurance and healthcare companies, hospitals, endowments and foundations, corporate and public treasurers, nuclear decommissioning trusts, non-U.S. institutions, defined benefit and defined contribution plans, high net worth individuals and investors in our mutual funds.

In addition to our asset management activities, through our BlackRock Solutions® we offer risk management services and enterprise investment system outsourcing to a broad base of institutional clients. We combine our expertise and analytics, systems, and capital markets with our knowledge of regulatory, accounting, and tax issues to meet unique client objectives. BlackRock Solutions services are an outgrowth of our long-standing investment in sophisticated, integrated systems to support risk management and investment approaches.

A Team of Experts

At BlackRock, we believe that experienced investment professionals using a disciplined investment process and sophisticated analytical tools will consistently add value to client portfolios. Accordingly, BlackRock has assembled a team of professionals with expertise in all areas of global fixed income and equity markets and, over the years, has continued to make significant investments in technology and analytics. By continually updating our analytics and systems, we are able to better quantify and evaluate the risk of each investment decision. We believe that our risk management process is unique in the investment management community, and we know of no other firm with such comprehensive capabilities in terms of technology and professional resources.

As of June 30, 2003, BlackRock employed 801 professionals whose disciplines include portfolio management, risk management, business development and client service, technology, operations and administration. Given BlackRock's focus on risk management to achieve our performance goals, our team of BlackRock Solutions risk management professionals is dedicated to developing and continually enhancing proprietarily-developed analytical tools.

BlackRock maintains a senior-level commitment to client service that fosters dynamic client relationships and enables us to assist clients with all aspects of their needs so that we can proactively develop a variety of suitable strategies to address them. As a result, more than 250 BlackRock clients have entrusted the firm with multiple assignments across and within asset classes.

Our commitment to client service extends to a high level of communication and reporting capabilities. We provide clients with password-protected access to portfolio reports and analytics via BlackRock's web site. Clients also receive a variety of BlackRock publications. More than 400 clients avail themselves of this opportunity, and some choose to receive their monthly or quarterly client reports via the Internet.

❖ ❖ ❖

MONEY MANAGEMENT FIRM PROFILES

Brandes Investment Partners, LLC
Contact: Brandes Private Client Services
11988 El Camino Real, Ste 500; San Diego, CA 92130
Tel: 858.755.0239 / 800.237.7119 ext 3502
http://www.brandes.com   Email: info@brandes.com

Brandes Investment Partners is an independent investment advisory firm and recognized leader in value equity management. Applying a "Graham & Dodd" value-oriented approach to global markets since our founding in 1974, we manage a broad range of private and institutional clients worldwide, including:

- Employee Benefit Plans
- Corporations
- Foundations
- Taft-Hartley Plans
- Endowments

As of September 30, 2003, assets under management totaled approximately US$63 billion.

As an independently owned firm committed to investment management, Brandes Investment Partners is focused on meeting our clients' objectives. To honor client mandates and complement other asset classes and investment styles, we adhere to our disciplined process. We believe the consistent application of our philosophy has rewarded patient, long-term investors with favorable results and reduced risk.

As a bottom-up, value-oriented, global equity manager, Brandes Investment Partners believes that buying businesses at a discount to their true value produces superior long-term results. Because we view a stock as a small piece of a business that is for sale, we focus on the fundamental characteristics of a company in order to develop an estimate of its intrinsic value.

We carefully evaluate the price we pay for the business. We analyze long-term rates of return, cash flows, balance sheet strength, management, asset values, and liquidation values. We also often look at private market transactions to determine intrinsic value. We look for a business with an attractive margin of safety – one selling at a price below our estimate of its underlying value.

Market Approach

Because of the volatile nature of global equity markets – where sentiment can shift rapidly between sweeping optimism and overwhelming uncertainty—prices of stocks tend to fluctuate much more than the intrinsic value of the companies they represent. We believe that a stock's price and its fair value often detach from one another in the short term. By choosing stocks that are selling at a significant discount to our estimates of their intrinsic business values, we seek to establish a margin of safety and an opportunity for superior performance with below-average risk. This combination of rational fundamental analysis with the discipline to take advantage of market price irrationality helps us to find securities which offer superior long-term potential. Brandes Investment Partners seeks to add value to the investment process through our willingness to take a long-term approach to a relatively concentrated portfolio of what we believe to be our best ideas.

We apply our investment philosophy consistently in all market conditions and in stock markets around the globe. Since our inception nearly 30 years ago, our investment process has remained consistent, personnel turnover has been low, and our investment approach has been sufficiently different so that we have tended to add return and diversification benefits over the long term when our portfolios are integrated with those of other managers.

Today, we offer a variety of value-oriented portfolios designed to meet the diverse needs of long-term investors.

Investment Vehicles:

- Separate Accounts
- Pooled Trusts
- Mutual Funds

Portfolio Styles:

- U.S. Value Equity
- U.S. Small Cap Value Equity
- U.S. Mid Cap Value Equity
- U.S. Balanced
- Emerging Markets Equity
- European Equity
- Global Small Cap Equity
- Global Mid Cap Equity
- International (non-U.S.) Small Cap Equity
- International (non-U.S.) Mid Cap Equity

Portfolio Styles Closed to New Clients:

- International (non-U.S.) Equity
- Global Equity
- Global Balanced

Brandes closed its International Equity strategy to new clients effective September 30, 1998. Effective November 30, 2001, Brandes Investment Partners closed both its Global Balanced and Global Equity strategies to new client relationships in North America. As of June 30, 2002, Brandes limited any additional client funding in the International Equity, Global Equity, and Global Balanced strategies.

The primary reason for closing these strategies was to give top priority to the interests of existing clients. We experienced significant growth in assets in these areas and, to maintain our ability to provide competitive returns and superior service, we believe that it was prudent to close well in advance of any potential capacity constraints.

Headquartered in San Diego with an office in Milwaukee, Brandes Investment Partners has non-U.S. affiliate companies in Toronto and Geneva and employs more than 475 employees worldwide. With every portfolio we manage, our objective remains constant – to exploit the difference between a company's current intrinsic worth and the security's price in the market.

❖❖❖

Brandes Investment Partners® is a registered trademark in the United States.

Eaton Vance
Larry Sinsimer, VP & Director of Managed Accounts
255 State Street; Boston, MA 02109
Tel: 877.207.8703 / 617.598.8822
http://www.eatonvance.com   Email: lsinsimer@eatonvance.com

Eaton Vance is one of the oldest financial services firms in the United States, with a history dating to 1924. Reflecting the traditional values of its home in Boston, Massachusetts, Eaton Vance established its reputation as an investment manager for wealthy individuals by offering a conservative approach to managing money and an uncompromising commitment to integrity and quality.

Having earned the confidence and trust of investors for more than seven decades, Eaton Vance holds a prominent place in the financial services industry at the beginning of the 21st century. Today, Eaton Vance offers innovative, comprehensive wealth management solutions that seek to deliver consistent performance, guided by our proven investment principles and our experience in both up and down markets. This compelling combination of tradition, experience, innovation, and performance has helped make Eaton Vance the investment manager of choice for many of today's individual and institutional investors.

The Disciplined Pursuit of Consistent Performance

Throughout its history, Eaton Vance has followed accepted, time-tested principles of investing that emphasize avoidance of unnecessary risk and the pursuit of consistent, long-term returns.

A Research-Driven Investment Process

Proprietary, hands-on fundamental research is the basis of our approach to security selection. We construct fixed-income and equity portfolios one security at a time, after intensive analysis of risk/reward characteristics and potential for long-term performance.

A Focus on Risk Management

Eaton Vance believes that effective risk management is key to strong investment performance. We seek to manage risk through rigorous research and analysis, by building highly diversified portfolios, and by adhering to our established investment disciplines.

Tax-Advantaged Treatment

Eaton Vance has been the leader in tax-managed funds, providing the investor the opportunity to invest in most asset classes with the goal of achieving superior after-tax returns. On the separate accounts side, Parametric Portfolio Associates has become the recognized leader in providing after-tax rates of return not only for their index enhanced portfolios, but also working in conjunction with investors and other asset managers. Many high net-worth individuals utilize Parametric in a core/satellite arrangement. Parametric, as the core manager, harvests losses to offset the gains generated by the satellite managers. These managers are usually in the international or small-cap sectors. In addition, Parametric is often coupled with hedge funds. Hedge funds historically generate short-term gains and Parametric can harvest short-term losses to offset those gains allowing the investor the benefit on an after-tax basis. Parametric also has the capability to make sure that qualifying dividends do, in fact, qualify for favorable tax treatment.

A Disciplined, Long-Term Perspective

We seek to deliver long-term returns for our investors by following a quality-oriented, buy-and-hold investment philosophy. Valuations and buy/sell decisions are governed by equity and fixed-income disciplines that encourage patience with successful investments and ensure diligence in pruning underperforming securities when necessary.

The Value of Experience

We rely on the individual and collective strengths of our seasoned portfolio managers and analysts. With an average of more than 15 years' experience in financial services, our staff of more than 70 investment management professionals is one of the most highly qualified in the industry.

Today, Eaton Vance provides core investment products and services, as well as specialized asset management for wealthy individuals and a variety of institutional investors, through the Eaton Vance Asset Management Companies: Eaton Vance Management, Atlanta Capital Management Company, LLC, Fox Asset Management, LLC, and Parametric Portfolio Associates.

As the global marketplace continues to grow in size and complexity, it gives rise to many exciting new opportunities for investors – along with new risks. Yet, in the midst of increasingly rapid change, the fundamental principles of sound money management have remained constant.

Eaton Vance has grown with the marketplace, adding value for our clients with our proven approach which incorporates extensive research, risk management and broad diversification, using a disciplined long-term perspective, yet remaining flexible and innovative in developing new products and services. In the new century, investors can turn to Eaton Vance with the confidence that our long history of experience, professionalism and performance are a solid foundation for the future.

❖ ❖ ❖

MONEY MANAGEMENT FIRM PROFILES

ING Investment Management
230 Park Avenue; New York, NY 10169
Tel: 800.640.3334
http://www.inginvestment.com   Email: clientservicenyc@inginvestment.com

ING Investment Management Americas comprises over 900 staff and approximately 350 investment professionals. We manage over $167 billion, with investment operations located in New York, Atlanta, Hartford, Minneapolis, Scottsdale, Canada and Latin America. Our clients include a diverse group of institutional clients, including corporate, public, and Taft-Hartley pension funds, endowments and foundations, healthcare organizations, insurance companies, mutual funds, and insurance and financial services companies from within our parent company, ING Group.

ING Investment Management Americas focuses on four business segments:

- ING Institutional investments– Investment management for institutional clients and mutual funds, primarily serving the defined benefit and defined contribution markets.

- ING Managed accounts – Investment management for institutional, high net worth and retail clients through sub-advisory of managed accounts at ING's financial intermediary partners and affiliates.

- ING Alternative assets –Investment management in alternative asset classes for institutions and high net worth individuals, including fund of hedge funds, private equity, real estate, single strategy hedge funds and structured fixed income products.

- Insurance Company assets – Investment management services for the proprietary assets of ING insurance companies.

The ING Managed Account Group provides financial advisors with a convenient, single source for access to ING products and services, especially the powerful lineup of separately managed account offerings from:

- Aeltus Investment Management
- Baring Asset Management
- Furman Selz Capital Management
- ING Advisors
- ING Investment Management
- ING Ghent Asset Management

When choosing a portfolio management team, exceptional customer service is as important as superior investment results. To help financial advisors build their business, we deploy regional client service teams for faster, personal support. We provide private client and institutional meetings, new business presentations, portfolio reviews and value-added training, as well as timely investment insights that can benefit advisors and their clients.

❖❖❖

MONEY MANAGEMENT FIRM PROFILES

Madison Investment Advisors
Contact: Mark Knipfer, Mktg Assoc
550 Science Drive; Madison, WI 53711
Tel: 608.274.0300
http://www.madisonadv.com

Madison Investment Advisors, Inc. was founded in December of 1973 as an employee-owned, independent investment management organization, and we remain completely independent. As of the end of 2003, Madison and its subsidiaries managed approximately $9 billion in both equity and fixed income assets for a variety of clients nationwide and abroad. Our main office is located in Madison, Wisconsin. Our subsidiaries include Madison Scottsdale, LLC, which specializes in managing the assets of insurance companies, Concord Asset Management located in Chicago, Illinois, and Madison Mosaic, LLC, serving as investment advisor to our Mosaic Funds family of no-load mutual funds.

Large-Cap and Mid-Cap Core Equity

We are bottom-up stock-pickers, focused on high-quality, consistent growth companies trading at reasonable valuations. Our goal is to beat the market over a market cycle by fully participating in up markets, while protecting principal in difficult markets. We strive to remain both objective and unemotional in our decision-making process through independent thinking.

We follow a rigorous three-step process when evaluating companies. We consider the business model, the management team and the valuation of each potential investment. When evaluating the business model we look for a sustainable, competitive advantage, cash flow that is both predictable and growing, as well as a rock-solid balance sheet. When assessing management we look to see how they have allocated capital in the past, their track record for enhancing shareholder value and the nature of their accounting practices. The final step in the process is assessing the proper valuation for the company. We strive to purchase securities trading at a discount to their intrinsic value as determined by discounted cash flows. We corroborate this valuation work with additional valuation methodologies. Often we find companies that clear the first or second hurdle, but not the third. Those companies are monitored for inclusion at a later date when the valuation is more appropriate.

Part of the overall valuation methodology is to establish an upside and downside target for each candidate. Typically, Madison will only invest in a stock with (1) triple the expected upside versus downside, and (2) at least a 25 percent return upside potential over the 12 months following purchase. This allows us to avoid the volatility associated with high growth/high multiple equities while still investing in high-quality growth companies. In the end, clients end up with a portfolio of high-quality growth companies with very attractive upside return potential and limited downside risk. This risk-reward ratio is the key element in our stock selection process.

Buy Discipline

The analyst prepares a buy report (which includes a one-page "thesis" summary outlining the key investment considerations for the stock) and then distributes it to the other members of the investment team. Upon review by the other members, the analyst must then verbally present the idea to the team at which time full debate on the stock takes place. After considering the input of all the team members, the lead portfolio manager will make the final decision. Incorporated in the thesis report is a confidence rating that is assigned by the lead portfolio manager and the analyst. Generally speaking, the higher the confidence level, the larger the position size in the portfolio.

Sell Discipline

There are three possible "events" that could trigger the selling of a security from our portfolios: (1) price target is achieved; (2) breakdown in fundamentals threatens the original investment thesis; or (3) a more attractive alternative is found to replace it. "Could" is important here because we do not employ any strict rules that say we must sell when any of the above events take place. However, the "events" demand action on the part of the analyst. The key to our sell discipline is that each "event" will always merit a re-evaluation of the investment by the team. The confidence rating has an impact on the sell discipline such that the lower the rating, the more likely we are to sell a security after a re-evaluation.

Portfolio Construction

The number of holdings will range from 25 to 35. The portfolio's weighting in any one economic sector shall not exceed double the weighting of that sector within the benchmark, at the time of purchase. The portfolio's weighting for any one industry shall not exceed 25 percent of the total market value of the portfolio at the time of purchase. We do not typically purchase any company with a market capitalization below $1 billion in market cap.

Equity Management Team

Jay Sekelsky is the lead equity portfolio manager and was responsible for the development of the core equity product. Portfolio manager Rich Eisinger has lead responsibilities for mid-cap portfolios, while Dave Halford, Haruki Toyama and Matt Hayner also play key roles in the management of Madison's equity portfolios.

❖❖❖

MONEY MANAGEMENT FIRM PROFILES

Mariner Investment Group, Inc.
Contact: Grey Perkins
780 Third Avenue, 16th Fl; New York, NY 10017
Tel: 212.758.6200

Mariner Investment Group, Inc., is an alternative asset management firm with over $3.5 billion in assets under management across multiple affiliated single strategy hedge funds, multi-strategy hedge funds, fund of hedge funds, and other alternative investments. Mariner was founded in 1992 and has a 10-year track record of consistently producing attractive risk-adjusted returns while preserving capital.

Mariner's senior investment professionals average 23 years' experience, mostly in Wall Street proprietary trading operations and risk management. Bill Michaelcheck, Mariner's founder, was a senior investment professional at the World Bank and then head of fixed income proprietary trading and risk management at Bear Stearns prior to Mariner. Other Mariner principals also have extensive experience in heading proprietary trading and risk management operations at major Wall Street firms, including Bear Stearns, Goldman Sachs, UBS, CSFB, and Deutsche Bank.

Mariner has 75 employees located in New York City, White Plains, Boston, and Tokyo. Mariner is 100 percent employee owned and the principals and employees have more than $100 million of their personal capital invested in Mariner affiliated funds. Mariner's global clients include insurance and re-insurance companies, plan sponsors, endowments, foundations, wealthy families, and professional money managers. Mariner was one of the managers originally selected by S&P to be included in the S&P Hedge Fund Index.

Investment Philosophy

Mariner's goal is to consistently produce attractive risk-adjusted returns with low volatility, preservation of capital, and no correlation to major market indices. To achieve this goal, Mariner seeks to avoid taking unnecessary directional risks and concentrates its efforts on investing in niche, arbitrage strategies. Mariner also seeks on an opportunistic basis to allocate to oversold markets, which are often the result of market dislocations.

The firm believes that to be successful, a hedge fund manager must fully understand the risks inherent in their strategy. In particular, Mariner seeks to identify and avoid managers that employ "short volatility" strategies. Short volatility strategies expose investors to the undue risk of large capital losses from low probability events. Since capital preservation is an objective for all Mariner funds, the firm seeks to avoid short volatility portfolios.

Risk Management

Mariner has a dedicated risk management and asset allocation team that conducts risk management on a daily basis with a fundamental understanding of trading, markets, and the strategies employed. The senior investment professionals in risk management and asset allocation have first-hand experience allocating proprietary capital in a variety of arbitrage strategies throughout the different phases of market and business cycles. In addition to looking at historical performance statistics and attribution, we proactively manage risk in the same manner that a proprietary trading desk would, which is to view portfolio positions in real time as market events are unfolding. The firm believes that there is no substitute for good qualitative judgment when evaluating position level information.

Talent

Mariner believes that it has an edge in attracting top-quality proprietary trading talent to manage our hedge funds. Mariner prefers proprietary traders (those who employ a firm's internal capital rather than third party investor money) because they often have experience using a variety of security types such as bonds, equities, futures, swaps, and other derivatives as well as experience shorting and using leverage. Mariner has been structured to attract and retain these professionals and has been doing so for 11 years.

Mariner's fund of hedge fund portfolios have traditionally been constructed with an emphasis on smaller-sized hedge fund managers. Mariner believes that there is significant alpha in smaller-sized, niche hedge fund managers. Smaller-sized managers can be more agile in difficult markets, have smaller short positions to keep outstanding, and often operate in strategies with limited capacity. If the risks of small fund investing are efficiently managed, the return potential and access to information is often greater than with managers of larger funds.

❖ ❖ ❖

MONEY MANAGEMENT FIRM PROFILES

Nuveen Investments, Inc.
Contact: Alan Brown, Chief Mktg Officer
333 West Wacker; Chicago, IL 60606
Tel: 312.917.7700
http://www.nuveen.com

Nuveen Investments is a premier investment management company that provides a range of high-quality services to help build well-diversified, core investment portfolios. With more than $90 billion in assets under management, the firm serves financial advisors and their high net worth clients, as well as a growing number of institutional clients.

Nuveen Investments markets its capabilities under four distinct brands: Nuveen, a leader in tax-free investments; NWQ, a leader in value-style equities; Rittenhouse, a leader in conservative growth-style equities; and Symphony, a leading institutional manager of market-neutral alternative investments.

Every day, from locations coast to coast, Nuveen Investments helps individuals and institutions pursue their financial goals. The firm's distinctive areas of expertise and unified investment philosophy are aimed at delivering "smarter ways to be conservative" that reflect a long-term view and balanced approach to constructing quality portfolios.

Nuveen Investments believes in the power of diversification. Together, the family of Nuveen Investments brands offers investors a wide range of investment styles and products, covering the spectrum of risk and reward. By offering investors choice, all within a conservative commitment to long-term performance, the firm can create diversified portfolios that reflect each investor's financial objectives and risk tolerance.

Fixed Income Investing

As a leading municipal bond manager, Nuveen seeks to meet an investor's need for both relatively low risk and attractive after-tax returns. Nuveen actively manages portfolios with the goal of generating consistent income over time.

Alternative Investing

Symphony pursues investment strategies designed to reduce or eliminate market-related risks. Toward this end, Symphony uses research and quantitative analysis of earnings quality, industry trends, trading characteristics and other market-neutral investing techniques.

Value Investing

NWQ seeks to capitalize on the appreciation potential of companies whose stock is undervalued and poised for positive change. NWQ managers and analysts look for catalysts such as new management, improving fundamentals, renewed focus, industry consolidation or company restructuring.

Growth Investing

Rittenhouse focuses on blue-chip companies with large market capitalizations, industry leadership and the potential to deliver consistent and predictable earnings growth over time. Rittenhouse identifies those with strong fundamentals that it believes are likely to increase their earnings and appreciate in value.

Founded in 1898 in Chicago, Nuveen Investments is a longtime champion of conservative investing and remains committed to helping financial advisors and their clients succeed by following three guiding principles: investment discipline, service excellence and continuous innovation.

The company's disciplined approach to investing begins with a perspective both broad and deep. Nuveen Investments combines time-tested investment specialization, extensive industry knowledge and active risk management to find investment opportunities that will be productive and promising over time. The firm integrates some of the industry's best thinking and resources while pursuing balanced diversification for individual and institutional investors.

Nuveen Investments adds value to the investing process through expert research, personalized service and comprehensive wealth management solutions. The company excels through one-to-one relationships with advisors and their clients and its customer-focused service approach.

Products are developed purposefully to give advisors and investors choice and flexibility in creating quality investment portfolios that can match each client's financial goals and risk tolerance. Through product innovation, the firm strives to offer advisors and their clients investment solutions that help provide an optimal return on their investments over time.

Over the years, dedication to these guiding principles has enabled Nuveen Investments to flourish and develop strong relationships with business partners and customers who have placed great trust in the quality and consistency of the firm's services.

Nuveen Investments now enjoys a market leadership position in the fast-growing area of separately managed accounts. Within this market the firm has won recognition for managing customized portfolios of large-cap growth stocks, multi-cap value equities and both taxable and tax-free fixed-income investments.

Nuveen Investments also leads the market in sponsoring closed-end exchange-traded funds, with 106 actively managed portfolios trading like stocks on the New York Stock Exchange or the American Stock Exchange. In an example of continuous innovation, the firm has recently broadened these closed-end ETF offerings from municipals to senior loans, real estate, preferred securities and convertible securities.

In the future, Nuveen Investments will continue to build on its reputation for quality and pursue its mission to help people grow and preserve their wealth in order to achieve their life goals – today and tomorrow.

❖ ❖ ❖

Benchmarks Used Include: Lehman Brothers 7-year Muni, Government Credit; Russell 1000 Value, Mid Cap Value, 1500 Value; MSCI EAFE; S&P 500.

Rorer Asset Management, LLC
Contact: Frank M. Natale, Principal, Senior VP
One Liberty Place, Ste 5100; Philadelphia, PA 19103
Tel: 800.544.6737 / ContactUs@rorerasset.com
Website: http://www.rorerasset.com

Rorer Asset Management, LLC (Rorer) is a Philadelphia-based firm specializing in portfolio management for equity, balanced, and fixed income accounts. The firm was founded in 1978 by Edward C. "Ted" Rorer and is an affiliate of the Affiliated Managers Group, Inc. (AMG).

In 1984, after 14 years of direct investment experience, Ted Rorer developed a highly disciplined approach to managing assets, emphasizing reduced risk and preservation of capital. The investment methodology employs strong buy and sell disciplines designed to remove as much emotion as possible from the investment decision process. Rorer uses a team approach to portfolio management, which maximizes our focus on the investment process.

Philosophy

The cornerstone of the investment philosophy at Rorer is to buy high quality, but currently "out of favor" securities with strong investment fundamentals that are positioned for growth. The firm has found that this approach reduces risk, while providing excellent risk-adjusted returns throughout the investment cycle.

Process

The Rorer approach to investing utilizes the concept of relative value. Stock selection starts with a universe of companies which are subjected to a rigorous quantitative screening process designed to filter out potential purchase candidates based on two factors: attractive relative valuation and earnings momentum. The valuation methodology identifies companies trading below historic norms relative to the market. The earnings momentum measure identifies companies that are experiencing upward earnings estimate revisions and have the best potential to provide positive earnings surprises.

Fundamental and economic analysis is performed on companies that meet the valuation, earnings momentum, and portfolio guidelines. Our fundamental analysis is extensive in scope and rigorous in its discipline. The due diligence process includes discussions with corporate management, interviews with Wall Street analysts, and a thorough review of fundamental data. Fundamental analysis, including interest rate and business cycle analysis, is always considered as a whole before the time of purchase. The research methodology is differentiated by the unique emphasis placed on quantitative research combined with qualitative research in the security selection process.

The Rorer sell process is highly disciplined, and designed to eliminate the emotion often associated with the decision of whether or not to sell a particular stock. The sell process seeks to realize substantial profits after they have been earned or, conversely, to conserve capital when circumstances so dictate. Specifically, an upside price objective is established at the time of purchase, and set at a level that the stock is reasonably expected to achieve over an 18 to 24 month period. Alternatively, a stock will be sold if its fundamentals deteriorate or if the holding exceeds our individual position, industry, or sector guidelines. Finally, a relative stop-loss provision forces the sale of any security that underperforms the portfolio's benchmark by a specified margin. Together, these disciplines form a solid investment process with the objective of recognizing and controlling risk.

Balanced

Our Balanced portfolio seeks to further reduce risk by investing a portion of the portfolio in bonds, with the remainder invested in equity securities using Rorer's disciplined investment process. For those clients that desire more or less exposure to the equity markets, the asset allocation percentages can be customized to suit an investor's specific needs.

Fixed Income

Bonds are utilized to reduce volatility and provide a consistent stream of income. We invest in intermediate term fixed income securities with an average maturity of four to five years. Our approach to fixed income management is highly disciplined. Factors that we evaluate include duration, yield curve placement, industry sector weightings, and investment quality. We invest in only high quality, "investment grade" bonds, which include government, Treasury, and Agency securities as well as high quality corporate bonds.

Team

Rorer uses a team approach to arrive at buy/sell decisions for the portfolio, and manages all portfolios based on a model. The result of this collective effort is seen when decisions are made to purchase or sell a stock, since decisions are uniformly applied to all accounts at the same time. This eliminates individual discretion by portfolio managers, which, over time, could result in a dissimilar portfolio structure and account performance. All Rorer portfolios receive the benefit of our investment process. Rorer's Investment Policy Committee, which includes our chief investment officer, director of research and equity analysts, establishes investment policy and strategy and makes the stock selection and sell decisions.

Our relative value investment approach has added measurable value by producing returns above the benchmark indices with lower performance volatility. We have achieved excellent risk- adjusted returns across investment cycles by implementing a clear investment process that incorporates highly focused stock selection parameters and rigid sell disciplines. By strictly following this approach, we have provided our clients with attractive performance results with controlled risk and downside protection.

❖❖❖

Roxbury Capital Management, LLC

Contact: Jon R. Foust, Dir of Mktg, Client Services
100 Wilshire Blvd, Ste 1000; Santa Monica, CA 90401
Tel: 800.227.6681
Website: http://www.roxcap.com

Roxbury Capital Management, LLC, was founded in 1986 to provide equity and fixed income management to a variety of clients, including public funds, corporations, endowments, foundations, Taft-Hartley plans, and individuals. As of December 31, 2003, assets under management totaled $3.2 billion.

Headquartered in Santa Monica, California, Roxbury manages client relationships from our offices in Boston, Chicago, Houston, Minneapolis; the small cap growth equity portfolio is managed from our Portland, Oregon, office.

Roxbury is majority owned by its employees. The firm has 17 investment professionals, 14 equity professionals and three fixed income professionals, with over 185 years of combined experience.

Our investment philosophy and process are applied consistently to all of our investment strategies, which include:

- Large Cap Growth Equity
- Socially Responsible Equity
- Small to Mid Cap Equity
- Balanced
- Focus Equity
- Science & Technology
- Small Cap Growth Equity
- Fixed Income

Roxbury's philosophy is to invest in high quality, sustainable growth stocks. We emphasize quality to provide a greater margin of safety and stability in our portfolios. Superior earnings growth ultimately translates into superior compounding of returns. Additionally, several proprietary tools are used to determine what we believe are fair valuations. Over time, we believe these favorable characteristics will produce superior returns with less risk than many growth stocks.

The objective of Roxbury's investment process is to combine people and process to facilitate optimal decision making and investment performance. There are four main components in the Roxbury process. They include Information, Insight, Implementation, and Oversight.

Information gathering is the primary role of our sector specific research analysts. Research is bottom-up and emphasizes company fundamentals. It is conducted in a two-stage process: basic research and advanced research. Analysts first conduct basic research on a potential stock by investigating the income statement, focusing on revenues, margins, and earnings per share. The financial strength of the company is also scrutinized by reviewing accounts receivable, inventories, debt, and the company's cash flow statement. The final stage of the analysts' basic research examines the industry size and growth as well as the company's return on invested capital (ROIC). We believe that EPS data can be misleading, and measuring cash returns on cash invested, or ROIC, tells a truer story of a company's financial viability.

Roxbury's advanced research looks at management execution, competitive position, business trends, and market expectations. We utilize both sell-side and buy-side contacts as well as meeting with company management to collect this information. Analysts also generate a discounted free cash flow analysis to determine the stock's price relative to history, industry, and the current market. This level of research allows our analysts to thoroughly understand the company and its industry.

Analysts and portfolio managers work together in the investment committee to provide *Insight* into the process of stock selection. Together they add perspective, context, and experience to the information gathered by the analysts.

The portfolio management team is ultimately responsible for *Implementing* the analyst recommendations by selecting investments for portfolios to balance both absolute and relative risk as well as return. Portfolio managers are also responsible for sell decisions. Stocks are sold if the original thesis is altered, i.e., fundamentals deteriorate, the company's competitive position is challenged, or ROIC declines; the stock approaches its price target; alternative investment ideas are identified; or the stock underperforms the market or its peer group.

The final stage of Roxbury's process is *Oversight*, which is a combined effort by both Roxbury executives as well as outside consultants. They monitor every strategy's compliance with our philosophy and process as well as suitability, dispersion, and portfolio performance.

For the last 17 years Roxbury's emphasis on investing in great businesses has been providing clients with the comfort and confidence to stay invested and benefit from the superior compounding power of stocks.

❖ ❖ ❖

This material is provided for informational and educational purposes only. The statements contained herein are the opinions of Roxbury Capital Management, LLC and are subject to change without notice.
This report contains no investment recommendations and should not be construed as specific tax, legal, financial planning, or investment advice. Clients should consult their professional advisors before making any tax or investment decisions. Investing entails risk including the loss of principal and there is no assurance that an investment will provide positive performance over any period of time. It is important to review investment objectives, risk tolerance, tax objectives, and liquidity needs before choosing an investment style or manager. Information was obtained from third party sources, which we believe to be reliable but not guaranteed. Past performance is no guarantee of future results.

MONEY MANAGEMENT FIRM PROFILES

Russell Investment Group
Contact: David Grieger, Mktg Director
909 A Street; Tacoma, WA
Tel: 253.596.3030
Website: http://www.russell.com

Russell Investment Group, global leaders in multi-manager investing, offers goal-oriented investors a full range of tailored solutions. Investors in 36 countries – from individuals to financial advisors to administrators of pension funds, foundations and endowments – look to Russell for their investment needs. Today they seek our advice on how to invest more than $1.6 trillion, and they have entrusted us with the management of $85 billion in assets.

Investors also draw on Russell's suite of stock market indexes to gain an objective measure of stock performance. In addition, many of the world's leading banks, brokerage firms, insurance firms and independent investment professionals turn to Russell to provide sophisticated investment programs for their clients.

Our success derives from several key aspects that distinguish Russell and set our investment programs and advice apart from those of other investment service companies.

Money Manager Research

From almost 3,500 money managers worldwide, our researchers select about 3.5 percent who meet our rigid standards to qualify as among the world's best. Our manager selection process uses highly sophisticated tools and is one of the most intensive and highly developed of any financial services company anywhere.

By using a number of managers for one fund, we intend to balance risk and investment style. Our team of specialists monitors the managers' investment processes and performance, researches capital markets, and handles administration of the funds.

Russell is a pioneer in this concept, known as multi-manager investing, which the company has implemented for more than three decades. Today it is a cornerstone of our fund operations.

Strategies for Individual Investors

Working through financial professionals who offer our multi-manager products, we provide our fund investors with time-tested investment strategies. This guidance is based on our pioneering philosophy of diversifying investments using our multi asset, multi style, multi manager approach, which is the core of our long-term investment strategy.

Research and Consulting Services for Those Who Run Large Pools of Capital

More than 700 clients benefit from our institutional services, which are available individually or packaged flexibly. All services tap our extensive and disciplined research into capital markets and money managers.

Our clients run large defined benefit and defined contribution retirement plans as well as foundations, endowments and financial institutions. Many outsource their investment management to us, entrusting us with efficient and thorough oversight of their multi-manager portfolios.

MONEY MANAGEMENT FIRM PROFILES

Transaction Services and Techniques

Believing that the best ideas are of no use unless they are implemented well, we provide institutional clients with pioneering implementation services designed to manage costs and reduce risks.

Our services cover a wide array of strategies and programs, some of which are the management of rebalancing, implementation of manager chances, trade execution improvement and cash flow management.

Statistical Analysis of Managers and Markets

Understanding performance helps investors of all sizes make better investment decisions for the future. Through Russell/Mellon Analytical Services – a joint venture between Russell and Mellon Financial Corporation – we provide the detailed investment information they need.

These tools help investors compare, analyze and understand a fund's performance, structure, risk, exposure and diversification. In addition, investors can monitor the markets through 21 Russell indexes, including the Russell 1000, 2000 and 3000 indexes, which objectively measure the top 3,000 U.S. securities. Investors have placed $200 billion in portfolios that use Russell's U.S. indexes as a model.

New Frontiers

Russell focuses on three key types of alternative investments: private equity, real estate and hedge strategies. We bring our proprietary multi-manager approach, diversification and discipline to these investment strategies.

❖❖❖

Note: In general, alternative investments involve a high degree of risk, including potential loss of principal, can be highly illiquid and can charge higher fees than other investments. Investing in specific market sectors such as real estate can be subject to different and greater risks than other investments. Hedge strategies and private equity investments are not subject to the same regulatory requirements as registered investment products. Hedge strategies often engage in leveraging and other speculative investment policies that may increase the risk of investment loss.

Benchmarks Used Include: Russell Indexes, S&P 500 index, AIM Composite Index, MSCI EAFE Index, MSCI Emerging Markets Free Index, Lehman Brothers Aggregate Bond Index, Citigroup 3-month Treasury Bill Index.

MONEY MANAGEMENT FIRM PROFILES

State Street Global Advisors
Contact: Gary MacDonald, Director of Mktg
State Street Financial Cntr; One Lincoln Street; Boston, MA 02111
Tel: 617.664.2296 / Email: gary_macdonald@ssga.com
Website: http://www.advisors.ssga.com

The world's largest institutional asset manager, with over $1 trillion in assets under management[*], State Street Global Advisors (SSgA) is the investment management arm of State Street Corporation. Combining our global reach and local market expertise with State Street's industry presence and resources permits us to focus single-mindedly on designing and delivering competitive investment strategies and integrated solutions to our clients worldwide, across virtually every asset class, capitalization range, investment approach, region, and style. SSgA commands a truly global presence, with 29 offices and nine investment centers across five continents.

SSgA Advisor Strategies Group

At SSgA we know that your business is as much about managing assets as it is about managing relationships. That is why we've developed the Advisor Strategies Group (ASG), an independent division within SSgA that is dedicated exclusively to serving the needs of sophisticated financial advisors.

The Advisor Strategies Group offers institutional caliber products and services to sophisticated financial advisors. SSgA's heritage as a "pure institutional manager" helps to ensure the highest level of discipline, investment expertise, risk control, and cost efficiencies when executing investment strategies on behalf of advisors and their clients.

Investment Capabilities

Ranging from broad-based market access vehicles to sector- and region-specific alternative services, SSgA provides financial advisors with a wide array of institutional caliber investment capabilities:

Fundamental Equity: Our fundamental equity approach blends top-down macroeconomic analysis with bottom-up security selection and is characterized by the selection of dominant companies and a risk-managed approach.

Our portfolios concentrate on leading companies within respective industries that typically have established records of success, strong management teams, sustained profitability, and competitive advantages. By employing tight risk controls, each portfolio targets an appropriate benchmark against which it manages risk. Broad diversification, prudent sector strategies, re-balancing, and a strict buy/sell discipline are used to cushion against impact during regional or sector-specific volatility.

Quantitative Equity: For more than two decades, SSgA has managed domestic and international quantitative equity portfolios. We focus on investments that are undervalued yet may have superior growth characteristics, repeatedly identifying and exploiting inaccurate valuations within equity markets. Our objective is to place the most attractive stocks into the portfolio while delivering the characteristics of a specific benchmark.

Passive Equity: SSgA developed its first indexed portfolio in 1978– a milestone that served as the foundation of our asset management business. The second-largest manager of domestic indexed equities and bonds– as well as the second-largest U.S. index manager– SSgA ranks as one of the largest providers of passively managed portfolios in the world. Our large and diverse asset and client bases, coupled with expedient, low-cost trading techniques, have helped to

* as of December 31, 2003

create strong economies of scale– resulting in cost efficiencies for clients.

Our services are offered in more than 50 equity markets worldwide, and track more than 170 benchmarks. We offer many domestic indexes– representing a vast range of markets, sectors, styles and capitalizations– as well as enhanced portfolios. Internationally, we provide local indexes and country funds for developed, pre-emerging and emerging markets.

Fixed Income: SSgA's fixed income capabilities seek to match or exceed relevant benchmark returns by exploiting inefficiencies, capturing excess returns overlooked or unattainable by less robust methodologies, and by minimizing portfolio risk exposure. SSgA has an array of fixed income capabilities, ranging from those that efficiently pinpoint opportunities in specific sectors or regions, to those that gain from broad market exposure.

Our dedicated management teams blend fundamental and quantitative analysis with local geographic perspectives and rigorous credit research to service fixed income clients worldwide.

Cash Management: SSgA is one of the leading currency managers in the world. Our resources and experience enable us to provide convenient, tax-sensitive cash management solutions. We do so by using both market and book value capabilities designed to generate a secure revenue stream and enhanced funding flexibility by maintaining liquidity, maximizing yield and controlling risk.

The buying power that our volume and economies of scale enable clients to realize is a benefit that comes from working with the world's largest institutional investment manager and global custodian. We utilize an approach that incorporates both fundamental and technical methodologies in managing currency risk and exchange rate movements. We also provide credit research capabilities.

Alternative Investments: Alternative investments can yield important portfolio management benefits, such as diversification, risk reduction and performance enhancement. Once reserved for institutional investors, alternative investments are now accessible to advisors and individual investors in search of non-correlated investment services.

SSgA provides a broad range of alternative investments that pursue competitive performance while reducing volatility. These investments are built for specialized clients who desire an element of non-traditional composition. SSGA's current services include hedge funds, real estate and private equity.

Separately Managed Account Strategies

SSgA's Advisor Strategies Group provides financial advisors access to our institutional and private investment expertise using separate account strategies. These tax-sensitive strategies are managed with a long-term investment philosophy to maximize after-tax returns.

At SSgA we always seek to minimize costs. However, we think that for taxable investors, a pooled vehicle is often not the best solution, as it fails to address individual tax situations. Instead, our approach focuses on forecasting risk for the individual and comparing that against the certainty of their tax situation.

We work with financial advisors to leverage SSgA's trading technology, extensive fiduciary experience, comprehensive global sub-custodial network and wide-ranging dealer relationships to help advisors and their clients best pursue their investment objectives through separate accounts.

Mutual Funds

SSgA offers a mutual fund family with a comprehensive selection of active, quantitative, or passive strategies. SSgA Funds include a broad range of domestic equity funds across all style and market capitalization ranges. Additionally, SSgA's fund family offers a complete line of income, high yield, and money market funds. Our expertise in global, international and emerging market strategies results in world class mutual funds that seek to enhance a client's investment over time.

To best pursue fund performance, we utilize advanced investment technologies; employ rigorous, disciplined decision-making; adhere to a highly structured portfolio construction process; and pay careful attention to risk parameters.

Exchange Traded Funds

SSgA is a recognized global force in exchange traded funds (ETFs), which combine the benefits of both indexing and mutual funds within a single-listed security. SSgA's size and breadth of offerings, our sophistication in passively managed products, and state-of-the-art technology backbone have created a solid foundation for continued leadership in the ETF marketplace.

Advisor Support and Business-Building Tools

The SSgA Advisor Strategies Group is collaboratively dedicated to providing advisors with the resources and tools they need to grow their business and meet their clients' evolving needs. By delivering educational tools, communications and value-added research on practice management, wealth management, and investment-related products, we're committed to helping advisors maintain a competitive edge in the marketplace.

❖ ❖ ❖

This material was been created for informational purposes only and does not constitute investment advice and it should not be relied on as such. It should not be considered a solicitation to buy or an offer to sell a security. It does not take into account any investor's particular investment objectives, strategies, tax status or investment horizon. There is no representation or warranty as to the current accuracy of, or liability for, decisions made based on this material. All material has been obtained from sources believed to be reliable, but its accuracy is not guaranteed. This presentation or any portion thereof may not be reprinted or redistributed without the written consent of SSgA. Information contained herein was obtained from, and is based upon, sources that SSgA believes to be reliable, however SSgA does not guarantee its accuracy, and any such information may be incomplete or condensed.

MONEY MANAGEMENT FIRM PROFILES

Templeton Private Client Group
Contact: Alexandra Weber, Asst VP, Nat'l Mktg Mgr
One Franklin Pkwy, #910   San Mateo, CA 94403
Tel: 650.822.8464 ext. 22271 / Email: aweber@frk.com
Website: http://www.franklintempletonpcg.com

The principal ownership and control of Templeton Private Client Group rests ultimately with Franklin Resources, Inc. (FRI). Key corporate officers and directors retain control and principal ownership and remain actively engaged in the business of investment advisory services. Directors, executive officers, and other beneficial owners (defined as owners of more than 5 percent of the outstanding common shares not acting as directors or officers) as a group owned 35.17 percent of the outstanding shares of Common Stock as of December 31, 2002.

An Impressive History

The founding of the Templeton organization dates back to 1940 when Sir John Templeton[1] became president of the investment counseling firm Templeton, Dobbrow and Vance, Inc. The Templeton Private Client Group (TPCG), a division of Templeton/Franklin Investment Services, Inc., has offered separate account management services to individuals and institutional clients since 1991.

The Templeton organization, a preeminent name in global investing, has focused on global and international investing for its entire 60-year history. As of December 31, 2003, it manages more than $109 billion in assets. TPCG, as an affiliate of Templeton Investment Counsel, LLC, Templeton Global Investors, Inc., Templeton Advisors, Ltd., and Templeton Worldwide, Inc., utilizes the experience, resources and extensive research capabilities of the Templeton organization in managing clients' separate accounts.

In 1992, Templeton merged with Franklin Resources, Inc. (FRI), and TPCG became a part of Franklin Templeton Investments which, as of December 31, 2003, manages more than $336 billion globally. Founded in 1947, FRI, which employs over 6,500 people in 28 nations worldwide, is comprised of several divisions, one of which is the Franklin Templeton Private Client Group (FTPCG). FRI, the ultimate parent corporation of TPCG (and all Templeton companies), is a public reporting company under Section 12 of the Securities Exchange Act of 1934.

In 1996, Franklin Resources, Inc., merged with Heine Securities Corporation, the investment adviser to Mutual Series Fund, Inc. Mutual Series is known for its distinctive domestic value equity investment approach, uncovering value in traditional value opportunities as well as risk arbitrage and bankruptcy situations.

In April 2001, Franklin Resources, Inc., completed acquisition of Fiduciary Trust Company International of New York. Fiduciary Trust is now an affiliate under Franklin Templeton's corporate structure, and will maintain its identity, independence and investment style. Fiduciary's recognized investment performance and superior service is expected to strengthen our presence in the institutional market, as well as the high net worth market. Moreover, Fiduciary's global growth products have the longest global growth track record in the industry, which is a critical consideration for institutional investors. Fiduciary's complementary product offerings include expertise in growth equity and global and U.S. fixed income separate account management as well as a sizable high net worth operation. Franklin's primary complementary product offerings include a substantial mutual fund presence and Templeton's value equity and emerging markets capabilities.

Separately Managed Accounts

The Franklin Templeton Private Client Group offers a wide range of separate account management products and services catering to high net worth individual, institutional and non-profit organization clients. Its portfolios are managed by either Franklin Private Client Group, Templeton Private Client Group, or the recently acquired Fiduciary Trust Corporation International –an investment management company recognized for its superior investment performance and outstanding service.

With a dedicated team of regional directors and separate account specialists, the Private Client Group offers separately managed accounts through the broker/dealer channel, in addition to Independent broker/dealers and bank channels. As a wholly owned subsidiary of Franklin Resources, Inc., the Private Client Group draws on the strengths of its 50-plus year-old parent company, with exceptional research capabilities and over 100 portfolio managers and analysts.

❖ ❖ ❖

---

[1] Sir John Templeton is retired from the Franklin Templeton organization and is no longer associated with it.